# Amazing meals
## for less than £2.50 a person

# Amaz

# ing
# meals

## for less than £2.50 a person

Published by the Reader's Digest Association, Inc.
London • New York • Sydney • Montreal

# using the recipes

To ensure perfect results every time, all recipes have been tested by professional cooks or home economists.

■ All oven-cooked recipes have been tested using metric measures and a conventional oven. For fan ovens, follow the manufacturer's guidelines. However, as a general guide, reduce the oven cooking temperature by 20°C and reduce the cooking time by 10 minutes in every hour.

## unless stated otherwise:

■ All spoon measurements are level and are based on proper measuring spoons.

■ All recipes have been tested in standard-sized dishes readily available in the UK. (To check the capacity of a cooking dish, fill it with water then tip the water into a measuring jug.) If you haven't got the exact size recommended in the recipe, use dishes of a similar size and keep an eye on the cooking times.

■ All recipes use medium-sized eggs.

■ All recipes use medium-sized vegetables and fruit unless otherwise stated.

■ All costings are based on using seasonal produce from local markets or suppliers, grocers or supermarkets.

■ For vegetarian meals, use the vegetable stock option where there is a choice.

■ Many vegetarians prefer not to eat cheese made with animal rennet, which includes Parmesan, Roquefort and Gruyère. Recipes containing these cheeses do not carry the vegetarian symbol Ⓥ. However, you can often omit the cheese or use a vegetarian alternative. For example, use Parmazano (a ready grated Parmesan-style, soya-based seasoning), or Italian-style premium cheese (a medium-fat, wedge-shaped cheese) in place of Parmesan. Alternatively, use a British hard cheese, such as Cheddar or Stilton, that carries the vegetarian symbol.

## nutritional information

The exact nutritional content of ingredients can vary so the nutritional notes should be used as a guideline only.

■ Where a recipe requires 'salt to taste', the quantity is variable so has not been included in the final sodium figure. Where a recipe states a specific amount of salt, this is included in the nutritional calculations. To find the figure for salt, multiply the amount for sodium by 2.5.

■ Serving suggestions and optional ingredients are included in the nutritional analysis.

■ If the recipe gives a choice of two or three ingredients – for example, 125ml chicken stock or white wine – the ingredient listed first is used in the nutritional analysis.

# intro

## metric measures

All food in the UK is now sold in metric units so it makes sense to cook using these measurements. However, if you feel happier or more confident using imperial measurements, you can use the conversion chart below. Remember though, use *either* metric *or* imperial and don't mix the two.

### weight

| Metric | Approx imperial |
|--------|-----------------|
| 5g | ⅛ oz |
| 10g | ¼ oz |
| 15g | ½ oz |
| 20g | ¾ oz |
| 25g | 1 oz |
| 35g | 1¼ oz |
| 40g | 1½ oz |
| 50g | 1¾ oz |
| 55g | 2 oz |
| 60g | 2¼ oz |
| 70g | 2½ oz |
| 75g | 2¾ oz |
| 85g | 3 oz |
| 90g | 3¼ oz |
| 100g | 3½ oz |
| 1kg | 2lb 4 oz |

### volume

| Metric | Approx imperial |
|--------|-----------------|
| 30ml | 1 fl oz |
| 50ml | 2 fl oz |
| 75ml | 2½ fl oz |
| 85ml | 3 fl oz |
| 90ml | 3¼ fl oz |
| 100ml | 3½ fl oz |
| 1 litre | 1¾ pints |

**YOU DON'T NEED TO SPEND A FORTUNE TO CREATE DELICIOUS, IMAGINATIVE AND IMPRESSIVE MEALS. ALL YOU NEED IS SOME PRE-PLANNING, SMART SHOPPING AND CLEVER COOKING, AND A LITTLE INSPIRATION, AND YOU WILL FIND YOUR MONEY GOES FURTHER THAN YOU EVER THOUGHT POSSIBLE.**

# duction

**With more than 260 tempting recipes** and pages packed with hints and tips on making the most of seasonal ingredients, it's easy to create fabulous meals at an amazing price. There are great ideas for making the most of good quality, good value ingredients when they're at their best, as well as delicious dishes for every occasion – from light lunches to hearty family meals. And for entertaining that will impress even the most discerning guests, there are some very special ideas.

**All recipes make the most of seasonal produce** that can be bought from supermarkets, grocers and local markets, or even bought direct from local growers or farmers. We have used many inexpensive ingredients that may be less familiar, but are better value and just as delicious as well-known but more expensive foods. Where more luxurious ingredients have been included, we have shown how to maximise their impact by mixing them with other delicious but more reasonably priced foods.

**No recipe should cost more than £2.50 per person,** and most of the starters, accompaniments and desserts cost less than £1.25 per person. All recipes have a £ sign rating so you can see at a glance how much you'll be spending. There's also a useful menu planner on pages 37–41 to help you put together two or three-course seasonal meals.

**All recipes include Cook Smart tips** with ingredient variations and alternative serving ideas, clever ways to avoid waste and delicious ideas for using leftovers.

**The more you use this invaluable book,** the better you'll become at getting the most for your money, enjoying the best of seasonal produce and meeting the daily challenge of preparing affordable, appetising, healthy food without sacrificing flavour or quality.

## price codes

£ less than £1.25

££ less than £2

£££ less than £2.50

**The £ signs indicate the cost of the recipe per person. All the prices have been based on widely available, good quality groceries and fresh produce bought in season from markets, grocers or cost-conscious supermarkets. To check the total cost, multiply the cost per person by the number of diners.**

# contents

## making the most of your food 10

# making

## of your

**fresh produce,
smart shopping
and clever
cooking**

# the most
# food

Planning and preparation are everything when you want to make the most of seasonal foods. Choose the best quality products, buying them when they are at their best and cheapest. What you don't use immediately for delicious, healthy meals for friends and family can be frozen or preserved to use out of season. This chapter contains a wealth of ideas to help you to create banquets out of budget buys.

# smart shopping

The key to cooking delicious dishes that won't break the bank lies in the raw ingredients. So before you shop, always think about the two main issues: cost and quality.

With each purchase, consider whether it's worth spending more on an ingredient and where you can cut corners. Experience is the best way to find bargains, but the tips below will help you on your way to getting the very best value for your money – in terms of quality, quantity, flavour and health.

## shop around

Supermarkets can be great for many things, offering economy packs, special offers and a one-stop shop, but you'll get better value for money if you shop around. This doesn't mean driving from one supermarket to another to save a penny here or there. What it means is shopping selectively and planning what you need.

■ Save on time and transport costs by visiting the supermarket less frequently – perhaps once a fortnight, or once a month – and stock up on bulk staples, such as pasta, rice, fruit juice and canned goods.

■ For fresh produce and specialist items, shop locally if you can. Find a good greengrocer, butcher and fishmonger who will recommend the day's best buys. Some areas have a van that comes round once a week selling fresh produce, and these are worth checking out. (Look in the supermarket too, but independent shops generally stock good-quality, well-priced fresh produce that is often supplied by local growers and producers.)

■ Wholefood stores or co-operatives stock well-priced grains, pulses, nuts and dried fruit. These dry staples have a fairly long shelf-life, so make a visit once a month or so, and stock up on what you need. (Nuts have a shorter shelf-life, so buy in smaller quantities.)

■ Ethnic grocers, especially those in the heart of a local ethnic community, sell a wide range of foods such as spices, fresh herbs, rice, unusual breads and exotic produce at much cheaper prices than the supermarket.

■ Open-air markets are great for good-value fruit and vegetables, as well as meat, cheese, fish and deli items such as olives. Farmers' markets sell local produce – particularly specialist cheeses, meats and seasonal fruit and vegetables; the food may not always be cheap, though. On the plus side, the quality is usually excellent and you can often taste before buying.

■ Mail order can be an economical way to buy specialist items such as preserved meats and fish, unusual spices and organic foods. Magazines often recommend good suppliers, but check the price of goods before you order.

## dare to try

Don't be afraid to try new things. Expanding your culinary repertoire is the best way to make the most of good quality, inexpensive ingredients. For example, if your local grocer has a big crate of lush, leafy pak choi for a great price, take the opportunity to add it to Oriental Stir-fried Vegetables (see page 266). Or if you have a good local Middle Eastern or Mediterranean store, buy some of the more unusual ingredients and try out exotic recipes such as Moroccan Braised Chicken (see page 192) or Roasted Vegetable Couscous (see page 111). If you're unfamiliar with an ingredient, ask the shopkeeper what it is and how to use it.

**GET TO KNOW YOUR LOCAL AREA, AND TRY OUT DIFFERENT SHOPS UNTIL YOU FIND OUT WHICH ONES ARE BEST. PERSONAL ADVICE FROM A SHOPKEEPER IS OFTEN THE MOST RELIABLE WAY TO FIND A BARGAIN.**

Save money on fresh produce by selecting your own. Pre-packed vegetables are often more expensive than those sold loose, and choosing your own allows you to check each item is in perfect condition.

# plan,
## plan,
### plan

Sensible planning and writing a proper shopping list will help you to avoid impulse buying, or simply buying more food than you need.

■ Make a menu for the week (breakfast, lunch, dinner and snacks), and work out what ingredients you will need.

■ Be prepared for the unexpected. Stock up on useful freezer and storecupboard basics that you can turn into instant meals when required.

■ Plan meals that incorporate leftovers from earlier in the week. For example, if you have a roast chicken with potatoes and leafy greens at the weekend, you could then make a Chicken Hash with Potatoes and Peppers (see page 188) during the week. Bubble and Squeak (see page 292) is the perfect way to use up any leftover greens and potatoes, and makes a great light lunch or supper served with poached eggs.

■ Spread the cost of meals. If you go over budget for one meal (perhaps for a special dinner), balance your budget with a more economical meal another night. Hearty dishes such as Sausage Hotpot with Lentils (see page 242) and Spaghetti with Blue Cheese and Walnuts (see page 127) make great choices for a cheap yet satisfying and enjoyable supper.

## but be
## flexible

Planning is sensible, but be flexible too. Be prepared to take advantage of great offers. If something you planned to buy isn't available, is too expensive or doesn't look good, choose an alternative. In most recipes, you can substitute ingredients – for example, cod for another firm white fish, pancetta for bacon, or one blue cheese for another. Alternatively, change the menu slightly. You'll find lots of suggestions for variations in the Cook Smart tips, but also experiment yourself.

# watch the price

It's easy to switch on to automatic pilot when you're doing a big food shop, tossing the same items into your trolley week after week, without thinking about what you're doing. But stop for a second and check the price first. Prices go up and down, perhaps with a special offer or promotion, so what might have been good value the previous week may not be the following week.

■ The price of fresh produce, in particular, fluctuates depending on whether it's in season, if it's locally grown or imported, or if there's been a good or bad harvest.

■ Avoid buying ready-prepared fruits, vegetables and salads. You pay a premium price for the convenience factor, and they're not as nutritious.

■ On packaged goods, many supermarkets list the price per kilogram as well as the pack price, so you can see if you're getting value for money. Generally, the bigger the pack, the lower the unit price so if it's a food that you eat regularly, it's worth buying the larger size.

## bulk bargains

Buying in bulk can appear to be cheaper but it's only an economy if you're going to use all that you've bought. A huge can of beans may seem cheap, but if you can't use them all up then you'll end up wasting food – and money.

■ If you've got a big freezer, use it to preserve fresh produce when it's cheap (see page 20).

■ When buying dry goods with a limited shelf life, remember that spices and herbs lose their flavour with age, and nuts can turn rancid. To avoid waste, buy smaller quantities more often, and keep an eye on the 'best before' dates.

■ Store ingredients properly so that they stay in peak condition. Invest in airtight containers to keep dry goods fresh, and label the container with the content and 'best before' date or purchase date. Most dry goods should be stored in a cool, dry place.

■ Supermarket special offers such as 'three for the price of two' or 'buy one, get one free' can often be worth taking advantage of – but only if they are ingredients that you use regularly.

## less is more

Sometimes you get better value by buying less of a more expensive, better quality item. For example, a small quantity of a good, tangy, mature cheese will give a better flavour than a large quantity of a cheaper, less tasty one, and you will need less of good-quality dark chocolate than a cheap chocolate with a low percentage of cocoa solids. Wholegrain bread is more satisfying and better for you than refined white bread.

## cost and quality

Although cost can be a good indicator of quality, this isn't always the case. Supermarket own-brand products are often just as good as the manufacturer's branded products – and sometimes better. Try out different products until you find the one you prefer.

## special extras

Some dishes require a small quantity of an expensive ingredient, such as a splash of liqueur in a dessert. If the flavour makes a significant difference and the ingredient has a long shelf-life, it's often worth buying.

■ Miniatures are an expensive way to buy spirits and liqueurs, so as long as you are likely to use the ingredient again, it may be cheaper to buy a whole or half bottle.

■ When it comes to spirits, brandy, dark rum and whisky are the most likely to be included in recipes. Use brandy and a little grated orange zest in place of orange liqueur. Dry sherry and/or Madeira are also useful standbys.

■ When you're abroad, look out for spirits and liqueurs, or special ingredients, such as saffron, which are often available more cheaply.

■ Some ingredients such as vanilla pods can be reused. If you use a vanilla pod to flavour a sauce, rinse it well after use and pat dry. Store in a jar of sugar and the sugar will become deliciously scented – perfect for desserts and baking.

# what to look for

When you buy fresh produce, choose carefully to ensure you get the freshest, best-quality ingredients.

## meat

Economical cuts usually come from parts of the animal that have done the most work, such as the legs. They have a good flavour and not too much waste in terms of fat, gristle and bone. However, they can be tough, so need long slow cooking and/or marinating. Don't be afraid to try cuts that you've never cooked before, and check with the butcher if you are unsure how to prepare them.

■ Red meat is not always a sign of quality – well-hung meat will be darker. When buying lamb, young lamb is pale pink, while older lamb should be brownish-pink.

■ Choose lean cuts, and neatly prepared meat trimmed of surplus fat. Weight for weight, you'll get better value because you're not paying for the weight of the fat.

## poultry

Generally, larger birds are better value because there is a higher proportion of meat to bone.

■ Look for plump birds with soft, blemish-free skin (the thinner the skin, the younger the bird).

■ Buy the best bird you can afford: although free-range birds are more expensive, the flavour will be superior to battery-reared birds. Corn fed birds have a yellowish flesh and a good, slightly gamey flavour.

## fish and shellfish

Seafood is best eaten very fresh and in season. If you are unfamiliar with different varieties or how to cook them, ask the fishmonger for advice and enjoy experimenting.

■ Choose fresh-smelling fish with glistening skins, bright eyes and firm flesh. For the best choice and quality, avoid buying seafood on a Monday.

## fruit and vegetables

Your eye is often the best judge so if something looks tired or wilted, leave it on the shelf – even if the price is reduced. If in doubt, ask your greengrocer for advice.

■ If there are still leaves attached, they should be fresh-looking.

■ Produce needn't be perfect-looking but fruit and vegetables should usually be firm, and not wrinkled, bruised or too soft.

■ Freshly-picked local produce is likely to have the best flavour.

■ You can check the ripeness of fruits in different ways. Some, such as melons and peaches, will smell sweet and aromatic when ripe, so have a sniff. Others, such as mangoes, avocados and plums, will give slightly when squeezed gently in the palm of the hand.

# seasonal sense

Once you start to eat seasonally, you'll appreciate the food you eat so much more. The summer months when fresh raspberries and strawberries are in season will be heaven, and the arrival of pumpkins and squash in autumn will be a real treat.

**Take advantage of fresh leafy greens while they're in season. They're great for your health and taste delicious.**

Although most fresh ingredients are now available all year round, they're at their cheapest and best when they're in season. Imported, out-of-season produce is usually more expensive and often has an inferior taste.

Meals made with seasonal ingredients seem to suit the weather too. Hearty dishes made with winter cabbage or butternut squash are perfect in the cold months, while sweet tomato tarts and soft berry desserts are just right for sunny summer days. But if you start craving a salad in winter, don't panic – there are plenty of seasonal salad leaves in the winter months, such as dark green watercress and pale, crunchy chicory.

Make seasonal buying work for you all year round. Take advantage of ingredients when they're cheap and plentiful, and freeze or preserve them in jams and chutneys (see pages 35 and 36), or make them into dishes that can then be frozen and enjoyed out of season. For example, what could be better than an Apple and Blackberry Cobbler (see page 328) in the middle of winter? Pick the blackberries from hedgerows in autumn and cook them with windfall apples for virtually no cost at all. Freeze in small portions, and enjoy whenever the mood takes you.

Buying imported food doesn't just hit your pocket – the rules about use of pesticides in other countries can be less stringent than in Europe, and the pollution produced by trucks and planes takes its toll on the planet. Buying locally and supporting the farmers and growers in your area is a good way to get to know and participate in your community.

**BUYING LOCALLY HELPS TO SUPPORT THE FARMERS AND GROWERS IN YOUR AREA, SO YOU'RE NOT JUST SAVING MONEY AND EATING BETTER, BUT INVESTING IN YOUR LOCAL COMMUNITY TOO.**

# what's in season?

| month | fish, meat & game | | vegetables | | fruit | |
|---|---|---|---|---|---|---|
| january | haddock<br>herring<br>ling<br>mussels<br>whiting | goose<br>guinea fowl<br>pheasant | Brussels sprouts<br>carrots<br>cauliflower<br>kale<br>leeks | parsnips<br>squash<br>swede | citrus fruits<br>conference pears<br>lychees<br>mangoes<br>physalis | |
| february | cod<br>halibut<br>herring<br>ling<br>mussels<br>plaice<br>skate | sole<br>whiting<br>wild salmon<br><br>guinea fowl<br>pheasant | Brussels sprouts<br>cauliflower<br>celeriac<br>chicory<br>Jerusalem<br>  artichokes<br>kale | leeks<br>parsnips<br>swede<br>turnips<br>winter cabbage | citrus fruits<br>  (especially<br>   Seville oranges,<br>   which are good<br>   for making<br>   marmalade)<br>forced rhubarb | pineapples |
| march | haddock<br>hake<br>halibut<br>ling | mussels<br>wild salmon<br><br>duckling | baking potatoes<br>carrots<br>savoy cabbage<br>spinach | spring greens<br>sprouting broccoli<br>watercress | early rhubarb<br>pineapples | |
| april | crab<br>hake<br>mackerel<br>oysters<br>sardines | wild salmon<br><br>British spring<br>  lamb<br>duckling | carrots<br>Chinese leaves<br>Jersey royals<br>kale<br>spinach | spring greens<br>watercress | Bramley cooking<br>  apples<br>rhubarb | |
| may | crab<br>gurnard<br>mackerel<br>plaice<br>sardines<br>sole | trout<br>wild salmon<br><br>British lamb<br>duckling | asparagus<br>broad beans<br>broccoli<br>cauliflower<br>cucumber<br>lettuce | new potatoes<br>spinach | cherries<br>melon<br>rhubarb<br>strawberries | |
| june | dab<br>gurnard<br>hake<br>herring<br>mackerel<br>mullet | sardines<br>trout<br>wild salmon<br><br>duckling | asparagus<br>beetroot<br>broad beans<br>broccoli<br>celery<br>cucumber | lettuce<br>mange-tout<br>new potatoes<br>peas | cherries<br>gooseberries<br>melons<br>peaches<br>raspberries<br>redcurrants | strawberries |
| july | crab<br>dab<br>gurnard<br>hake<br>herring<br>lobster<br>mackerel<br>mullet | plaice<br>sardines<br>scallops<br>sole<br>trout<br>wild salmon<br><br>duckling | broccoli<br>cauliflower<br>courgettes<br>cucumber<br>fennel<br>lettuce<br>peas<br>peppers | runner beans<br>tomatoes | apricots<br>black/red<br>  currants<br>cherries<br>gooseberries<br>melons<br>nectarines<br>peaches | plums<br>raspberries<br>strawberries |
| august | dab<br>gurnard<br>herring<br>mackerel<br>mullet<br>plaice | sardines<br>trout<br><br>wild duck<br>wild salmon<br>grouse | beans in the pod<br>beetroot<br>broccoli<br>corn cobs<br>courgettes<br>cucumber | fennel<br>globe artichokes<br>peppers<br>spinach<br>tomatoes | currants<br>gooseberries<br>greengages<br>melons<br>nectarines<br>peaches | plums<br>raspberries<br>strawberries |
| september | crab<br>dab<br>gurnard<br>mackerel<br>mussels<br>oysters | plaice<br>red mullet<br>sardines<br><br>grouse<br>wild duck | beans in the pod<br>beetroot<br>corn cobs<br>courgettes<br>fennel<br>marrow | peppers<br>pickling onions<br>savoy cabbage<br>sprouting broccoli<br>tomatoes | apples<br>blackberries<br>conference pears<br>damsons<br>greengages<br>melons | nectarines<br>peaches<br>raspberries<br>victoria plums |
| october | dab<br>gurnard<br>red mullet<br>mussels<br>sardines | grouse<br>guinea fowl<br>pheasant<br>wild duck | aubergine<br>celeriac<br>courgettes<br>marrow<br>peppers | pumpkin/squash<br>red cabbage<br>watercress | apples<br>grapes<br>pears<br>quinces<br>sloes | |
| november | dab<br>halibut<br>lemon sole<br>ling<br>mussels<br>skate<br>whiting | goose<br>grouse<br>guinea fowl<br>pheasant<br>venison<br>wild duck | broccoli<br>cauliflower<br>celeriac<br>Jerusalem<br>  artichokes<br>leeks<br>parsnips | pumpkin/squash<br>swede<br>winter cabbage | apples<br>chestnuts<br>dates<br>grapes<br>mangoes<br>pears<br>pineapples | pomegranates<br>satsumas<br>tangerines |
| december | dab<br>ling<br>mussels<br><br><br>goose | grouse<br>guinea fowl<br>pheasant<br>turkey<br>venison | Brussels sprouts<br>carrots<br>chicory<br>parsnips<br>red cabbage | savoy cabbage<br>swede<br>sweet potatoes<br>watercress | apples<br>chestnuts<br>cranberries<br>dates<br>pineapples | satsumas<br>tangerines |

■ Availability of fish varies depending on the catch.

# grow
# your own

From the smallest pot of basil on a sunny windowsill to a vegetable patch or an abundant allotment – growing your own produce makes sound economic sense.

## from
## tiny seeds

For the cost of a few packets of seeds and some compost, you can grow dozens of plants and harvest many kilos of produce. Compare this with the cost of the equivalent quantity of produce from the supermarket and you'll find you have made a significant saving.

■ Growing plants from seed is usually the cheapest way to grow your own, while growing from seedlings or young plants is more reliable and less time-consuming. Trays of seedlings can be bought cheaply in most garden centres and DIY stores.

■ Tubs, window boxes and small pots placed in a sunny position are great for growing herbs and spicy chillies. Delicate herbs such as coriander and basil can be more difficult to grow,

but hardy ones such as chives, sage, rosemary and thyme really do grow like weeds. You can pick the herbs as you need them, which is much cheaper and less wasteful than buying cut fresh herbs.

■ Grow-bags (available from most garden centres and DIY stores) are good for growing tomatoes, courgettes, aubergines and runner beans. You don't need much space so these are ideal for small gardens or sunny balconies. You will need to train runner beans up a wall or trellis.

■ If you have a larger garden or allotment, dig a vegetable patch and grow root vegetables, brassicas

(such as cabbages and broccoli), salad vegetables and summer berries. Take time deciding which plants to grow, checking when they should be planted and harvested, then plan your vegetable patch accordingly. Avoid gluts by planting a variety of produce that will be ready to harvest at different times throughout the year.

■ If you have a large garden, a fruit tree can be a great investment. It will produce fruit year after year, providing you with a free supply of fruit for cooking and preserving.

## sprouting beans

**1** Soak a handful of beans or seeds (such as mung, soya, alfalfa or cress) overnight in cold water. Rinse well under cold running water, and transfer to a large jar; they should fill about one quarter of the jar.

**2** Cover the jar with a square of muslin and fasten with string. Lay the jar on its side in a warm, well-ventilated place, out of direct sunlight.

**3** Twice a day, uncover the jar, fill with cold water, swirl, then cover again and drain off the water through the muslin. The seeds should start to sprout on the second day. After a few days, when the sprouts have grown 1–2 cm long, they are ready to eat.

## food for free

From blackberries, elderberries and sloes to mushrooms and wild garlic, there is an abundance of fresh, wild produce growing in fields and hedgerows that can be picked free. Take care though (particularly with mushrooms) and only pick foods that are safe to eat; always check using a good identification guide, and if in doubt – don't eat it. Next time you go for a walk in the countryside, be sure to take a container with you, so that you can bring home a feast for free.

## pick-your-own and farm boxes

More farmers are inviting people to pick their own produce, which is an economical and fun way to buy vegetables and fruit. If you end up with more produce than you can use, freeze the extra (see page 20), or make preserves.

■ Many farms and organic producers run farm box schemes. Each week, they deliver a box of fresh, seasonal produce to your door. Boxes contain a good range of fresh produce but for flexibility, remember that many vegetables can be substituted for each other in recipes – try using cauliflower in place of broccoli, carrots for parsnips, or leeks instead of onions.

# freezer know-how

The freezer is your best friend when it comes to making the most of fresh produce all year round. And it's a real help to have ingredients or dishes available when there's no time to shop.

## perfect freezing

Take advantage of bulk buys and cheap, seasonal produce by freezing for a later date. Most fresh produce freezes well, and keeping stocks, sauces and pastry in the freezer can be a great time-saver.

■ to avoid waste, freeze foods in useful, portion-sized quantities so that you thaw only what you need.

■ freeze food quickly on the day of purchase, but thaw it slowly.

■ never refreeze food once it has been thawed.

■ when buying meat or fish to freeze, check that it has not already been frozen.

■ label containers with the content and date of freezing, and arrange the oldest food towards the front of the freezer so you use it up first.

■ try to use foods within 2–3 months of freezing.

## fruit

Choose ripe, good quality fruit for freezing, and only wash if necessary, drying it well before freezing. Never freeze fruit directly on a metal surface, as the juice could react with the metal – line trays first with greaseproof paper.

■ Soft fruits such as berries, currants and gooseberries freeze well, but can become soft when thawed so are best used for cooking. To freeze, spread out the fruit in an even layer on a lined tray, then freeze. Once frozen, pack into bags or containers.

■ Orchard and stone fruits such as apples and apricots can turn brown when they thaw, so should be frozen in an acidulated syrup (450g caster sugar dissolved in 1 litre water with the juice of one lemon). Allow 300ml of syrup for every 450g fruit. Prepare the fruit, peeling, stoning and cutting into bite-sized pieces, then place in containers, pour over the syrup and freeze.

## herbs

Fresh herbs freeze well, so you can preserve cut herbs that you don't need immediately. Chop the herbs, then freeze in a polythene bag; stir spoonfuls of the herb into dishes at the last minute. Alternatively, place 1 tsp of the chopped herb into each compartment of an ice cube tray and top up with water. Freeze, then transfer the cubes to a small bag; stir into hot soups, sauces and stews as required.

# vegetables

To preserve the colour, flavour and texture of vegetables, they should be blanched before freezing. Allow 3 litres of boiling water and 2 tsp salt per 500 g vegetables.

- Trim the vegetables, cut into bite-sized pieces and place in a wire basket.

- Plunge into the boiling salted water, return to the boil, then cook according to the chart below.

- Drain the vegetables, then plunge into iced water to prevent them cooking further. Drain again and pack into bags or containers and freeze.

## preparing vegetables for the freezer

| vegetable | preparation | blanching time |
| --- | --- | --- |
| asparagus | Arrange spears of similar length and thickness in bundles and tie together. | thin – 2 minutes<br>medium – 3 minutes<br>thick – 4 minutes |
| beans | Wash and cut into 1 cm slices. Leave French and string beans whole. Slice runner beans. | 2 minutes |
| broad beans | Choose young beans only and shell. | 2 minutes |
| broccoli | Trim the heads into florets and remove tough stalks. | 2 minutes |
| brussels sprouts | Wash, trim and remove outer leaves. | 2 minutes |
| carrots | Leave young carrots whole; peel and slice larger ones. | 2 minutes |
| cauliflower | Wash and divide into florets. Add 1 tbsp lemon juice to the boiling water. | 2 minutes |
| celeriac | Peel and dice. | 2 minutes |
| corn on the cob | Remove the husks and silks and trim the ends. | small – 4 minutes<br>large – 8 minutes |
| courgettes | Trim and cut into 1 cm slices. | 1 minute |
| leeks | Remove the outer leaves and wash the leeks well to remove any grit. Slice if thick. | 2–4 minutes, depending on size |
| parsnips | Choose young parsnips. Scrape off the skin, wash and slice. | 2 minutes |
| peas | Choose young peas only and shell. | 1 minute |
| spinach | Rinse well and pat dry. Remove the tough ribs and freeze the tender leaves. | 1 minute |

# fish

Frozen fish is a useful standby and retains the nutritional value of fresh. It's a particularly good choice when wild fish is out of season. (Farmed fish is available all year round.) Only freeze very fresh fish.

# meat

For quality and value for money, try to buy direct from the producer. Many small producers, rearing organic and non-intensively farmed animals, sell at farmers' markets, in farm shops, by mail order, or can deliver locally. The quality is usually excellent, and by buying direct and in bulk, prices can work out to be very competitive. You will often see good deals, such as a great price for half a lamb. Ask the butcher to joint it for you but be sure you're going to want all the cuts. The same applies to selection packs – only buy them if you're interested in all the cuts. When freezing cutlets, chops, steaks and burgers, interleave with waxed paper so they can be separated easily.

# poultry

All poultry, especially chicken portions, are versatile and great for family meals. Frozen birds may have added water, which will drain out as the meat thaws, so weigh after thawing to calculate the cooking time. Poultry must be thawed slowly in the fridge to make sure it's thoroughly defrosted (although if you're in a hurry, you can speed up the process by leaving it wrapped and submerging it in cold water). Never refreeze raw poultry that has already been frozen. However, you can freeze a cooked dish that contains previously frozen poultry.

# bread and breadcrumbs

■ If a loaf of bread often goes stale before you have time to use it all, cut the fresh loaf in half and wrap one half in a plastic bag and freeze for later. If you mainly use bread for toast, slice the loaf, wrap and freeze; you can put the frozen slices straight into the toaster.

■ Loaves of bread are often sold off cheaply at the end of the day and can be made into breadcrumbs. Break the loaf into chunks, whizz in a food processor to make crumbs and pack into a plastic bag or container. They will freeze as a loose mixture so you can use as little as you need.

# pastry

Freeze leftover fresh shortcrust, puff or filo pastry for another day. If you're making shortcrust pastry for a pie, make up a double or triple quantity and freeze the extra batches. You can do the same with crumble toppings.

# stocks, soups and sauces

Home-made stock (see page 31) tastes much better than stock cubes and is cheaper than buying the fresh supermarket varieties. The same is true of soups and sauces, which are a great way of using up a glut of seasonal produce. Make up several batches and freeze in useful quantities.

■ To freeze stock, soups and sauces, line a square container with a polythene bag, then ladle the mixture into the bag and freeze. Once frozen, the bags can be removed from the container, sealed and labelled, and the solid blocks stacked neatly in the freezer.

■ Soups containing cream, cheese and eggs often do not freeze well. If the recipe calls for these ingredients to be stirred in at the end of cooking, make the soup but do not add the final ingredients. Freeze, then stir in the extra ingredients after thawing and reheating.

■ To save freezer space, reduce stock right down by rapid boiling, then freeze the concentrated stock in ice cube trays. To use, simply drop the ice cubes into a little hot water then dilute to the desired concentration.

**If you grow your own vegetables, freeze some so you can enjoy fresh-tasting produce all year round.**

# larder basics

Every kitchen needs a store of basic supplies. Even if the initial expenditure seems high, you'll use them all the time, and very few will be wasted if you buy wisely.

**Pasta and noodles** Although fresh pasta and noodles are available, dried ones often make a better, cheaper choice. Pasta comes in three main types – short, long and sheets. Most short pastas are interchangeable so if a recipe calls for penne, you can usually use farfalle or fusilli instead. The same is true of long pasta and pasta sheets, so keep one of each type in store. There are many different types of noodle – wheat, egg, rice – all of which are good served as an accompaniment, or in stir-fries and Asian-style soups.

Allow 50–75 g pasta, couscous or rice per person. If you cook too much, use it up in another meal (see page 28).

**Couscous** This North African staple makes a delicious alternative to pasta, rice and potatoes, and is great as an accompaniment to stews and casseroles, or used in stuffings and salads.

**Rice** Regular long-grain rice is good value and can be used in countless dishes. Fragrant basmati rice and creamy risotto rices are more expensive, but worth investing in if you enjoy making specific dishes such as pilafs and risottos.

**Pulses** Dried pulses are cheaper than canned and are a useful addition to soups, casseroles and salads. Lentils and split peas are fairly quick to cook and do not need pre-soaking. However, dried beans and chickpeas need to be soaked overnight and require lengthy cooking, so canned may be more convenient.

**Dried fruit and nuts** These don't last indefinitely so buy in small quantities as and when you need them.

**Flour** Many dishes require a small amount of flour so keep a bag of plain flour in store. Cornflour is useful for thickening sauces; self-raising flour is good for baking (alternatively, add baking powder to plain flour). For bread-making, you will need a strong 'bread' flour.

**Storecupboard staples form the basis of many satisfying, economical meals.**

**Sugar** Useful for baking, desserts, preserves, and some savoury dishes. Different types of sugar have different uses and flavours. Unrefined sugars have a better flavour.

**Oil** Olive oil is good for flavouring dressings and drizzling over cooked dishes. Extra virgin olive oil is expensive but has the best flavour. Light olive oil is good for frying and Mediterranean-style dishes; otherwise use flavourless vegetable oil, such as groundnut, sunflower, safflower or rapeseed. Save money by making your own dressings (see page 33) and flavoured oils. To make flavoured oil, add fresh herbs, garlic, chillies or lemon zest to a bottle of oil and leave it to infuse for at least a week.

# herbs and spices

Fresh herbs are usually best but dried are a good standby and can work out cheaper. Dried spices are invaluable. Most dishes only need a small amount, so a packet or jar will last a long time. However, dried herbs and spices lose their flavour with age, so buy in small quantities to avoid waste, and store in airtight containers in a cool, dark place.

**Herbs** Delicate herbs such as basil and coriander do not dry well, but

more robust herbs such as thyme and oregano retain their flavour and are a convenient, cheap alternative to fresh. If you don't have the right herb for a recipe, you can often substitute another of a similar strength.

**Spices** Buy spices as required. Whole spices such as coriander and cumin seeds retain their flavour and aroma longer than ground, so may make a better investment. Grind them in a spice grinder or mortar.

# canned and bottled goods

Unopened, canned and bottled goods have a very long shelf life. Once opened, canned goods can be transferred to a plastic container and stored in the fridge for a few days. Bottled goods such as sauces and condiments will last longer – but always check the label.

**Vegetables** Often cheaper than fresh, because they are canned when the ingredients are abundant and cheap, these are a great kitchen standby. Canned tomatoes and sweetcorn are particularly versatile. Try to choose vegetables canned without salt.

**Fruit** For fruits such as pineapple that involve a lot of waste during preparation, the canned alternative can often work out cheaper than fresh. Fruits in unsweetened juice are useful for desserts and breakfast, or as an ingredient in some savoury dishes.

They are also ideal when fresh fruit is out of season and unavailable frozen.

**Fish and shellfish** Fish such as tuna and sardines and shellfish such as crab are good canned and can be used in many dishes which require cooked fish – from sandwiches and salads to pasta and rice dishes. Canned fish and shellfish are usually cheaper than the fresh equivalent.

**Pulses** Canned beans, peas and lentils are nutritious and great for quick pâtés and dips, salads, soups, stews and casseroles. They are usually more expensive than dried, but more convenient.

**Bottled vegetables** Jars of sun-dried tomatoes and bottled roasted peppers are ideal for bruschetta and pizza toppings, soups, sauces and casseroles.

**Mustard and condiments** Bottled sauces and flavourings such as mustard, tomato ketchup, Worcestershire sauce and soy

sauce are brilliant for boosting the flavour of stews, sauces, dressings and marinades. They have a strong flavour, so you only need to use a little, and have a long shelf life.

**Vinegar** There are many different types available and they keep well so if you can, buy a few and experiment a little. For basic dressings and cooking, red or white wine vinegar is the best choice; red has a slightly more robust flavour. Cider vinegar is milder and less acidic with a fragrant apple flavour and is good for lighter salads. Rich, dark, balsamic vinegar is expensive but you only need a little to enjoy its mellow, sweet-sour flavour.

# useful skills

Although many fresh ingredients can be purchased ready for use, it's often cheaper to prepare them yourself.

## meat and poultry

In general, cheaper cuts of meat are tougher than prime cuts and are best suited to gentle, slow cooking methods, such as pot-roasting, braising and stewing. They may also be marinated before cooking to help tenderise them. More expensive cuts of meat may be 'stretched' to go further, for example by stuffing a boned joint. You can also supplement the meat with pulses or vegetables, or with toppings like dumplings and pastry.

## smart cooking methods

**Marinating**  This technique helps to break down the fibres and tenderise meat, so it is ideally suited to cheaper, tougher cuts. It also adds flavour and helps to keep the flesh moist during cooking. A typical marinade includes oil, wine or vinegar, herbs and spices.

**Braising**  Used for smaller cuts of meat, such as less tender chops and steaks, or cubed meat that doesn't require the long cooking of stewing cuts. The meat (or poultry) is usually fried briefly until brown all over, then placed in a casserole on a bed of vegetables with enough stock to come about halfway up the meat. The pan is then covered tightly and the meat or poultry cooked slowly until tender and juicy. Good value, suitable cuts include chuck, blade, skirt (or meat sold as braising beef), shoulder of lamb or neck fillet, pork spare-rib, chops, lamb's or pig's liver, and chicken and rabbit joints. Italian Braised Beef with Mushrooms (see page 223) is a delicious example.

**Stewing**  Excellent for very tough cuts. Chuck and shin are good beef choices; supermarkets often label them as stewing beef. Be sure to cut the meat into similar sized pieces for even cooking. For a lamb stew, neck fillets are good value. Stews are easy to make and can be left to cook on the hob or in the oven on a low heat

for several hours. Try Beef Stew with Rosemary Dumplings (see page 222) and Fruity One-pot Lamb (see page 230).

**Pot-roasting**  Whole large cuts or boned and rolled joints make excellent pot-roasts and cost less than a roasting cut. They are slow-cooked in a covered casserole using a well-flavoured stock, often with wine or cider, vegetables, herbs and/or spices. Topside, silverside, brisket and flank make good choices. Try Pot Roast Beef with Braised Vegetables (see page 224).

**Stir-frying**  This quick cooking technique is an excellent way to stretch a small amount of a prime, tender meat, such as steak or pork fillet. Tender meat only requires brief cooking, so cut into small, bite-sized pieces and fry quickly over a high heat with lots of vegetables and

## making a marinade

**Use this basic marinade with beef or lamb. For pork, poultry or fish, use white wine instead of red.**

300 ml dry red wine
3 tbsp olive oil
1 tbsp lemon juice
1 small onion, chopped
1 carrot, peeled and sliced
1 stick celery, chopped
1–2 cloves garlic, crushed
1 bouquet garni (including bay leaf, rosemary, parsley and thyme)
6 black peppercorns

Combine the ingredients in a shallow dish, add the food to be marinated and toss to coat. Leave to stand for several hours. (Fish should be marinated for no more than 30 minutes.)

noodles to make a delicious, filling, low-fat meal. Why not spice up your mid-week repertoire and treat the family to exotic recipes such as Chinese Crispy Beef Stir-fry (page 219), Linguine with Pork, Greens and Peas (page 132), and Spicy Pork Fajitas (see page 235).

**Stuffing** Stuffing a boned joint with a tasty filling is a good way to make an expensive cut go further. Some cuts are sold ready-boned but if not, ask the butcher to bone a joint for you. He'll be happy to help and won't charge as long as you don't ask while the shop is busy. A Middle Eastern-style stuffing of dried apricots, spices, nuts and bulghur wheat makes a good choice for a boned leg or shoulder of lamb. Stuffing is also excellent for poultry; see Roast Chicken with Herb Stuffing (page 196) and Stuffed Pheasant (page 211).

# jointing a chicken

Cutting a whole chicken into joints is cheaper than buying legs, wings and breasts separately. If you don't need all the portions, you can freeze the rest for a later date (see page 22). Use the carcass to make stock (see page 31).

**1** Place the chicken, breast side up, on a board. Pull one leg gently away from the body and use a heavy cook's knife to cut through the skin between the body and leg. Bend the leg outwards until the ball pops out of the socket joint, then carefully cut through the flesh under the joint. Repeat with the second leg.

**2** To separate the drumstick from the thigh, stand one leg on the board so that it forms a natural V-shape. Firmly hold the end of the drumstick in one hand and cut through the joint where the two bones meet at the centre of the V. Repeat with the second leg.

**3** To separate the wings from the body of the chicken, make a deep cut into the breast meat near to the inside of each wing. As you do this, angle the knife diagonally across the neck end of the bird so that the uncut breast forms a diamond shape. Cut down into the meat far enough to expose the bones.

**4** To free the wings from the carcass, use a pair of poultry shears or strong kitchen scissors to cut between the ball and socket joints and through the remaining flesh and bone. Make sure there are no sharp splinters of bone embedded in the cut portions.

**5** To remove the breast meat, lay the carcass on its side then use shears or scissors to cut through the thin rib cage on either side of the backbone.

**6** Divide the breast into two, cutting crossways or lengthways through the bird's flesh using a knife and then through the bones and cartilage with the shears or scissors. If the bird is large, each portion can be further divided into two to give four pieces of breast meat.

# preparing meat for stewing

Cheaper cuts such as chuck, shin and neck are perfectly suited to long, slow cooking. Before cutting into equal-sized cubes, you will need to trim off any excess fat and connective tissue.

**1** Place the meat on a board and, using a very sharp knife with a non-slip handle, cut and pull the surrounding fat away from the meat.

**2** Cut out the connective tissue, membrane and gristle from each of the smaller pieces of meat.

**3** Cut the meat into equal-sized cubes, cutting across the grain to shorten the fibres and help to tenderise the meat.

# fish

The thought of preparation puts many people off buying fish, but there are several ways around this, and it need cost you little more than if you'd done it yourself. You can find 'pan-dressed' fish in most supermarket chiller cabinets (which means that it has been trimmed, scaled, gutted, boned or filleted and is ready for the pan). If buying whole fish from a supermarket wet fish counter or fishmonger, you can usually ask them to prepare it for you. There is unlikely to be any charge and it will save you the bother of gutting and filleting yourself. There are a few money-saving techniques though, such as slicing your own smoked salmon.

# slicing smoked salmon

If you are buying a large quantity of smoked salmon – for example, for a party – buy a whole side and slice it yourself.

**COOK SMART**
• Reserve any scraps of smoked salmon that aren't good enough to serve at the party. You can stir them into scrambled eggs for a special breakfast, or add them to a creamy sauce to serve with pasta.

**1** First chill the salmon until firm, then, using a long thin filleting knife, cut off any dry surface flesh and skin. Pull out any small pin bones that are embedded in the length of the salmon, using a pair of tweezers.

**2** With the sharp edge of the knife facing the tail of the fish, cut wafer-thin slices of smoked salmon, starting with small slices cut from the tail end and gradually working up to full-length slices. Keep the knife parallel with the fish and use a gentle sawing action.

**3** Interleave the slices between sheets of greaseproof paper as you go. Keeping the slices flat, wrap in cling film and chill until ready to serve.

# clever cooking

Planning your meals carefully and using ingredients effectively
will help you to get the best value for money.

## making more from less

There are many ways to make affordable dishes using luxurious ingredients, or to dress up cheaper ingredients with a small quantity of more pricey ones. Combining expensive ingredients with cheaper ones will help them to go further and will make you feel that you're not missing out or compromising on taste, quality or quantity.

For example, asparagus is relatively expensive, but by using it in Summer Risotto (page 107), you can make an elegant dish that feels like a treat but without the cost. Similarly, Tagliatelle with Smoked Salmon (page 126) combines smoked salmon trimmings with pasta and cream to make a luxurious pasta dish that won't make a dent in your pocket.

However, stretching ingredients isn't always just about the cost. Sometimes it's just a matter of an extra guest, or not having quite enough of a key ingredient. Or perhaps you've seen something on special offer but there's not quite enough to go round. Try some of the following ideas to make things go further.

■ To make a small roasting chicken feed more people, stuff it with well-flavoured couscous and surround the bird with grilled sausages. Alternatively, joint the chicken and use the pieces to make a casserole or curry, such as Easy Chicken Curry (page 190), and serve with rice or naan bread and a vegetable side dish.

■ If you don't have enough fish to go round, cut it into pieces and use in French Fish Soup (page 63) or make Fish Stew with Vegetables (page 147) for a chunky one-pot meal. Alternatively, poach the fish and combine with mashed potato to make fishcakes.

■ If you're short of potatoes, try mashing them with an equal quantity of carrots for a tasty, healthy mash. Alternatively, roast the potatoes with other root vegetables such as carrots and parsnips.

■ There are plenty of ways to make desserts go further or make it look as though a small portion was deliberate. Serve an elegant sliver of tart with a dollop of crème fraîche and dust with icing sugar, or scoop a modest portion of ice-cream into an elegant stemmed glass, drizzle with a Fruit Coulis (page 34) or Chocolate Sauce (page 35) and serve with dessert biscuits.

■ Dress up a plain cake and make it bigger by cutting it into layers, spreading with cream and piling on fruit.

■ If you're throwing a party but your budget won't run to Champagne, offer guests a glass of Buck's Fizz made with half sparkling wine and half orange juice. Also remember that if you're entertaining for large numbers, you will need less food per person than for an ordinary meal. This is particularly true for buffets.

## something from nothing

Throwing away leftovers is a waste of food and money when you could transform them into new meals instead. Store any remains in a sealed container in the fridge and use them up the next day or in two days at the most. Most leftovers make a great addition to a chunky soup, but try these ideas too.

**Cooked rice** Toss leftover rice with chopped raw vegetables and dressing to make a salad, or stir-fry with vegetables and a little chicken or pork or a handful of prawns.

**Cooked Pasta** If there's enough pasta left over for another serving or two, stir it into tomato sauce, add some cooked vegetables and perhaps some chopped ham, then spoon into individual dishes, sprinkle over grated cheese and bake until golden and bubbling. If you haven't got enough for a whole dish, add the pasta to Minestrone-style Soup (page 46).

**Cooked meat or poultry** Leftovers from a roast are a boon to the economic cook and can be added to almost anything: sandwiches, salads, sauces, fillings for pies or pancake parcels, omelettes, hashes and rice and pasta dishes. Scraps are also great combined with mashed potato and shaped into croquettes or patties and fried.

**Cooked fish and shellfish** Small amounts of fish and shellfish are versatile and good added to salads, sauces, soups, stir-fries, risottos or pizza toppings, or used in fish cakes, tarts and pastry parcels.

**Cooked vegetables** These can make a great filling for an omelette, or add them to a tortilla or vegetable quiche.

They're also great fried with leftover potatoes to make a Bubble and Squeak-style dish, or stirred into a sauce to go with pasta. Stir them into a creamy sauce, top with breadcrumbs, savoury crumble topping or grated cheese and grill to make a tempting gratin.

**Dry plain cake and stale bread** Use dry cake as the base for a trifle, or turn into cakecrumbs in a food processor and freeze for later use in crumbles or dessert bakes. Dry bread can be made into Apricot Bread & Butter Pudding (page 338) or breadcrumbs for stuffings, gratin toppings or crispy coatings. Or, cut into cubes, fry until crisp and golden and sprinkle over salads or soup.

# all-important presentation

No matter how simple the dish, the way a meal is presented can transform it from a cheap supper into an elegant feast.

**Citrus zest** Use a zester to remove fine strips of zest, which can adorn sweet and savoury dishes.

**Fresh herbs** Sprigs, whole leaves or chopped – herbs are one of the cheapest and easiest ways to smarten up a dish.

**Crisp, golden breadcrumbs** Fry breadcrumbs in a little butter and scatter over vegetables to add a lovely crunchy bite.

**Nuts and seeds** A handful of toasted nuts or seeds looks great scattered over a savoury salad, while chopped or flaked nuts look attractive sprinkled over desserts.

**Soup garnishes** A swirl of cream or sprinkling of chopped fresh herbs adds a simple yet elegant finish to a bowl of soup, while a handful of tortilla chips or French bread and grated cheese can turn

it into a hearty meal. Other ideas include crispy bacon pieces, chunky croûtons or a spoonful of salsa.

**Fresh fruit** From a twist of citrus fruit to a fanned, sliced strawberry or kiwi fruit, fresh fruit garnishes can add the finishing touch to a dessert. Grated chocolate or a dusting of icing sugar are good too.

**Individual portions** Many dishes can be cooked or served in elegant, individual dishes. Particularly good for entertaining, the food will look great.

# saving fuel costs

Inefficient cooking is a waste of money. Use the tips and tricks below to save on your fuel bill.

■ While you're cooking, why not make a double quantity? You can freeze half for another day.

■ If you have the oven on, make several baked dishes at the same time. If you're roasting a chicken,

make roast vegetables as an accompaniment. Or if you're making a baked dessert, roast some peppers at the same time to put in a salad the next day.

■ Use good quality heavy-based pans with tight-fitting lids to keep in the heat for economic cooking.

■ Modern pressure cookers are simple and safe to use and can cook dried pulses, sponge puddings and slow-simmered stocks, soups and stews in

about one-third of the time of conventional cooking.

■ A layered steamer that can be placed over a single pan of simmering water is an economical way of cooking several different ingredients at the same time.

■ For speed, economy and efficiency, a microwave is unbeatable. It's ideal for cooking fish, sponge puddings, scrambled eggs, jacket potatoes, porridge, sauces and vegetables.

# one ingredient:
## so many options

If you're worried that eating seasonally will mean lack of variety, then you're in for a pleasant surprise. Take a look at the humble leek. In winter when leeks are in season, you can ring the changes with so many different dishes that you'll never get bored. Try a main meal Cock-a-Leekie Soup (page 65) using up leftover chicken from a roast, or a one-bowl Mediterranean Fish Stew (page 168)

with chunks of crusty bread. Salmon and Leek Parcels (page 157) and Creamy Rabbit Casserole (page 206) make elegant dishes for entertaining. For a simple supper, make quick Turkey and Leek Fritatta (page 205) or Chinese Crispy Beef Stir-fry (page 219), or for a hearty winter feast try Vegetable Medley with Bacon and Kidney Beans (page 272), or chunky Country Cassoulet (page 240). Sliced leeks can also be added to vegetable risottos and paellas, sautéed in butter and used as an omelette or jacket potato filling with grated cheese, tossed into a stir-fry, scattered over a pizza or baked with a creamy cheese sauce until golden and bubbling.

vegetable medley with bacon and kidney beans

turkey and leek fritatta

salmon and leek parcels

cock-a-leekie soup

mediterranean fish stew

creamy rabbit casserole

country cassoulet

crispy beef stirfry

# making the basics

Although you can buy stocks, sauces and preserves ready-made, it's usually cheaper, healthier and tastier to prepare them yourself.

## stocks

Meat, fish and vegetable stocks are used as the base of many dishes, including soups, stews and casseroles. Home-made stock made with bones and trimmings is much cheaper than bought stock. Make a big pot of stock, then freeze in small batches to use when required (see page 22 for tips on freezing).

### meat stock

**Makes 1 litre**
Preparation 5 minutes
Cooking 2 hours

750 g–1 kg meat bones
1 onion, roughly chopped
1 carrot, peeled and roughly chopped
1 celery stick, chopped
1 bouquet garni
6 black peppercorns
½ tsp salt

1 Put the bones in a large pan and pour over 2.5 litres cold water. Bring to the boil, skimming off any scum that rises to the surface, then add the vegetables, bouquet garni, peppercorns and salt.

2 Half cover the pan, reduce the heat and simmer for 2 hours, or until the liquid has reduced by just over half.

3 Remove the pan from the heat and strain the stock, discarding the bones and vegetables. Leave to cool, then skim off the fat that has risen to the surface.

4 Store in a plastic container in the fridge for up to 4 days or freeze for up to 6 months.

• Meat bones can be used raw or cooked but they should always be fresh. You may have bones left over from a roast joint, otherwise ask your butcher for some.

• For a richer flavour, first roast the vegetables in a little oil in a very hot oven for 30–40 minutes before using as above.

### chicken stock

**Makes 1 litre**
Preparation 5 minutes
Cooking 2 hours

1 chicken carcass (raw or remains from a roasted chicken)
chicken giblets, but not the liver (optional)
1 onion, roughly chopped
1 carrot, peeled and roughly chopped
1 celery stick, roughly chopped
1 leek, sliced (optional)
1 bouquet garni (bay leaf, parsley and thyme)
6 black peppercorns
½ tsp salt

**COOK SMART**
• A few chopped mushrooms, if you have some, can also be added to the stock with the rest of the vegetables for extra flavour.

1 Break up the carcass into several pieces and put in a large pan. Add 2 litres of cold water and bring to the boil. Skim off any scum that rises to the surface, then add the vegetables and flavourings.

2 Half cover the pan, reduce the heat and simmer gently for 2 hours or until the stock has reduced by half. Remove the pan from the heat and strain the stock, discarding the bones and vegetables. Leave to cool.

3 Once cool, skim off any fat that has risen to the surface. Keep chilled in the fridge for up to 4 days or store in the freezer for up to 6 months.

# fish stock

**Makes 1 litre**
Preparation 5 minutes
Cooking 30 minutes

900 g trimmings from
  white fish
1 onion, sliced
125 ml dry white wine
1 bouquet garni (bay leaf,
  parsley and thyme)
1 tbsp lemon juice
4 black peppercorns

1 Put the fish trimmings in a large pan, add the onion and cook gently over a low heat for 5 minutes. Pour over 1.25 litres cold water and the wine, then bring to the boil. Skim off any scum that rises to the surface, then add the bouquet garni, lemon juice and peppercorns.

2 Half cover the pan, reduce the heat, then simmer gently for 30 minutes.

3 Remove from the heat, strain the stock and discard the fish trimmings and vegetables. Cool then keep chilled in the fridge for up to 4 days or store in the freezer for up to 3 months.

### COOK SMART
• Ask your fishmonger for fish trimmings, including skin, bones and heads without gills. Alternatively you can use an inexpensive white fish such as pollack or coley – you'll need about 400 g fish fillet.

# vegetable stock

**Makes 1 litre**
Preparation 5 minutes
Cooking 1 hour

750 g–1 kg vegetables
  (such as beans, broccoli,
  cauliflower, celery,
  fennel, leeks,
  mushrooms, onions and
  any root vegetables),
  trimmed and roughly
  chopped
bunch of fresh herbs
  (such as bay leaf,
  dill, parsley stalks,
  rosemary, tarragon
  and thyme)
large strip of lemon zest
6 black peppercorns
1 tsp salt

### COOK SMART
• To make a darker vegetable stock, include aubergines, mushroom stalks and clean onion skins in the selection of vegetables

1 Put all the ingredients in a large pan and pour over 1.5 litres cold water. Bring to the boil, then reduce the heat, half cover the pan and simmer gently for 1 hour or until reduced by about one third.

2 Remove the pan from the heat, strain the stock and discard the vegetables.

3 Leave to cool, then chill in the fridge for up to 4 days or store in the freezer for 6 months.

# savoury sauces

## white sauce

This versatile sauce is used in many dishes. Use this recipe as a base, then add other flavourings such as cheese or herbs. Make it just before you need to use it.

**Makes 600 ml**
Preparation 5 minutes
Cooking 25 minutes

50 g butter
50 g plain flour
600 ml semi-skimmed
  milk
salt and freshly ground
  black pepper

1 Melt the butter in a small pan and stir in the flour. Cook, stirring continuously, for 1 minute, until the mixture forms a smooth 'roux'.

2 Remove the pan from the heat and gradually pour in the milk, stirring or whisking constantly. Return the pan to the heat and bring to the boil, still stirring or whisking.

3 Reduce the heat and simmer the sauce gently for 2 minutes, stirring occasionally, until it is smooth and thick. Season to taste with salt and pepper.

### COOK SMART
• To make a lightly flavoured béchamel sauce, first warm the milk in a pan with a roughly chopped, small onion, a bay leaf, six black peppercorns and a pinch of grated nutmeg. Bring just to the boil, then remove from the heat, cover and set aside to infuse for 10 minutes. Strain then use to make the white sauce, as above.

• To make a cheese sauce, stir 50 g grated cheese (such as mature Cheddar, Gruyère or Parmesan) into the sauce just before serving. A sprinkling of cayenne pepper or nutmeg or 1 tsp mustard improves the flavour.

• To make a mushroom sauce, gently cook 100 g thinly sliced mushrooms in the butter before stirring in the flour.

• To make an onion sauce, gently cook a finely chopped, small onion in the butter for 5 minutes or until softened then stir in the flour.

• To make a parsley sauce, stir 2–3 heaped tbsp chopped fresh parsley into the sauce. Alternatively, use other chopped fresh herbs such as chives or tarragon.

# tomato sauce

A key ingredient in many dishes, serve with pasta or use in speedy stews and casseroles.

**Makes  500ml**
Preparation  10 minutes
Cooking  30–45 minutes

**1 tbsp olive oil**

**1 onion, chopped**

**1 large garlic clove, crushed**

**700g ripe tomatoes, skinned and chopped, or 2 x 400g cans chopped tomatoes**

**2 tsp chopped fresh basil or oregano or 1 tsp dried oregano**

**1 tsp sugar**

**salt and freshly ground black pepper**

**1** Heat the oil in a large saucepan, add the onion and fry gently for 5 minutes until softened. Add the garlic and cook, stirring, for a further 1 minute.

**2** Add the tomatoes with their seeds and juice, then stir in the herbs and sugar and season with salt and pepper. Bring to the boil, then reduce the heat, cover and simmer gently for 30–45 minutes, stirring occasionally, until the sauce is thick.

**3** Purée the sauce in a blender or food processor until smooth. Taste to check the seasoning.

# mayonnaise

Serve with poached or grilled fish, fish cakes, cold roast chicken and salads, or spread on sandwiches. (Note: Foods containing raw eggs should not be served to the very young, pregnant women, the elderly or those with a compromised immune system.)

**Makes  150ml**
Preparation  20 minutes

**1 large egg yolk**

**½ tsp dry mustard**

**pinch of caster sugar**

**salt and freshly ground black pepper**

**150ml olive oil**

**1 tbsp white wine vinegar**

**1** Whisk the egg yolk in a bowl until thick. Whisk in the mustard, sugar and salt and pepper.

**2** Add the oil, a drop at a time, whisking well between each addition. As the mayonnaise thickens and becomes shiny, the oil may be added in a thin stream.

**3** Blend in the vinegar and store in a covered container in the fridge for up to 1 month.

**COOK SMART**

• Flavour the mayonnaise with 1 tbsp chopped fresh herbs, such as chives or tarragon, or 1–2 crushed cloves of garlic.

• To make lemon mayonnaise, use lemon juice in place of the vinegar and add the grated zest of ½ lemon.

• To make a spicy mayonnaise, stir in 1 tsp mild curry paste and 1 tbsp mango or peach chutney.

• To make tartare sauce, stir in three chopped cocktail gherkins, 2 tsp capers, and 1 tsp snipped chives.

# vinaigrette

Salad dressing is easy to make and cheaper than bought dressing. For extra flavour, add 1 tsp mustard.

**Makes  150ml**
Preparation  5 minutes

**120 ml olive oil**

**2 tbsp red or white wine vinegar, or lemon juice**

**pinch of caster sugar**

**1 tsp made mustard**

**salt and freshly ground black pepper**

Put all the ingredients in screw-top jar, seasoning with salt and pepper, and shake well to combine.

# sweet sauces

## apple sauce

Serve with roast pork, gammon and goose, grilled sausages and bacon.

**Makes  300 ml**
Preparation  5 minutes
Cooking  10 minutes

500 g Bramley cooking apples, peeled, cored and sliced

25 g unsalted butter, softened

caster sugar (to taste)

**1** Put the apples in a pan with 3 tbsp cold water and cook over a low heat for 10 minutes until soft.

**2** Mash the apples with a large fork or vegetable masher or for a smoother sauce, purée in a blender or food processor.

**3** Stir in the butter and sweeten to taste with caster sugar.

## custard sauce

Sometimes called crème anglaise, serve this sauce with sweet pies, tarts and puddings.

**Makes  600 ml**
Preparation  5 minutes
Cooking  5 minutes

4 egg yolks

4 tsp cornflour

4 tbsp caster sugar

600 ml semi-skimmed milk

few drops of pure vanilla extract (optional)

**1** Put the egg yolks, cornflour and sugar in a heatproof bowl and beat until smooth.

**2** Pour the milk into a saucepan and bring to the boil. Slowly pour the milk onto the egg yolk mixture, stirring all the time.

**3** Return the mixture to the pan and cook over a low heat, stirring constantly until thickened to a custard consistency. Flavour with a few drops of vanilla extract, if liked. Remove from the heat and strain into a jug.

**4** Serve hot or leave to cool before using or serving.

**COOK SMART**
• Vanilla adds a lovely flavour to custard but you can add other flavourings such as a little grated orange zest or 2 tbsp rum, brandy or flavoured liqueur to the finished custard.

## fruit coulis

Serve drizzled over tarts, stewed or poached fruits or ice-cream. Use seasonal berries and freeze the coulis, or freeze the berries and make the coulis later.

**Serves  6**
Preparation  10 minutes

300 g soft summer fruits (such as strawberries, raspberries, blackberries or stoned cherries)

1 tbsp lemon juice

icing sugar, to taste

1–2 tbsp fruit liqueur (optional)

**1** Place the fruit in a food processor or blender and process to a smooth purée.

**2** For a smooth coulis, press the purée through a sieve to remove seeds.

**3** Stir in the lemon juice and sweeten to taste with sugar.

**4** Add a little fruit liqueur if liked or, if the coulis is too thick, stir in a little water to thin to the desired consistency.

# chocolate sauce

Serve warm over ice-cream or pancakes.

**Serves 6**
Preparation  5 minutes
Cooking  5 minutes

**100 g plain chocolate, broken into pieces**

**15 g unsalted butter**

**3 tbsp golden syrup or runny honey**

1 Put the chocolate in a small pan with the butter, syrup or honey and 2 tbsp water. Warm gently over a low heat until the chocolate has melted.

2 Remove pan from the heat and serve warm.

# butterscotch sauce

For a sticky treat, pour over ice-cream, sliced bananas and chopped walnuts or pecans.

**Serves  6**
Cooking  5–10 minutes

**50 g unsalted butter**

**150 g light muscovado sugar**

**170 g can evaporated milk**

1 Gently heat the butter in a small saucepan until melted, add the sugar and stir until dissolved, then cook gently for 3 minutes.

2 Remove the pan from the heat and stir in the evaporated milk. Return to the heat and bring back to the boil. Serve warm, or cool and chill. Then reheat gently when required.

# preserves

Jams, jellies and chutneys are great for preserving fresh, seasonal produce when it is cheap and in plentiful supply. They're also a good way to use up bruised or squashy fruits.

## tomato and apple chutney

**Makes about 1.8 kg**
Preparation  25 minutes
Cooking  2½ hours

**1 kg ripe tomatoes, skinned**

**1 kg cooking apples, peeled and cored**

**450 g onions**

**4 garlic cloves, crushed**

**400 ml malt or cider vinegar**

**300 g demerara or light muscovado sugar**

**225 g sultanas**

**2 tsp salt**

**15 g whole pickling spices, e.g. a mixture of allspice berries, dried chillies, ginger, celery seeds and peppercorns, tied in a muslin bag (optional)**

### COOK SMART

• Pears or plums may be substituted for some of the apples. They'll make a sweeter chutney, but don't be tempted to reduce the amount of sugar, or the chutney won't keep well.

• To sterilise jars, first wash, rinse and drain them, then place in a warm oven at 110°C (gas ¼) for 15 minutes. Keep warm until ready to fill.

1 Roughly chop the tomatoes, apples and onions and put them in a preserving pan or large, heavy-based, stainless steel saucepan with the garlic and vinegar. Slowly bring to the boil, then reduce the heat and simmer for 30 minutes or until the fruit and vegetables are tender, stirring the mixture occasionally.

2 Add all the remaining ingredients, including the pickling spices, if using, and heat gently, stirring frequently until the sugar has dissolved. Bring back to the boil, then simmer uncovered for 2 hours, stirring often towards the end of the cooking time, to prevent sticking. By this time the chutney should be well-reduced and very thick – if necessary, cook for a few more minutes.

3 Spoon the chutney into warm, sterilised jars. Cover the chutney with discs of waxed paper, waxed-side down to cover the surface completely. Cover the jars with cellophane or plastic screw-topped lids (not metal lids, as they will corrode). Tighten the lids when the chutney is completely cold, and label.

4 Store in a cool dark place and leave to mature for at least 1 month, before eating. Use within 1 year of making. Once opened, store in the fridge and use within 1 month.

# citrus fruit marmalade

**Makes about 2.5 kg**
Preparation 30 minutes
Cooking 2¼ hours

**900 g oranges or a mixture of oranges and grapefruit**
**2 lemons**
**1.75 kg granulated sugar**

1 Wash the fruit, then halve and squeeze the juice into a preserving pan or large, heavy-based stainless steel saucepan. Tie the pips and membranes in a muslin bag. Cut the peel into thin shreds (or coarse ones, if preferred) and then add to the saucepan with the bag of pips and 2.25 litres of water.

2 Bring to the boil, then simmer gently, uncovered for about 2 hours or until the contents of the pan are reduced by about half and the peel is really tender. Remove the muslin bag, leave to cool, then squeeze any liquid back into the pan.

3 Add the sugar to the saucepan and stir over a very low heat, until completely dissolved. Bring to the boil and boil rapidly for about 15 minutes or until setting point is reached (105°C on a sugar thermometer).

4 Remove the saucepan from the heat and skim off any scum from the surface with a draining spoon. Leave to cool, for about 5 minutes, or until a thin skin starts to form on top of the marmalade. Stir gently, to distribute the peel evenly.

5 Ladle into warm, sterilised jars, then cover and seal. When cold, label, then store in a cool dark place. Use within 1 year of making. Once opened, store in the fridge and use within 1 month.

## COOK SMART

· Seville oranges, which are available in late January/ February, have a particularly good flavour for marmalade making. You will need about 1 kg of fruit.

· If you haven't got a sugar thermometer, spoon a little of the marmalade onto a chilled saucer, cool for a few seconds then push a finger across it. If the surface wrinkles, it has reached setting point. If not, boil the marmalade for a further 5 minutes, then test again.

# microwave summer berry jam

**Makes about 750 g**
Cooking 15–20 minutes

**500 g strawberries or raspberries**
**50 ml lemon juice**
**500 g jam sugar**

1 Put the strawberries in a large, microwaveable bowl with the lemon juice. Cook on full power for 4 minutes, or until the fruit is soft.

2 Stir in the sugar and when completely dissolved, cook for 15–20 minutes, stirring every 3 minutes.

3 To test when the jam is ready, after 15 minutes, spoon a little jam onto a chilled saucer, cool for a few seconds then push a finger across it. If the surface wrinkles, it has reached setting point, if not, cook the jam for a further 3 minutes, then test again. Continue testing every 3 minutes until setting point is reached.

4 Stand for 5 minutes, then pour into warm sterilised jars, seal and label.

## COOK SMART

· Cooking time will vary depending on the power of the microwave and ripeness of the fruit.

· Jam sugar contains a balanced amount of natural pectin and citric acid, which overcomes the problem of setting encountered with some fruits, like strawberries with low pectin levels. You can therefore be sure of a perfect set.

# seasonal menu ideas

Entertaining friends and family on a budget is easy, especially when you use fresh ingredients and seasonal produce. In order to take the hassle out of planning, we've come up with a selection of year-round menus that you can vary and adapt according to your own taste. Most recipes and menus serve four, although there are also ideas included for buffet parties and picnics when you'll want to serve a wider selection of dishes to feed more people. Many recipes can be adapted for smaller or larger numbers, either by making a double quantity or by changing the proportions of ingredients to suit your needs. Alternatively, you could make a meal go further and add variety by cooking an extra dish.

**autumn
fireside food**

## informal supper

**blt pasta**
(page 129)

**warm ciabatta**

**mixed leaf salad**

**pineapple pudding**
(page 332)

## vegetarian dinner

**tomato and lentil soup**
(page 54)

**vegetable paella**
(page 106)

**orange mousse**
(page 313)

## easter sunday lunch

**grapefruit salad shells**
(page 77)

**roast chicken with
herb stuffing** (page 196)

**roast potatoes and
seasonal vegetables**

**spiced crème brûlée**
(page 317)

## easy for mid-week

**chilli pots with cheese**
(page 215)

**crusty bread or tortillas**

**mixed green salad**

**normandy baked apples**
(page 303)

## a taste of the east

**prawn crackers**

**stir-fried chicken and
broccoli with coconut milk**
(page 184)

**boiled rice**

**juicy orange wedges**

## quick lunch for friends

**spicy pork fajitas**
(page 235)

**caramel ice-cream
with apricots**
(page 304)
(make the ice-cream ahead)

## lazy weekend lunch

**artichoke crostini**
(page 91)

**pasta puttanesca**
(page 128)

**mixed leaf salad**

**fresh peaches or mixed
summer berries**

## picnic hamper

**chicken liver paté with
crusty bread** (page 84)

**hummus dip with pitta and
vegetable crudités**
(page 82)

**summer pasta salad** (page 118)

**devilled chicken drumsticks**
(page 185)

**chocolate chip cookies**
(page 341)

**fresh seasonal fruit**

## al fresco get-together

**guacamole with a kick**
(page 81)

**marinated cucumber
yoghurt** (page 82)

**salmon terrine with
tarragon sauce** (page 85)

**bulghur wheat salad**
(page 102)

**filo fruit baskets** (page 326)

## light and simple

**pesto rice salad with tuna**
(page 104)

**floating islands on
berry coulis**
(page 309)

## sunshine holiday menu

**mediterranean fish stew**
(page 168)

**crusty baguette or
garlic bread**

**baked bananas** (page 303)
**with vanilla ice-cream**

## vegetarian special

**chilled summer vegetable
soup** (page 71)

**roasted vegetable
couscous** (page 111)

**cherry sponge layer cake**
(page 339)

## brunch party

**smoked fish kedgeree**
(page 166)

**champion hash browns**
(page 281)

**balsamic baked tomatoes
with parmesan crumbs**
(page 260)

**fresh fruit salad**

## family sunday lunch

**gardener's chicken**
(page 191)

**creamy polenta** (page 115)
**and seasonal greens**

**autumn crumble**
(page 327)

**custard sauce**
(page 34)

## easy supper

**grissini (breadsticks)**

**turkey and vegetable
pasta bake**
(page 203)

**leafy green salad**

**chocolate and
coconut mousse**
(page 310)

## veggie treat

**baked stuffed marrow**
(page 290)

**wholegrain or
granary bread**

**apple and blackberry
pancakes** (page 307)

**crème fraîche or
greek-style yoghurt**

## fireside food

**spicy pumpkin and
apple soup** (page 51)

**toad-in-the-hole** (page 239)

**boston baked beans**
(page 277)

**chocolate caramel cream**
(page 311)

## super one-pot meal

**pot-roast beef with
braised vegetables**
(page 224)

**jam tart** (page 319)

**custard sauce**
(page 34)

## drinks party

double cheese bites (page 88)

chicken satay (page 174)

buckwheat blinis (page 92)
with taramasalata (page 83)

spicy aubergine caviar
with toast fingers (page 80)

crispy fish goujons with
lemon and caper dip
(page 143)

tempting tex-mex nachos
(page 93)

(suitable for 8 guests)

## celebration lunch

blue cheese and
apple salad (page 77)

salmon and spinach
pastries (page 158)

seasonal vegetables

pears with chocolate
sauce (page 305)

## fork buffet

sausage-stuffed chestnut
mushrooms (page 87)

turkey and leek frittata (page 205)

spinach and mushroom roulade
(page 297)

red, white and green bean
salad (page 253)

quinoa pilaff with
cherries and walnuts (page 114)

luscious lemon tart (page 321)

sponge cake (page 337)

(suitable for 6–8 guests)

## quick light supper

chicken hash with
potatoes and peppers
(page 188)
or tagliatelle with
smoked salmon (page 126)

crisp wedges of apple

## spicy tastes

keema curry (page 232)

potato curry with peas
and mushrooms (page 279)

basmati rice or naan bread

yoghurt raita

slices of fresh mango
or mango purée swirled with
creamy yoghurt

## cold comfort

picadillo with rice
(page 232)
or lentil stew with
browned onions (page 299)

apricot bread and butter
pudding (page 338)

WINTER MENU IDEAS

41

# so

**fabulous
flavours, luscious
textures**
and **glorious
colours**

# ups

Piping hot or cool and chilled, soup is the perfect way
to take advantage of great-value seasonal ingredients
when they're in abundance. Whatever the weather or the
occasion, a bowl of soup is always irresistible, and it is
a great way to transform the simplest ingredients into
the most stunning dish. Whether you're looking for a meal
in a bowl or a sophisticated starter, a warming lunch or
a simple supper, versatile soup is always the way to go.

THE ROBUST FLAVOURS OF SWEET ORANGE CARROTS AND DELICIOUSLY CREAMY CELERIAC MAKE THE PERFECT BASE FOR THIS HEARTY, WARMING SOUP.

# autumn root vegetable soup

**£**

**Serves 4** Ⓥ
Preparation 15 minutes
Cooking 25 minutes

**3 carrots, peeled and chopped**

**600 g celeriac, peeled and chopped**

**1 large onion, chopped**

**1 garlic clove, crushed**

**4 tbsp crème fraîche**

**1 tbsp finely snipped fresh chives**

**salt and freshly ground black pepper**

**fresh chives to garnish (optional)**

## COOK SMART

• Chop the celeriac and carrots into roughly equal-sized pieces, so that they take the same amount of time to cook.

• You can make an equally flavourful and creamy soup by substituting pumpkin for the celeriac.

**Per serving**
kcal 119, protein 3g, fat 7g (of which saturated fat 4g), carbohydrate 12g (of which sugars 10g), fibre 7g, sodium 0.2g

**1** Bring 1 litre of lightly salted water to the boil in a large saucepan while preparing the carrots, celeriac and onion. Tip the vegetables into the water. Bring water back to the boil, then reduce the heat and cover the pan. Simmer gently for 25 minutes or until tender.

**2** Remove from the heat, add the garlic and allow to cool slightly. Purée the soup in a blender or food processor until smooth. Return to the pan.

**3** Stir in the crème fraîche and reheat gently. Do not allow the soup to boil. Add the snipped chives and season to taste. Garnish with extra chives, if liked.

# fresh tomato soup

£

**Serves 4**  Ⓥ
Preparation  25 minutes
Cooking  20 minutes

**Per serving**
kcal 216, protein 4g,
fat 14g (of which saturated
fat 7g), carbohydrate 19g
(of which sugars 9g),
fibre 4g, sodium 0.1g

**COOK SMART**
• When fresh tomatoes
are not in season, you can
use 1 litre tomato juice or
2 x 400g cans of tomatoes
with their juice instead of
the fresh tomatoes.

1 tbsp olive oil

2 leeks, trimmed and
   sliced

1 kg well-ripened
   tomatoes, skinned,
   seeded and chopped

3 sprigs of flat-leaf parsley

1 celery stalk

2 sprigs of fresh thyme

1 bay leaf

1 tsp tomato purée

2 garlic cloves, crushed

pinch of sugar

50 g vermicelli or
   spaghetti, broken
   into short lengths

20 g butter, diced

salt and freshly ground
   black pepper

fresh sprigs of thyme
   to garnish (optional)

**1** Heat the oil in a saucepan. Add the leeks and cook gently for 10 minutes until softened.

**2** Tip the chopped tomatoes into a blender or food processor and whizz them into a pulp.

**3** Fincly chop the parsley leaves. Tie together the parsley stalks, celery, thyme and bay leaf to make a bouquet garni.

**4** Add the tomatoes to the leeks, together with the tomato purée, chopped parsley, garlic, sugar and bouquet garni. Season with salt. Cover and simmer gently for 15 minutes.

**5** Remove the bouquet garni. Add the vermicelli or spaghetti to the soup and cook for 5 minutes until just tender.

**6** Add the butter, stir and season to taste. Garnish with fresh thyme sprigs, if liked.

**MAKE THE MOST OF HOME-GROWN TOMATOES WHEN THEY'RE PLUMP, JUICY AND PLENTIFUL, AND BURSTING WITH FLAVOUR.**

# minestrone-style soup

£

**Serves 4**
Preparation 15 minutes
Cooking 25 minutes

**Per serving**
kcal 424, protein 30 g,
fat 15 g (of which saturated
fat 4 g), carbohydrate 40 g
(of which sugars 10 g),
fibre 8 g, sodium 0.8 g

ADDING CHUNKY RED
KIDNEY BEANS AND
MACARONI TO THIS
HEALTHY VEGETABLE
SOUP TRANSFORMS
IT INTO A SATISFYING
MEAL-IN-A-BOWL.

2 tbsp olive oil

1 large onion, diced

2 carrots, peeled and diced

1 leek, trimmed and sliced

100 g lean smoked bacon,
derinded and diced

1 garlic clove, crushed

1 litre vegetable or
chicken stock

1 bay leaf

a few stalks of fresh parsley

1 tbsp tomato purée

400 g can red kidney beans,
drained and rinsed

100 g small macaroni

100 g green beans, chopped

salt and freshly ground
black pepper

sprigs of parsley to garnish
(optional)

**1** Heat the oil in a large saucepan. Add the onion, carrots, leek, bacon and garlic and cook gently over a low heat for 5 minutes, stirring often until softened.

**2** Add the stock, bay leaf and parsley stalks and bring to a gentle boil. Add a good pinch of salt, cover, reduce the heat and cook gently for 10 minutes.

**3** Stir in the tomato purée, kidney beans and macaroni, bring back to a gentle boil and cook for another 10 minutes, stirring often to prevent the pasta from sticking. Add the green beans after 5 minutes.

**4** When the macaroni is cooked, remove the bay leaf and taste to check the seasoning. Serve garnished with extra parsley, if liked.

# creamy celery and potato soup

STARCHY POTATOES MAKE A CREAMY,
FILLING BASE FOR THIS WARMING SOUP,
WHILE DISTINCTIVELY-FLAVOURED CELERY
ADDS A TANGY BITE.

£

**Serves 4** V
Preparation 15 minutes
Cooking 25 minutes

**Per serving**
kcal 245, protein 21 g,
fat 14 g (of which saturated
fat 8 g), carbohydrate 9 g
(of which sugars 5 g),
fibre 1 g, sodium 0.2 g

25 g butter

5 celery sticks, chopped,
leaves reserved

200 g potatoes, peeled and
chopped

1 leek, trimmed and sliced

700 ml vegetable stock

1 bay leaf

300 ml semi-skimmed milk

salt and freshly ground
black pepper

**To serve**
50 g Stilton, crumbled
(optional)

**1** Melt the butter in a large saucepan over a low heat. Add the celery, potatoes and leeks and cook gently for 5 minutes.

**2** Pour the stock into the pan and add the bay leaf. Bring to the boil, then reduce the heat, cover and simmer for 20 minutes or until all the vegetables are tender. Remove the bay leaf.

**3** Cool slightly. Using a draining spoon, lift out the vegetables and put them into a blender or food processor with some of the liquid. Whizz to a purée.

**4** Return the purée to the pan with the rest of the liquid, add the milk and heat gently. Season to taste with salt and pepper.

**5** Ladle the soup into warm bowls and grind a little more pepper over the top. Scatter over the chopped celery leaves to garnish and add some crumbled Stilton, if liked.

**COOK SMART**

• Serve with hot garlic and herb bread. Thickly slice a baguette, leaving the slices attached at the base. Hold the slices apart and spread each one thinly with garlic, chive and parsley butter (add chopped herbs and crushed garlic to softened butter). Reshape the loaf, wrap in foil and bake in a moderate oven for 10 minutes.

• Some crispy, grilled pieces of bacon would also make a tasty garnish.

46

DARK GREEN, PEPPERY WATERCRESS IS
PACKED WITH HEALTHY NUTRIENTS SO YOU
CAN ENJOY THIS DIVINELY CREAMY SOUP
WITH NONE OF THE GUILT.

# watercress
## soup

£

**Serves 4** V

Preparation 15 minutes
Cooking 20 minutes

**2 bunches or packs
watercress, about 85g
each**

**40g butter**

**1 onion, finely chopped**

**2 tbsp flour**

**500ml semi-skimmed milk**

**100ml crème fraîche**

**salt and freshly ground
black pepper**

**Garlic toast**
**2 medium slices white
bread (from a sandwich
loaf)**

**1 garlic clove**

### COOK SMART
● For a thicker
consistency, cook a
little diced potato with
the watercress. You could
also stir in 1 or 2 egg
yolks in step 4.

● For a lighter soup, omit
the crème fraîche and
simply add a little more
milk or stock.

**Per serving**
kcal 309, protein 8g,
fat 21g (of which saturated
fat 13g), carbohydrate 23g
(of which sugars 9g),
fibre 1.5g, sodium 0.2g

1 Set aside four fresh sprigs of watercress for garnish,
then finely chop half of the rest. Tip the unchopped
watercress into boiling, lightly salted water and cook
for 5 minutes. Drain, reserving the cooking water,
then tip the watercress into a blender or food
processor with 250ml of the reserved cooking
water and blend to a purée.

2 Melt the butter in a saucepan. Add the onion, stir,
and cook gently for 5 minutes.

3 Sprinkle the flour over the onion and stir for
2 minutes, without letting it colour. Gradually add
the milk and another 250ml of the reserved cooking
water. Bring to the boil, stirring constantly. Simmer
for 5 minutes. Season with salt and pepper.

4 Add the puréed watercress, the chopped raw
watercress and the crème fraîche to this mixture.
Stir together well and season to taste. Keep warm.

5 Toast the bread on both sides. Rub the toast with
the peeled, whole clove of garlic, then cut the toast
into slim fingers.

6 Serve the soup garnished with the reserved sprigs of
watercress and the garlic toast fingers.

# broccoli soup

(£)

**Serves 4**
Preparation  15 minutes
Cooking  20 minutes

**1 litre chicken or
   vegetable stock**
**600 g broccoli, cut into
   florets and stalks
   chopped**
**1 onion, roughly chopped**
**2 garlic cloves, crushed**
**2 tbsp long-grain rice**
**2 tbsp crème fraîche**
**1 tbsp flaked almonds,
   toasted**
**salt and freshly ground
   black pepper**

### COOK SMART
• If preferred, you
can substitute milk or
single cream for the
crème fraîche.

• Add a few ice cubes
to the water in which you
refresh the broccoli florets
in step 2: the cold will set
their deep green colour.

**Per serving**
kcal 262, protein 29 g,
fat 11 g (of which saturated
fat 4 g), carbohydrate 12 g
(of which sugars 4 g),
fibre 3 g, sodium 0.1 g

**1** Bring the stock to the boil in a large saucepan.
Set aside a few florets of broccoli for the garnish,
then add the rest to the saucepan with the onion
and garlic. Bring back to the boil and tip the rice into
the saucepan. Cover and cook over a low heat for
20 minutes or until the broccoli and rice are tender.

**2** Meanwhile, cook the reserved broccoli florets in
a little lightly salted, boiling water for 5 minutes
until just tender. Refresh in cold water and drain
on kitchen paper.

**3** Blend the soup in a blender or food processor,
then return the soup to the pan. Add the crème
fraîche and season to taste.

**4** Serve garnished with the separately cooked broccoli
florets and the toasted almonds.

THERE'S NO WASTE WITH THIS SOUP. USE
THE WHOLE BROCCOLI HEAD, INCLUDING
THE STALKS, TO REALLY MAKE THE MOST
OF THOSE VALUABLE ANTIOXIDANTS.

ADDING STUFFED PASTA TO THIS DELICATELY FLAVOURED SOUP TURNS
IT INTO A FILLING LUNCH OR SUPPER. MAKE IT IN LATE SUMMER AND
EARLY AUTUMN WHEN COURGETTES ARE AT THEIR BEST.

💷💷

**Serves 4**
Preparation  15 minutes
Cooking  about 20 minutes

**700 ml chicken or
   vegetable stock**

**700 g courgettes, peeled
   and chopped**

**2 garlic cloves, crushed**

**15 g fresh flat-leaf parsley,
   finely chopped**

**6 fresh chives, snipped**

**300 g fresh cheese and
   tomato ravioli**

**salt and freshly ground
   black pepper**

**Per serving**
kcal 246, protein 23 g,
fat 7 g (of which saturated
fat 1 g), carbohydrate 23 g
(of which sugars 4 g),
fibre 2.5 g, sodium 0.2 g

---

**COOK SMART**

• If the courgettes are
very fresh and sufficiently
young, don't peel them:
you'll have a lovely deep-
green soup punctuated by
the white of the ravioli.

• Substitute spinach
ravioli for the cheese
ravioli.

• Offer round a little
freshly grated Parmesan
to sprinkle on top.

---

**1** Bring the stock to the boil in a saucepan, add the courgettes, reduce
the heat, then cover and cook gently for 15 minutes or until tender.

**2** Remove from the heat and add the garlic to the soup. Blend until
smooth in a blender or food processor. Return to the pan and stir
in the herbs. Season to taste. Cover and keep warm, then reheat
gently before serving.

**3** Bring a saucepan of lightly salted water to the boil. Add the ravioli
and cook according to the packet instructions. (Take care not to
overcook the ravioli, as they could break up and lose their filling in
the cooking water.)

**4** Drain the ravioli and divide among the bowls. Ladle over the soup
and serve at once.

# courgette
## soup with
### ravioli

# spicy pumpkin and apple soup

ENJOY THIS SPICY SOUP AT HALLOWEEN. CARVE THE PUMPKIN SHELL INTO A SPOOKY-LOOKING LANTERN, AND USE THE SCOOPED-OUT FLESH TO MAKE THE SOUP.

£

**Serves 4** V
Preparation 20 minutes
Cooking 25 minutes

**2 tbsp vegetable oil**

**1 onion, chopped**

**1 tsp mild or medium curry paste**

**600 g pumpkin flesh, cubed**

**1 cooking apple, peeled, cored and diced**

**2 tomatoes, skinned and chopped**

**1 litre vegetable stock**

**2 tbsp chopped fresh coriander**

**salt and freshly ground black pepper**

**fresh coriander leaves to garnish**

**To serve**
**crispy croûtons**

## COOK SMART

• To make croûtons, cut off the crusts from three to four thick slices of wholemeal bread, then cut the bread into small cubes. Heat a little oil in a non-stick frying pan, then sauté the bread cubes until golden and crispy. Drain on kitchen paper.

• If buying a wedge of pumpkin to make this soup, you'll need about 1.25 kg to give 600 g flesh. Alternatively you can use butternut squash.

**Per serving**
kcal 227, protein 22 g, fat 11 g (of which saturated fat 2.5 g), carbohydrate 11 g (of which sugars 10 g), fibre 3 g, sodium 0.1 g

1 Heat the oil in a large saucepan, add the onion and cook gently for 5 minutes until softened. Stir in the curry paste and cook gently over a low heat for 3–4 minutes.

2 Add the pumpkin and stir to coat with the onion mixture. Stir in the apple and tomatoes. Pour in the stock and bring to the boil. Then reduce the heat, cover and simmer for 25 minutes or until the pumpkin is tender.

3 Allow to cool slightly, then purée the soup in a blender or a food processor until smooth. Reheat gently, season to taste and stir in the chopped coriander.

4 Serve with some freshly ground black pepper and scatter over the croûtons and coriander leaves.

WITH ITS VIBRANT TASTE AND COLOUR, THIS HEALTHY SOUP OFFERS A REFRESHING LIGHT WINTER LUNCH OR SUPPER.

# green pea soup

£

**Serves 4**
Preparation  5 minutes
Cooking  30 minutes

**10 g butter**
**1 large leek, trimmed and thinly sliced**
**750 ml chicken or vegetable stock**
**2 x 300 g cans garden peas, drained**
**pinch of sugar**
**salt and freshly ground black pepper**

**To serve**
**4 tbsp whipping cream**

**Per serving**
kcal 270, protein 23 g fat 12 g
(of which saturated fat 6 g)
carbohydrate 19 g (of which
sugars 3 g) fibre 5 g, sodium 0.5 g

1 Melt the butter in a large saucepan. Add the leek, cover and cook over a low heat for 5 minutes. Add 3 tbsp water and cook gently for 10 more minutes.

2 Pour the stock over the leeks, stir, then cover and continue to cook gently for 10 minutes.

3 Put aside a few peas for garnish, then tip the rest into the pan. Add the sugar and heat for 5 minutes, without boiling, allow to cool slightly, then tip into a blender or food processor and purée until smooth. Season to taste. Return to the pan and reheat gently.

4 Garnish each serving with a swirl of cream and a few of the reserved peas.

**COOK SMART**

• If liked, serve the soup with some crisp toast croûtons, some diced lean ham or some crisply fried, smoked bacon lardons.

• You can also make this soup using about 450 g frozen peas. Minted peas give an especially good flavour.

# greek spinach, egg and lemon soup

**Serves 4**
Preparation  5 minutes
Cooking  10–15 minutes

**Per serving**
kcal 194, protein 22g,
fat 6g (of which saturated
fat 2g), carbohydrate 14g
(of which sugars 2g),
fibre 1.5g, sodium 0.5g

**750 ml chicken or
    vegetable stock**
**3 spring onions, thinly
    sliced**
**3 garlic cloves, crushed**
**300 g frozen chopped
    spinach, thawed
    and drained**
**½ tsp dried oregano**
**150 g cooked rice**
**1 tsp grated lemon zest**
**3 tbsp lemon juice**
**1 large egg, plus 2 egg
    whites**
**salt and freshly ground
    black pepper**

**A VELVETY, MEDITERRANEAN-STYLE SOUP
ENRICHED WITH EGG AND BOOSTED WITH COOKED
RICE TO MAKE A REALLY SATISFYING BOWLFUL.**

**1** Combine 50 ml of the stock with the spring onions and garlic in a medium saucepan. Cook over a moderate heat for about 2 minutes until the spring onions are tender.

**2** Add the remaining 700 ml stock, spinach and oregano, and bring to the boil. Reduce heat, cover and simmer for 3–4 minutes until the spinach is tender.

**3** Stir in the rice, lemon zest and juice, season to taste and continue to gently simmer.

**4** Lightly whisk the whole egg and egg whites in a heatproof bowl then whisk in 125 ml of the soup. Pour the egg mixture into the simmering soup, stirring constantly to make egg 'threads'. Serve immediately.

---

**COOK SMART**

• Perfect for using up leftover rice from another meal but if you need to cook some for this recipe, use 50g (dry weight) rice and cook it first, until just tender.

• If you'd like to use fresh spinach, cook 500g in a large pan, with just the washing water clinging to the leaves, for 2 minutes until just wilted. Cool, press out excess moisture, then finely chop. Add to the soup in step 2.

# tomato and lentil soup

£

**Serves 4** V
Preparation 10 minutes,
   plus 20 minutes soaking
Cooking 25–30 minutes

**15g dried porcini or
   shiitake mushrooms**

**2 tbsp olive oil**

**1 large onion, finely
   chopped**

**3 garlic cloves, crushed**

**400g can chopped
   tomatoes**

**1 tsp ground ginger**

**1 tbsp chopped fresh
   tarragon or 1 tsp dried**

**90g brown or green lentils,
   rinsed**

**salt and freshly ground
   black pepper**

**COOK SMART**

• This recipe can be made
ahead, then chilled or
frozen. Thaw, if necessary,
then reheat gently, adding
a little water if too thick.

• You could use red
split lentils, but they
tend to cook down to a
purée, whereas the brown
and green varieties hold
their shape.

**Per serving**
kcal 152, protein 7g,
fat 6g (of which saturated
fat 1g), carbohydrate 18g
(of which sugars 4.5g),
fibre 3g, sodium 0.05g

**1** Put the mushrooms in a bowl and pour over 250ml
boiling water. Leave to soak for 20 minutes until
softened, then drain in a sieve with a double layer of
kitchen paper, reserving the soaking liquid. Roughly
chop the mushrooms.

**2** Meanwhile, heat the oil in large saucepan over a
medium heat. Add the onion and garlic, and cook
gently for 7–8 minutes, stirring frequently, until the
onion is golden.

**3** Stir in the mushrooms and their soaking liquid, the
tomatoes with their juice, the ginger, tarragon and
500ml water. Add the lentils and bring to the boil.
Reduce heat, cover and simmer for 25–30 minutes
or until the lentils are tender. Season to taste.

**NOTHING BEATS A HEARTY LENTIL
SOUP. THE DRIED MUSHROOMS ADD
A REAL DEPTH OF FLAVOUR AND,
ALTHOUGH THEY'RE EXPENSIVE, YOU
ONLY NEED A SMALL QUANTITY.**

# brussels sprout and almond soup

£

**Serves 6** V
Preparation 20 minutes
Cooking 10–15 minutes

**50g butter**

**1 large onion, chopped**

**75g flaked almonds**

**500g Brussels sprouts,
   quartered**

**1.2 litres vegetable stock**

**1 bouquet garni**

**freshly grated nutmeg**

**freshly ground black
   pepper**

**2 tbsp single cream
   (optional)**

**snipped fresh chives or
   toasted flaked almonds
   to garnish**

**COOK SMART**

• For a more substantial,
richer soup, serve the
soup sprinkled with some
grated mature Cheddar
over the top.

• For freezing, omit
the cream then cool and
chill. Pour into a plastic
container. Use within
3 months. Reheat then
add the cream, if liked.

**Per serving**
kcal 290, protein 22g,
fat 20g (of which saturated
fat 7g), carbohydrate 6g
(of which sugars 5g),
fibre 4g, sodium 0.1g

**1** Melt the butter in a large saucepan over a low heat,
add the onion and almonds and cook gently for
3–4 minutes, until the onion is softened and
the nuts are golden. Stir in the sprouts.

**2** Pour in the stock, bring to the boil and add the
bouquet garni. Reduce heat, cover and simmer for
10–15 minutes, until the sprouts are tender.

**3** Using a draining spoon, lift out the sprouts,
onion and nuts and transfer to a blender or food
processor. Remove and discard the bouquet garni.
Add a little of the liquid to the sprouts then whizz
to a smooth purée. Pour back into the pan, stir and
season to taste with nutmeg and pepper.

**4** Stir in the cream, if using, and warm through.
Serve garnished with a sprinkling of chives or
toasted almonds.

**MAKE THE MOST OF BRUSSELS SPROUTS WHILE THEY'RE IN SEASON.
THIS DELICIOUS, NUTRITIOUS SOUP IS PERFECT WINTER FOOD – SO
ENJOY IT WHEN SPROUTS ARE PILED HIGH IN THE SHOPS.**

# hearty split pea soup

£

**Serves 6**
Preparation  20 minutes
Cooking  45 minutes

**Per serving**
kcal 234, protein 22g,
fat 6g (of which saturated
fat 2g), carbohydrate 23g
(of which sugars 5g),
fibre 2.5g, sodium 0.1g

2 tsp vegetable oil

1 large onion, finely
    chopped

3 garlic cloves, crushed

2 carrots, peeled, halved
    lengthways and thinly
    sliced crossways

125g split peas

1 litre vegetable stock

2 tbsp tomato purée

½ tsp dried sage

50g small pasta shapes
    (such as macaroni)

salt and freshly ground
    black pepper

**To serve**
30g Parmesan, grated

**1** Heat the oil in a large, heavy-based saucepan over a medium heat. Add the onion and garlic to the pan and cook gently for about 7 minutes, stirring frequently until the onion is golden. Add the carrots to the pan and continue to cook for 4–5 minutes, stirring frequently until just beginning to soften slightly.

**2** Stir in the split peas, stock, tomato purée, sage, and seasoning and bring to the boil. Reduce heat, then cover and simmer for 30 minutes.

**3** Add the pasta and cook for a further 15 minutes, until the pasta and split peas are tender. Serve sprinkled with Parmesan.

**THIS IS COMFORT FOOD AT ITS BEST – AND GREAT VALUE TOO. THICK, CHUNKY AND ROBUSTLY FLAVOURED, SERVE STEAMING BOWLFULS WHEN IT'S ICY OUTSIDE AND YOU NEED TO KEEP CHILLS AT BAY.**

56

**COOK SMART**

• A little smoked bacon is good in this soup – gently cook 1 chopped, rindless rasher with the onions or you could add some chunks of cooked ham to the finished soup to make a main meal. Using ham stock will add extra flavour.

• This soup can be made ahead. Prepare the soup to the end of step 2, then cool and chill. Reheat to a simmer before adding the pasta.

££

**Serves 6**

Preparation 20 minutes
Cooking about 1¼ hours

1 tbsp vegetable oil
375 g lean braising steak, cut into
    2.5 cm cubes
3 onions, roughly chopped
300 g chestnut mushrooms, sliced
3 large carrots, peeled and sliced
100 g pearl barley
1.75 litres beef stock
250 ml red wine or tomato juice
150 g frozen peas, thawed
2 tsp lemon juice
salt and freshly ground black pepper

**Per serving**
kcal 400, protein 42 g, fat 12 g
(of which saturated fat 4 g),
carbohydrate 25 g (of which
sugars 8 g), fibre 4 g, sodium 0.2 g

**MORE OF A STEW THAN A SOUP – A BIG BOWL OF THIS SUSTAINING, MEATY BROTH IS GUARANTEED TO KEEP YOU GOING UNTIL THE NEXT MEAL.**

1 Heat the oil in a large heavy-based saucepan over a medium heat. Add the beef and sauté for about 5 minutes until browned all over. Remove the beef to a plate, using a draining spoon.

2 Add the onions to the pan and cook gently for 5 minutes, then stir in the mushrooms and cook for a further 3–4 minutes. Return the beef to the pan. Stir in the carrots, barley, stock, wine or tomato juice and seasoning and bring to the boil.

3 Reduce the heat, partially cover the pan and simmer for 1–1¼ hours or until the beef and barley are tender.

4 Stir in the peas and cook, uncovered, for 5 minutes. Add the lemon juice and season to taste.

# beefy mushroom and barley soup

57

£

Serves 4   V

Preparation  20 minutes, plus
   15 minutes soaking
   (for mushrooms)
Cooking  20–25 minutes

**15 g dried shiitake mushrooms**

**2 tbsp vegetable oil**

**1 large onion, finely chopped**

**4 garlic cloves, crushed**

**1 large carrot, peeled and thinly
   sliced**

**1 large parsnip, peeled and thinly
   sliced**

**½ small head green cabbage,
   about 400 g, shredded**

**300 g can broad beans, drained
   and rinsed**

**5 tbsp tomato purée**

**3 tbsp red wine vinegar**

**1 tsp dried dill (optional)**

**salt and freshly ground black pepper**

**Per serving**
kcal 170, protein 8 g, fat 7 g (of which
saturated fat 1 g), carbohydrate 21 g
(of which sugars 10 g), fibre 7 g,
sodium 0.2 g

# mushroom and winter vegetable soup

**WHOLESOME VEGETABLES, CHUNKY
BEANS AND EARTHY SHIITAKE
MUSHROOMS COMBINE TO MAKE
A DELICIOUS, HEARTY MEAL.**

### COOK SMART
• Any canned beans could be added, such as red kidney
or cannellini beans or alternatively, frozen broad beans
– whatever you happen to have. Some ordinary cultivated
mushrooms, about 150 g, could replace the dried variety.

**1** In a small bowl, cover the mushrooms with 375 ml
boiling water. Let them stand for 15 minutes or until
softened. Then, with a spoon, remove the mushrooms
from the soaking liquid, reserving the liquid. Trim any
stems from the mushrooms and roughly chop the caps.
Strain the reserved liquid through a sieve and set aside.

**2** Meanwhile, heat the oil in a large saucepan, over a
medium heat. Add the onion and garlic and cook for
about 5 minutes, stirring occasionally until the onion
is light golden. Add the carrot and parsnip and cook for
5 minutes, then stir in the cabbage. Cover and cook
for a further 5 minutes or until the cabbage begins
to wilt.

**3** Stir in the mushrooms and the reserved soaking liquid,
the beans, tomato purée, vinegar, dill, if using, and
750 ml water. Bring to the boil, then reduce to a simmer;
cover and cook for 20–25 minutes, until well flavoured.
Season to taste.

THIS FRENCH CLASSIC, MADE WITH CARAMELISED ONIONS AND TOPPED WITH OOZINGLY CHEESY TOAST, IS ALWAYS A FAVOURITE.

£

**Serves 4**
Preparation 1 hour 10 minutes
Cooking 15 minutes

1 kg onions, thinly sliced
2 tbsp olive oil
1 tbsp sugar
1 tbsp chopped fresh thyme or 1 tsp dried
125 ml dry white wine
1.3 litres vegetable stock
4 thick slices French bread
50 g Gruyère cheese, grated
salt and freshly ground black pepper

**COOK SMART**
• It's not essential to use wine in this soup although it does boost the flavour. You can just use more vegetable stock instead.

**Per serving**
kcal 400, protein 14 g, fat 11 g (of which saturated fat 4 g), carbohydrate 55 g (of which sugars 22 g), fibre 6 g, sodium 0.5 g

**1** Preheat the oven to 220°C (gas 7). Toss the onions with the oil, sugar and seasoning in a large bowl. Spread in a large roasting tin and drizzle with 50 ml water. Cover with foil and roast for 30 minutes, then uncover and roast for 10 minutes. Add the thyme and roast for a further 20 minutes, stirring often, until the onions are brown and tender.

**2** Place the roasting tin on the hob, over a high heat. Add the wine and stir for 2 minutes with a wooden spoon, scraping the onions and browned bits from the bottom of the tin, until the wine is syrupy.

**3** Transfer the onions and pan juices to a large saucepan. Stir in the stock, bring to the boil, then reduce the heat and simmer for 15 minutes until the flavours are blended.

**4** Meanwhile, preheat a moderate grill. Place the bread slices on a baking sheet and toast for 2 minutes on each side.

**5** Ladle the soup into four heatproof bowls. Float a bread slice in each bowl and sprinkle with cheese. Place the bowls in the grill pan or a shallow baking tin and grill on a low shelf for 2 minutes or until the cheese is melted and bubbling. Serve immediately.

# oven-roasted onion soup

# spicy kale soup with sausage

£

**Serves 6**
Preparation  20 minutes
Cooking  30 minutes

**300g spicy pork sausages**
**1 tbsp vegetable oil**
**1 small onion, roughly chopped**
**2 garlic cloves, crushed**
**1 tsp ground cinnamon**
**½ tsp ground allspice**
**2 carrots, peeled, halved**
   **lengthways and thinly**
   **sliced crossways**
**1 small red pepper, seeded**
   **and diced**
**1 litre chicken or vegetable**
   **stock**
**125g fresh kale, stems**
   **removed and torn into**
   **small pieces**
**2 x 400g cans chickpeas,**
   **drained and rinsed**
**salt and freshly ground**
   **black pepper**

**To serve**
**4 tbsp freshly grated Parmesan**

**Per serving**
kcal 286, protein 22g, fat 18g
(of which saturated fat 6g),
carbohydrate 12g (of which
sugars 7g), fibre 3g,
sodium 0.5g

**1** Grill the sausages until evenly browned all over, cool, then cut into thick slices and set aside.

**2** Heat the oil in a large saucepan over a medium heat, add the onion and cook gently for 7 minutes or until softened and lightly golden. Stir in the garlic, cinnamon and allspice.

**3** Add the carrots and the red pepper to the pan, then stir in the stock. Bring to the boil, then reduce heat and simmer for 10 minutes, partially covered. Toss in the kale and simmer for a further 10 minutes until the vegetables are just tender.

**4** Stir in the chickpeas and sausage slices, warm through, then serve sprinkled with Parmesan.

### COOK SMART

• When kale is not available, you could add other shredded leafy greens or even some small broccoli florets. Some pan-fried, sliced, spicy sausage, like chorizo, would also be good in place of the grilled fresh sausages.

**THE IDEAL DISH FOR THOSE COLD MONTHS WHEN CURLY KALE IS IN SEASON. SERVE WITH HUNKS OF CRUSTY BREAD FOR A WARMING FEAST.**

# fennel and prawn bisque

💷💷

**Serves 6**

Preparation 15 minutes
Cooking 25 minutes

**50g butter**

**1 large onion, chopped**

**1 large bulb of fennel,
finely sliced**

**3 tbsp plain flour**

**600ml semi-skimmed milk**

**425ml fish or vegetable
stock**

**1 bay leaf**

**225g cooked, peeled
frozen prawns, thawed
and drained**

**2 tomatoes, skinned,
seeded and diced**

**juice of ½ lemon**

**salt and freshly ground
black pepper**

**chopped fennel fronds
to garnish**

### COOK SMART

• There's no need to pay
a premium price for extra
large king or tiger prawns.
The small Atlantic variety is
fine for flavouring a soup.

• To serve chilled, stir
in the chopped prawns
and tomatoes just
before serving.

**Per serving**

kcal 221, protein 19g,
fat 10g (of which saturated
fat 6g), carbohydrate 13g
(of which sugars 7g),
fibre 1.5g, sodium 0.7g

**1** Melt the butter in a saucepan, and gently cook
the onion and fennel for 5–8 minutes, to soften
but not colour. Sprinkle on the flour, and cook for
a further minute.

**2** Remove from the heat, and blend in the milk and
stock. Return to the heat, bring to the boil, add
the bay leaf, then cover and simmer very gently
for 15 minutes.

**3** Remove the bay leaf, add half the prawns, then
purée in a blender or food processor until smooth
Season to taste.

**4** Roughly chop the remaining prawns. Reserve a few
for garnish, then add the rest to the soup with the
diced tomatoes and the lemon juice. Heat through
gently, then serve garnished with the reserved
prawns and fennel fronds scattered over the top.

**THIS SOPHISTICATED BISQUE FEELS LIKE THE ULTIMATE
LUXURY. SERVE IT IN LATE SUMMER WHEN SWEET, ANISEED-
FLAVOURED FENNEL IS IN ABUNDANCE.**

# french fish soup

££

**Serves 6**
Preparation  15 minutes
Cooking  30 minutes

**Soup**
2 tbsp olive oil
2 leeks, trimmed and sliced
2 tomatoes, chopped
100 g white fish fillet
     (such as hake or hoki)
1.3 litres fish stock
1 bay leaf
3 sprigs of fresh parsley
1 tsp turmeric
pinch of chilli powder
salt and freshly ground black pepper

**Rouille**
3 tbsp mayonnaise
1 garlic clove, crushed
½ tsp tomato purée
few drops of brandy (optional)
pinch of cayenne pepper
     or chilli powder

**To serve**
1 small baguette
2 tbsp olive oil
50 g Gruyère, grated

**Per serving**
kcal 357, protein 13g, fat 25g
(of which saturated fat 6g),
carbohydrate 20g (of which
sugars 6g), fibre 3g, sodium 0.9g

**COOK SMART**
 • To make a great-tasting fish soup
you need a good flavoursome stock
(see page 32).

SOUPS

63

**SERVED IN TRUE FRENCH STYLE, THIS HEARTY SOUP IS
TOPPED WITH CRISP BAGUETTE TOASTS SPREAD WITH
SPICY ROUILLE AND A SPRINKLING OF GRATED GRUYÈRE
– PERFECT FOR A ONE-BOWL-MEAL.**

**1** Heat the oil in a saucepan. Add the leeks, cover, and cook gently
for 3 minutes over a low heat. Add the tomatoes and fish, stir, then
cover and continue to cook gently for a further 5 minutes.

**2** Pour in the fish stock, add the bay leaf and parsley, bring gently
to the boil, then reduce the heat and simmer for 20 minutes.

**3** Remove the bay leaf, tip the soup into a blender or food processor
and blend together. Return the soup to the pan, add the turmeric
and chilli powder and seasoning to taste.

**4** To prepare the rouille, mix together the mayonnaise, garlic, tomato
purée, brandy if using and the cayenne or chilli powder. Blend in
1 tbsp of the fish soup.

**5** Preheat the grill. Cut the baguette into diagonal slices, just under
1cm thick. Brush sparingly with oil, and grill for a few seconds on
both sides until golden. Spread them with a little rouille.

**6** Reheat the soup gently and serve with the rouille toasts. Put
the grated Gruyère and any remaining rouille into ramekins, for
everyone to help themselves.

A REAL SCOTTISH CLASSIC – SERVE THIS HEARTY COMBINATION OF CHICKEN, LEEKS, RICE AND PRUNES WITH WEDGES OF WARM SODA BREAD SPREAD THICK WITH BUTTER.

# cock-a-leekie
## soup

£ £

**Serves 4**
Preparation 15 minutes
Cooking 50 minutes

**Per serving**
kcal 315, protein 42g,
fat 12g (of which saturated
fat 4g), carbohydrate 10g
(of which sugars 4g),
fibre 0.5g, sodium 0.2g

15g butter

1 tbsp vegetable oil

270g chicken quarter

2 leeks, about 350g in
   total, trimmed

1.2 litres chicken stock

2 tbsp long-grain rice

1 bouquet garni (fresh
   or dried)

8 stoned, ready-to-eat
   prunes, chopped

salt and freshly ground
   black pepper

chopped fresh parsley
   or thyme to garnish
   (optional)

**1** Melt the butter with the oil in a large non-stick saucepan. Add the chicken to the pan and sauté quickly for 5 minutes until evenly browned all over. Remove the chicken and drain on kitchen paper.

**2** Cut off the green parts of the leeks and put aside. Cut the white parts in half lengthways, wash thoroughly, then slice crossways. Add the sliced leeks to the pan and fry for 5 minutes until soft.

**3** Add the stock, rice and bouquet garni and return the chicken to the pan. Season with salt and pepper, then bring to the boil, reduce heat, cover and simmer for 30 minutes or until the chicken is tender.

**4** Shred the green parts of the leeks, then add to the pan with the prunes. Cover and simmer for a further 10 minutes.

**5** Take out the bouquet garni, remove the chicken and shred the flesh into bite-sized pieces, discarding the skin and bone. Return the chicken meat to the pan.

**6** To serve, ladle the soup into warm bowls and scatter with some chopped fresh parsley or thyme, if liked.

### COOK SMART

• You can buy dried bouquet garni in convenient sachets but if you have fresh herbs available, make your own for a better flavour. Tie together sprigs of fresh parsley and thyme with a fresh or dried bay leaf and secure with kitchen string to make a little bundle.

• You could use leftover roast chicken instead of starting from scratch – just cook the soup for only 20 minutes in step 3. Some diced carrot and/or turnip could be added.

# creamy
# avocado
## soup

£ £

**Serves 4**
Preparation 5 minutes
Cooking 5 minutes

2 ripe avocados

2 tbsp lemon juice

1 tbsp crème fraîche

½ tsp mild curry powder

1 garlic clove, crushed

500 ml chicken or
   vegetable stock

salt and freshly ground
   black pepper

### COOK SMART

• For a celebratory meal, make little wholemeal croûtons and garnish each serving with a few of them plus three cooked, peeled prawns.

**Per serving**
kcal 220, protein 12g,
fat 18g (of which saturated
fat 5g), carbohydrate 2g
(of which sugars 0.7g),
fibre 2.5g, sodium 0.04g

**1** Halve the avocados lengthways, stone and peel them. Cut the flesh into chunks and place in a blender or food processor. Add the lemon juice and blend.

**2** Add the crème fraîche, curry powder and garlic and blend again.

**3** Heat the stock in a saucepan. Gradually add several spoonfuls of the chicken stock to the avocado purée and blend together. Add the avocado mixture to the remaining stock in the pan and heat gently, without boiling. Season to taste and serve in small soup bowls.

**A DELICATE FLAVOUR HEIGHTENED BY A LIGHT SPICY NOTE, THIS SOUP IS QUICK TO COOK AND PERFECT FOR USING UP VERY RIPE AVOCADOS.**

# creamy
# cauliflower
# soup

£

**Serves 4** V
Preparation 10 minutes
Cooking 20 minutes

**1 cauliflower, cut into
small florets**

**1 onion, chopped**

**100 ml whipping cream,
lightly whipped**

**pinch of ground nutmeg**

**salt and freshly ground
white pepper**

**snipped fresh chives to
garnish**

### COOK SMART

• You don't need a perfect
cauliflower for making
this soup so don't worry
if the florets are slightly
blemished – it's the flavour
you are after.

• For a garnish, scatter
some finely chopped hard-
boiled egg over the soup.

**Per serving**
kcal 134, protein 4g,
fat 11g (of which saturated
fat 7g), carbohydrate 6g
(of which sugars 5g),
fibre 2g, sodium 0.01g

CAULIFLOWER MAKES THE MOST DIVINELY
CREAMY, MILD, SWEET-TASTING SOUP AND
LOOKS PARTICULARLY PRETTY SPRINKLED
WITH FRAGRANT, DARK GREEN CHIVES.

**1** Bring 1 litre of lightly salted water to the boil. Add
the cauliflower and onion and cook for 15 minutes
until tender.

**2** Drain, reserving the cooking water. Purée the
cauliflower and onion in a blender or food processor
in two batches, with 150ml of the cooking water
each time.

**3** Pour the purée back into the saucepan with the
remaining cooking water and reheat gently over a
low heat. Stir in the cream, add nutmeg and season
to taste. Serve garnished with chives.

£ £ £

**Serves 4**
Preparation 30 minutes
Cooking 30 minutes

**250 ml dry white wine**

**2 celery sticks with leaves,
    stalks thinly sliced**

**1 kg mussels, scrubbed, beards
    removed and washed thoroughly**

**20 g butter**

**200 g leeks, trimmed and
    thinly sliced**

**1 onion, thinly sliced**

**1 carrot, peeled and grated**

**½ tsp curry powder**

**1 tsp tomato purée**

**600 ml fish stock**

**100 ml crème fraîche**

**pinch of cayenne pepper**

**salt and freshly ground black pepper**

**Per serving**
kcal 350, protein 28 g, fat 19 g
(of which saturated fat 10 g),
carbohydrate 8 g (of which sugars
7 g), fibre 2.5 g, sodium 0.3 g

**COOK SMART**
• Once the mussels have been
cooked, discard any that remain closed
– a sign that they were dead before
cooking, and might well be toxic.

**1** Pour the white wine into a large saucepan. Add the celery leaves and bring to the boil. Add the mussels, cover and cook for 4–5 minutes, shaking the pan regularly, until the mussels open.

**2** Once the mussels have opened, drain them, reserving their cooking liquid. Shuck the mussels, setting aside the meat and reserving a few attractive shells. Strain the cooking liquid through a fine sieve into a large jug.

**3** Melt the butter in a saucepan. Add the celery, leeks, onion and carrot, reserving a few thin slices of leek and some grated carrot for garnishing. Stir, cover and cook gently for 5 minutes. Sprinkle in the curry powder and stir. Pour over the mussels' cooking liquid. Add the tomato purée and fish stock. Bring to the boil and simmer for 20 minutes.

**4** Allow to cool slightly, then tip the contents of the pan into a blender or food processor and blend until smooth. Add the crème fraîche and blend once more. Season to taste.

**5** Reheat the soup, add the mussels and heat through gently in the soup for 1 minute, taking care not to boil.

**6** Serve sprinkled with a little cayenne pepper and garnish with reserved leeks and carrots and a few of the mussels returned to their shells.

# mussel soup

**MUSSELS ARE A REAL BARGAIN AND MAKE A SUPERB SOUP THAT LOOKS IMPRESSIVE FOR ENTERTAINING. RESERVE THE PRETTIEST SHELLS TO FLOAT ON TOP OF THE SOUP AS A GARNISH.**

# creamy butternut squash soup

£ £

**Serves 4**
Preparation 15 minutes
Cooking 35 minutes

1 butternut squash, about 780 g,
    peeled, seeded and cut into
    chunks

1 large carrot, peeled and thickly
    sliced

1 red pepper, seeded and chopped

1 large onion, thinly sliced

3 garlic cloves, crushed

80 g full-fat soft cheese

1 tbsp finely snipped fresh chives

salt and freshly ground black pepper

2 tbsp chopped fresh parsley

**To serve**
40 g blue cheese (such as Roquefort,
    Stilton or Danish blue), crumbled
sprigs of flat-leaf parsley to garnish

**Per serving**
kcal 190, protein 4 g, fat 10 g
(of which saturated fat 6 g),
carbohydrate 22 g (of which
sugars 14 g), fibre 4.5 g,
sodium 0.07 g

**VIBRANT ORANGE AND
VELVETY SMOOTH, THIS
INTENSELY FLAVOURED
SOUP IS AN ABSOLUTE
TREAT. THE SHARP FLAVOUR
OF THE BLUE CHEESE SETS
OFF THE SWEET TASTE OF
THE SOUP PERFECTLY.**

**1** Bring 1 litre of lightly salted water to the boil in a large saucepan. Add the prepared vegetables and the garlic, cover and cook gently for 30 minutes or until the vegetables are tender.

**2** Allow to cool slightly, then tip into a blender or food processor and purée. Add the garlic and soft cheese and blend once more.

**3** Return the soup to the pan, stir in the herbs and reheat gently. Season to taste.

**4** Serve the soup with little pieces of the blue cheese scattered over the top and garnish with sprigs of parsley.

### COOK SMART

• Don't throw out the squash seeds: wash carefully, toast in a lightly oiled frying pan and sprinkle over a salad.

• The soft cheese can be either full-fat or reduced-fat. For extra flavour, use one flavoured with garlic and herbs.

# thick vegetable soup with poached eggs

£

**Serves 4** V
Preparation  20 minutes
Cooking  35–40 minutes

**200g turnips, peeled and chopped**
**200g carrots, peeled and chopped**
**300g celeriac, peeled and chopped**
**4 eggs**
**2 tbsp crème fraîche**
**salt and freshly ground black pepper**

**To serve**
**4 tsp crème fraîche**
**few chopped capers or 25g chopped
    walnuts (optional)**

**Per serving**
kcal 220, protein 10g, fat 16.5g
(of which saturated fat 6g),
carbohydrate 9g (of which sugars 8g),
fibre 5g, sodium 0.2g

**1** Bring 1 litre of lightly salted water to the boil in a large saucepan. Add the vegetables, cover and cook for 30 minutes or until tender.

**2** Allow to cool slightly, then purée the soup in a blender or food processor. Tip back into the pan and bring back to a gentle simmer.

**3** Break one egg into a cup and slide it into the soup; lift the white over the yolk with a slotted spoon. Do the same with the other three eggs. Lower the heat and simmer gently for 3–4 minutes, taking care not to allow the soup to boil. (If your saucepan isn't big enough to cook all the eggs at the same time, poach them separately in a sauté pan filled with boiling water to which 1 tbsp of vinegar has been added.)

**4** Lift one egg into each bowl. Add the crème fraîche to the soup and season to taste with salt and pepper. Gently ladle the soup over the eggs and serve at once with an extra tsp of crème fraîche on each serving. Scatter a few chopped capers or walnuts over the soup, if liked.

**COOK SMART**
- Be sure to use very fresh eggs, otherwise they won't stay together in the soup.
- If liked, you could jazz up the flavour with 1 tbsp sherry or Madeira.

SOUPS

69

ADDING A PERFECTLY POACHED EGG TO EACH BOWL TRANSFORMS
THIS SIMPLE SOUP INTO A NUTRITIOUS, WHOLESOME MEAL.

# creamy corn chowder

1 tbsp vegetable oil

3 rindless, smoked streaky bacon rashers, chopped

1 large onion, chopped

450 g waxy potatoes, peeled and quartered

625 ml chicken stock

6 large corn cobs, shucked

625 ml semi-skimmed milk

¼ tsp hot pepper sauce, or to taste

pinch of salt

chopped fresh parsley to garnish

££

**Serves 6**
Preparation 20 minutes
Cooking 20–25 minutes

**Per serving**
kcal 271, protein 18 g,
fat 10 g (of which saturated
fat 3 g), carbohydrate 30 g
(of which sugars 8 g),
fibre 2 g, sodium 0.2 g

**COOK SMART**
• You could substitute
frozen sweetcorn for fresh,
or use the canned variety,
drained.

1 Heat the oil in a large saucepan and fry the bacon over a medium heat until crisp. Remove with a spatula, allow to cool, then chop roughly.

2 Add the onion to the remaining bacon fat in the pan and cook gently for 5 minutes until softened. Stir in the potatoes and stock and bring to the boil. Reduce the heat and simmer for 15 minutes or until the potatoes are just tender.

3 Meanwhile, stand the cobs upright and cut off the kernels with a serrated knife – you'll need about 700 g of kernels. (To make a corn garnish, cut a few slices off the cobs and cook them in a pan of boiling water for 8–10 minutes until tender.)

4 Tip about half of the cooked potatoes with some of the stock into a blender or food processor and process briefly to a purée. Stir back into the pan, add the milk, sweetcorn, hot pepper sauce and seasoning to taste.

5 Simmer for 5–10 minutes. Serve scattered with the crispy bacon pieces, corn and chopped parsley.

IDEAL IN LATE SUMMER WHEN FRESH CORN COBS ARE SWEET, TENDER AND PLENTIFUL, THIS CREAMY SOUP IS ALWAYS A FAMILY FAVOURITE.

# chilled red pepper soup

MAKE THIS BURSTING-WITH-FLAVOUR SOUP WHEN PEPPERS ARE IN SEASON. THEY'LL BE SWEET, JUICY AND – BEST OF ALL – CHEAP.

2 tbsp olive oil

1 onion, chopped

4 red peppers, seeded and chopped

1 courgette, peeled and chopped

750 ml vegetable stock

pinch of sugar

2 garlic cloves, crushed

½ tbsp red wine or sherry vinegar

good pinch of paprika

pinch of salt

fresh basil leaves to garnish

**£ £**

**Serves 4**  V

Preparation  10 minutes, plus at least 2 hours chilling before serving

Cooking  20–25 minutes

**Per serving**

kcal 200, protein 17 g, fat 10 g (of which saturated fat 2 g), carbohydrate 11 g (of which sugars 10 g), fibre 2.5 g, sodium 0.06 g

**1** Heat half the oil in a saucepan and sauté the onion, peppers and courgette for 5 minutes until softened.

**2** Pour over the stock, add the sugar and bring to the boil. Reduce heat, then cover and cook gently for 15–20 minutes. Add the garlic, allow to cool slightly, then tip into a blender or food processor and blend until smooth.

**3** Add the vinegar and paprika, season to taste, then allow to cool. Chill in the fridge for at least 2 hours.

**4** Serve the soup in bowls, drizzled with a little of the remaining olive oil and garnished with a few basil leaves.

# chilled summer vegetable soup

**£**

**Serves 4**  V

Preparation  20 minutes, plus at least 2 hours chilling before serving

1 slice from a white sandwich loaf (several days old)

1 tbsp red wine vinegar

600 g well-ripened tomatoes, skinned, chopped and seeded

½ cucumber, peeled and diced

½ red pepper, seeded and diced

1 onion, chopped

1 garlic clove, crushed

2 tbsp olive oil

½ tsp curry powder

pinch of sugar

150 g whole milk yoghurt

salt and freshly ground black pepper

shredded fresh basil to garnish (optional)

## COOK SMART

● If you prefer the tomato to be cooked, cook it gently over a low heat for 20 minutes with the onion, garlic and olive oil, and let it cool before adding the other ingredients.

**Per serving**

kcal 150, protein 5 g, fat 7 g (of which saturated fat 1.5 g), carbohydrate 16 g (of which sugars 11 g), fibre 2.5 g, sodium 0.09 g

**1** Crumble the bread and sprinkle with the vinegar. Set aside for 5 minutes.

**2** Put all the prepared vegetables in a blender or food processor with 50 ml cold water and whizz to a purée. Add the soaked bread, oil, curry powder and sugar. Blend again and season to taste. Chill in the fridge for at least 2 hours.

**3** Just before serving, stir the yoghurt into the soup. Thin the soup with a little cold water if too thick. Serve chilled, sprinkled with the basil.

MADE WITH FRESH, RAW SALAD VEGETABLES AND THICKENED WITH BREAD, THIS TANGY SOUP IS INSPIRED BY THE SPANISH CLASSIC, GAZPACHO.

WONDERFULLY REFRESHING IN SUMMER, THE FRAGRANT AROMA OF DILL COMPLEMENTS THE DELICATE TASTE OF CUCUMBER BEAUTIFULLY. FRESH, ZESTY MINT WOULD MAKE A GOOD ALTERNATIVE.

# chilled cucumber and yoghurt soup

£

**Serves 4** V
Preparation  20 minutes, plus at least 2 hours chilling before serving

**1 cucumber, peeled and grated (reserve a few slices for garnishing)**
**½ tsp salt**
**½ tsp sugar**
**50 g white bread, crust removed**
**2 garlic cloves, crushed**
**50 ml olive oil**
**1 tbsp lemon juice**
**300 g Greek-style yoghurt**
**3 tbsp single cream**
**15 g fresh dill, finely chopped**
**fronds of fresh dill to garnish (optional)**

**Per serving**
kcal 208, protein 6 g, fat 17 g (of which saturated fat 5 g), carbohydrate 12.5 g (of which sugars 7.5 g), fibre 3 g, sodium 0.5 g

1 Spread the cucumber on a large plate, sprinkle it with the salt and sugar, then leave to drain in a sieve for 15 minutes.

2 Soak the bread in 100 ml of cold water for 5 minutes.

3 Squeeze the water out of the bread and place in a blender or food processor with the garlic. Let the motor run while pouring in the olive oil. Add the lemon juice. Transfer this mixture to a large serving bowl. Add the yoghurt and cream and stir carefully to combine.

4 Stir the cucumber into the yoghurt mixture and season to taste. Thin the soup with a little cold water if too thick. Put in the fridge and chill for at least 2 hours.

5 Just before serving, stir the chopped dill into the soup. Serve garnished with extra dill and a little sliced cucumber, if liked.

## COOK SMART
• To make pretty cucumber rounds for garnishing the soup, score the skin of a small section of cucumber from top to bottom at regular intervals with a cannelle knife or the tip of a paring knife. Then finely slice the cucumber over the slanted blade of a box grater.

# chilled borscht

**£**

**Serves 4** Ⓥ
Preparation  10 minutes, plus at least
2 hours chilling before serving

**400g cooked fresh beetroot, peeled
and chopped**

**2 shallots, roughly chopped**

**400ml vegetable stock**

**2 tbsp lemon juice**

**2 tbsp soured cream or crème fraîche**

**salt and freshly ground black pepper**

**fresh mint to garnish (optional)**

**Per serving**
kcal 116, protein 11g, fat 3.5g
(of which saturated fat 1.5g),
carbohydrate 11g (of which sugars
10g), fibre 2g, sodium 0.1g

**1** Blend the beetroot with the shallots, stock and lemon juice in a blender or food processor. Add the soured cream or crème fraîche and blend once more. Season to taste. (Rinse out the blender or processor bowl immediately after use so that it doesn't stain.)

**2** Chill in the fridge for at least 2 hours. Serve in small cups or individual bowls. Fresh mint makes a pretty garnish that contrasts well with the vivid red of the soup.

### COOK SMART
• If using raw beetroot, scrub them under running water, cover with plenty of cold water, add salt, and cook for at least 2½ hours (or 1 hour in a pressure cooker). Alternatively, bake small beetroot in a baking tin with a little water for 2 hours at 180°C (gas 4).

• You can buy vacuum-packed cooked beetroot readily from the supermarket salad selection. Don't use the type preserved in vinegar.

**RUBY-RED AND INTENSELY FLAVOURED, THIS SOUP LOOKS STUNNING
SWIRLED WITH SOUR CREAM. SERVE AS A STARTER OR LIGHT LUNCH
WITH SLICES OF RYE BREAD.**

# star

mouthwatering morsels and tantalising dishes to whet the appetite

# spicy aubergine caviar

THIS SWEETLY SPICED,
MELT-IN-THE-MOUTH PÂTÉ
IS GREAT FOR VEGETARIANS,
BUT MEAT-EATERS WILL
LOVE IT TOO. IT IS GOOD
AS AN APPETISER OR A
LIGHT SUPPER.

£ £

**Serves 4** Ⓥ
Preparation 30 minutes
Cooking 5 minutes

1 large aubergine
1 tbsp olive oil
1 tbsp tomato purée
1 garlic clove, crushed
1 tsp ground coriander
1 tsp ground cumin
pinch of chilli powder
   (optional)
1 tsp sugar
salt and freshly ground
   black pepper

**To serve**
toast fingers

## COOK SMART

- This dish is perfect for using slightly damaged or over-ripe aubergines.
- Serve with Hummus Dip, Marinated Cucumber Yoghurt and Taramasalata (see pages 82 and 83) for Mediterranean-style casual dining.

**Per serving**
kcal 40, protein 0.6g,
fat 3g (of which saturated
fat 0.5g), carbohydrate 3g
(of which sugars 2.5g),
fibre 1g, sodium 0.01g

1 Place the whole aubergine under a preheated moderate grill and grill for 20 minutes, turning it halfway through cooking.

2 Allow to cool slightly, then cut the aubergine in half, scoop out the flesh with a spoon and place in a sieve over a bowl to drain for a few minutes.

3 Heat the oil in a non-stick frying pan, add the tomato purée, garlic, coriander and cumin and stir over a gentle heat for 30 seconds. Add the chilli powder if liked, for a spicier note.

4 Add the aubergine, sprinkle over the sugar and season with salt and pepper. Crush the aubergine with a fork and keep stirring for about 5 minutes until you have a creamy purée. Serve hot, warm or chilled with toast fingers.

# guacamole with a kick

£

**Serves 8** Ⓥ
Preparation 20 minutes

2 plum tomatoes, chopped
   and seeded
1 red pepper, seeded and
   diced
1 small onion, finely
   chopped
1 red chilli, seeded and
   finely chopped
1 garlic clove, crushed
2 tbsp chopped fresh
   coriander
pinch of salt
150g natural low-fat
   yoghurt
150g soured cream
2 large ripe avocados
2 tbsp lime juice

**To serve**
tortilla chips

## COOK SMART

- Very ripe avocados, which are perfect for this recipe, are often sold at a reduced price. If bought hard, place in a paper bag and ripen at room temperature a few days in advance.
- Plum tomatoes are the best to use here as they have a firm flesh and are less watery than other tomatoes.

**Per serving**
kcal 245, protein 4.5g,
fat 18g (of which saturated
fat 5g), carbohydrate 17g
(of which sugars 5g),
fibre 3.5g, sodium 0.2g

1 Combine the tomatoes, pepper, onion, chilli, garlic and coriander in a large bowl and season with a pinch of salt.

2 Mix together the yoghurt and soured cream. Halve, stone and peel the avocados. Mash with a potato masher or large fork until almost smooth, but still a little chunky. Sprinkle with the lime juice to prevent the avocado from discolouring, then stir into the yoghurt mixture.

3 Quickly fold in the tomato mixture. Keep covered with cling film until ready to serve. Serve with tortilla chips.

**STARTERS**

**81**

A SMOOTH, CREAMY DIP MAKES A WONDERFUL INFORMAL APPETIZER AND THIS RECIPE HELPS A LITTLE AVOCADO TO GO A LONG WAY.

# hummus dip

THIS CREAMY, GARLICKY MIDDLE EASTERN DIP IS UNBELIEVABLY SIMPLE TO MAKE – AND YOU CAN DO IT FOR A FRACTION OF THE PRICE OF THE STORE-BOUGHT VERSIONS.

82

£

**Serves 4** Ⓥ
Preparation 10 minutes

**400 g can chickpeas**
**3 tbsp olive oil**
**juice of ½ lemon**
**1 fat garlic clove, crushed**
**pinch of ground cumin**
**1 tbsp sesame seeds,
    toasted (optional)**

**To serve**
**pitta bread (white or
    wholemeal)**

> **COOK SMART**
> • There's no need to buy sesame seeds just for garnishing. Alternative garnishes could include black olives, lemon zest, a little paprika or a drizzle of olive oil.

**Per serving**
kcal 180, protein 6 g,
fat 13 g (of which saturated
fat 2 g), carbohydrate 12 g
(of which sugars 0.5 g),
fibre 3.5 g, sodium 0.2 g

**1** Tip the chickpeas into a sieve and rinse under cold running water. Drain, then transfer to a food processor or blender.

**2** Add the olive oil, lemon juice, garlic and cumin to the chickpeas and blend together. Taste to check the balance of flavours and, if liked, add a little extra of any of these ingredients. If the mixture is very thick, add 1–2 tbsp hot water to thin the consistency a little.

**3** Spoon the hummus into a dish and chill until ready to serve. Sprinkle with toasted sesame seeds, if you have some, to garnish. Serve with warm pitta bread.

# marinated cucumber yoghurt

£

**Serves 4** Ⓥ
Preparation 10 minutes,
    plus 24 hours marinating

**1 cucumber**
**½ tsp salt**
**1 tsp sugar**
**¼ tsp dried dill**
**1 garlic clove, crushed**
**2 tbsp lemon juice**
**2 tbsp olive oil**
**200 g Greek-style yoghurt**

**To serve**
**crusty bread**

> **COOK SMART**
> • If you don't have dried dill, use dried mint. In the summer, when fresh herbs are plentiful, use finely chopped fresh dill or mint and add to the cucumber with the yoghurt.

**Per serving**
kcal 120, protein 4 g,
fat 11 g (of which saturated
fat 3 g), carbohydrate 3 g
(of which sugars 3 g),
fibre 0.5 g, sodium 0.3 g

**1** Using a canelle knife, if you have one, remove strips of peel along the entire length of the cucumber to give a striped effect. (If you don't have one, simply use a vegetable peeler.) Next, slice the cucumber into paper-thin rounds.

**2** Put the cucumber into a plastic container, add the salt, sugar, dill, garlic, lemon juice and olive oil and mix gently. Cover and marinate in the fridge for 24 hours.

**3** Just before serving, drain the cucumber and mix with the yoghurt. Serve in individual dishes with crusty bread.

**QUICK AND EASY TO MAKE, SERVE THIS
CLASSIC SMOKED COD'S ROE DIP AS A
SNACK WITH DRINKS OR AS A MORE FORMAL
STARTER WITH STRIPS OF PITTA BREAD.**

💷

**Serves 4**

Preparation  10 minutes,
    plus 1 hour soaking
    (for the roe)

**200 g smoked cod's roe**

**40 g (1 thick slice) stale
white bread, crusts
removed**

**2 tbsp semi-skimmed milk**

**5 tbsp vegetable oil**

**3 tbsp olive oil**

**3 tbsp lemon juice**

**1 garlic clove, crushed**

**freshly ground black
pepper**

**To garnish
wedge of lemon**

**sprigs of flat-leaf parsley**

**COOK SMART**

• Smoked cod's roe is
sold at fishmongers and
delis. It varies in saltiness:
taste during preparation
and adjust the amount
of oil and lemon juice
accordingly.

• Using mainly vegetable
oil for the creamy
consistency and just a little
olive oil for flavour reduces
the cost.

**Per serving**
kcal 280, protein 12g,
fat 23g (of which saturated
fat 3.5g), carbohydrate 5g
(of which sugars 0.5g),
fibre 0g, sodium 0.1g

**1** First soak the roe in a bowl of cold water for about
1 hour to remove some of the saltiness.

**2** When ready to prepare, soak the stale bread in
the milk for 5 minutes. Rinse and drain the roe
thoroughly, cut in half lengthways, then, with the
skin side down on a board, scrape the roe off
the skin with a knife. Put the roe in a blender or
food processor.

**3** Squeeze the bread dry and add it to the roe. Blend
together, trickling in first the vegetable oil, then the
olive oil, while the motor is running.

**4** Now add the lemon juice, a little at a time, adding a
little extra, if liked, for a sharper taste. If the mixture
is slightly thick, you can slacken it with a little boiling
water, rather than adding more oil or lemon juice.
Add the garlic and season to taste with pepper.

**5** Spoon the taramasalata into a bowl, cover with
cling film and chill in the fridge until ready to serve.
Garnish with a lemon wedge and sprigs of parsley.

# taramasalata

£

**Serves 6**
Preparation  40 minutes, plus 4 hours
    or overnight marinating, plus at
    least 4 hours chilling
Cooking  20 minutes

**250 g chicken livers, (thawed
    if bought frozen), trimmed,
    washed and drained**
**150 ml red wine**
**2 garlic cloves, crushed**
**2 tsp chopped fresh thyme**
**generous pinch of ground nutmeg**
**1 onion, finely chopped**
**1 tsp powdered gelatine**
**50 g butter**
**salt and freshly ground black pepper**
**small sprigs of fresh thyme to garnish**

**Per serving**
kcal 123, protein 8 g, fat 8 g (of which
saturated fat 4.5 g), carbohydrate
1.5 g (of which sugars 1 g), fibre 0.3 g,
sodium 0.06 g

**84**

**1** Place the chicken livers in a bowl with the red wine, garlic, chopped thyme and nutmeg. Leave to marinate in the fridge for 4 hours or overnight.

**2** Lift the livers out of the marinade using a draining spoon and set aside. Pour the marinade into a saucepan. Add the onions and cook over a low heat for 15 minutes or until the onions are soft and the liquid has completely evaporated.

**3** Meanwhile, put 1 tbsp hot water in a small bowl, sprinkle over the gelatine and stir briskly until dissolved. If the gelatine does not fully dissolve, stand the bowl in a pan of hot water and stir until the gelatine has fully dissolved.

**4** Heat the butter in a non-stick frying pan and sauté the livers for 3 minutes over a moderate heat. Season with salt and pepper. Cool slightly, then tip the livers with the buttery juices into a blender or food processor and purée until smooth. Add the onions and the gelatine liquid. Blend again and taste to check the seasoning.

**5** Transfer the pâté to a small earthenware dish, cover and chill for at least 4 hours until firm. Serve garnished with thyme.

**COOK SMART**
• If you happen to have a bottle of port in the cupboard, maybe left from Christmas, use it instead of the red wine for a really gutsy flavour.

# chicken liver pâté

**CHICKEN LIVERS ARE SO ECONOMICAL, BUT YOU'D NEVER KNOW IT WHEN YOU TASTE THIS RICH AND DELICIOUS PÂTÉ. IT FEELS LIKE THE ULTIMATE INDULGENCE, SPREAD ON ELEGANT TOASTS.**

A CREAMY FISH
TERRINE MAKES
A SOPHISTICATED
STARTER FOR A
SPECIAL OCCASION
– AND REQUIRES A
SURPRISINGLY SMALL
QUANTITY OF SALMON.

# salmon terrine with tarragon sauce

£ £

**Serves 6**

Preparation  15 minutes, plus
    overnight chilling, plus 30 minutes
    standing before serving
Cooking  40–50 minutes

**1 tbsp butter, melted**

**200 g salmon fillet, cut into chunks**

**4 eggs**

**250 ml full-fat milk**

**pinch of mixed spice**

**1 tbsp brandy**

**dash of Tabasco**

**2 tsp chopped fresh tarragon**

**½ tsp salt**

**¼ tsp freshly ground white pepper**

**Tarragon sauce**

**200 ml whipping cream, chilled**

**pinch of salt**

**1 tsp lemon juice**

**1 tsp chopped fresh tarragon**

**To serve**

**leafy herb salad**

**small sprigs of fresh tarragon
    to garnish**

**Per serving**

kcal 300, protein 14 g, fat 25 g
(of which saturated fat 13 g),
carbohydrate 3 g (of which sugars 3 g),
fibre 0.4 g, sodium 0.1 g

**1** Preheat the oven to 160°C (gas 3). Thoroughly grease a
750 ml loaf tin with the melted butter.

**2** Put the salmon in a blender or food processor with the eggs,
milk, mixed spice, brandy, Tabasco and chopped tarragon.
Blend together, then season with salt and pepper.

**3** Pour the mixture into the loaf tin, cover with buttered foil and
place in a roasting pan. Pour sufficient boiling water into the
pan to come about half way up the sides of the loaf tin. Bake
for 40–50 minutes until set – insert a knife point and it should
come out clean. Leave to cool in the tin, then place in the fridge
and chill overnight.

**4** Remove the terrine from the fridge 30 minutes before serving
so that it isn't too cold. Just before serving, prepare the sauce.
Add a pinch of salt to the cream and beat until thick. Blend in
the lemon juice and tarragon.

**5** Carefully run the blade of a knife all around the inside of the tin,
then turn the terrine out onto a long platter, so that it comes
out cleanly. Slice and arrange on individual plates. Place a small
spoonful of dressing on each serving, then offer the remaining
sauce in a separate dish. Serve with salad leaves and garnish
with tarragon sprigs.

**COOK SMART**

• You can buy fresh tarragon during the summer months. Even better,
grow some yourself and freeze for year-round use (see page 20).

THESE MEDITERRANEAN VEGETABLE STACKS DRIZZLED WITH AROMATIC PESTO MAKE A STUNNING STARTER. MAKE THEM WHEN AUBERGINES ARE IN PLENTIFUL SUPPLY.

# summer vegetable pyramids

£ £

**Serves 4**  V
Preparation  25 minutes
Cooking  8–10 minutes

**1 large aubergine**
**1 large firm tomato**
**200 g mozzarella**
**2 tbsp pesto sauce**
**1 tbsp olive oil**
**freshly ground black pepper**

**To garnish (optional)**
**fresh basil leaves**
**chopped, stoned black olives**

**Per serving**
kcal 203, protein 10 g, fat 17 g
(of which saturated fat 7 g),
carbohydrate 2.5 g (of which
sugars 2 g), fibre 1 g, sodium 0.2 g

1 Preheat the oven to 200°C (gas 6). Top and tail the aubergine and slice into twelve 1 cm rounds. Arrange the aubergine slices on a lightly greased, non-stick baking sheet, without overlapping them. Bake for 8 minutes on each side.

2 Cut the tomato into four even rounds, trimming off the top and bottom of the tomato. Cut the mozzarella into four slices, then cut each slice in half widthways.

3 Spread one side of the aubergine rounds with a little of the pesto sauce, then stack into four towers, each with three slices, on the baking sheet. Top each stack with a slice of tomato and two slices of mozzarella, overlapping to fit. Lightly season with pepper.

4 Drizzle with olive oil, then bake for 8–10 minutes or until the cheese is just beginning to melt.

5 Serve immediately with any remaining pesto sauce spooned on top and garnish, if liked, with fresh basil leaves and chopped, stoned olives.

£

**Serves 6**
Preparation 20 minutes
Cooking 8–10 minutes

**250g (12 large) chestnut mushrooms**
**50g plain dry breadcrumbs**
**2 tbsp freshly grated Parmesan**
**2 tbsp vegetable oil**
**75g sausage meat**
**1 large onion, finely chopped**
**1 garlic clove, crushed**
**1 small red pepper, seeded and finely chopped**
**1 tbsp olive oil**
**freshly ground black pepper**

**Per serving**
kcal 165, protein 6.5g, fat 11g (of which saturated fat 3g), carbohydrate 11g (of which sugars 3g), fibre 2g, sodium 0.2g

**1** Preheat the oven to 200°C (gas 6). Wipe the mushrooms clean with a damp kitchen towel. Remove the stalks and finely chop them. Mix 2 tbsp of the breadcrumbs with the Parmesan in small bowl.

**2** Heat the vegetable oil in a large frying pan. Add the sausage meat and cook over a medium heat for 5 minutes, breaking it up with the side of a spatula, until it's beginning to brown.

**3** Stir in the chopped onion, garlic, red pepper and mushroom stalks and cook gently for about 5 minutes until the vegetables are soft. Stir in the remaining breadcrumbs and season with black pepper. Remove the pan from the heat.

**4** Mound the stuffing into the mushroom caps and arrange, stuffing side up, in a large shallow baking dish. Sprinkle with the Parmesan mixture and drizzle over the olive oil. Bake for 8–10 minutes until heated through and golden and crispy on top.

# sausage-stuffed chestnut mushrooms

CHESTNUT MUSHROOMS HAVE A PARTICULARLY GOOD TASTE AND THEY ARE FABULOUS STUFFED. YOU DON'T NEED TO PEEL THEM, JUST WIPE WELL, THEN FILL AND BAKE.

ABSOLUTELY IRRESISTIBLE,
THESE ELEGANT MORSELS
MAKE PERFECT PRE-DINNER
CANAPÉS. SERVE THEM WITH
DRINKS BEFORE SITTING
DOWN TO THE MAIN MEAL.

# double cheese bites

💷💷

**Serves 4**
Preparation  20 minutes,
      plus 3 hours chilling

**12 firm cherry tomatoes**

**75 g soft cheese with
    garlic and herbs**

**75 g rindless goat's cheese**

**1 tbsp crème fraîche**

**few drops of lemon juice**

**5 fresh chives, snipped**

**125 g smoked trout**

**2 tbsp chopped fresh basil**

**fresh chives to garnish**

## COOK SMART
• You can use smoked
salmon instead, but
smoked trout is generally
less expensive.

• Any leftover cheese can
be spread on canapés or
added to a savoury sauce
instead of cream.

**Per serving**
kcal 200, protein 12 g,
fat 17 g (of which saturated
fat 10 g), carbohydrate 1 g
(of which sugars 1 g),
fibre 0.5 g, sodium 0.2 g

**1** Put the tomatoes in a bowl and pour over boiling
water to cover. Leave for 10 seconds, then drain
and cool under cold water. Peel off the skins using
a sharp knife. Crush the soft cheese on a plate with
a fork and roll each tomato in it (first wetting your
hands slightly), covering them completely. Transfer
to a plate lined with greaseproof paper.

**2** Carefully blend the goat's cheese with the crème
fraîche, lemon juice and snipped chives. Lay the
slices of trout out on the work surface and spread
them with the cheese mixture. Roll them up, starting
from the thinner end. Transfer these rolls to a plate
and cover with cling film.

**3** Chill the tomatoes and trout rolls in the fridge for
at least 3 hours to firm them up.

**4** Roll the tomatoes in the basil, then carefully cut
them in half. Spear each tomato half with a cocktail
stick. Return to the fridge until ready to serve.

**5** Cut the trout rolls into little pinwheels using a sharp
knife. Spear each pinwheel with a cocktail stick and
return these to the fridge also.

**6** Arrange the tomatoes and trout pinwheels on small
serving plates and garnish with extra chives.

# cheese soufflé

💷

**Serves 8** Ⓥ
Preparation  20 minutes,
    plus 10 minutes cooling
Cooking  15 minutes

**40 g butter**

**40 g plain flour**

**250 ml semi-skimmed milk**

**100 g mature Cheddar,
    grated**

**pinch of chilli powder**

**2 tsp chopped fresh thyme
    or 1 tsp dried**

**4 eggs, separated**

**salt and freshly ground
    pepper**

**small sprigs of fresh thyme
    to garnish**

---

**COOK SMART**
• To make 1 large soufflé, pour the mixture into a greased 1.7 litre soufflé dish. Bake for 25 minutes until risen and golden.

---

**Per serving**
kcal 160, protein 8g,
fat 11g (of which saturated
fat 5g), carbohydrate 5.5g
(of which sugars 1.5g),
fibre 0.2g, sodium 0.2g

**1** Preheat the oven to 190°C (gas 5). Generously grease eight 250 ml soufflé dishes and place them on a baking tray.

**2** Melt the butter in a saucepan, add the flour and stir to blend for 1 minute. Add the milk gradually and bring to the boil, stirring all the time until thickened. Add the grated cheese, chilli powder, thyme and a generous grinding of pepper. Stir and leave to cool for about 10 minutes.

**3** Blend the egg yolks into the cheese sauce, two at a time.

**4** Sprinkle the egg whites with a pinch of salt and whisk until stiff peaks form. Whisk one quarter of the egg whites into the sauce, then gently fold in the remainder, using a large metal spoon.

**5** Divide the mixture among the dishes and bake for 15 minutes until risen and golden. Serve at once, garnished with fresh thyme.

INDIVIDUAL SOUFFLÉS MAKE A STUNNING START TO A MEAL. TRY TO USE A WELL-FLAVOURED CHEESE TO GET THE MAXIMUM IMPACT.

# florentine baked eggs

SPINACH AND EGGS ARE A CLASSIC COMBINATION, AND DRIZZLING A LITTLE CREAM OVER EACH DISH ADDS A LOVELY RICHNESS.

£

**Serves 4** V
Preparation  10 minutes
Cooking  10–12 minutes

10 g butter, melted

1 garlic clove, peeled

250 g fresh spinach,
thoroughly washed,
drained and chopped

pinch of ground nutmeg

pinch of ground cinnamon

4 eggs

4 tbsp whipping cream

salt and freshly ground
white pepper

## COOK SMART
• If you happen to have some leftover cooked rice, add this to the spinach.

• Alternatively, replace the spinach with some chopped fresh tomatoes or mushrooms sautéed in a little olive oil.

**Per serving**
kcal 183, protein 10g,
fat 15g (of which saturated
fat 7g), carbohydrate 1.5g
(of which sugars 1.5g),
fibre 1g, sodium 0.2g

1 Preheat the oven to 200°C (gas 6). Brush four 150 ml ramekins with the melted butter.

2 Spear the garlic clove on the end of a fork. Tip the spinach into a non-stick frying pan and wilt it over a high heat, stirring with the fork to flavour with the garlic. Discard the garlic.

3 Drain and press out any excess moisture from the spinach, then season to taste with nutmeg, cinnamon, salt and pepper. Divide the spinach evenly among the ramekins, making a hollow in the middle. Break one egg into each hollow and top each one with 1 tbsp of the cream. Season with pepper.

4 Place the ramekins in a baking tin and pour boiling water around them to come about half way up the sides of the ramekins. Carefully place in the oven and bake for 10–12 minutes until the eggs are just set.

5 Remove the ramekins from the water bath, wipe dry and serve at once.

90

# potato charlottes with smoked trout

SOPHISTICATED, SIMPLE, YET INCREDIBLY GOOD VALUE – THESE ELEGANT STACKS ARE PERFECT FOR ENTERTAINING.

**Per serving**
kcal 160, protein 9g,
fat 7g (of which saturated
fat 1g), carbohydrate 16g
(of which sugars 1g),
fibre 1g, sodium 0.04g

£

**Serves 4**
Preparation  35 minutes,
plus overnight chilling

400 g waxy potatoes

2 tbsp olive oil

1 tbsp white wine vinegar

2 tsp chopped fresh dill

125 g smoked trout

4 tsp lemon juice

salt and freshly ground
white pepper

**To garnish**
1 lemon, cut into wedges

sprigs of fresh dill

1 Place the potatoes in a saucepan with cold water to cover, add salt, and bring to the boil. Cook for 20 minutes until just tender. Drain and leave to cool, then peel the potatoes and crush them with a fork.

2 Blend the oil and vinegar with some salt and pepper. Add the chopped dill to the dressing and mix in to the potatoes.

3 Place half of this mixture in four 150 ml, lightly oiled ramekins, pressing it down well.

4 Flake the trout with a fork and lay it on top of the potatoes in the ramekins. Drizzle 1 tsp lemon juice over each charlotte. Cover with the rest of the potatoes and press down. Chill in the fridge overnight and until just before serving.

5 Run a knife around the edge of each ramekin and carefully ease the charlottes onto serving plates. Garnish with lemon wedges and dill.

# artichoke crostini

ENJOY THESE CLASSIC ITALIAN TOASTS WITH DRINKS BEFORE DINNER OR AS A STARTER. USING BOTTLED ARTICHOKES MEANS YOU CAN ENJOY THEM ALL YEAR ROUND.

**£**

**Per serving**
kcal 100, protein 2g, fat 5g
(of which saturated fat 0.5g),
carbohydrate 10.5g
(of which sugars 1.5g),
fibre 0.5g, sodium 0.2g

**Makes 8** Ⓥ
Preparation 12–15 minutes

280g jar marinated
  artichokes, well drained
  and coarsely chopped
2 large tomatoes, seeded
  and coarsely chopped
50g stoned black olives,
  coarsely chopped
2 tbsp chopped fresh
  parsley
1 tbsp olive oil
1 garlic clove, crushed
½ ciabatta loaf
salt and freshly ground
  black pepper

**1** In a medium bowl, combine the artichokes, tomatoes, olives, parsley, oil and garlic with salt and pepper to season. Cover and keep in the fridge until ready to serve.

**2** Cut the crusty end off the ciabatta, then cut 8 slices, each about 1cm thick. Toast the bread on both sides.

**3** Just before serving, divide the artichoke mixture equally among the toast slices. Serve immediately

**COOK SMART**
• Crostini, like bruschetta, are cut from good French or Italian breads. Crostini are usually thinner, about 1cm thick, but you could cut the bread slightly thicker to make bruschetta. Smaller crostini are easiest to eat as a nibble with drinks whereas the slightly larger bruschetta make a more generous first course.

# goat's cheese purses

2 tbsp olive oil

250 g onions, thinly sliced

1 garlic clove, crushed

pinch of sugar

25 g butter, melted

8 sheets filo pastry, about 115 g, cut in half

50 g walnut pieces, chopped into small pieces

2 goat's cheeses, about 70 g each, cut in half horizontally

2 tsp chopped fresh thyme

freshly ground black pepper

fresh thyme sprigs to tie purses (optional)

£ £

**Serves 4** V

Preparation 50 minutes

Cooking 10–15 minutes

**Per serving**

kcal 380, protein 12 g, fat 28 g (of which saturated fat 11 g), carbohydrate 18 g (of which sugars 0.7 g), fibre 0.5 g, sodium 0.3 g

> **COOK SMART**
> • If you don't have a non-stick baking sheet, line any baking sheet with grease-proof or baking paper.

1 Heat half the oil in a heavy-based saucepan. Add the onions, garlic and a pinch of sugar. Stir, cover and cook gently over a low heat for 30 minutes. Leave to cool.

2 Preheat the oven to 200°C (gas 6). Mix the remaining oil and butter together. Take a half sheet of filo and brush with a little of the oil mixture, then place three more pieces on top at angles to each other to form a star shape, lightly oiling each sheet.

3 Scatter a quarter of the onions in the centre of the pastry and sprinkle with a quarter of the walnuts. Place one half of a goat's cheese on top. Scatter over ½ tsp of the thyme leaves and season with pepper. Gather up the edges of the pastry and pinch tightly together to enclose the filling and make the shape of a purse. Repeat to make three more purses.

4 Place the purses on a non-stick baking sheet. Brush lightly with the remaining oil mixture. Bake for 10–15 minutes until golden. If liked, tie each purse with a sprig of thyme. Serve immediately.

# buckwheat blinis

£

**Serves 4** V
**(makes 8)**

Preparation 10 minutes, plus 1 hour rising

Cooking 25 minutes

60 g buckwheat flour

60 g plain flour

pinch of salt

1 sachet easy-blend dried yeast, about 7 g

250 ml semi-skimmed milk, warmed

2 eggs, separated

knob of butter for frying

> **COOK SMART**
> • Well wrapped, these blinis keep very well in the fridge. Reheat them in a low oven, wrapped in foil. You could also reheat them in a grill pan, taking care not to overheat.

**Per serving**

kcal 200, protein 9 g, fat 7 g (of which saturated fat 3 g), carbohydrate 27 g (of which sugars 3 g), fibre 1 g, sodium 0.09 g

1 Sift the two flours with a good pinch of salt into a bowl. Add the yeast and the warm milk and beat with a hand whisk until smooth. Add the egg yolks to the batter. Cover with a tea towel and leave to rest for 1 hour, in a warm place away from draughts, until risen.

2 When ready to cook, add a pinch of salt to the egg whites and whisk until they form slightly soft peaks. Stir the batter, then fold in the beaten egg whites.

3 Heat a heavy-based frying pan. Grease sparingly with butter, then pour in a small ladleful of the blini mixture. Cook for 1½ minutes on each side. Place the blini on a dish, cover and keep warm. Make seven more blinis (each about 12 cm in diameter) in the same way, using the rest of the mixture.

4 Serve warm topped with Taramasalata (see page 83), smoked salmon trimmings and crème fraîche, Guacamole With A Kick (see page 81), or Spicy Aubergine Caviar (see page 81).

**THESE LITTLE RUSSIAN PANCAKES HAVE A DELICIOUSLY DISTINCTIVE FLAVOUR. FOR A MORE LUXURIOUS STARTER, TOP WITH A SPOONFUL OF DIP OR SOUR CREAM.**

# tempting
# tex-mex nachos

£

**Serves 6** V
Preparation 10 minutes
Cooking 4–5 minutes

250g cherry tomatoes
1 tbsp olive oil
1 onion, chopped
120g packet tortilla chips
8 spring onions, sliced
250g mild Cheddar, grated

**COOK SMART**
• Be creative with other exciting toppings. Try red kidney beans with chopped green peppers, or chopped cooked chicken breast with tomato and chilli salsa.

**Per serving**
kcal 300, protein 13g,
fat 20g (of which saturated
fat 10g), carbohydrate 16g
(of which sugars 4g),
fibre 2g, sodium 0.5g

1 Preheat the oven to 230°C (gas 8). Slice the tomatoes into quarters, then cut the quarters in half.

2 Heat the oil in a frying pan over a medium heat. Add the onion and sauté for 5 minutes until soft. Stir in the tomatoes, then remove the pan from the heat.

3 Arrange the tortilla chips in single layers on two baking trays. Top the chips evenly with the vegetable mixture and spring onions. Sprinkle with the cheese.

4 Bake briefly for 4–5 minutes, just until the cheese melts. Serve immediately, hot from the oven.

**MAKE A BATCH OF THESE MOREISH NACHOS, LOADED WITH TOMATO SALSA AND GRATED CHEESE, TO GET EVERYONE MUNCHING. THEY'RE FUN TO MAKE AND READY TO EAT IN MINUTES.**

# french toast with onions

**WEDGES OF FRENCH TOAST TOPPED WITH CARAMELISED ONIONS, SMOKED BACON AND MELTING GRUYÈRE MAKE AN UNUSUAL BUT UTTERLY DELICIOUS STARTER.**

£

**Serves 4**
Preparation  30 minutes
Cooking  20 minutes

**Per serving**
kcal 360, protein 15g,
fat 22g (of which saturated
fat 8g), carbohydrate 28g
(of which sugars 9g),
fibre 2g, sodium 0.7g

**100g rindless smoked
    back bacon, chopped**
**2 tbsp vegetable oil**
**500g onions, thinly sliced**
**pinch of sugar**
**2 eggs**
**3 tbsp single cream**
**4 fresh chives, snipped**
**4 thick slices stale white
    bread, crusts removed**
**15g butter, softened**
**30g Gruyère, grated**
**salt and freshly ground
    black pepper**
**flat-leaf parsley to garnish
    (optional)**

---

**COOK SMART**
• Gruyère cheese works
particularly well for this
dish as it has good melting
qualities and a strong nutty
flavour. Emmenthal would
give a similar result.

---

**1** Preheat the oven to 200°C (gas 6). Brown the bacon in a large non-stick frying pan over a low heat for 5 minutes. Lift out with a draining spoon and put aside. Add the oil to the pan, then tip in the onions, add the sugar and season with salt and pepper. Cook for 20–25 minutes until soft and golden.

**2** Meanwhile, lightly beat the eggs with the cream. Add the chives and a little seasoning.

**3** Toast the slices of bread and butter them sparingly. Place them side-by-side in a shallow ovenproof dish.

**4** When the onions are soft, remove from the heat and mix them with the bacon and the egg mixture.

**5** Pour the onion mixture over the toast and sprinkle with cheese. Bake for 20 minutes until golden brown. Serve hot, straight from the baking dish, garnished with flat-leaf parsley, if liked.

£

**Serves 4**
Preparation  about 1 hour,
    plus 1 hour rising
    (for the dough)
Cooking  15 minutes

**200 g strong white bread
    flour**

**¹⁄₂ sachet easy-blend dried
    yeast, about 4 g**

**3 tbsp olive oil**

**700 g onions, thinly sliced**

**1 bay leaf**

**1 tsp dried oregano**

**50 g can anchovy fillets,
    drained and chopped**

**20 stoned black olives,
    halved**

**salt and freshly ground
    black pepper**

**Per serving**
kcal 300, protein 6 g,
fat 8 g (of which saturated
fat 1 g), carbohydrate 53 g
(of which sugars 10 g),
fibre 3.5 g, sodium 0.2 g

# provençal pizza

**A WEDGE OF PIZZA TOPPED WITH SAUTÉED
ONIONS, ANCHOVIES AND OLIVES IS GREAT
AS A DELICIOUS AND UNUSUAL STARTER.**

**1** Put the flour into a large bowl and stir in the yeast
and a pinch of salt. Make a well in the centre and
add 125 ml tepid water and 1 tbsp of the olive oil.
Mix with a round-bladed knife until the mixture
forms a soft dough, adding a little more water if
it feels too dry.

**2** Turn the dough out on to a lightly floured surface
and knead for about 5 minutes until the dough is
soft and supple. Place in a lightly greased bowl,
cover with a tea towel and leave to rise in a warm,
draught-free place for 1 hour or until doubled in size.

**3** Meanwhile, heat the remaining 2 tbsp of olive oil in
a deep frying pan. Add the onions and cook gently
over a medium heat for 5 minutes without letting
them colour. Add the bay leaf and oregano, and
season with salt and pepper. Cover and continue to
cook gently, stirring occasionally for 35–40 minutes
(the onions should remain transparent).

**4** Preheat the oven to 230°C (gas 8). Add the chopped
anchovies to the onions. Let them cook gently for
2–3 minutes, then remove the pan from the heat.
Remove the bay leaf. Lightly oil two baking sheets.

**5** Turn out the risen dough onto the floured surface,
and knock it back, then knead very lightly. Divide
into four, then roll out to make four rounds, each
about 15 cm in diameter. Put on the baking sheet.
Spread the onions on top to within 1 cm of
the edges.

**6** Bake for 10 minutes, then scatter the olives over
the pizzas and bake for a further 5 minutes, or until
the pizza bases are lightly risen and golden brown.

**COOK SMART**
• Reseal the sachet of yeast as tightly as possible with
sticky tape and put it back in the box to use another time.
Alternatively, why not make eight individual pizzas while
you are at it and put some in the freezer?

**MAKE THESE LITTLE UPSIDE-DOWN TARTS IN THE SUMMER, WHEN TOMATOES ARE AT THEIR RIPEST, JUICIEST AND MOST PLENTIFUL.**

£

**Makes 4** Ⓥ
Preparation  20 minutes, plus 1½ hours
    caramelising (for the tomatoes)
Cooking  10 minutes

**1 kg ripe, but firm tomatoes**
**3 tbsp olive oil**
**1 tbsp chopped fresh thyme**
**½ tsp sugar**
**2 garlic cloves, thinly sliced**
**200 g ready-made puff pastry**
**salt and freshly ground black pepper**
**sprigs of fresh thyme to garnish**

**Per serving**
kcal 305, protein 5 g, fat 21 g (of which
saturated fat 7 g), carbohydrate 27 g
(of which sugars 9 g), fibre 2.5 g,
sodium 0.2 g

96

**1** Preheat the oven to 140°C (gas 1). Scald the tomatoes in a bowl of boiling water for 30 seconds, then refresh them under cold running water. Peel off the skins, then cut them into quarters and remove their seeds.

**2** Pour 2 tbsp of the oil onto a large non-stick baking sheet and sprinkle over the thyme leaves, sugar and seasoning. Turn the tomatoes in this mixture two or three times, then spread them out in a single layer. Scatter over the garlic. Bake for 1½ hours for the tomatoes to caramelise. Leave to cool.

**3** Increase the oven temperature to 200°C (gas 6). Lightly grease the base of four individual tart tins, 10 cm in diameter. Roll out the puff pastry. Cut out four circles, each measuring 10 cm in diameter, to fit the tart tins. Spread the tomatoes evenly over the base of the tins. Top the tomatoes with a circle of pastry. Bake for 10 minutes until the pastry is puffed and golden.

**4** Turn the tartlets out, upside down onto individual plates so that the tomatoes are now on the top with the pastry underneath. Drizzle with the remaining olive oil and serve at once, garnished with fresh thyme.

# tomato tartes tatin

**COOK SMART**

• During the summer months when home-grown tomatoes are in season and full of flavour, it makes sense to prepare a larger quantity of '*confit*' tomatoes (see step 2). Cooked and drizzled with a layer of olive oil, they will keep for several days in the fridge. Use them to add a burst of flavour to salads, pasta, rice and fish dishes.

• To make one large tart, spread the tomatoes in a 25 cm flan tin, top with pastry and bake at 200°C (gas 6) for 15–20 minutes. Cut into quarters.

# cheese and walnut soufflé tart

£

**Serves 6**

Preparation  20 minutes
    plus 15 minutes resting
    (for the pastry)
Cooking  25–30 minutes

**200 g ready-made puff
  pastry**

**4 eggs, beaten**

**300 ml single cream**

**pinch of ground nutmeg**

**150 g Stilton or other
  similar blue cheese,
  crumbled**

**50 g walnut pieces,
  chopped**

**1 thick slice lean ham,
  about 40 g, diced**

**freshly ground black
  pepper**

**Per serving**
kcal 440, protein 17 g,
fat 36 g (of which saturated
fat 17 g), carbohydrate 13 g
(of which sugars 2 g),
fibre 0.5 g, sodium 0.5 g

**1** Preheat the oven to 200°C (gas 6) and place a baking sheet in the oven to warm. Roll out the pastry on a lightly floured surface and use to line a 23 cm flan dish, about 5 cm deep. Prick the base with a fork. Put the pastry case in the fridge for 15 minutes to rest – this will prevent the pastry from shrinking as it bakes.

**2** Beat the eggs with the cream and season with nutmeg and pepper. Crumble the cheese evenly over the pastry, then scatter over the walnuts and ham. Place the flan dish on the preheated baking sheet and pour over the egg mixture.

**3** Bake for 25–30 minutes until the tart is puffed and golden. Serve hot. (It's also delicious served cold.)

AN ELEGANT SLIVER OF THIS TANGY BLUE CHEESE TART IS DIVINE
SERVED AS A MOUTH-WATERING FIRST COURSE.

## COOK SMART
• Make a quick snack with any leftover pastry. Roll it out, then scatter half of it with grated cheese, chopped olives or chopped anchovy fillets, then fold the rest over the top. Cut into bite-sized pieces and bake at 200°C (gas 6) for 10 minutes.

• For a vegetarian version, omit the ham and add an extra 25 g chopped walnuts.

• This tart would also make a delicious main course to serve four with salad or seasonal vegetables.

££

**Serves 4**
Preparation  15 minutes
Cooking  20 minutes

**30 g butter**
**1½ tbsp flour**
**300 ml semi-skimmed milk**
**juice of 1 small lemon**
**2 small avocados**
**4 soft flour tortillas**
**100 g smoked salmon trimmings**
**salt and freshly ground black pepper**

**Per serving**
kcal 410, protein 14 g, fat 20.5 g (of which
saturated fat 8 g), carbohydrate 44 g
(of which sugars 4.5 g), fibre 3.5 g,
sodium 0.7 g

# smoked salmon and avocado enchiladas

**1** Preheat the oven to 190°C (gas 5). Melt the butter in a small saucepan, add the flour and stir for several seconds, then gradually add the milk. Bring to the boil, season with salt and pepper, and cook for 2 minutes. Remove from the heat. Add 2 tbsp lemon juice, then set this white sauce aside.

**2** Cut the avocados in half, remove the stone, peel, then slice the flesh thinly lengthways. Sprinkle lightly with the remaining lemon juice.

**3** Spread the tortillas out flat on the work surface. Place some smoked salmon and avocado slices on each one. Roll them up and place them, side by side, in a shallow ovenproof dish. Pour over the sauce.

**4** Bake for 20 minutes until golden. Serve immediately.

**INSPIRED BY THE CLASSIC MEXICAN DISH, THESE LUXURIOUS TORTILLA WRAPS MAKE A LOVELY START TO ANY MEAL.**

# red pepper, feta and olive cake

**£ £**

**Serves 4**

Preparation  35 minutes
Cooking  35 minutes

2 tbsp olive oil

2 onions, sliced

3 red peppers, seeded and thinly sliced

2 sprigs of fresh thyme or ½ tsp dried

2 garlic cloves, crushed

50 g stoned black olives, chopped

200 g feta cheese, roughly chopped

3 large eggs, lightly beaten

freshly ground black pepper

**Per serving**
kcal 300, protein 15 g,
fat 22 g (of which saturated
fat 9 g), carbohydrate 11 g
(of which sugars 10 g),
fibre 2.5 g, sodium 1 g

**1** Preheat the oven to 190°C (gas 5). Grease and line the base of a 20 cm sandwich tin.

**2** Heat the oil in a deep heavy-based frying pan. Gently cook the onions for 5 minutes until transparent, then add the peppers and thyme. Add the garlic and cook for 20 minutes over a medium heat, stirring occasionally.

**3** Add the olives and cheese to the vegetables, remove the thyme sprigs, if using fresh, and take the pan off the heat.

**4** Season the beaten eggs with black pepper, then stir into the vegetables and mix well. Pour into the tin and bake for 35 minutes until golden and firm to the touch.

**RATHER LIKE AN ITALIAN FRITTATA, THIS OVEN-BAKED OMELETTE IS GREAT CUT INTO WEDGES AND SERVED WITH CRISP SALAD LEAVES.**

**5** Remove cake from the oven and let it rest for 3 minutes. Turn it out onto a large plate, then flip it back onto a platter so it is right side up. Cut into wedges. It's delicious served hot, warm or cold.

**COOK SMART**

• If you have any leftover feta cheese, dice it finely with some stoned olives, drizzle with a little olive oil and chopped fresh herbs and use to fill hollowed-out cherry tomatoes. Serve as a nibble with drinks.

# rice, gr

sensational salads and hearty, wholesome one-pot wonders

# pasta, ains

Healthy, low-fat, cheap and sustaining, rice, pasta and grains make up the backbone of hundreds of meals. From creamy risottos and fluffy pilaffs and paellas to wholesome couscous, sensational stir-fries, summer salads and hearty pasta bakes – you'll soon see how versatile these ingredients can be. They're also great for stretching more expensive ingredients, such as prime pork fillet or sweet, juicy crab meat – helping you to keep to your budget while still enjoying unbeatable meals.

# bulghur wheat
## salad

£

**Serves 4 as an accompaniment**  Ⅴ
Preparation  20 minutes, plus about
   3 hours chilling

**150 g bulghur wheat**
**2 large tomatoes**
**½ cucumber, peeled and coarsely grated**
**1 carrot, peeled and coarsely grated**
**3 sprigs of flat-leaf parsley, finely chopped**
**10 fresh mint leaves, finely chopped**
**1 tbsp lemon juice**
**sprig of fresh mint to garnish**

**Dressing**
**5 tbsp olive oil**
**2 tbsp red or white wine vinegar**
**1 garlic clove, crushed**
**salt and freshly ground black pepper**

**Per serving**
kcal 280, protein 4.5 g, fat 14 g (of which
saturated fat 2 g), carbohydrate 33 g (of
which sugars 4 g), fibre 1 g, sodium 0.02 g

**A VARIATION ON THE CLASSIC MIDDLE EASTERN SALAD, TABBOULEH, THIS DELICIOUS DISH MADE WITH CRACKED WHEAT MAKES A HEALTHY LIGHT LUNCH OR SUPPER.**

**1** Tip the bulghur wheat into a heatproof bowl, pour over 300 ml boiling water, cover, and leave to rest for 20 minutes, until most of the water has been absorbed. Tip into a sieve and drain off any excess water.

**2** Scald the tomatoes in a bowl of boiling water for 30 seconds, drain and refresh under cold running water, then peel away the skins. Halve and deseed the flesh, then cut into dice.

**3** Mix the tomatoes with the cucumber and carrot. Rub the bulghur between your fingers to separate the grains, then toss with the vegetables and herbs. Add the lemon juice.

**4** Put the oil, vinegar, garlic and seasoning into a screw-top jar and shake well. Pour the dressing over the salad and toss gently. Cover with cling film and chill for at least 3 hours before serving. Garnish, with a sprig of fresh mint.

**COOK SMART**
• If you don't have any bulghur wheat, substitute an equal amount of couscous.
• If liked, add 2 or 3 chopped spring onions and a little crumbled feta.

# gorgonzola and bacon risotto

£ £

**Serves 4**
Preparation  10 minutes
Cooking  20–25 minutes

3 tbsp olive oil

2 shallots, finely chopped

275 g risotto rice

100 ml dry white wine

850 ml chicken stock, hot

2 rindless smoked bacon
    rashers, chopped

75 g Gorgonzola, cubed

2 tbsp crème fraîche

salt and freshly ground
    black pepper

**Per serving**
kcal 570, protein 30 g, fat 23 g
(of which saturated fat 9 g),
carbohydrate 57 g (of which
sugars 1.5 g), fibre 0.5 g,
sodium 0.5 g

**1** Heat the oil in a deep frying pan. Add the shallots and cook over a low heat for 3 minutes. Add the rice and stir with a wooden spoon until the grains become translucent and have absorbed most of the oil.

**2** Pour in the wine and stir constantly until it is absorbed. Add sufficient hot stock to just cover the rice, stir, and cook until all the liquid has been absorbed, stirring occasionally. Repeat this process two or three times until the stock is used up.

**3** Meanwhile, gently cook the bacon in a frying pan or grill until crispy.

**4** Stir the Gorgonzola and crème fraiche into the risotto. Grind over some pepper and taste to check the seasoning. Scatter over the bacon and serve immediately.

**COOK SMART**
• If the risotto turns out too thick, add a little extra hot stock at the end of cooking.

• Replace the Gorgonzola with Roquefort, add some crushed walnut pieces and substitute smoked ham for the bacon.

**COMFORT FOOD AT ITS BEST, THIS RICH AND CREAMY RISOTTO, FLAVOURED WITH TANGY BLUE CHEESE AND SMOKEY BACON, IS A REAL FEAST.**

# pesto rice salad with tuna

£

**Serves 4**
Preparation 10–15 minutes
Cooking 12–15 minutes

300 g long-grain white rice

4 tbsp pesto sauce

1 tbsp lemon juice

4 rindless smoked streaky bacon rashers, chopped

185 g can tuna, drained

100 g baby spinach leaves

1 yellow pepper, seeded and cut into strips

---

### COOK SMART

• If you want to prepare the salad ahead, keep in a covered bowl in the fridge for up to 24 hours, but leave out the spinach and bacon until ready to serve. Cooked rice shouldn't be kept for longer than 48 hours.

• You could also make this salad with small pasta shapes and toss in some halved cherry tomatoes.

---

**Per serving**
kcal 430, protein 22 g,
fat 7 g (of which saturated
fat 1.5 g), carbohydrate 68 g
(of which sugars 3 g),
fibre 1.5 g, sodium 0.9 g

104

1 Cook the rice in plenty of boiling water for 12–15 minutes or until just tender. Drain, rinse in a sieve under cold running water for a few seconds to cool slightly and stop further cooking, then tip into a large mixing bowl.

2 Whisk the pesto sauce and lemon juice together, drizzle over the warm rice and stir to coat in the dressing. Leave to cool.

3 Meanwhile, fry the bacon in a non-stick frying pan, without added fat, for 4–5 minutes, until lightly browned and crisp. Remove and drain on kitchen paper. Set aside.

4 Break the tuna fish into large chunks. Add to the rice with the spinach leaves, yellow pepper and half the crispy bacon. Gently mix together, taking care not to break up the tuna too much.

5 Transfer to a serving bowl, sprinkle over the remaining bacon as a garnish and serve within 1 hour of making.

# vegetable paella

£

**Serves 4**  Ⅴ
Preparation  15 minutes
Cooking  25–30 minutes

3 tbsp olive oil

1 onion, chopped

2 garlic cloves, crushed

2 courgettes, trimmed and diced

2 carrots, peeled and diced

250 g paella or risotto rice

227 g can chopped plum tomatoes

½ tsp turmeric

pinch of paprika

800 ml vegetable stock, hot

100 g French beans, trimmed and cut into short lengths

100 g frozen peas

2 tbsp chopped, fresh flat-leaf parsley

salt and freshly ground black pepper

sprig of flat-leaf parsley to garnish

**Per serving**
kcal 485, protein 25 g,
fat 15 g (of which saturated
fat 3 g), carbohydrate 66 g
(of which sugars 9 g),
fibre 4 g, sodium 0.1 g

**1** Heat the oil in a paella pan or deep frying pan. Add the onion and garlic and cook gently for 2 minutes without letting them brown. Add the courgettes and carrots. Sauté everything for 5 minutes over a high heat, stirring constantly.

**2** Tip in the rice, stir, then add the tomatoes with their juice. Add the turmeric and paprika to the stock and pour into the pan. Bring to the boil, then reduce the heat and cook for 20 minutes, stirring occasionally, until the rice is tender.

**3** Meanwhile, cook the beans and peas in boiling water for 5 minutes. Drain and add to the rice 5 minutes before the end of cooking.

**4** Stir in the parsley and season to taste. Turn off the heat, cover and leave to rest for 5 minutes before serving. Garnish with flat-leaf parsley.

### COOK SMART

• Leftover diced chicken or cooked vegetables could be used. Sauté quickly in a little oil before adding to the paella three-quarters of the way through cooking.

**PERFECT FOR VEGETARIANS, BUT GREAT FOR MEAT-EATERS TOO, THIS HEARTY RICE DISH MADE WITH STARCHY SHORT-GRAIN RICE IS WONDERFULLY RICH AND SATISFYING.**

££

**Serves 4**
Preparation 10 minutes
Cooking 30–35 minutes

**25g butter**

**1 onion, chopped**

**275g risotto rice**

**125ml dry white wine**

**1.2 litres vegetable stock, hot**

**225g asparagus, tips trimmed
off and stems sliced**

**1 courgette, thinly sliced**

**75g fresh or frozen peas**

**50g Parmesan, freshly grated**

**salt and freshly ground black
pepper**

**chopped fresh parsley or
snipped chives to garnish**

**Per serving**
kcal 580, protein 38g, fat 18g
(of which saturated fat 8g),
carbohydrate 66g (of which
sugars 4g), fibre 2g,
sodium 0.3g

# summer risotto

**1** Melt the butter in a large heavy-based saucepan over a medium heat. Add the onion and sauté for 3 minutes until just soft, then stir in the rice and sauté for 2 minutes until the rice is opaque.

**2** Pour in the wine and continue cooking for 3 minutes or until the wine has reduced by half. Now start to add the stock, about 125ml at a time, stirring almost continuously, gradually adding more of the stock as it is absorbed, until you've used about 500ml of the stock.

**3** Stir in the asparagus stems and another 125ml stock and cook, stirring constantly, until the stock is absorbed. Now add the courgettes, asparagus tips and a further measure of stock.

**4** Continue cooking, stirring constantly and gradually adding the remaining stock. Add the peas with the last measure. By the time all the stock is absorbed, the rice should be creamy and tender but still firm. Remove from the heat and stir in the Parmesan. Season to taste, then serve immediately, sprinkled with chopped parsley or snipped chives.

**COOK SMART**
• If you have a can or jar of artichoke hearts in the cupboard, drain and cut them into quarters, then add them to the risotto with the onion.

107

MAKE THIS RISOTTO IN EARLY SUMMER WHEN LOCALLY-GROWN ASPARAGUS IS IN PLENTIFUL SUPPLY. IMPORTED VARIETIES ARE EXPENSIVE, AND DON'T TASTE AS GOOD BECAUSE THEY ARE LESS FRESH.

# caribbean coconut rice with beans

THIS FABULOUS STORECUPBOARD DISH TASTES FANTASTIC AND IS SO SIMPLE TO MAKE. THE ADDITION OF COCONUT MILK GIVES IT A REAL TASTE OF THE CARIBBEAN.

**£**

**Serves 4** Ⓥ
Preparation 10 minutes
Cooking 15–20 minutes

**1 tbsp vegetable oil**
**1 small onion, chopped**
**1 garlic clove, crushed**
**1 red chilli, seeded and finely chopped**
**1 tbsp chopped fresh thyme or 1 tsp dried**
**200 g long-grain rice**
**400 ml can coconut milk**
**100 ml vegetable stock**
**420 g can red kidney beans, drained and rinsed**
**salt and freshly ground black pepper**
**fresh thyme leaves to garnish**

### Per serving
kcal 640, protein 14 g, fat 40 g (of which saturated fat 31 g), carbohydrate 60 g (of which sugars 7.5 g), fibre 4.5 g, sodium 0.3 g

**1** Heat the oil in a large saucepan, add the onion and cook gently for 3–4 minutes until softened. Stir in the garlic, chilli and thyme and cook for 1 minute, then stir in the rice.

**2** Pour over the coconut milk and stock, bring to the boil and stir, then cover the pan. Reduce the heat and simmer for 12–15 minutes until all the liquid has been absorbed and the rice is just tender. Add a little more boiling stock or water if the stock has all been absorbed before the rice is cooked.

**3** Stir in the beans, season to taste and scatter over some fresh thyme leaves to garnish.

### COOK SMART
• For a more substantial main meal, serve topped with prawns. Quickly sauté 200 g raw peeled prawns in a little garlic butter, with one seeded and finely chopped red chilli, if liked. Toss in some snipped chives then heap on top of the rice to serve.

# couscous with chickpeas

£ £

**Serves 4** V
Preparation 30 minutes
Cooking 35 minutes

1 tbsp olive oil

2 onions, sliced

1 green pepper, seeded
and diced

4 carrots, peeled and cut
into small sticks

2 courgettes, cut in half
lengthways and sliced

200g celeriac, peeled
and diced

1 tsp ground cumin

⅓ tsp each chilli powder,
turmeric, ground
cinnamon and ginger

500ml vegetable stock

1 tbsp tomato purée

1 bouquet garni

400g can chickpeas,
drained and rinsed

300g couscous

pinch of salt

25g butter, diced

sprigs of fresh mint to
garnish (optional)

## COOK SMART

• Good alternative
vegetables might include
turnips, leeks, pumpkin,
red peppers, aubergines or
broad beans. Some frozen
mixed vegetables,
combined with fresh, are
also useful in such dishes.

• If you happen to have
couscous spices, use
1 tbsp in place of the
individual spices.

**Per serving**
kcal 460, protein 23g,
fat 13g (of which saturated
fat 4g), carbohydrate 67g
(of which sugars 15g),
fibre 9g, sodium 0.3g

1 Heat the oil in a large saucepan. Sauté the
onions and pepper for 5 minutes. Add the carrots,
courgettes and celeriac, then sprinkle over the
spices and cook for a few seconds.

2 Pour in the stock. Bring to a gentle boil and add
the tomato purée and bouquet garni. Reduce the
heat, then cover and cook gently for 35 minutes.
Add the chickpeas to the vegetables 10 minutes
before the end of cooking.

3 Meanwhile, put the couscous in a large heatproof
bowl and pour over 500ml boiling water. Stir in
a pinch of salt, then cover and leave to swell for
5 minutes or until the couscous has absorbed all
the water.

4 Add the butter to the warm couscous, fork through,
then tip into a warmed deep dish. Using a draining
spoon, pile the vegetables on top of the couscous,
removing the bouquet garni. Pour over some of the
vegetable cooking juices, then serve the remainder
in a jug. Serve piping hot, garnished with sprigs
of fresh mint, if liked.

**TAKING ITS INSPIRATION FROM NORTH AFRICAN CUISINE,
THIS HEALTHY, WHOLESOME VEGETARIAN DISH MAKES A
SATISFYING MAIN COURSE.**

# roasted vegetable couscous

💷💷

**Serves 4** 🅥
Preparation 20 minutes
Cooking 45–50 minutes

**2 courgettes, thickly sliced**

**1 aubergine, cut into chunks**

**1 large red pepper, quartered and seeded**

**4 large ripe tomatoes, halved**

**2 red onions, cut into wedges**

**2 carrots, peeled and cut into chunks**

**4 large garlic cloves**

**2 tbsp olive oil**

**300 g couscous**

**25 g butter**

**2 tbsp chopped fresh parsley or coriander**

**salt and freshly ground black pepper**

To serve
**harissa or chilli sauce, to taste**

**Per serving**
kcal 350, protein 7.5 g,
fat 12.5 g (of which
saturated fat 4 g),
carbohydrate 54 g
(of which sugars 14 g),
fibre 5 g, sodium 0.06 g

**COUSCOUS IS THE NATIONAL DISH OF MOROCCO, AND THIS AUTHENTIC-TASTING VERSION, WITH ROASTED VEGETABLES AND HOT SAUCE, WILL TRANSPORT YOU THERE.**

## COOK SMART
• Harissa is a fiery North African sauce made from a mix of red chillies, garlic, coriander, cumin, caraway, mint and olive oil. You'll find it in larger supermarkets or you can use any chilli sauce or spicy tomato sauce.
• A creamy yoghurt raita, pepped up with diced green chillies and cooling cucumber would also make a good accompaniment.

**1** Preheat the oven to 200°C (gas 6). Arrange all the vegetables in a large shallow roasting tin, leaving the garlic cloves whole but peeled. Drizzle over the olive oil and season well with black pepper.

**2** Roast the vegetables for 45–50 minutes, turning them occasionally, until tender.

**3** Meanwhile, put the couscous in a deep ovenproof dish, pour over 500 ml boiling water, cover, and leave for 5 minutes to allow the grains to soak up the water. Cover tightly with foil and put in the oven with the vegetables for their final 15 minutes, to keep warm.

**4** Fluff up the cooked couscous with a fork, stir in the butter and herbs and season to taste. Serve the roasted vegetables piled on top of the couscous. Sprinkle with harissa or chilli sauce, to taste.

# noodles with tofu & green vegetables

THIS DELICIOUS VEGETARIAN STIR-FRY IS PACKED WITH LIGHTLY COOKED VEGETABLES, LOW-FAT TOFU AND HEALTHY NOODLES – PERFECT FOR A HEALTHY LUNCH OR SUPPER.

£ £

Serves 4   V
Preparation  15 minutes
Cooking  10 minutes

250 g Chinese medium egg noodles
125 ml vegetable stock
2 tbsp soy sauce
2 tsp cornflour
1 tsp toasted sesame oil
1 tbsp vegetable oil
4 spring onions, chopped
4 garlic cloves, crushed
1 red chilli, seeded and finely chopped (optional)
1 large courgette, halved lengthways then sliced crossways
250 g firm tofu, cubed
40 g watercress, tough stems removed
2 tbsp chopped fresh coriander

## COOK SMART
• Soba (Japanese buckwheat noodles) would also be good in this dish. Cook for 6 minutes or according to the packet instructions until al dente, then combine in step 5.
• If preferred, use peeled, cooked prawns or diced, skinned, cooked chicken or turkey instead of the tofu.

**Per serving**
kcal 350, protein 15 g, fat 11.5 g (of which saturated fat 2 g), carbohydrate 49.5 g (of which sugars 3 g), fibre 2 g, sodium 0.7 g

**1** Place the noodles in a large pan of lightly salted boiling water. Return to the boil and simmer for 4 minutes, stirring occasionally with a fork to separate the noodles. Drain, reserving 50 ml of the liquid. Rinse the noodles under cold running water. Put aside.

**2** Meanwhile, whisk together the stock, soy sauce, cornflour and sesame oil in a small bowl until smooth.

**3** Heat the vegetable oil in a wok or large non-stick frying pan over a medium heat. Reserve some of the dark green parts of the spring onions for garnish, then add the remaining spring onions, garlic, chilli if using, and courgettes to the frying pan. Stir-fry for 3–4 minutes until softened.

**4** Add the tofu, stock mixture and reserved noodle soaking liquid to the cooking pan. Bring to the boil, stirring constantly for 1–2 minutes or until the sauce thickens.

**5** Add the noodles and quickly toss together. Remove pan from the heat, toss in the watercress, coriander and reserved spring onions and serve immediately.

YOU ONLY NEED A LITTLE CHICKEN TO MAKE THIS
MOUTHWATERING PILAFF, SO IT IS THE PERFECT DISH
TO USE UP LEFTOVERS FROM A ROAST.

# spicy almond pilaff with chicken

£ £

**Serves 4**
Preparation 20 minutes
Cooking 15–20 minutes

2 tbsp olive oil

1 onion, chopped

2.5 cm piece fresh root ginger, finely grated

2 garlic cloves, crushed

1 red pepper, seeded and diced

1 tsp ground cumin

1 tsp ground cinnamon

¼ tsp ground turmeric

350 g basmati rice, rinsed

600 ml chicken or vegetable stock, hot

150 g cooked chicken, shredded

1 tbsp lemon juice

2 tbsp chopped fresh coriander

50 g flaked almonds, toasted

salt and freshly ground black pepper

fresh coriander leaves to garnish

**Per serving**
kcal 620, protein 32 g, fat 21 g
(of which saturated fat 4 g),
carbohydrate 81 g (of which
sugars 4.5 g), fibre 2 g,
sodium 0.08 g

1 Heat the oil in a large heavy-based saucepan and gently cook the onion for 5 minutes. Add the ginger, garlic and red pepper and cook for a further 2 minutes, stirring frequently, until the onion is translucent and beginning to soften. Stir in the cumin, cinnamon and turmeric and cook for a further minute, stirring all the time.

2 Add the rice and stir to coat in the spices, then pour in the hot stock and season with salt and pepper. Bring to the boil, then lower the heat so that the mixture bubbles gently. Cover and cook for 12–15 minutes or until the rice is just tender and nearly all the stock has been absorbed.

3 Stir in the chicken and lemon juice and gently heat for 2–3 minutes until the chicken is hot. Remove the pan from the heat and toss in the chopped coriander and most of the flaked almonds. Taste and adjust the seasoning if necessary, then cover again and leave to stand for 3–4 minutes.

4 Spoon the pilaff into a warmed serving dish or onto individual plates. Serve hot, scattered with the remaining toasted flaked almonds and garnished with coriander leaves.

## COOK SMART
• For a vegetarian version, leave out the chicken and increase the amount of toasted, flaked almonds to 75 g. Stir in 50 g seedless raisins or chopped, dried apricots when adding the stock.

QUINOA IS A SUPER-HEALTHY GRAIN, NATIVE TO SOUTH AMERICA. IT HAS A WONDERFUL TASTE AND TEXTURE THAT IS PERFECT FOR PILAFFS, SO IT IS WELL WORTH TRYING.

# quinoa pilaff with cherries and walnuts

**£**

**Serves 6 as an accompaniment** Ⓥ
Preparation  10 minutes
Cooking  30 minutes

**Per serving**
kcal 200, protein 6 g,
fat 8 g (of which saturated
fat 1 g), carbohydrate 26 g
(of which sugars 9 g),
fibre 0.5 g, sodium 0.03 g

**2 tsp olive oil**

**1 onion, finely chopped**

**200 g quinoa**

**2 tsp chopped fresh thyme or ½ tsp dried**

**50 g dried cherries or cranberries**

**50 g walnut pieces, toasted and coarsely chopped**

**salt and freshly ground black pepper**

**1** Heat the oil in a saucepan, add the onion and cook over a medium heat for 7 minutes, stirring frequently, until golden brown.

**2** Meanwhile, place the quinoa in a large frying pan (not greased) over a medium heat and cook for 5 minutes, stirring often, until lightly toasted.

**3** Add the quinoa to the onion in the pan, stir in 500 ml boiling water, the thyme and salt and pepper to season. Cover and simmer gently for 10 minutes. Uncover and cook, stirring occasionally, for a further 10–12 minutes, until all the liquid has been absorbed and the quinoa is tender.

**4** Remove the pan from the heat and stir in the cherries or cranberries and walnuts. Serve hot or at room temperature.

### COOK SMART

• To turn this side dish into a main course meal for four, add some shredded leftover chicken breast or strips of roast pork tenderloin. Other dried fruits and nuts could be tossed in.

• Quinoa can be found in health food stores and larger supermarkets. Brown rice makes a good alternative, but it takes 30–35 minutes to cook. Add more boiling water, as needed.

£

**Serves 4 as an accompaniment**
Preparation and cooking
15 minutes

**200g quick-cooking (instant) polenta**

**1 tbsp olive oil**

**40g butter**

**60g Parmesan, freshly grated**

**2 tbsp crème fraîche**

**salt and coarsely ground black pepper**

## COOK SMART

• Buy Parmesan in a piece and grate it yourself. This works out far cheaper than ready grated and has a better flavour.

• Cooked polenta can be left to sit in a shallow tin, then cut into wedges and grilled to use as a base for bruschetta.

**Per serving**
kcal 380, protein 11g,
fat 21g (of which saturated
fat 11g), carbohydrate 37g
(of which sugars 5g),
fibre 1g, sodium 0.2g

# creamy polenta

**1** Bring 1 litre of lightly salted water to the boil in a heavy-based saucepan. Add the oil. Gradually tip in the polenta, reduce the heat to a simmer and stir vigorously with a long-handled wooden spoon until the mixture is thick and all the water has been absorbed. Stand back as you do this, as polenta splutters quite dramatically.

**2** Scrape the polenta away from the sides of the pan. Remove from the heat and leave covered for 5 minutes.

**3** Add the butter in thin slices, the Parmesan and the crème fraîche. Season to taste and mix. Serve hot.

THIS CLASSIC ITALIAN DISH MAKES A GREAT ACCOMPANIMENT TO MEAT DISHES, PARTICULARLY THOSE WITH A RICH SAUCE OR GRAVY.

# toasted buckwheat pilaff with dried fruit

£

**Serves 4 as a main course** V
**or 6 as an accompaniment**
Preparation  20 minutes
Cooking  15 minutes

**50 g walnut pieces**

**1 tbsp olive oil**

**1 red pepper, seeded and
diced**

**4 garlic cloves, crushed**

**200 g toasted buckwheat
(kasha)**

**90 g red split lentils**

**½ tsp dried rosemary**

**50 g ready-to-eat dried
apricots, diced**

**50 g ready-to-eat dried figs,
diced**

**4 tbsp chopped fresh parsley**

**salt and freshly ground black
pepper**

**Per serving (as a main course)**
kcal 422, protein 12.5 g,
fat 13 g (of which saturated
fat 1 g), carbohydrate 69 g
(of which sugars 14 g),
fibre 4.5 g, sodium 0.02 g

**1** Preheat a moderate grill. Scatter the walnuts in a grill pan or on a baking sheet then toast under the grill for 5–7 minutes, turning frequently, until crisp and fragrant. When cool enough to handle, coarsely chop, then set aside.

**2** Heat the oil in a large frying pan over a medium heat. Add the pepper and garlic, and cook for 4 minutes or until the pepper is tender.

**3** Stir in the buckwheat and lentils and cook for 3 minutes, until the grains are well coated.

**4** Add 750 ml boiling water, the rosemary and salt and black pepper to season and bring to the boil. Reduce the heat, cover and simmer for 15 minutes or until the buckwheat and lentils are tender and all the water is absorbed.

**5** Toss through the walnuts, apricots, figs and parsley, then serve hot.

### COOK SMART

• Toasted buckwheat (kasha) is sold in some supermarkets or you'll find it in health food shops, continental grocers or delis. Alternative grains could be used instead, such as brown rice or bulghur wheat for an equally tasty and nutritious result.

**BUCKWHEAT, POPULAR IN MUCH EASTERN EUROPEAN COOKING, HAS A LOVELY NUTTY FLAVOUR AND MAKES THE WHOLESOME BASE FOR THIS FRAGRANT, HERBY PILAFF.**

# fresh egg pasta

300g strong plain flour
3 eggs
1 tbsp olive oil
pinch of salt

£

Serves 4   V

Preparation  25 minutes,
      plus 30 minutes resting

**Per serving**
kcal 346, protein 12.5g,
fat 9g (of which saturated
fat 2g), carbohydrate 58g
(of which sugars 1g),
fibre 2g, sodium 0.07g

**COOK SMART**
• If the dough still seems
sticky after kneading, add
a little flour – not too much,
it must remain supple.

1 Heap the flour on a clean work surface, making
a well in the centre. Crack the eggs into the well
and add the oil and salt. Gently beat the eggs with
a fork, drawing in the flour a little at a time, until
the mixture forms a dough. If necessary, add a
few drops of water. (Alternatively, place all the
ingredients in a food processor and whizz together
until the mixture forms a smooth dough.)

2 Knead the dough by hand on the work surface,
stretching it as much as possible. Roll back into a
ball and repeat the stretching and kneading operation
for at least 5 minutes, until the pasta is smooth and
elastic and no longer sticks to your fingers. Wrap in
cling film and chill for 30 minutes.

3 Divide the ball of dough in half. Lightly flour the
work surface and the rolling pin. Roll out each
piece of dough as thinly and evenly as possible.

4 Cut the dough into whatever shape you desire,
using a knife or a pasta machine (following the
manufacturer's instructions).

5 Cook immediately or allow to dry for up to
30 minutes before cooking in a large pan of
lightly salted boiling water.

# summer pasta salad

£ £

Serves 4

Preparation  25 minutes,
      plus 30 minutes chilling
Cooking  10–12 minutes

**Per serving**
kcal 340, protein 12g,
fat 14.5g (of which
saturated fat 4g),
carbohydrate 42g (of which
sugars 6g), fibre 3g,
sodium 0.4g

½ cucumber
200g elbow macaroni
4 tomatoes
4 spring onions, trimmed
   and sliced
12 stoned black olives,
   halved
50g fresh Parmesan, pared
   into shavings

**Dressing**
3 tbsp olive oil
1 tbsp red or white wine
   vinegar
1 tsp prepared mustard
salt and freshly ground
   black pepper

**COOK SMART**
• If preferred, leave the
peel on the cucumber.
• For strict vegetarians,
omit the Parmesan and
use an alternative cheese
(see page 4).

1 Peel the cucumber and halve lengthways, then
scoop out the seeds with a small spoon. Cut into
thin slices. Place the cucumber in a sieve, sprinkle
with a little salt and allow to drain.

2 Bring a large pan of lightly salted water to the boil.
Tip in the pasta and cook for 10–12 minutes or
following the packet instructions, until al dente.

3 Meanwhile, scald the tomatoes in a bowl of boiling
water for 30 seconds, drain and cool quickly under
cold running water. Peel away the skins using a
sharp knife. Halve and seed the tomatoes, then
dice. Tip them into a salad bowl and add the onions
and olives.

4 Put the oil, vinegar and mustard in a screw-top jar
and shake well together. Pour over the salad.

5 Drain the pasta and rinse under cold running water
to cool quickly. Add to the salad and toss together
to combine. Chill for 30 minutes.

6 Add the cucumber and Parmesan to the salad just
before serving and toss together.

HEALTHY, LOW-FAT PASTA MAKES A GREAT BASE FOR SALADS. ENJOY THIS ONE FOR A LIGHT SUMMER LUNCH OR SUPPER, OR SERVE WITH A BARBECUE.

# sunshine twists

MAKE THIS GORGEOUS SALAD IN SUMMER WHEN AUBERGINES AND PEPPERS ARE AT THEIR SWEETEST AND MOST DELICIOUS.

£ £

**Serves 4**
Preparation  20–25 minutes
Cooking  about 20 minutes

**2 aubergines**

**3 tbsp olive oil**

**1 large avocado**

**2 tbsp lemon juice**

**300 g pasta twists or spirals (such as fusilli or rotini)**

**1 red pepper, seeded and diced**

**50 g feta in oil and herbs, diced**

**salt and freshly ground black pepper**

---

**COOK SMART**

• Replace the avocado with a courgette, baked in the same way as the aubergines.

• Crank up the flavour of the avocado by sprinkling it with a few drops of hot pepper sauce.

• Make this dish even more colourful by using coloured pasta, flavoured with tomato or spinach.

---

**Per serving**
kcal 490, protein 13 g, fat 23 g (of which saturated fat 5 g), carbohydrate 61 g (of which sugars 5 g), fibre 5 g, sodium 0.2 g

**1** Preheat the oven to 200°C (gas 6). Cut the aubergines lengthways into slices about 12 mm thick. Place on a non-stick baking sheet, brush on both sides with 1 tbsp of the olive oil, salt sparingly, and bake for 8–10 minutes on each side until golden and tender. Set aside.

**2** Cut the avocado in half, remove the stone and dice the flesh. Sprinkle with 1 tbsp of the lemon juice and a little salt.

**3** Bring a large pan of lightly salted water to the boil. Add the pasta and cook for 10 minutes, or according to the packet instructions, until al dente.

**4** Dice the aubergine. Skim off and reserve 1 tbsp of the pasta cooking water and drain the pasta. Tip the pasta into a large deep bowl with the reserved tablespoon of water. Add the aubergine, avocado, red pepper and feta. Gently toss to mix. Pour over the remaining olive oil and lemon juice. Season with pepper and toss once more. Serve immediately.

# vegetable fettuccine

£ £

**Serves 4**
Preparation 15 minutes
Cooking 10–12 minutes

375 g fettuccine or
  tagliatelle

150 g broccoli florets

250 g baby carrots,
  scraped, trimmed and
  cut in half lengthways

150 g fresh or frozen peas,
  thawed if frozen

1 large red pepper, seeded
  and thinly sliced

25 g butter

1 garlic clove, crushed

2 tbsp plain flour

375 ml semi-skimmed milk

100 ml whipping cream

50 g Parmesan, grated

salt and freshly ground
  black pepper

## COOK SMART
- To avoid waste, chop the broccoli stems and toss them into a soup or casserole. Or thinly slice and blanch them for a salad.

**Per serving**
kcal 670, protein 26 g,
fat 24 g (of which saturated
fat 14 g), carbohydrate 94 g
(of which sugars 16 g),
fibre 8 g, sodium 0.3 g

1 Cook the pasta in a large pan of lightly salted boiling water for 10–12 minutes, or according to the packet instructions, until al dente.

2 Meanwhile, cook the broccoli and carrots in another large saucepan of boiling water for 5 minutes. Add the peas and red pepper and cook for a further 3 minutes until all the vegetables are just tender. Drain and keep warm.

3 Melt the butter in a saucepan over a gentle heat. Add the garlic, cook for 2 minutes, then stir in the flour and cook for 1 minute, stirring occasionally.

4 Remove the pan from the heat and gradually stir in the milk and cream. Return the pan to the heat and bring to the boil, stirring continuously. Reduce the heat and simmer for 1–2 minutes, stirring occasionally, until the sauce thickens. Stir in the cheese until just melted and smooth, and season to taste.

5 Drain the pasta well, then toss with the vegetables and the sauce. Transfer to a large dish and serve immediately.

FRESH VEGETABLES, A LITTLE CREAM AND FRESHLY GRATED PARMESAN ARE ALL THAT ARE NEEDED TO MAKE THIS PASTA DISH REALLY LUXURIOUS.

# spaghetti with fresh tomato sauce

300 g spaghetti

4 tomatoes

1 small green pepper, seeded and diced

2 garlic cloves, crushed

3 tbsp olive oil

½ tsp dried crushed chillies (optional)

2 tbsp chopped fresh parsley

salt and freshly ground black pepper

£

Serves 4  Ⓥ

Preparation  5 minutes
Cooking  10–12 minutes

**Per serving**
kcal 356, protein 10 g,
fat 10 g (of which saturated
fat 1 g), carbohydrate 60 g
(of which sugars 7 g),
fibre 3.5 g, sodium 0.01 g

**1** Bring a large pan of lightly salted water to the boil. Tip in the pasta and cook for 10–12 minutes, or according to the packet instructions, until al dente.

**2** Meanwhile, scald the tomatoes in a bowl of boiling water for 30 seconds, drain and refresh under cold running water, then peel off the skins. Deseed and roughly chop the flesh.

**3** Mix the tomatoes with the diced pepper, garlic, olive oil, chillies, if liked, parsley and seasoning in a saucepan. Warm this sauce over a low heat.

**4** Drain the pasta, tip into a heated serving dish and season with pepper. Pour over the warm sauce, toss with the pasta and serve at once.

# spaghetti with almond pesto

£

Serves 4

Preparation  10 minutes
Cooking  10–12 minutes

30 g blanched almonds

3 garlic cloves, coarsely chopped

10 fresh basil leaves

50 g Parmesan, freshly grated

5 tbsp olive oil

300 g spaghetti

salt and freshly ground black pepper

To serve

Parmesan shavings

fresh basil leaves (optional)

**COOK SMART**

• Nuts are best bought in small quantities and should be used soon after purchase to prevent them going rancid. Wrap tightly and store in an airtight container in a cool place.

**Per serving**
kcal 483, protein 15 g,
fat 23 g (of which saturated
fat 5 g), carbohydrate 56 g
(of which sugars 3 g),
fibre 3 g, sodium 0.1 g

**1** To prepare the pesto, put the almonds, garlic, basil and Parmesan in a food processor and grind in some pepper. Add the olive oil and whizz until you have a smooth paste.

**2** Bring a large pan of lightly salted boiling water to the boil. Put the spaghetti into the boiling water and cook for 10–12 minutes, or according to the packet instructions, until al dente.

**3** Pour 2 tbsp of the cooking water into a heated serving dish, drain the pasta and tip into the dish. Add the pesto and toss gently to mix. Serve immediately, with some extra Parmesan. If liked, scatter over some fresh basil leaves to garnish.

**THERE'S NOTHING BETTER THAN PASTA TOSSED WITH HOME-MADE PESTO. ALMONDS ARE JUST AS GOOD AS TRADITIONAL PINE NUTS, BUT MUCH LESS EXPENSIVE.**

**THIS VEGETARIAN VERSION OF THE ITALIAN CLASSIC USES NO-PRECOOK PASTA SHEETS SO IT IS REALLY QUICK TO ASSEMBLE.**

**Serves 6**

Preparation 20 minutes, plus 10 minutes standing before serving

Cooking 55 minutes

**750 g ricotta cheese or fromage frais**

**125 g Parmesan, freshly grated**

**1 large egg**

**1 litre chunky tomato pasta sauce**

**220 g (12 sheets) no-precook egg lasagne**

**600 g frozen chopped spinach, thawed and squeezed dry**

**250 g mozzarella cheese, coarsely grated**

**Per serving**

kcal 627, protein 39 g, fat 34 g (of which saturated fat 19 g), carbohydrate 43 g (of which sugars 14 g), fibre 3 g, sodium 1.4 g

**1** Preheat the oven to 180°C (gas 4). Mix together the ricotta, Parmesan and egg in a large bowl.

**2** Spread 250 ml of the pasta sauce over the base of a lightly oiled, large baking dish, measuring about 23 x 33 cm and about 7 cm deep.

**3** Arrange three of the lasagne sheets side by side in the dish. Spread with a quarter of the ricotta mixture then top with a third of the spinach. Repeat layering twice more with the sauce, lasagne, ricotta mixture and spinach. Top with remaining three sheets of lasagne.

**4** Spread the remaining ricotta mixture and sauce over the top, then gently press the lasagne sheets down into the dish, so the sauce comes up around the sides. Cover the dish with foil.

**5** Bake for 35 minutes, then uncover, sprinkle with the mozzarella and bake for a further 20 minutes until golden and bubbling.

**6** Allow to stand for 10 minutes before cutting into rectangles to serve warm.

**COOK SMART**

• You can make this lasagne with other ingredients. Try 250 g sliced pepperoni sausage with 250 g sliced mushrooms; frozen, chopped broccoli and some diced, cooked ham; or drained, canned tuna in place of the spinach layers.

# easy one-step spinach lasagne

# tagliatelle with smoked salmon

£ £

**Serves 4**
Preparation 5 minutes
Cooking 10–12 minutes

**300 g tagliatelle**

**150 ml single cream**

**200 g smoked salmon trimmings, cut into small strips**

**8 fresh chives, snipped**

**salt and freshly ground black pepper**

**Per serving**
kcal 405, protein 23 g, fat 11 g (of which saturated fat 5 g), carbohydrate 58 g (of which sugars 2.5 g), fibre 2 g, sodium 1 g

1. Bring a large pan of lightly salted water to the boil. Add the pasta and cook for 8–10 minutes, or according to the packet instructions, until al dente.

2. Meanwhile, heat the cream gently in a small pan. Season sparingly with salt.

3. Drain the pasta, tip into a serving dish and add the salmon and cream. Toss to mix. Grind over some pepper, sprinkle with the chives and serve at once.

**USING SMOKED SALMON TRIMMINGS GIVES YOU ALL OF THE FLAVOUR OF MORE EXPENSIVE CUTS BUT AT A FRACTION OF THE COST.**

### COOK SMART

• If using fresh pasta, double the quantity and cook for just 2–3 minutes.

• Wrap any surplus smoked salmon in cling film. It will keep for 4–5 days in the fridge, and can be used on canapés, or in a sauce, salad or quiche.

RICH, CREAMY AND ABSOLUTELY DELICIOUS, THIS DISH IS A NO-HASSLE TREAT FOR ANY DAY OF THE WEEK.

# spaghetti with blue cheese and walnuts

£

**Serves 4** V
Preparation 5 minutes
Cooking 10–12 minutes

**75 g walnut pieces**
**300 g spaghetti**
**100 g Stilton or other blue cheese**
**3 tbsp single cream**
**salt and freshly ground black pepper**

**Per serving**
kcal 510, protein 18 g, fat 25 g
(of which saturated fat 8 g),
carbohydrate 57 g (of which
sugars 3 g), fibre 3 g, sodium 0.2 g

**1** Preheat the oven to 180°C (gas 4). Spread the walnuts on a baking sheet and bake for 5 minutes until lightly browned. Remove them from the oven and leave to cool, then crush coarsely.

**2** Bring a large pan of lightly salted water to the boil. Tip in the spaghetti, bring back to the boil and cook for 10–12 minutes, or according to the packet instructions, until al dente.

**3** Meanwhile, crumble the cheese into a saucepan. Add the cream, mix, and heat gently for 2–3 minutes, stirring constantly.

**4** Drain the pasta, setting aside 2 tbsp of the cooking water. Tip the pasta into a heated serving dish. Add the reserved cooking water to the blue cheese mixture. Pour this sauce over the pasta and stir until incorporated. Add the nuts, grind over some pepper and serve at once.

# pasta puttanesca

A GOOD GUTSY SAUCE USING
CANNED TOMATOES, CHILLIES,
ANCHOVIES, CAPERS AND OLIVES
FOR A MEDITERRANEAN FLAVOUR.

**Serves 4**
Preparation 10 minutes
Cooking 10–12 minutes

375 g penne (tubes) or
   fusilli (spirals)
1 tbsp olive oil
2 garlic cloves, crushed
2 x 400 g cans chopped
   tomatoes
1 tbsp capers, drained and
   rinsed
4 anchovy fillets, drained
   and finely chopped
¼ tsp dried crushed
   chillies, or to taste
50 g stoned black olives,
   roughly chopped
1 tbsp chopped flat-leaf
   parsley

**COOK SMART**
• Turn this into a complete
Italian meal with warm
ciabatta and a rocket salad
as accompaniments. For
dessert, serve poached
pears with little almond
biscuits (amaretti).

**Per serving**
kcal 402, protein 14 g,
fat 6 g (of which saturated
fat 1 g), carbohydrate 77 g
(of which sugars 8 g),
fibre 4.5 g, sodium 0.5 g

128

1 Cook the pasta in a large pan of lightly salted boiling
water for 10–12 minutes, or according to the packet
instructions, until al dente.

2 Meanwhile, heat the oil in large frying pan over a
medium heat. Sauté the garlic for 1 minute, then
stir in the tomatoes, capers, anchovies and chillies.
Cook gently for 10 minutes, stirring from time to
time until the sauce thickens slightly, then stir in
the olives.

3 Drain the pasta and tip into a large serving dish.
Pour over the sauce and toss to coat well. Sprinkle
with parsley and serve immediately.

# tagliatelle with ham and mushrooms

SUPER-SPEEDY,
AND RELYING ON
THE MOST BASIC
INGREDIENTS, YOU
CAN WHIP UP THIS
DISH IN A FLASH.

**Serves 4**
Preparation 5 minutes
Cooking 10–12 minutes

300 g tagliatelle
10 g butter
290 g can sliced
   mushrooms, drained
200 g lean smoked ham,
   chopped
100 ml crème fraîche
salt and coarsely ground
   black pepper

**Per serving**
kcal 440, protein 20 g,
fat 15 g (of which saturated
fat 9 g), carbohydrate 59 g
(of which sugars 3 g),
fibre 2 g, sodium 0.8 g

1 Bring a large pan of lightly salted water to the boil.
Add the tagliatelle and cook for 8–10 minutes, or
according to the packet instructions, until al dente.

2 Melt the butter in a large deep-sided frying pan and
sauté the mushrooms for 2 minutes over a medium
heat. Add the ham and toss with the mushrooms.

3 Drain the pasta and tip into the frying pan with the
ham and mushrooms. Stir in the crème fraîche,
season with pepper and serve at once.

**COOK SMART**
• Buy ham end cuts, which are cheaper than sliced ham.
Always compare prices by weight. Pre-packed ham is quite
often more expensive per kg than ham sold loose on the deli
counter, and you can buy just the amount you need.

# blt pasta

£ £

**Serves 4**

Preparation  15 minutes
Cooking  15 minutes

**Per serving**
kcal 493, protein 23g,
fat 13g (of which saturated
fat 5g), carbohydrate 75.5g
(of which sugars 5g),
fibre 4.5g, sodium 0.6g

### COOK SMART
• You could serve this as
a hot pasta salad on a bed
of lettuce leaves.

**375g tri-colour fusilli
(pasta spirals)**
**2 tsp olive oil**
**4 rindless, smoked back
bacon rashers, chopped**
**1 large onion, chopped**
**3 garlic cloves, crushed**
**250g cherry tomatoes,
halved**
**225g baby spinach leaves**
**50g Parmesan, grated**
**freshly ground black
pepper**

1. Cook the pasta in a large pan of lightly salted boiling water for 10–12 minutes, or according to the packet instructions, until al dente.

2. Meanwhile, heat the oil in a large frying pan over a medium heat. Add the bacon, onion and garlic. Sauté for 7 minutes, stirring frequently, until the onion is golden.

3. Add the tomatoes to the frying pan and cook gently for 5 minutes until the tomatoes are beginning to soften but still holding their shape.

4. Drain the pasta, reserving 125ml of the cooking water. Pour the water over the tomatoes in the frying pan and bring to the boil. Season with black pepper.

5. Place the spinach in a large serving bowl, pour over the hot tomato mixture, add the pasta and Parmesan and toss to combine. Serve immediately.

**ANOTHER THROW-IT-ALL-TOGETHER DISH THAT IS PERFECT MID-WEEK WHEN YOU NEED A HEALTHY, COMFORTING DISH IN MINUTES.**

# penne with crab

£ £

**Serves 4**

Preparation 15 minutes
Cooking 30 minutes

250g penne or other pasta shapes

2 tsp olive oil

2 smoked turkey or rindless bacon
rashers, roughly chopped

1 red onion, finely chopped

2 garlic cloves, crushed

1 green pepper, seeded and diced

1 small bulb of fennel, thinly sliced
crossways

400g can chopped tomatoes

125ml orange juice

170g can white crab meat, drained

salt and freshly ground
black pepper

**Per serving**
kcal 345, protein 19g, fat 5g
(of which saturated fat 1g),
carbohydrate 58g (of which
sugars 11g), fibre 4g, sodium 0.5g

130

**1** Cook the pasta in a large pan of lightly salted boiling water for 10–12 minutes, or according to the packet instructions, until al dente.

**2** Meanwhile, heat the oil in large frying pan over a medium heat. Add the smoked turkey or bacon and sauté for 4 minutes until lightly crisped. Add the onion and garlic to the pan and cook for 5 minutes, stirring frequently, until the onion is tender. Add the pepper and fennel and cook for 7 minutes until softened.

**3** Drain the pasta and keep warm, reserving 125ml of the cooking liquid. Stir this liquid into the pan with the tomatoes and their juice and the orange juice. Season with salt and pepper, and bring to the boil. Reduce to a simmer, cover and cook for 5 minutes or until the fennel is tender and the sauce is a good coating consistency.

**4** Stir in the crab meat and heat gently for just 2–3 minutes. Transfer to a serving dish. Add the pasta, toss to combine and serve.

**COOK SMART**
• There is no need to buy a premium, chilled orange juice for this sauce. Use a long-life juice or squeeze your own fresh oranges.
• Multi-packs of canned tomatoes are often on 'special offer' so buy them when keenly priced and keep several cans in your storecupboard.

CANNED CRAB MEAT IS PERFECT FOR THIS DISH, AND MAKES AN ECONOMICAL, FUSS-FREE ALTERNATIVE TO FRESH.

**RICH WITH THE FLAVOURS OF TUSCANY, THIS ROBUST PASTA DISH MAKES A GREAT LAID-BACK SUPPER.**

££

**Serves 4**
Preparation  10 minutes
Cooking  10–12 minutes

**375g small pasta shells (such as conchigliette or orecchiette)**

**1 tbsp olive oil**

**1 small red onion, chopped**

**1 small carrot, peeled and grated**

**3 garlic cloves, crushed**

**2 x 400g cans chopped tomatoes in rich juice**

**250ml vegetable stock, hot**

**300g can cannellini beans, drained and rinsed**

**4 tbsp freshly grated Parmesan**

**50g rocket, roughly torn into pieces**

**4 tbsp chopped fresh basil**

**4 tbsp dry breadcrumbs**

**salt and freshly ground black pepper**

**Per serving**
kcal 605, protein 30g, fat 11g (of which
saturated fat 4g), carbohydrate 100g
(of which sugars 13g), fibre 8g, sodium 0.6g

# pasta with cannellini beans and rocket

**1** Cook the pasta in a large pan of lightly salted boiling water for 10–12 minutes, or according to the packet instructions, until al dente.

**2** Meanwhile, heat the oil in a large saucepan, add the onion, carrot and garlic and sauté for 5 minutes, over a medium heat, until tender.

**3** Add the tomatoes with their juice, the stock and beans and half the Parmesan. Season with salt and pepper, then simmer, uncovered, for 5 minutes.

**4** Drain the pasta and tip into a large serving dish. Add the rocket and half the basil to the sauce, then pour over the pasta and toss together.

**5** Mix the breadcrumbs with the remaining Parmesan and basil and scatter over the top.

**COOK SMART**
• If you don't have any fresh basil, add 2 tbsp pesto to the tomato sauce.
• Grissini (Italian breadsticks) make a good accompaniment to an Italian-style meal.

# linguine with pork, greens and peas

💷💷

**Serves 6**

Preparation 20 minutes
plus 15 minutes
marinating
Cooking 10 minutes

1 tbsp dry sherry or
rice wine

1 tbsp soy sauce

375 g pork fillet
(tenderloin), thinly
sliced across the grain

350 g linguine

1 tbsp vegetable oil

2 garlic cloves, crushed

2 tsp finely chopped fresh
root ginger

185 g pak choi or spring
greens, shredded

150 g frozen peas, thawed

6 spring onions, thinly
sliced

175 ml chicken stock

2 tbsp oyster sauce

1 tsp cornflour

100 g bean sprouts

1 tsp toasted sesame oil

## COOK SMART

• Linguine are long, flat
ribbon noodles. Spaghetti
or Chinese egg noodles
could be used instead
– cook according to packet
instructions.

**MAKE THE MOST OF PRIME PORK FILLET BY STIR-FRYING WITH FRESH, CRUNCHY VEGETABLES AND NOODLES.**

**Per serving**
kcal 362, protein 27 g,
fat 7 g (of which saturated
fat 1.5 g), carbohydrate 51 g
(of which sugars 3.5 g),
fibre 4 g, sodium 0.5 g

**1** Stir together the sherry and soy sauce in a medium bowl, add the pork and toss to coat. Leave to marinate at room temperature for 15 minutes (or longer if more convenient).

**2** Cook the linguine in a large pan of lightly salted boiling water for 10 minutes, or according to the packet instructions, until al dente. Drain and cool under cold running water.

**3** Meanwhile, heat 2 tsp of the oil in a wok or large frying pan, add the garlic and ginger and stir-fry over a medium heat for 15 seconds. Add the pork with the marinade mixture and stir-fry for 3–4 minutes until cooked through. Transfer the pork to a plate.

**4** Add the remaining 1 tsp oil to the pan, add the pak choi or greens and stir-fry over a medium heat for 2 minutes. Next, add the peas and spring onions, stir-fry for 1 minute, then add the stock and oyster sauce. Bring to the boil. Blend the cornflour with 2 tsp water, stir into the pan, lower the heat and simmer for 30 seconds or until the sauce is thickened.

**5** Add the pork and linguine, heat through for 1–2 minutes, then stir in the bean sprouts and sesame oil. Toss together and serve at once.

**Serves 4**
Preparation 20–25 minutes
Cooking 30 minutes
(20 minutes for
individual dishes)

**300 g macaroni**

**200 g chicken breast fillet**

**200 ml single cream**

**250 ml semi-skimmed milk**

**pinch of ground nutmeg**

**100 g mature Cheddar,
grated**

**25 g Parmesan, grated**

**salt and freshly ground
black pepper**

**Per serving**
kcal 584, protein 33 g,
fat 24 g (of which saturated
fat 14.5 g), carbohydrate
61 g (of which sugars 5.5 g),
fibre 2 g, sodium 0.3 g

# baked macaroni cheese with chicken

1 Preheat the oven to 200°C (gas 6). Bring a large pan of lightly salted water to the boil. Tip in the macaroni, and cook for 3 minutes less than it says on the packet instructions.

2 Cook the chicken breast in a non-stick frying pan over a low heat for 10 minutes, turning once. Season, then remove from the pan.

3 Pour the cream into the frying pan and bring to the boil, scraping the bottom with a wooden spatula to incorporate any browned bits. Add the milk, nutmeg and salt and pepper to season and heat gently. Cut the chicken into small dice.

4 Drain the macaroni, tip back into the pan, and add the diced chicken, grated Cheddar and the creamy milk mixture. Mix well.

5 Pour into a lightly buttered 1.5 litre ovenproof dish or four 375 ml individual dishes. Sprinkle over the Parmesan and bake a large dish for 30 minutes, or individual dishes for 20 minutes, until golden brown.

133

ADDING CHICKEN TO THIS FAMILY FAVOURITE TRANSFORMS IT INTO A SATISFYING MEAL. KEEP IT HEALTHY BY SERVING WITH A GREEN SALAD.

# fi

**versatile, delicious, and essential for good health**

# sh

From the simplest baked, grilled and poached dishes
to more complex casseroles, curries, parcels, soufflés
and pastries, there are countless fish and shellfish
recipes that are great for every occasion. You can vary
the fish in many recipes, asking your fishmonger for
advice and choosing what's in season and the best
value that day. Smoked and frozen fish and shellfish
can be an economical way of enjoying seafood without
compromising on taste.

# crab and avocado salad

££

**Serves 4 as a main course
or 6 as a starter**
Preparation  15 minutes

**3 tbsp mayonnaise**

**1 tsp finely grated lime zest**

**1½ tbsp lime juice**

**170 g can white crab meat, drained**

**2 avocados**

**1 tbsp olive oil**

**pinch of caster sugar**

**175 g cherry tomatoes, halved**

**140 g mixed salad leaves, such as frisée,
lamb's lettuce, mizuna and rocket**

**½ medium cucumber, halved and
thinly sliced**

**salt and freshly ground black pepper**

**fine strips of lime zest to garnish**

**Per serving (as a main course)**
kcal 300, protein 10 g, fat 27 g
(of which saturated fat 5 g),
carbohydrate 5 g (of which
sugars 3.5 g), fibre 3.5 g,
sodium 0.3 g

THIS LUXURIOUS DISH MAKES A STYLISH LUNCH OR
SUPPER, BUT USING CANNED CRAB MEAT MEANS THAT
IT DOESN'T COST THE EARTH.

1 Put the mayonnaise in a bowl with the grated lime zest and 1 tbsp lime juice. Mix well, then set 1 tbsp of the lime mayonnaise aside. Add the crab meat to the remaining lime mayonnaise and mix well.

2 Peel the avocados, remove the stones and cut the flesh into cubes. Whisk the oil and remaining lime juice together with the sugar and a little salt and pepper to season. Add the avocado cubes and toss together to coat in the dressing. Add the cherry tomatoes and gently mix again.

3 Arrange the salad leaves and cucumber slices in a shallow salad bowl or serving platter, then scatter with the cubes of avocado and cherry tomatoes.

4 Spoon the crab meat in a pile in the middle of the salad, then top with the reserved spoonful of lime mayonnaise. Scatter over strips of lime zest to garnish.

# smoked mackerel salad

££

**Serves 4 as a main course
or 6 as a starter**
Preparation  10 minutes
Cooking  5 minutes

**Per serving
(as a main course)**
kcal 425, protein 15 g,
fat 27 g (of which saturated
fat 0.5 g), carbohydrate
32 g (of which sugars 4 g),
fibre 2 g, sodium 0.5 g

**750 g new potatoes,
scrubbed**

**2 small smoked mackerel
fillets, about 225 g
in total**

**100 g radishes**

**1 tsp lemon juice**

**4 cos lettuce leaves,
roughly torn**

**Horseradish dressing**
**4 tbsp soured cream**

**2 tbsp mayonnaise**

**2 tsp creamed horseradish**

**6 mini gherkins, finely
chopped**

**salt and freshly ground
black pepper**

1 Cut the potatoes into 5 mm thick slices, then cook them in a saucepan of lightly salted boiling water for 5 minutes or until just tender. Drain, briefly rinse with cold water and drain again.

2 Meanwhile, make the dressing. Mix together the soured cream, mayonnaise, horseradish and two-thirds of the gherkins in a mixing bowl. Season to taste with salt and pepper. Add the warm potato slices and gently mix together.

3 Skin the smoked mackerel and break into large flakes, removing any bones. Slice the radishes and toss in the lemon juice. Add to the potatoes with the mackerel. Gently toss together to coat in the dressing.

4 Arrange the lettuce leaves on a serving platter. Pile the mackerel mixture on top, then scatter with the remaining chopped gherkins.

SMOKED MACKEREL FILLETS ARE GOOD VALUE AND REQUIRE
LITTLE PREPARATION, MAKING THIS A GREAT NO-FUSS MEAL.

## COOK SMART

• New potatoes are cheaper bought loose rather than pre-packed in bags; you also have the opportunity to select those of a similar size.

• For a spicier flavour, use peppered smoked mackerel fillets instead of plain.

💷💷
**Serves 4**
Preparation  15 minutes
Cooking  20 minutes

**8 small herrings, about 100 g each
(or 4 large herrings, about
200 g each), cleaned, scaled
and heads removed**

**1 bay leaf**

**2 sprigs of fresh thyme**

**1 tbsp English or French mustard**

**200 ml dry white wine**

**3 garlic cloves, finely chopped**

**2 tbsp chopped fresh parsley**

**salt and freshly ground
black pepper**

**sprigs of fresh thyme to garnish**

**Per serving**
kcal 370, protein 31 g,
fat 23 g (of which saturated
fat 5.5 g), carbohydrate 1 g
(of which sugars 0.5 g), fibre 0 g,
sodium 0.3 g

# wine-baked herring with herbs and garlic

**1** Preheat the oven to 200°C (gas 6). Rinse the herrings under cold water and pat dry. Salt and pepper them inside and out. Place them in a single layer in a lightly buttered and seasoned baking dish, tucking in the bay leaf and thyme.

**2** Mix the mustard with the wine and pour into the dish. Put the dish in the oven and bake for 15 minutes.

**3** Remove the bay leaf and thyme sprigs. Combine the chopped garlic and parsley, sprinkle over the fish and return to the oven for a further 5 minutes to finish cooking. Serve garnished with sprigs of fresh thyme.

### COOK SMART

• If the herrings are not already scaled, this is simple to do yourself. Just wipe off the thin layer of scales with kitchen paper.

• Serve with some nice crusty bread to mop up the delicious juices.

**OILY FISH IS AN ESSENTIAL IN EVERYONE'S DIET, AND HERRINGS ARE GREAT VALUE FOR MONEY. THE ACIDITY OF THE WINE COMPLEMENTS THE RICH FLESH PERFECTLY.**

# salade niçoise

£ £ £

**Serves 4**
Preparation and cooking
30 minutes

350 g small waxy new
   potatoes, scrubbed

225 g French or fine green
   beans, trimmed

2 fresh tuna steaks, each
   about 200 g

1 tbsp olive oil

1 lettuce heart or 2 little gem
   lettuces

1 red onion, thinly sliced

½ cucumber thinly sliced

225 g ripe tomatoes, quartered

50 g can anchovies, drained
   and halved lengthways

3 lightly-boiled eggs, quartered

12 black olives, stoned

**Vinaigrette dressing**
1 small garlic clove, crushed

1 tsp Dijon mustard

4 tbsp olive oil

1 tbsp white wine vinegar

salt and freshly ground
   black pepper

**Per serving**
kcal 460, protein 36 g, fat 26 g
(of which saturated fat 5 g)
carbohydrate 21 g (of which
sugars 6.5 g), fibre 3.5 g,
sodium 0.8 g

1 Cook the potatoes in a saucepan of lightly salted boiling water for 12 minutes. Add the beans and cook for a further 3–4 minutes until both vegetables are tender. Drain and briefly refresh under cold running water. Cut the potatoes in half, then transfer the potatoes and beans to a large bowl.

2 For the dressing, whisk the ingredients together in a small bowl or shake together in a screw-top jar. Pour about two-thirds of the dressing over the warm vegetables and toss to coat.

3 Brush the tuna steaks with the olive oil and lightly season with pepper. Heat a ridged, cast-iron grill pan or non-stick frying pan and cook the tuna steaks over a moderately high heat for 3–4 minutes on each side until just tender. Remove from the pan and set aside.

4 Separate the lettuce leaves, tear into bite-sized pieces and place in a shallow bowl, serving platter or individual plates. Add the onion, cucumber, tomatoes and anchovies to the potato and bean mixture, gently toss together, then spoon on top of the lettuce. Arrange the egg quarters around the edge of the dish.

5 Cut the tuna steaks into strips and arrange on top of the salad. Scatter over the olives, then drizzle with the remaining dressing before serving.

---

**COOK SMART**

• Use waxy 'salad' potatoes such as Pink Fir Apple or Charlotte, as they keep their shape when cooked.

• Olives bought from the deli counter, rather than in a jar or can, tend to have a better flavour and you can buy the exact quantity you need.

• Use canned tuna for a storecupboard alternative.

PACKED WITH HEALTHY FRESH VEGETABLES,
THIS PIQUANT CHINESE-STYLE DISH IS THE
PERFECT WAY TO ENJOY FRESH TUNA STEAKS.

£ £ £

**Serves 4**
Preparation and cooking
30 minutes

**2 fresh tuna steaks, each
    about 200 g**
**2 tsp olive oil**

**Sweet and sour vegetables**
**100 ml vegetable stock**
**3 tbsp red wine vinegar**
**4 tbsp orange juice**
**3 tbsp dry sherry**
**1½ tbsp soy sauce**
**1 tbsp tomato purée**
**1 garlic clove, finely chopped**
**2.5 cm piece fresh root ginger,
    peeled and finely chopped**
**1½ tbsp light muscovado sugar**
**1 tbsp cornflour**
**2 tbsp vegetable oil**
**2 carrots, peeled and thinly sliced**
**1 red pepper, seeded and thinly
    sliced**
**1 yellow pepper, seeded and
    thinly sliced**
**100 g mange-tout, halved
    lengthways**
**freshly ground black pepper**

**Per serving**
kcal 311, protein 28 g, fat 12.5 g
(of which saturated fat 2.5 g),
carbohydrate 20 g (of which
sugars 15.5 g), fibre 2.5 g,
sodium 0.5 g

1 Brush the tuna steaks with the olive oil and season with
pepper. Put on a plate and set aside while preparing
the vegetables.

2 Put the stock, vinegar, orange juice, sherry, soy sauce, tomato
purée, garlic, ginger and sugar in a small saucepan. Slowly
bring to the boil, stirring until the sugar has dissolved, then
simmer for 2–3 minutes.

3 Blend the cornflour to a smooth paste with 2 tbsp cold water.
Stir into the hot sauce then continue stirring over a low heat
until the sauce has cleared and thickened. Remove from the heat.

4 Heat a ridged, cast-iron grill pan or non-stick frying pan
and cook the tuna steaks over a moderately high heat for
3–4 minutes on each side until just tender. (Alternatively,
cook the steaks under a preheated, moderately hot grill.)

5 Meanwhile, heat the oil in a wok or large frying pan and
add the carrots. Stir-fry for about 30 seconds, then add
the red and yellow peppers. Cook for 1 minute, then add the
mange-tout. Continue stir-frying for 1–2 minutes or until all the
vegetables are cooked – they should still be slightly crisp. Pour
in the sauce and bring to the boil.

6 Flake the tuna into large, bite-sized pieces, toss into the stir-fry
then serve straight away.

**COOK SMART**
• Plain steamed or boiled rice makes a good accompaniment to this dish.

• This sweet and sour vegetable mixture works equally well with other
firm oily fish, such as swordfish, and meats such as turkey stir-fry or
fillet slices or pork steaks.

# sweet and sour vegetables with tuna

# gurnard
## with tomato, lemon and basil dressing

💷💷💷

**Serves 4**

Preparation  15–20 minutes
Cooking  12–15 minutes

1 large beef tomato

1 lemon

4 tbsp olive oil

2 red gurnard, about 500 g
    each, scaled, gutted
    and heads removed

1 tbsp chopped fresh basil

**salt and freshly ground
    black pepper**

### COOK SMART

• Good alternative fish for
this dish are rainbow trout,
mackerel and salmon.

• Gurnard is a good fish
for adding to soup. Use the
head for making stock.

**Per serving**
kcal 348, protein 42 g,
fat 19 g (of which saturated
fat 1.5 g), carbohydrate 1 g
(of which sugars 1 g),
fibre 0.5 g, sodium 0.2 g

**GURNARD HAVE FIRM TASTY FLESH AND
ARE GREAT VALUE. GREY AND YELLOW
GURNARD ARE GOOD, BUT LOOK OUT FOR
RED ONES FOR THE BEST FLAVOUR.**

1 Scald the tomato in boiling water for 30 seconds,
then drain and refresh under cold running water.
Peel off the skin, squeeze to extract the seeds
and cut the flesh into small dice.

2 Cut away the lemon rind and all the white pith.
Then free the individual segments by running the
thin blade of a knife on either side of each segment.
Work over a bowl to collect the juice. Cut the flesh
into small dice and add to the tomatoes with the
lemon juice.

3 Mix the diced tomato and lemon with the olive oil,
season with salt and pepper and put aside to
marinate while cooking the fish.

4 Rinse the fish and wipe them dry with kitchen paper.
Lay them in a steamer or on a lightly oiled plate,
then cover with a lid or foil and cook over a pan of
simmering water for 12–15 minutes until tender.

5 Add the basil to the tomato and lemon dressing
and mix gently. Remove the skin from the cooked
fish and separate into fillets, using a pair of
tweezers to remove any stray bones. Flake the
fish into chunky pieces.

6 Arrange the fish on a serving dish and spoon over
the dressing. Serve immediately.

# tuna and courgette frittata

£

**Serves 4**
Preparation  15 minutes
Cooking  10–12 minutes

**8 eggs**
**2 tbsp snipped fresh chives**
**2 tbsp olive oil**
**2 courgettes, about 400 g in
    total, sliced**
**1 garlic clove, finely chopped**
**185 g can tuna, drained**
**75 g frozen peas, thawed**
**salt and freshly ground
    black pepper**

**Per serving**
kcal 300, protein 28 g,
fat 19 g (of which saturated
fat 4.5 g), carbohydrate 3 g
(of which sugars 1 g), fibre 1 g,
sodium 0.3 g

1 Break the eggs into a bowl and beat lightly with a fork. Stir in 2 tbsp cold water and the chives. Season with salt and pepper and set aside.

2 Heat the oil in a large heavy-based frying pan. Add the courgette slices and cook over a medium heat for 3–4 minutes, turning the courgettes until light golden on both sides and just tender when pierced with a knife. Add the garlic and cook for a few more seconds.

3 Add the tuna and peas and stir to break up the tuna into chunks. Pour in the beaten egg mixture, mix quickly into the other ingredients, then stop stirring.

4 Lower the heat slightly and cook the frittata for 6–8 minutes or until the base is golden. Take a large plate and place it upside down over the pan. Wearing oven gloves, turn the pan and the frittata over on to the plate. Slide the frittata back into the pan and continue cooking for 3–4 minutes or until golden brown on the second side. (Alternatively, it can be finished off under a moderate grill for 5 minutes, if cooked in a pan with a heatproof handle.)

5 Remove the pan from the heat, cut the frittata into four wedges and serve hot or cold.

**COOK SMART**
• For a more substantial frittata, leftovers such as diced cold potato or cooked beans or pulses may be added. Other vegetables could also be included.

• Served cold, it makes a tasty addition to a lunch box or picnic basket.

**THIS ITALIAN-STYLE OMELETTE IS PERFECT SERVED WITH A SIMPLE SALAD AND CRUSTY BREAD OR NEW POTATOES – GREAT FOR AN EASY FAMILY SUPPER.**

# crispy fish goujons

£

**Serves 4**
Preparation 25 minutes,
 plus 30 minutes chilling
Cooking 15 minutes

**450g firm white fish fillet,
 skinned**

**3 tbsp plain flour**

**¼ tsp cayenne pepper**

**1 large egg, beaten**

**80g fine, fresh white
 breadcrumbs**

**2 tbsp sesame seeds**

**salt and freshly ground
 black pepper**

**25g butter, melted**

**Lemon and caper dip**
**8 tbsp mayonnaise**

**1 tsp Dijon mustard**

**1 tbsp bottled capers,
 drained and chopped**

**finely grated zest and juice
 of ½ lemon**

**Per serving**
kcal 532, protein 28g,
fat 36g (of which saturated
fat 8g), carbohydrate 24.5g
(of which sugars 1g),
fibre 1g, sodium 0.4g

---

**COOK SMART**
• Bread which is a day or
two old is ideal for making
breadcrumbs. To give the
goujons a cheesy flavour,
add 25g finely grated
Parmesan to the
breadcrumbs in place of
the sesame seeds.

---

**1** Cut the fish fillets across their width
into thick, finger-like strips, about
2cm wide.

**2** In a shallow bowl, mix together the
flour and cayenne with some salt
and pepper to season.

**3** Put the egg in a separate bowl. Mix
the breadcrumbs with the sesame
seeds in a third bowl or on a plate.

**4** Toss the fish in the seasoned flour
mixture, then dip each piece first
in the beaten egg and then in the
breadcrumbs. Place on a lightly oiled,
non-stick, baking tray and chill for
30 minutes until required. Preheat
the oven to 220°C (gas 7).

**5** For the dip, mix together the
mayonnaise, mustard, capers and
lemon juice. Season to taste, then
cover and chill.

**6** Bake the goujons for 10 minutes,
turning halfway through cooking.
Brush with the melted butter and
return to the oven for a further
5 minutes until golden and crispy.
Serve immediately with the dip.

**YOU CAN USE ANY WHITE FISH
FOR THESE HOME-MADE FISH
FINGERS COATED IN A SESAME
SEED CRUMB, SO SEE WHAT IS
ON OFFER AND BUY THE BEST
OF THE DAY.**

# steamed fish with ginger

**Serves 4**
Preparation  20 minutes
Cooking  10 minutes

**1 tbsp grated fresh root ginger**

**2 garlic cloves, crushed**

**½ tsp grated lemon zest**

**½ tsp salt**

**4 white fish fillets, about 150 g each**

**1 tbsp toasted sesame oil**

**2 tbsp lemon juice**

**1 tsp cornflour**

**1 tbsp chopped fresh coriander**

**3–4 spring onions, shredded**

**fresh coriander sprigs to garnish**

**Per serving**
kcal 152, protein 27 g,
fat 3.5 g (of which
saturated fat 0.5 g),
carbohydrate 1.5 g (of
which sugars 0.5 g),
fibre 0.1 g, sodium 0.3 g

144

1 Combine the ginger, garlic and lemon zest in a small bowl. Lay the fish, skinned side up, on a work surface and sprinkle with salt and the ginger mixture. Fold the fillets in half widthways. Place the folded fish on a heatproof plate or a shallow dish and drizzle over the sesame oil.

2 Set up a steamer or put a round rack into a wok or deep frying pan. Fill it with water to a level just below the rack (it's important that the water doesn't come into contact with the fish while cooking) and bring to the boil.

3 Put the plate with the fish on the rack or in the steamer, cover tightly with foil and steam for 10 minutes or until the fish is just cooked. It should look opaque and flake lightly but still remain moist. Using a draining spoon, transfer the fish to a serving dish and cover loosely to keep warm. Reserve the juices left on the plate.

4 Pour these juices into a small saucepan. Add the lemon juice and 100 ml of water. Blend the cornflour with a little water to make a smooth paste, then stir into the pan, bring to the boil, stirring, and cook for 1 minute until the sauce is lightly thickened. Stir in the chopped coriander.

5 Drizzle the sauce over the fish, scatter with spring onions and garnish with coriander sprigs.

STEAMING IS A GREAT TECHNIQUE FOR COOKING FISH, GIVING MOIST, HEALTHY, DELICIOUS RESULTS. FRESH GINGER ADDS A SUBTLE BUT DISTINCTIVE NOTE.

**COOK SMART**
• Any white fish fillets can be steamed. You could choose cod, haddock, plaice, hake, hoki or whiting. Supermarkets also often sell frozen white fish fillets, which could include any species, and are good value for money.

# lemon-glazed plaice fillets

**ZESTY LEMONS AND FRAGRANT HERBS TRANSFORM THESE SIMPLE FISH FILLETS INTO A SENSATIONAL MEAL THAT'S JUST RIGHT FOR ENTERTAINING.**

£ £ £

**Serves 4**
Preparation 15 minutes
Cooking 6 minutes

**5 large lemons**
**6 large fresh basil leaves**
**1 tbsp olive oil**
**1 garlic clove, crushed**
**4 small plaice fillets, about 150 g each**
**125 ml fish or chicken stock**
**1½ tsp cornflour**
**2 tsp sugar**
**salt and freshly ground black pepper**

**Per serving**
kcal 173, protein 28 g,
fat 5 g (of which saturated
fat 1 g), carbohydrate 3.5 g
(of which sugars 2 g),
fibre 0 g, sodium 0.2 g

**1** Roll one lemon on the work surface to get the juices flowing, then grate the zest and squeeze the juice. Cut three of the lemons into four 5 mm slices each, discarding the ends. Cut the remaining lemon into eight wedges.

**2** To make a basil *chiffonade*, stack the basil leaves and roll up tightly, to resemble a cigar. Slice across the roll, making cuts about 2 mm apart. Set aside for garnish.

**3** Heat the oil in a small saucepan over a medium heat. Add the garlic and cook gently for 2 minutes until golden. Stir in the lemon juice, then remove the pan from the heat.

**4** Preheat a moderate grill. Lay the lemon slices in a lightly oiled grill pan or on a non-stick baking sheet and put the fish on top. Lightly brush the fish with the lemon and garlic mixture and season with salt and pepper. Leave any leftover lemon mixture in the saucepan.

**5** Put the lemon wedges alongside, then grill the fish for 5–6 minutes, without turning, until just opaque. The lemon wedges will become lightly golden.

**6** Meanwhile, blend together the stock and cornflour until smooth. Stir into the pan used for the lemon mixture, add the sugar and a little of the lemon zest. Bring to the boil over a medium heat and cook for about 1 minute, stirring, until the sauce thickens.

**7** Transfer the fish to warm serving plates, with the lemon slices underneath. Spoon the sauce over the fish and sprinkle with basil *chiffonade* and remaining lemon zest. Garnish with grilled lemon wedges.

**COOK SMART**
• You can use fillets of any other white flat fish – fresh or frozen – in this recipe. Dab fillets make a good choice.

• Stir-fried strips of courgettes and carrots make a colourful accompaniment.

HEARTY ONE-POT DISHES LIKE THIS ARE GREAT FOR FAMILY AND FRIENDS. USE ANY FIRM-FLESHED FISH AND SERVE WITH CRUSTY BREAD.

££££

**Serves 4**

Preparation  10 minutes
Cooking  about 30 minutes

**2 tbsp olive oil**

**2 onions, finely chopped**

**3 garlic cloves, thinly sliced**

**1 large red pepper, seeded and thinly sliced**

**450 g sweet potatoes, peeled and cubed**

**500 ml fish or vegetable stock**

**1 tsp chopped fresh thyme**

**225 g frozen peas**

**175 g frozen sweetcorn**

**600 g skinless white fish fillet, cut into bite-sized pieces**

**salt and freshly ground black pepper**

**fresh thyme leaves to garnish (optional)**

**Per serving**

kcal 450, protein 45 g,
fat 11 g (of which saturated
fat 2 g), carbohydrate 45 g
(of which sugars 14 g),
fibre 7 g, sodium 0.2 g

# fish stew with vegetables

**1** Heat the oil in a large deep frying pan over a medium heat. Add the onions and garlic, and cook for 5 minutes, stirring frequently, until the onions are light gold.

**2** Add the pepper and sweet potatoes, cover and cook for 5 minutes or until the sweet potatoes begin to soften. Stir in the stock, thyme and a pinch of salt. Bring to the boil, reduce the heat, cover and simmer for 10 minutes or until the sweet potatoes are just tender. Stir in the peas and sweetcorn.

**3** Place the fish on top of the vegetables, cover and cook gently for 8–10 minutes or until the fish is cooked through. Season to taste with black pepper, then serve immediately sprinkled with fresh thyme leaves if you are using them.

---

**COOK SMART**

• Cod and haddock are favourite round white fish but scarcity has pushed the price up, so take the pressure off and check out other similar fish, such as huss or coley. Compare prices and choose whatever offers the best value. Ask a fishmonger for advice if trying something different.

• If you have a bottle of white wine open, use 150 ml to replace part of the stock.

# portuguese-style fish casserole

COOKING THE FISH IN LAYERS WITH SLICED ONIONS, POTATOES AND TOMATOES GIVES THIS SATISFYING CASSEROLE A DIFFERENT FEEL TO A CLASSIC FISH STEW.

£ £ £

**Serves 4**
Preparation  25 minutes
Cooking  40 minutes

2 tbsp olive oil

2 onions, sliced into rings

750 g waxy potatoes, peeled and sliced into rounds

500 g tomatoes, sliced into rounds

600 g white fish fillets, cut into large chunks

1 sprig of fresh thyme

1 bay leaf

200 ml fish stock

salt and freshly ground black pepper

fresh thyme to garnish

### COOK SMART
• You could cook 1 sliced red pepper and 2 crushed garlic cloves with the onions in step 1, and in step 2 sprinkle the layers with a pinch of chilli powder for a spicy flavour.

• Use thawed, frozen white fish steaks for convenience mid-week.

**Per serving**
kcal 365, protein 36 g, fat 8.5 g (of which saturated fat 1.5 g), carbohydrate 38 g (of which sugars 9 g), fibre 3.5 g, sodium 0.1 g

1 Heat 1 tbsp of the oil in a large flameproof casserole dish and cook the onions gently for about 15 minutes until transparent. Lift out half and set aside. Remove the casserole from the heat.

2 Place a layer of potato slices on top of the onions in the casserole, followed by a layer of tomatoes, then fish, then the remaining onions. Repeat until the ingredients are used up, finishing with a layer of potatoes. Season each layer with salt and pepper and place the thyme and bay leaf on top.

3 Pour over the fish stock and add the rest of the oil. Put the casserole back on the heat and bring to the boil. Reduce the heat, cover, and simmer for 40 minutes or until the fish and potatoes are tender. Garnish with fresh thyme.

THIS LIGHT, CREAMY CURRY MAKES A LUXURIOUS MEAL SERVED
WITH A BASMATI RICE. MAKE IT AS MILD OR SPICY AS YOU LIKE.

# quick white fish curry

**Serves 4**
Preparation 15 minutes
Cooking 25 minutes

**600 g white fish fillets**
**1 tbsp vegetable oil**
**2 garlic cloves, 1 thinly sliced
and 1 crushed**
**1 onion, finely chopped**
**2 tsp curry powder (mild
or medium)**
**1 tbsp tomato purée**
**½ tsp sugar**
**1 bay leaf**
**2 tbsp crème fraîche**
**salt and freshly ground
black pepper**

**Per serving**
kcal 193, protein 28 g, fat 7 g
(of which saturated fat 2.5 g),
carbohydrate 4 g (of which
sugars 2.5 g), fibre 1 g,
sodium 0.1 g

1 Season the fish on both sides with salt and pepper. Cut into four equal pieces, if bought whole.

2 Heat the oil in a deep heavy-based frying pan with the sliced garlic. Cook until the garlic is golden, then lift out and discard, using a draining spoon.

3 Sauté the onion in the garlicky oil for about 5 minutes until transparent. Sprinkle over the curry powder and add the crushed garlic. Stir for 1 minute. Add 200 ml boiling water and the tomato purée, followed by the sugar and bay leaf. Stir, cover and cook for 15 minutes over a low heat.

4 Place the fish in the sauce, cover, and simmer for 8–10 minutes or until tender.

5 Carefully lift out the fish with a draining spoon and place on a heated serving plate. Stir the crème fraîche into the sauce and taste to check seasoning. Remove the bay leaf. Pour the sauce over the fish and serve immediately.

**COOK SMART**
• Coley is an excellent economical substitute for cod. Don't be put off by the dark meat of the raw fish – it turns white when cooked.

# stuffed sardines with feta

£ £

**Serves 4**
Preparation 40 minutes
Cooking 10 minutes

12 plump sardines, scaled,
    gutted and heads removed
2 tbsp chopped fresh parsley
2 garlic cloves, crushed
40 g slightly stale, white
    breadcrumbs
1 egg, lightly beaten
40 g feta cheese
salt
lemon wedges to garnish

**Per serving**
kcal 288, protein 30 g,
fat 15 g (of which saturated
fat 5 g), carbohydrate 8 g
(of which sugars 0.5 g),
fibre 0 g, sodium 0.4 g

**150**

**SARDINES ARE IN SEASON FROM SPRING UNTIL EARLY AUTUMN SO ENJOY THEM AT THEIR BEST, STUFFED WITH HERBY BREADCRUMBS AND CREAMY FETA CHEESE.**

**1** Preheat the oven to 200°C (gas 6). Slit the sardines open lengthways using a sharp knife. Remove the central backbone (see below), leaving the tail fin attached. Rinse and dry the fish. Place them opened out, flesh-side-up, on the work surface, and season lightly with salt.

**2** Mix the parsley and garlic with the breadcrumbs. Add the egg and mix everything together.

**3** Fold back over to reshape the sardines, press them down firmly, then crumble over the feta. Fold back over to reshape the sardines, then arrange them in a single layer in a lightly greased baking dish.

**4** Bake for 10 minutes. Serve piping hot garnished with lemon wedges for diners to squeeze over.

**COOK SMART**

• To remove the backbone from the sardines, simply place the fish on a board, skin side up, then press down along the length of the bone to loosen it. Turn fish over, snip the bone at the tail end and tease it out, removing any small stray bones with a pair of kitchen tweezers.

£

**Serves 4**
Preparation 45 minutes
Cooking 25 minutes
(15 minutes for
individual soufflés)

150g waxy potatoes
(such as Charlotte or
Bintje), scrubbed

300g coley fillet (thawed if
bought frozen), skinned

40g butter, softened

2 shallots, finely chopped

4 tbsp whipping cream

3 eggs, separated

1 tsp wholegrain mustard

salt and freshly ground
black pepper

**Per serving**
kcal 292, protein 21g,
fat 20g (of which saturated
fat 10g), carbohydrate 8g
(of which sugars 2g),
fibre 0.5g, sodium 0.3g

# fish soufflé

**LIGHT, FLUFFY AND UTTERLY DELICIOUS – ALL YOU NEED IS A SIMPLE SALAD TO CREATE A BALANCED, HEALTHY MEAL FOR ALL THE FAMILY.**

**1** Place the potatoes in a saucepan with cold water to cover and a pinch of salt. Cover, bring to the boil, and cook for 25 minutes or until tender.

**2** Meanwhile, place the fish in a large shallow pan with cold water to cover and a pinch of salt. Bring gently to the boil and reduce the heat immediately. Cover and simmer for 3 minutes. Leave the fish to cool in its cooking liquid.

**3** Heat 10g of the butter in a small pan, add the shallots and cook gently over a low heat for 5 minutes. Add the cream and remove from the heat.

**4** Preheat the oven to 200°C (gas 6). Use 10g of the butter to grease a soufflé dish, about 16cm in diameter, or four 300ml large ramekins or individual soufflé dishes.

**5** Drain and peel the potatoes and crush with a fork. Add the remaining butter, the shallot-cream mixture and some pepper. Beat in the egg yolks and mustard.

**6** Drain and flake the fish and coarsely crush it with a fork. Check that no bones remain. Fold the fish into the potato mixture.

**7** Add a pinch of salt to the egg whites, whisk until stiff then fold into the potato-fish mixture. Pour into the soufflé dish(es) and smooth the surface with a spatula. Bake a large soufflé for 25 minutes or individual soufflés for 15 minutes, until puffed and golden. Serve immediately.

**COOK SMART**
• Spice up the mixture with a pinch of chilli powder and 1 tsp chopped fresh dill, if available.

• You could make this recipe with some leftover cooked fish, especially smoked haddock or smoked mackerel. Canned tuna would also be good.

EVERYONE LOVES KEBABS AND THESE MAKE A GREAT FAMILY MEAL SERVED WITH PITTA BREAD AND SALAD. COOK THEM ON A BARBECUE IN THE SUMMER.

# bacon and fish kebabs

**Serves 4**
Preparation 20 minutes
Cooking 12–15 minutes

**700 g chunky white
    fish fillet, cut into
    24 bite-sized cubes**
**1 tbsp lemon juice**
**4 tbsp olive oil**
**½ tsp dried oregano**
**1 garlic clove, crushed**
**8 thin rindless, smoked,
    streaky bacon rashers**
**2 courgettes, thickly
    sliced and halved**
**salt and freshly ground
    black pepper**

To serve
**1 lemon, cut into wedges**

**Per serving**
kcal 390, protein 41 g,
fat 24 g (of which saturated
fat 8 g), carbohydrate 12 g
(of which sugars 7 g),
fibre 3 g, sodium 0.8 g

**FISH**

**153**

1 Put the fish into a bowl. Whisk together the lemon juice, oil, oregano, garlic and salt and pepper to season in a small bowl, or shake together in a screw-top jar. Drizzle 2 tbsp over the fish and turn it with your hands to coat in the marinade. Set aside.

2 Put the bacon onto a board and gently stretch it with the back of a knife. Cut each rasher into three pieces. Wrap a piece of bacon around each piece of fish, then thread onto eight oiled skewers, alternating the bacon-wrapped fish with slices of courgette.

3 Preheat the grill to medium. Brush the kebabs all over with the reserved marinade mixture and place on the grill rack.

4 Grill for 12–15 minutes, turning from time to time, until the courgettes are tender and the bacon is browned and crispy. To keep the courgettes moist, baste them while cooking with leftover marinade. Check that the fish is cooked inside its bacon wrapping by sliding a piece off a skewer and cutting it open; it should be opaque and flake easily. Serve hot, with lemon wedges to squeeze over.

# salmon cakes with mustard and dill sauce

(£)

**Makes 4**
Preparation  15–20 minutes
Cooking  8 minutes

1 large baking potato, about 250 g, peeled and thinly sliced
6 tsp Dijon mustard
2 tbsp chopped fresh dill
2 tbsp cider vinegar
1 tsp light muscovado sugar
2 tbsp mayonnaise
1 tsp grated lemon zest
1 tbsp lemon juice
420 g can pink salmon, drained
2 tbsp plain dry breadcrumbs
2 tbsp chopped fresh parsley
1 tbsp vegetable oil for frying

**Per serving**
kcal 326, protein 24 g, fat 18 g (of which saturated fat 3 g), carbohydrate 17.5 g (of which sugars 3 g), fibre 0.5 g, sodium 0.9 g

**COOK SMART**
• Choose canned pink salmon rather than the more expensive red salmon for these fish cakes. They can be prepared ahead up to the end of step 4 and chilled, then cooked just before serving. If you don't have dill, add some snipped chives to the sauce.

**154**

1 Cook the potato in a small pan of lightly salted, boiling water for 6–7 minutes or until tender. Drain well, transfer to a large bowl and mash with a potato masher. Set aside to cool to room temperature.

2 Meanwhile, stir together 4 tsp of the mustard, the dill, vinegar, sugar and 2 tbsp of water in a small bowl. Set this mustard and dill sauce aside.

3 Add the mayonnaise, the remaining 2 tsp mustard, lemon zest and lemon juice to the mashed potato. Add the salmon and mix together. Shape the mixture into four even-sized cakes.

4 Combine the breadcrumbs and parsley on a plate or sheet of greaseproof paper. Dredge the fish cakes in the crumb mixture, patting it on.

5 Heat the oil in a large non-stick frying pan, over a medium heat. Add the salmon cakes and fry gently for 4 minutes on each side until crisp and golden.

6 Serve hot with the mustard and dill sauce drizzled over the top.

# spiced grilled salmon with sweetcorn relish

(£)(£)

**Serves 4**
Preparation and cooking  15–20 minutes

¼ tsp plus 2 tbsp sugar
1 tsp ground coriander
½ tsp salt
½ tsp ground cinnamon
¼ tsp crushed cardamom seeds
¼ tsp freshly ground black pepper
4 salmon steaks, about 150 g each
½ tsp yellow mustard seeds
75 ml white wine vinegar
1 courgette, diced
1 orange or red pepper, seeded and diced
175 g sweetcorn, canned or thawed if bought frozen

**Per serving**
kcal 306, protein 30 g, fat 16 g (of which saturated fat 3 g), carbohydrate 11 g (of which sugars 11 g), fibre 1.5 g, sodium 0.3 g

1 Preheat the grill to medium and lightly oil the grill pan. Combine the ¼ tsp of sugar, coriander, salt, cinnamon, cardamom seeds and black pepper in a small saucepan. Measure out 1¼ tsp of the spice mixture and rub into one side of each salmon steak.

2 Add the remaining 2 tbsp sugar, mustard seeds and vinegar to the spice mixture left in the saucepan, and bring to the boil over a medium heat. Add the courgette, pepper, and sweetcorn, and cook for 6–8 minutes until the vegetables are just tender and most of the liquid has been absorbed.

3 Meanwhile, place the salmon, spice-side down, on the grill pan and cook, without turning, for 6–8 minutes or until just tender and cooked through. Serve the salmon topped with the relish.

**COOK SMART**
• To prepare cardamom, crush the pods slightly and peel off the tough, green outer skin to release the seeds.

SALMON IS A SURPRISINGLY AFFORDABLE TREAT, AND IT IS GOOD FOR YOU TOO. THE SPICE RUB AND REFRESHING RELISH USED HERE REALLY HELP TO SET IT OFF.

# poached salmon with cucumber and dill sauce

£££

**Serves 4**

Preparation and cooking
10–15 minutes

**Per serving**
kcal 339, protein 27g,
fat 21g (of which saturated
fat 7g), carbohydrate 2.5g
(of which sugars 2.5g),
fibre 0.5g, sodium 0.08g

**200ml dry white wine**
**2 spring onions, sliced**
**8 black peppercorns**
**4 salmon fillets, about**
**    125g each**
**150g soured cream**
**¼ cucumber, diced**
**2 tbsp chopped fresh dill**
**1 tbsp lemon juice**
**salt and freshly ground**
**    black pepper**

**To serve**
**mixed salad leaves**
**lemon wedges to garnish**

**POACHING GIVES WONDERFULLY MOIST,
DELICATE RESULTS AND HELPS TO BRING OUT
THE FLAVOUR OF THE FISH, SO ALL IT NEEDS
IS A SPOONFUL OF FRAGRANT SAUCE.**

**1** Pour 375ml water into a large frying pan, stir in the wine, spring onions and peppercorns, then put the salmon in the pan in a single layer. Bring to the boil, then immediately reduce the heat, cover and simmer gently for 5–6 minutes until the fish flakes when tested with a fork.

**2** Meanwhile, stir together the soured cream, cucumber, dill and lemon juice in a medium bowl and season to taste with salt and pepper.

**3** Arrange the salad leaves on four serving plates. Carefully lay the salmon fillets on top, using a draining spoon. Garnish with lemon wedges and serve hot with the cucumber and dill sauce drizzled over.

**COOK SMART**

• The wine can be replaced with fish or chicken stock.

• This recipe works equally well served hot or cold. To serve cold, squeeze lemon juice over the poached fillets, cover with cling film, and chill for at least 2 hours or overnight. The sauce can be made ahead, then covered and chilled until ready to serve.

• Don't throw out the poaching liquid; strain and cool then freeze it to use as stock for a fish soup or casserole.

**WRAPPING THE FISH IN PAPER SEALS IN ALL THE FLAVOURS AND JUICES TO GIVE FABULOUSLY SUCCULENT RESULTS – AND ALSO OFFERS A FUN WAY TO SERVE.**

£ £

**Serves 4**
Preparation 35 minutes
Cooking 10 minutes

4 leeks, trimmed and thinly sliced
good pinch of sugar
2 salmon fillets, about 300 g each, skinned
1 tbsp chopped fresh dill
juice of 1 lemon
salt and freshly ground black pepper

**To garnish (optional)**
strips of thinly sliced lemon
sprigs of fresh dill

**Per serving**
kcal 295, protein 32 g, fat 17 g
(of which saturated fat 3 g),
carbohydrate 3.5 g (of which
sugars 2.5 g), fibre 2 g,
sodium 0.07 g

**1** Place the leeks in a heavy-based saucepan with 3 tbsp water, and sprinkle with sugar, salt and pepper. Cover and cook for 25 minutes over a low heat.

**2** Preheat the oven to 200°C (gas 6). Prepare four large sheets of greaseproof paper, measuring 30 x 37.5 cm.

**3** Cut the salmon fillets in half and season on both sides with salt and pepper.

**4** Once the leeks are soft, spread them over the centre portion of the greaseproof paper sheets. Place the salmon fillets on top, then sprinkle with chopped dill and drizzle with the lemon juice.

**5** Seal the parcels, bringing the two long edges together and roll down, stopping short of the fish, then twist the ends. Place the parcels in a baking tin and bake for 10 minutes.

**6** Serve as soon as soon as they're out of the oven, in their paper parcels. Garnish, if liked, with strips of thinly sliced lemon and sprigs of dill.

# salmon and leek parcels

**COOK SMART**
• Salmon fillets are sold in good value freezer packs, individually wrapped, so you can just take out as many as you need.

• Some snipped chives or chopped fresh parsley could be used in place of the fresh dill.

• Minted new potatoes and fresh young peas would be lovely served with this dish.

SALMON FILLETS AND BABY SPINACH
BAKED IN CRISP, GOLDEN PUFF
PASTRY TASTE DIVINE SERVED WITH
PIQUANT TARTARE SAUCE.

# salmon and spinach pastries

£ £ £

**Serves 4**

Preparation 40 minutes,
plus 30 minutes chilling

Cooking 25 minutes

**Per serving**

kcal 918, protein 50g,
fat 61g (of which saturated
fat 21g), carbohydrate 49g
(of which sugars 3.5g),
fibre 1.4g, sodium 0.9g

1 tbsp vegetable oil

4 rindless streaky bacon
rashers, chopped

1 small onion, chopped

225g baby spinach leaves

pinch of nutmeg

500g ready-made puff
pastry

4 salmon fillets, about
175g each

freshly ground black
pepper

beaten egg, to glaze

**To serve**
tartare sauce

**1** Preheat the oven to 200°C (gas 6). Heat the oil in a large frying pan and gently fry the bacon and onion until the bacon is browned and the onion softened. Stir in the spinach and cook for a further 2 minutes, to wilt the spinach. Season with a little nutmeg and pepper. Take the pan off the heat and remove the mixture to a plate, using a draining spoon to drain off all the excess moisture. Leave to cool.

**2** Divide the block of pastry into four rectangles. Roll out each piece on a lightly floured surface so that it measures about 20 x 15cm. Lay the salmon fillet on one side of each piece of pastry. Divide the spinach mixture equally over each salmon fillet.

# trout with almonds

£ £ £

**Serves 4**
Preparation and cooking
30 minutes

**4 rainbow trout, about
200 g each, gutted**

**3 tbsp semi-skimmed milk**

**3 tbsp plain flour**

**2 tbsp olive oil**

**50 g unsalted butter**

**juice of 1 lemon**

**2 tbsp chopped fresh
parsley**

**50 g flaked almonds,
toasted**

**salt and freshly ground
black pepper**

**COOK SMART**

• Using scissors, cut a
V-shaped notch in the end
of the tail in two places to
stop it curling up during
cooking.

• Don't buy toasted flaked
almonds – they are more
expensive than regular
flaked almonds. Toast
them quickly under the grill
until golden.

**Per serving**
kcal 512, protein 43 g,
fat 33 g (of which saturated
fat 10 g), carbohydrate 10 g
(of which sugars 1 g),
fibre 1 g, sodium 0.2 g

**1** Rinse the trout under cold running water, then
pat dry with kitchen paper. Season inside with salt
and pepper.

**2** Pour the milk into a deep plate. Season the flour
with salt and pepper on another plate. Dip the trout
in the milk, then dredge them in the flour, tapping
off the excess.

**3** Heat the oil in a large frying pan. Add 20 g of the
butter, and once it foams, add the fish to the pan.
Cook for 7–8 minutes on a fairly low heat until the
underside is golden brown, then turn the fish over
using a fish slice and brown on the other side for
a further 7–8 minutes.

**4** Lift the trout onto a serving dish and cover with foil
to keep warm. Discard the pan juices and wipe out
the pan with kitchen paper. Melt the rest of the
butter, season with salt and pepper and add the
lemon juice, followed by the parsley and almonds.
Spoon over the trout and serve at once.

**FISH**

159

**3** Brush the edges of the pastry with beaten egg, then
fold over the pastry to enclose the filling. Seal the
edges with a fork. Ideally, leave the parcels to 'rest'
in the fridge for 30 minutes.

**4** Transfer the parcels to two non-stick baking sheets,
brush with the beaten egg and bake for 25 minutes
or until the pastry is well risen and golden brown.
Serve warm with tartare sauce.

**COOK SMART**

• If you have some pine nuts, scatter some into each parcel,
at the end of step 2.

• To make a quick tartare sauce, blend together 3 tbsp each
of crème fraîche and mayonnaise with 1 tsp lemon juice,
½ tsp prepared mustard, 1 tbsp chopped capers and 4 finely
chopped gherkins.

# baked mackerel
# with rhubarb
# and orange sauce

TART, TANGY RHUBARB AND ORANGE
SAUCE COMPLEMENTS THE RICH FLESH
OF MACKEREL WONDERFULLY.

£ £

**Serves 4**
Preparation  15 minutes
Cooking  20–25 minutes

4 mackerel, about 200 g
   each, cleaned, boned
   and heads removed
1 orange
4 sprigs of fresh thyme
1 tbsp olive oil
50 g sugar
300 g rhubarb, trimmed
   and roughly chopped
2 tbsp shredless orange
   jelly marmalade
salt and freshly ground
   black pepper

**COOK SMART**
• Fresh rhubarb has a
relatively short season, so
is worth buying while it is at
its cheapest and freezing for
future use (see page 20).
Use for pies and crumbles.
• Forced rhubarb is
available in early spring
and main crop a little later.
It's easy to grow, too.

**Per serving**
kcal 494, protein 33g,
fat 31g (of which saturated
fat 6g), carbohydrate 21.5g
(of which sugars 21.5g),
fibre 1g, sodium 0.1g

1 Preheat the oven to 190°C (gas 5). Thinly pare about
   half the zest from the orange. Squeeze out the juice.

2 Season the cavity of the fish with salt and pepper,
   then place a sprig of thyme inside each. Make
   3–4 slashes on each side of the fish, then place
   on a foil-lined ovenproof dish or baking tray.

3 Mix the oil with 1 tbsp of the orange juice and brush
   over the fish. Bake, uncovered, in the oven for
   20–25 minutes or until the flesh will flake easily.

4 Meanwhile, put the remaining orange juice in a
   saucepan with the sugar and pared orange zest
   and gently heat, stirring frequently, until the sugar
   has dissolved. Add the rhubarb, cover with a
   tight-fitting lid and gently simmer for 10 minutes
   or until the fruit is soft and pulpy. Stir occasionally
   to prevent the rhubarb sticking to the pan.

5 Rub the rhubarb through a sieve or purée in a
   blender or processor until smooth. Return the purée
   to the cleaned out saucepan, add the marmalade
   and season with salt and pepper. Reheat until the
   marmalade has melted, then taste. It should have
   a pleasant, slightly sharp flavour but if too acidic,
   add a little more sugar

6 Transfer the fish to warmed dinner plates and spoon
   over a little of the sauce. Serve the remaining sauce
   in a sauceboat or jug.

# braised herrings in cider

£ £

**Serves 4**
Preparation  25 minutes
Cooking  40 minutes

**Per serving**
kcal 656, protein 38g,
fat 38g (of which saturated
fat 15g), carbohydrate 39g
(of which sugars 10g),
fibre 3g, sodium 0.4g

**COOK SMART**
• Cook some roasted
courgettes or braised
cabbage at the same time.

65 g butter, softened
8 small potatoes, about
   800 g in total
4 herrings, about 200 g
   each, filleted and
   skinned
1½ tbsp wholegrain
   mustard
2 eating apples
150 ml fish or vegetable
   stock
150 ml dry, fruity cider
salt and freshly ground
   black pepper
snipped fresh chives to
   garnish

1 Preheat the oven to 190°C (gas 5). Use 10g of the
   butter to grease a baking dish, in which the rolled
   up fish fillets will fit snugly side by side.

2 Cook the potatoes in boiling water for 15 minutes
   or until almost tender, but still firm. Drain and cool,
   then peel off the skins and slice them thinly.

3 Rinse the herring fillets and pat dry on kitchen
   paper. Place them, skinned-side up, on a board. Mix
   the remaining butter and mustard together. Reserve
   a third of the mustard butter, then thinly spread the
   rest over the fillets. Roll them up from the tail end.

4 Peel, quarter, core and thinly slice the apples. Put
   a layer of potato slices in the bottom of the baking
   dish, topped by a layer of apple slices. Mix together
   the stock and cider and season with a little salt and
   pepper. Pour a little over the apple slices to just
   cover them and stop them from discolouring.

5 Continue layering the potato and apple slices until
   you have used about two-thirds, adding a little liquid
   after each apple layer. Place the rolled herring fillets
   on top, seam-side down, and add the rest of the
   potato and apples, finishing with a layer of potatoes.

6 Pour over the remaining stock and cider – it should
   just cover the potato topping, so add a little more
   stock if necessary. Dot the reserved mustard butter
   over the top and bake for 40 minutes or until the
   potatoes and apples are tender and the fish is
   cooked. Serve hot, sprinkled with fresh chives.

# moules marinière

£ £

**Serves 2 as a main course
or 4 as a starter**
Preparation  10 minutes
Cooking  10 minutes

**Per serving
   (as a main course)**
kcal 155, protein 13g,
fat 8g (of which saturated
fat 4.5g), carbohydrate 1g
(of which sugars 1g),
fibre 0.5g, sodium 0.2g

**COOK SMART**
• Choose wine that you
enjoy drinking; it is a false
economy to buy cheap
'cooking' wine as this spoils
the flavour of the dish.
Alternatively, dry cider
works well in this dish.

25g butter

2 shallots or 1 small onion,
   finely chopped

2 garlic cloves, finely
   chopped

1 bay leaf

2 stalks of fresh parsley

150ml dry white wine

1kg mussels in shell,
   scrubbed and beards
   removed

4 tbsp crème fraîche

2 tbsp chopped fresh
   parsley

freshly ground black
   pepper

162

1 Melt the butter in a large heavy saucepan, add
the onion and cook gently for 5 minutes until
tender, but not coloured. Add the garlic, bay leaf
and parsley stalks and cook for a further minute.

2 Pour in the wine and bring to a rapid boil. Add the
mussels, all at once, and immediately cover the pan
with a tight-fitting lid. Cook over a medium heat,
shaking the pan occasionally for 3–5 minutes until
the mussels have opened. Discard the bay leaf,
parsley stalks and any mussels that have not opened.

3 Strain the cooking juices through a fine-meshed
sieve into a small saucepan. Add the crème fraîche
and 1½ tbsp of the chopped parsley and boil for a
minute or two to reduce slightly. Season to taste
with black pepper.

4 Meanwhile, transfer the mussels to a warmed
serving dish or individual bowls. Pour over the hot
sauce, sprinkle with the remaining parsley and
serve straight away.

**MUSSELS ARE GREAT VALUE AND THERE'S
NOTHING BETTER THAN SITTING DOWN TO
A HUGE BOWLFUL, AND MOPPING UP THE
SAUCE WITH CHUNKS OF BAGUETTE.**

# smoked fish
# and corn tart

£ £

**Serves 4**
Preparation  30 minutes,
   plus 30 minutes chilling
Cooking  30 minutes

**Shortcrust pastry**
**175g plain flour**
**pinch of salt**
**85g cool butter, diced**

**Fish filling**
**225g smoked haddock**
**1 bay leaf**
**3 black peppercorns**
**100ml semi-skimmed milk**
**3 eggs, lightly beaten**
**150ml single cream**
**2 tsp wholegrain mustard**
**pinch of freshly grated
   nutmeg**
**1 tbsp chopped fresh parsley**
**150g sweetcorn, thawed if
   bought frozen**

**COOK SMART**
• This tart can also be
made with 225g cooked,
flaked kippers or smoked
mackerel. Leave out steps
2 and 3 and simply whisk
the cold unflavoured milk
with the eggs and cream
in step 6.

• For a lighter filling,
replace the cream with an
equal amount of extra milk.

• Serve with a salad and
baked tomatoes.

**Per serving**
kcal 522, protein 24g,
fat 30g (of which saturated
fat 15g), carbohydrate 42g
(of which sugars 4g),
fibre 2g, sodium 0.7g

**1** To make the pastry, sift the flour and salt into a large bowl or a food processor with a pastry-making blade. Add the butter, rub in using your fingertips or whizz until crumbly, using the pulse action. Sprinkle 2½ tbsp cold water over the dry ingredients and stir with a round-bladed knife until the mixture comes together, or whizz quickly until bound together. If it seems a little dry, add an extra ½ tbsp water. Knead gently on a floured surface for a few seconds until smooth. Wrap and chill for 20 minutes before using.

**2** Meanwhile, put the fish in a small pan, cutting it to fit if necessary. Add the bay leaf and peppercorns, then pour over the milk.

**3** Cover the pan with a tight-fitting lid, then bring to the boil over a medium heat. Turn down the heat and simmer for 2 minutes or until the fish is opaque and almost cooked. Remove with a draining spoon, then break into large flakes, removing any skin and bones. Set the milk aside.

**4** Preheat a baking sheet in the oven at 200°C (gas 6). Roll out the pastry on a lightly floured surface and use to line a 23 cm loose-based flan tin. Prick the base all over with a fork, and chill for 10 minutes.

**5** Line the pastry case with greaseproof paper and baking beans and bake on the hot baking sheet for 10 minutes. Remove the paper and beans, brush the base with 2 tsp of beaten egg and bake for a further 8 minutes, then remove from the oven. Turn down the oven temperature to 190°C (gas 5).

**6** While the pastry is cooking, mix the eggs, reserved milk and cream together. Strain the mixture into a jug, discarding the bay leaf and peppercorns. Whisk in the mustard, nutmeg and parsley and extra seasoning if needed.

**7** Scatter the flaked fish and sweetcorn over the base of the pastry case. Pour the egg mixture into the case. Bake for 30 minutes or until golden and lightly set. Allow to stand for 10 minutes before serving warm, or cool completely and serve cold.

**SMOKY CHUNKS OF HADDOCK AND SWEET, JUICY KERNELS OF CORN MAKE A FABULOUS FILLING FOR THIS LUSCIOUS TART. USING FROZEN SWEETCORN MEANS THAT YOU CAN ENJOY IT ALL YEAR ROUND.**

# fish pie with watercress mash

£ £ £

**Serves 4**
Preparation  30 minutes
Cooking  25 minutes

**700 g floury potatoes, peeled
and cut into chunks**

**65 g butter**

**25 g plain flour**

**450 ml semi-skimmed milk,
plus 2 tbsp**

**1 bay leaf**

**2 tbsp chopped fresh parsley,
plus a few stalks**

**350 g firm white fish fillet,
cubed**

**100 g cooked peeled prawns,
thawed if bought frozen**

**1 tbsp snipped fresh chives**

**1 tbsp lemon juice**

**85 g watercress, stalks
trimmed and finely chopped**

**salt and freshly ground black
pepper**

**Per serving**
kcal 420, protein 30 g, fat 17 g
(of which saturated fat 10 g),
carbohydrate 39 g (of which
sugars 8 g), fibre 2 g,
sodium 0.6 g

1 Preheat the oven to 180°C (gas 4). Put the potatoes in a saucepan, cover with lightly salted boiling water and cook for 15 minutes or until tender.

2 Meanwhile, put 40 g of the butter in a saucepan with the flour, 450 ml milk, bay leaf and parsley stalks. Cook over a medium heat, whisking all the time until the sauce bubbles and thickens. Turn down the heat as low as possible and cook for 2–3 minutes, stirring frequently.

3 Turn off the heat and remove the bay leaf and parsley stalks. Stir in the fish, prawns, chopped parsley, chives and lemon juice. Season to taste with salt and pepper, then spoon into a 1.5 litre buttered baking dish.

4 When the potatoes are tender, drain them well and mash with the remaining butter. Stir in the chopped watercress and 2 tbsp milk, then beat with a wooden spoon for a minute or two until fluffy.

5 Spoon the mashed potato over the fish mixture, then spread it evenly right to the edge of the dish. Fork up the surface. Bake for 25 minutes or until bubbling and browned. Serve hot.

## COOK SMART

• Leave out the prawns, if preferred, and use smoked haddock with two chopped, hard-boiled eggs instead.

• If you happen to have a carton of cream in the fridge which needs using up or plan to make this pie for a special occasion, add it either to the sauce or mashed potatoes, in place of some of the milk, for a more luxurious result.

A HUGE DISH OF PIPING HOT FISH PIE IS THE ULTIMATE IN COMFORT FOOD, AND THIS VERSION WITH ITS GREEN-FLECKED WATERCRESS MASH IS NO EXCEPTION.

USING FROZEN
SEAFOOD FOR THIS
SPICY MEXICAN-STYLE DISH
MAKES IT AN AFFORDABLE,
NO-FUSS FEAST.

£££

**Serves 4 (makes 8)**
Preparation 30 minutes
Cooking 20 minutes

**400 g can chopped tomatoes**
**pinch of chilli powder, or to taste**
**1 tbsp vegetable oil**
**3 spring onions, thinly sliced**
**2 garlic cloves, crushed**
**400 g frozen seafood selection,**
**thawed and drained**
**60 ml whipping cream**
**8 flour or corn tortillas**
**125 g mature Cheddar, grated**
**2 tbsp chopped pickled jalapeños**

**Per serving**
kcal 620, protein 37 g, fat 20 g
(of which saturated fat 11 g),
carbohydrate 76 g (of which
sugars 4.5 g), fibre 3.5 g, sodium 1.5 g

---

**COOK SMART**
• Add the drained juice from the thawed
seafood to the sauce in step 4 for
extra flavour.

• For delicious Tex-Mex chicken
enchiladas, substitute 450 g boneless,
skinless chicken breasts, cut into
bite-sized pieces, in place of the
seafood. Add in Step 2, sautéing for
about 5 minutes or until the juices
run clear.

---

# seafood enchiladas

**1** Preheat the oven to 200°C
(gas 6). Pulse the tomatoes in
a food processor or blender
until smooth. Add chilli powder
to taste, then set aside.

**2** Heat the oil in a large frying
pan, add the spring onions and
garlic and sauté for 1 minute
or until soft.

**3** Stir in the seafood, then add
150 ml of the puréed tomatoes
and 1 tbsp of the cream and
heat through. Transfer to a bowl
and cover with foil to keep warm.

**4** Pour the remaining tomatoes
and cream into the frying pan
and bring to a simmer; lower
the heat to keep the sauce at
a gentle simmer.

**5** To make the enchiladas, dip
one tortilla at a time into the
sauce in the frying pan for
about 10 seconds until just
pliable. Allow excess sauce
to drip off, then lay on a board
and top with a spoonful of the
seafood mixture. Roll up the
tortilla and place, seam-side
down, in a large baking dish,
measuring about 28 x 18 cm.
Repeat with the remaining
tortillas and seafood mixture.

**6** Stir any remaining seafood
mixture into the sauce in
the frying pan and pour over
the tortillas. Sprinkle with
cheese and jalapeños. Bake the
enchiladas for 20 minutes or
until heated through. Serve hot.

**Serves 4**
Preparation  20 minutes
Cooking  15 minutes

**350 g skinless smoked haddock fillet
    (preferably undyed)**
**1 bay leaf**
**3 tbsp chopped fresh parsley plus 2 stalks**
**600 ml vegetable stock, hot**
**1 tsp olive oil**
**15 g butter**
**300 g basmati rice**
**½ tsp curry powder or paste**
**¼ tsp garam masala**
**¼ tsp ground coriander**
**150 g frozen peas, thawed**
**freshly ground black pepper**

**To garnish**
**2 hard-boiled eggs, quartered**
**sprigs of fresh parsley**

**Per serving**
kcal 542, protein 41 g, fat 13 g (of which
saturated fat 4 g), carbohydrate 65 g (of
which sugars 1 g), fibre 1.5 g, sodium 0.8 g

---

**COOK SMART**

• If you don't have garam masala or ground
coriander to hand, simply use an extra ½ tsp
of your favourite curry powder or paste.

• Naan bread, spread with garlic butter and
baked in a moderate oven for 5–6 minutes,
makes a great accompaniment. Cut into
strips to serve.

---

THIS LIGHTLY SPICED ANGLO-INDIAN RICE
DISH IS AN ABSOLUTE CLASSIC AND MAKES
A GREAT ONE-POT LUNCH OR SUPPER.

1 Put the haddock in a saucepan, cutting to fit if
necessary. Add the bay leaf and parsley stalks,
then pour in the stock. Cover and simmer gently for
7–8 minutes, until the fish flakes easily. Remove
the fish using a fish slice and set aside. Reserve
the cooking liquid and bay leaf.

2 Heat the oil and butter in the rinsed out pan until
melted, then add the rice and stir until coated in
the mixture. Add the spices and cook over a low
heat for 2 minutes, stirring all the time.

3 Make up the reserved cooking liquid to 600 ml
with boiling water, then pour this stock into the pan.
Add the bay leaf, cover and simmer for 10 minutes,
adding a little more boiling water if needed. Stir
in the peas, cover again and continue cooking for
2–3 minutes or until the rice is tender and the
liquid has been absorbed.

4 Meanwhile, break the fish into large flakes,
discarding any skin and bones. Gently stir into
the hot rice with the chopped parsley, season with
pepper and heat gently for about 30 seconds to
ensure the dish is piping hot. Remove the bay leaf.

5 Transfer the kedgeree to a warmed serving dish
or individual plates and serve garnished with egg
quarters and sprigs of parsley.

# smoked
# fish
# kedgeree

# cajun prawn and crab jambalaya

**£ £ £**

**Serves 6**
Preparation 20 minutes
Cooking 20 minutes

**Per serving**
kcal 389, protein 30.5 g,
fat 7 g (of which saturated
fat 2 g), carbohydrate 54 g
(of which sugars 7 g),
fibre 1 g, sodium 1 g

1 tbsp vegetable oil

2 onions, chopped

1 large green pepper, seeded and chopped

2 celery sticks, sliced

100 g lean gammon, diced

1 tbsp plain flour

2 x 400 g cans chopped tomatoes

500 ml chicken or fish stock

300 g long-grain white rice

2 tsp Cajun seasoning

250 g peeled raw tiger prawns

170 g can white crab meat, drained

2 tbsp chopped fresh coriander

**1** Gently heat the oil in a large heavy-based pan or flameproof casserole. Stir in the onions and cook for 5 minutes, then add the green pepper, celery and gammon and cook for a further 4–5 minutes until the vegetables are soft.

**2** Sprinkle over the flour and cook, stirring for 2–3 minutes. Stir in the tomatoes, with their juice, the stock, rice and Cajun seasoning. Bring to the boil, then reduce the heat. Cover and simmer for 15 minutes or until most of the liquid is absorbed and the rice is almost tender.

**3** Stir in the prawns, cover again and cook gently for 3–4 minutes or until the prawns have turned pink and are, therefore, just cooked.

**4** Gently stir in the crab meat, cover the pan and cook for 1 minute. Remove the pan from the heat and let stand for 3 minutes, then serve sprinkled with chopped coriander.

**COOK SMART**

• Use cooked prawns if they are a better price. Add in step 4, so they just heat through gently for 1–2 minutes or they will toughen. Use some chopped smoked bacon or chorizo sausage in place of the gammon, if preferred.

WARMLY SPICED AND PACKED WITH SEAFOOD, THIS HEARTY RICE DISH FROM LOUISIANA IS PERFECT FOR A HUNGRY CROWD.

# coconut prawn and vegetable curry

££

**Serves 4**
Preparation 20 minutes
Cooking 25 minutes

**Per serving**
kcal 410, protein 22g,
fat 27g (of which saturated
fat 16g), carbohydrate 21g
(of which sugars 12g),
fibre 4g, sodium 1g

200g small, even-sized
new potatoes,
scrubbed
2 tbsp vegetable oil
1 onion, sliced
3 garlic cloves, finely
chopped
3 tbsp mild curry paste
100g creamed coconut,
roughly chopped
227g can chopped
tomatoes
200g carrots, peeled and
sliced
200g cauliflower, divided
into bite-sized florets
200ml vegetable stock
200g French beans, cut
into short lengths
200g peeled raw tiger
prawns, thawed and
drained if bought frozen
3 tbsp chopped fresh
coriander
salt and freshly ground
black pepper

> **COOK SMART**
> • Spinach is also good in
> this curry. Reduce the
> stock to 150ml and add
> 250g washed, drained and
> roughly chopped spinach
> with the French beans.
> • For a simple
> accompaniment, serve
> with a cucumber raita:
> mix together half a finely
> chopped cucumber, 300ml
> Greek-style yoghurt and
> 2 tbsp chopped fresh
> coriander or mint.

**1** Cook the potatoes in a saucepan of lightly salted,
boiling water for 10 minutes. Drain and set aside.

**2** Meanwhile, heat the oil in a large heavy-based
saucepan, add the onion and fry gently for
5 minutes, stirring occasionally. Add the garlic
and curry paste and cook for a further 2 minutes,
stirring all the time.

**3** Add the creamed coconut and stir until it has
melted, then add the tomatoes with their juice.
Simmer uncovered for 2–3 minutes until the
mixture resembles a fairly thick paste.

**4** Add the carrots, cauliflower florets and stock, bring
to the boil, then cover and simmer for 15 minutes.
Add the beans and potatoes and cook for a further
8 minutes.

**5** Stir in the prawns and simmer for 2–3 minutes
or until they turn pink (simply heat through for
1–2 minutes if using cooked). Season to taste, stir
in the chopped coriander and serve straight away.

# mediterranean fish stew

£££

**Serves 4**
Preparation 25 minutes
Cooking 40 minutes

2 tbsp olive oil
1 onion, chopped
1 leek, trimmed and sliced
2 garlic cloves, finely chopped
1 celery stick, sliced
400g can chopped tomatoes
1 tbsp tomato purée (preferably sun-dried)
450ml fish stock
150ml dry white wine
1 bay leaf
250g whiting fillets, cut into chunks
250g haddock fillets, cut into chunks
125g chilled seafood selection
2 tbsp Pernod (optional)
salt and freshly ground black pepper
2 tbsp shredded fresh basil to garnish

**Per serving**
kcal 310, protein 39g, fat 9g (of which saturated
fat 1.5g), carbohydrate 7g (of which sugars 6g),
fibre 1.5g, sodium 0.2g

**1** Heat the oil in a large heavy-based saucepan. Add
the onion and leek and cook over a moderate heat,
stirring frequently, for 5 minutes, until beginning to
soften. Stir in the garlic and celery and cook for
2 more minutes.

**2** Add the tomatoes with their juice, the tomato purée,
fish stock, wine and bay leaf. Bring to the boil, then
lower the heat, cover and simmer for 30 minutes.
Season with salt and pepper.

**3** Stir in the white fish, cover and cook for 5 minutes,
then stir in the seafood. Re-cover and cook gently
for a further 2–3 minutes until the white fish is
cooked and the seafood is heated through.

**4** Remove the bay leaf and stir in the Pernod, if using.
Ladle the stew into a warmed tureen or individual
bowls and sprinkle with shredded basil to serve.

**COOK SMART**
• If buying from a wet fish counter, ask for the fish bones
and use them to make stock (see page 32).

A FABULOUS YET SURPRISINGLY INEXPENSIVE
DISH – SERVE WITH CRUSTY BREAD TO MOP UP
THE DELICIOUS JUICES.

# pou
# ga

tasty,
healthy
and great value
for any
meal

# poultry & game

Chicken is excellent value and always a favourite for family meals, but turkey, duck, pheasant and rabbit are also good choices, ideal for entertaining or for informal meals. Hearty casseroles and stews cooked with healthy vegetables, tangy fruit or pulses make substantial suppers, while a creamy curry served with plenty of steamed rice and naan bread is great with friends. For lighter meals, try grilled skewers, a refreshing salad, or a healthy stir-fry served with noodles.

# chicken parcels

**CREAMY CHICKEN WRAPPED UP INSIDE ELEGANT GOLDEN FILO PASTRY PARCELS MAKES A MARVELLOUS DISH FOR A SPECIAL OCCASION.**

172

£

**Serves 4**
Preparation 25–30
minutes, plus 1 hour
cooling (for the sauce)
Cooking 15–20 minutes

**26 g packet garlic,
mushroom and cream
sauce mix**

**1 tbsp crème fraîche**

**1 tbsp lemon juice**

**1 tbsp snipped fresh
chives**

**40 g butter**

**2 chicken breast fillets,
about 150 g each**

**1 tbsp vegetable oil**

**8 sheets filo pastry, about
115 g, cut in half**

**salt and freshly ground
black pepper**

**To serve**
**mixed salad leaves**

---

**COOK SMART**

• For an attractive finish,
tie the cooked parcels with
fresh chive stalks or sprigs
of parsley with long stems.

• Filo pastry varies in
thickness, size and
weight. If using a thicker
filo, six sheets will be
enough. Each half sheet
should measure about
24 cm square.

• Packets of sauce mix
are readily available from
supermarkets and make
a convenient standby to
keep in the cupboard.
Alternatively, make a
home-made sauce
(see page 32). You will
need 300 ml.

---

**Per serving**
kcal 380, protein 12 g,
fat 28 g (of which saturated
fat 11 g), carbohydrate 18 g
(of which sugars 0.7 g),
fibre 0.5 g, sodium 0.3 g

---

**1** Blend the sauce mix with 300 ml cold water in a saucepan. Bring to the boil, stirring, and cook gently for 3 minutes until thickened. Remove pan from the heat, add the crème fraîche, lemon juice and chives and season to taste. Set aside to cool for 1 hour.

**2** Melt 15 g of the butter in a frying pan and gently cook the chicken breasts for 7–8 minutes on each side, over a medium heat, until cooked through. Remove chicken from the pan, chop into small pieces and stir into the mushroom sauce, along with any pan juices. Preheat the oven to 200°C (gas 6).

**3** Melt the remaining butter and mix with the oil. Take half a sheet of filo (measuring about 24 cm square) and brush with a little of the oil mixture, then place three more pieces of the filo on top, at angles to each other, to form a star shape, lightly oiling each sheet.

**4** Place a quarter of the chicken mixture in the centre, then gather up the pastry edges, pinching tightly to form a parcel. Repeat to make three more parcels.

**5** Place the parcels on a non-stick or lightly greased baking sheet and bake for 15–20 minutes until the pastry is crisp and golden. Serve immediately, garnished with salad leaves.

# citrus chicken with pineapple salsa

**Serves 4**

Preparation 25 minutes, plus 30 minutes or overnight marinating
Cooking 12–15 minutes

2 limes

2 tsp soy sauce

1 tbsp vegetable oil

1 garlic clove, crushed

1 tsp runny honey

2 fresh red chillies, seeded and finely chopped

4 chicken breast fillets, about 150 g each

½ small fresh pineapple, peeled, cored and diced

½ small red onion, finely chopped

2 tbsp chopped fresh mint

100 g baby spinach leaves

12 cherry tomatoes, halved

salt and freshly ground black pepper

**WAKE UP YOUR TASTEBUDS WITH THIS ZINGY, ZESTY CHICKEN.**

## COOK SMART

• You can make salsas with all kinds of different fruits, according to what is in season. Try chopped peaches or mango, or cantaloupe melon sprinkled with lime juice, a little finely chopped stem ginger, if liked, and some chopped fresh mint, basil or coriander.

**Per serving**

kcal 225, protein 37 g, fat 5 g (of which saturated fat 1 g), carbohydrate 8.5 g (of which sugars 8 g), fibre 1.5 g, sodium 0.3 g

**1** Stir together the juice of one of the limes with the soy sauce, oil, garlic, honey, half the chopped chilli and salt and pepper to season in a shallow dish. Add the chicken and turn to coat. Marinate for at least 30 minutes or overnight in the fridge.

**2** Preheat a moderate grill. Combine the pineapple with the grated zest and juice of the second lime, the red onion, the rest of the chopped chilli and the mint in medium bowl. Season to taste, then set aside.

**3** Lift the chicken from the marinade and place on the grill rack. Grill for 12–15 minutes, turning and basting with the marinade, until the juices run clear when the chicken is pierced with a knife.

**4** Transfer the chicken to a board and cut diagonally into strips. Divide the spinach leaves among four plates, scatter over the tomatoes and arrange the chicken on top. Spoon over the salsa and serve immediately.

# chicken brochettes with pitta

**Serves 4**

Preparation 10 minutes
Cooking about 15 minutes

4 chicken breast fillets, about 150 g each

1 large green pepper, seeded

1 tbsp olive oil

juice of 1 lemon

4 pitta breads

50 g soft cheese with herbs and garlic

4 crisp lettuce leaves

2 tomatoes, sliced

salt and freshly ground black pepper

## COOK SMART

• Instead of just chicken, use 300 g cubed chicken breast and 2 sliced spicy sausages. Serve in hunks of baguette, spread with mustard and filled with tomato slices.

• Leftover pittas can be toasted and used in a salad instead of croûtons.

**Per serving**

kcal 426, protein 38 g, fat 11 g (of which saturated fat 4.5 g), carbohydrate 45 g (of which sugars 6 g), fibre 3 g, sodium 0.5 g

**1** Soak eight wooden skewers in cold water for at least 30 minutes. Alternatively, use metal skewers.

**2** Cut the chicken into even, bite-sized pieces. Cut the pepper into pieces the same size as the chicken. Preheat a moderate grill.

**3** Thread alternate pieces of chicken and pepper on to the skewers, pushing the ingredients close together so that they stay juicy. Brush with oil.

**4** Grill the brochettes for 7–8 minutes on each side until the chicken is cooked through. Squeeze over the lemon juice.

**5** Warm the pitta bread, either under the grill or in a toaster. Spread the soft cheese on the lettuce leaves.

**6** To serve, split the pittas open and insert the lettuce and tomato slices. Season the brochettes, then slip the chicken and peppers into the pitta pockets.

# chicken satay

174

£ £

**Serves 6 (makes 24)**
Preparation  15 minutes,
   plus 2 hours or
   overnight marinating
Cooking  about 10 minutes

**Per serving**
kcal 245, protein 33g,
fat 10g (of which saturated
fat 4g), carbohydrate 7g
(of which sugars 6.5g),
fibre 1g, sodium 0.6g

---

**COOK SMART**
• Both Quorn and tofu
could be marinated in
place of the chicken.

• Serve the kebabs with
new potatoes or rice and
a cool cucumber salad.

• Satay sauce also makes
a delicious accompaniment
to grilled or barbecued
vegetable kebabs.

---

4 chicken breast fillets,
   about 150g each

**Marinade**
3 tbsp lemon juice
2 tbsp soy sauce
1 tbsp light muscovado
   sugar
1 garlic clove, crushed
2cm piece fresh root
   ginger, peeled and
   finely chopped

**Satay sauce**
2 tbsp desiccated coconut
4 tbsp peanut butter
   (smooth or crunchy)
½ tsp chilli powder
2 tsp soy sauce
1 tbsp light muscovado
   sugar
grated zest and juice of
   1 lime
lemon or lime wedges
   to garnish

1  Cut each chicken breast lengthways into six strips.
   Blend together all the ingredients for the marinade
   in a shallow dish. Add the chicken, turn several
   times to coat, then cover and chill in the fridge
   for several hours or overnight.

2  Soak 24 wooden skewers in cold water for
   30 minutes. Alternatively, use metal skewers.
   For the sauce, put the coconut in a jug, pour
   over 100ml boiling water and leave to infuse for
   15 minutes. Strain, reserving the coconut-flavoured
   liquid. Discard the coconut. Preheat a medium grill.

3  Put all the ingredients for the sauce, including the
   coconut liquid, in a blender or food processor and
   whizz together. Transfer to a small serving bowl.

4  Thread the strips of chicken onto the skewers
   concertina-style, then grill for 10 minutes or until
   cooked through.

5  Serve the chicken skewers, four per person, with
   the sauce. Garnish with lemon or lime wedges.

---

**LITTLE THAI-STYLE KEBABS ARE GREAT FOR A SIMPLE SUPPER, OR AS A NIBBLE WITH DRINKS.**

# chicken kebabs with chilli dipping sauce

£ £

**Serves 4 (makes 12)**
Preparation  15 minutes,
   plus 2 hours or
   overnight marinating
Cooking  about 10 minutes

**Per serving**
kcal 292, protein 39g,
fat 10g (of which saturated
fat 1.5g), carbohydrate 13g
(of which sugars 13g),
fibre 0g, sodium 0.2g

**Chicken kebabs**
1 tbsp balsamic vinegar
1 tsp soy sauce
3 tbsp vegetable oil
1 garlic clove, crushed
finely grated zest and
   juice of 1 lime
4 chicken breast fillets,
   about 600g in total,
   cubed
lime wedges to garnish
   (optional)

**Chilli dipping sauce**
50g caster sugar
90ml white wine or
   rice vinegar
1 tsp crushed dried chillies

**1** In a bowl, whisk together the balsamic vinegar, soy sauce, oil, garlic and lime zest and juice. Add the cubed chicken, mix well, then cover and marinate in the fridge for at least 2 hours, or preferably overnight.

**2** Soak twelve wooden skewers for 30 minutes in a shallow dish of water. This helps to prevent them from burning and stops them absorbing juices from the chicken. Alternatively, use metal skewers.

**3** For the dipping sauce, place all the ingredients in a small saucepan and heat gently, stirring frequently, until the sugar has dissolved. Simmer gently for 5 minutes, then remove from the heat and leave to cool.

**4** Remove the chicken from the marinade and thread onto the skewers. Place under a preheated hot grill or on a hot, ridged grill pan and cook for about 10 minutes, brushing the kebabs after 5 minutes

with the leftover marinade mixture, to keep the chicken moist. Turn the kebabs occasionally so that the chicken becomes tender and slightly charred all over.

**5** Arrange the chicken kebabs on a warmed platter. Pour the dipping sauce into a small bowl and serve straight away with lime wedges to garnish and squeeze over, if liked.

**COOK SMART**
• These kebabs also work well using lean pork steaks, cut across the grain into thin strips and threaded onto skewers, concertina-style.

• A simple tabbouleh salad makes a good accompaniment. Put 75g bulghur wheat into a healproof bowl and cover with double its volume of boiling water. Soak for 20 minutes, drain thoroughly, then stir in some chopped cucumber, tomatoes and red onion. Toss in French dressing and plenty of chopped fresh mint or parsley.

# chicken liver pilaff

💷

**Serves 4**
Preparation  15 minutes
Cooking  about 20 minutes

**2 tbsp olive oil**

**1 large onion, finely chopped**

**200 g long-grain rice**

**450 g chicken livers, thawed
if bought frozen**

**1 garlic clove, thinly sliced**

**½ tsp ground cumin**

**¼ tsp paprika**

**1 tbsp red wine vinegar**

**salt and freshly ground
black pepper**

**Per serving**
kcal 360, protein 24 g, fat 10 g
(of which saturated fat 2 g),
carbohydrate 46 g (of which
sugars 2 g), fibre 1 g,
sodium 0.09 g

## COOK SMART

• For special occasions,
marinate the chicken livers for
1 hour in 2–3 tbsp brandy with
the leaves from 2 sprigs of
fresh thyme. Flambé the livers
with the brandy marinade when
cooked. Add 2–3 rashers
chopped streaky bacon, if liked.

• Add some colour to the rice
with strips of char-grilled red
pepper and petits pois.

CHICKEN LIVERS ARE FANTASTIC VALUE
AND ABSOLUTELY DELICIOUS PAN-FRIED
WITH GARLIC AND SPICES IN THIS
MOREISH PILAFF.

**1** Heat 1 tbsp of the oil in a saucepan, add the onion
and sauté gently for 5 minutes, until softened. Add
the rice and stir for 1 minute until the grains become
transparent, then add 500 ml boiling water and a
pinch of salt. Cover and cook gently for 18 minutes
or until the rice is tender.

**2** Meanwhile, rinse the chicken livers, pat dry on
kitchen paper, then cut into small, even-sized
pieces, removing any gristly bits. Heat the remaining
oil in a non-stick frying pan, add the garlic, sauté for
a minute or two until golden, then remove and
discard it.

**3** Add the chicken livers to the oil and cook over
a medium heat for 3–4 minutes, turning regularly.
Sprinkle over the cumin, paprika and salt
and pepper to season. Do not cook for any longer
or the livers will become tough. Remove the livers
to a dish.

**4** Add the vinegar and 2 tbsp water to the frying pan
used for cooking the livers and bring to the boil,
scraping the bottom of the pan with a wooden
spatula. Return the livers to the pan to keep warm
in the juices, while serving the rice.

**5** Drain the rice, if necessary, then heap it onto four
serving plates. Spoon over the livers with the pan
juices and serve immediately.

£ £ £

**Serves 4**
Preparation 30 minutes
Cooking 15–18 minutes

**2 tbsp olive oil**

**1 large portobello mushroom,
    coarsely chopped**

**4 spring onions, sliced**

**250 g fresh young spinach,
    coarsely chopped**

**2 tbsp dry breadcrumbs
    (made from stale bread)**

**2 tbsp freshly grated Parmesan**

**4 skinless, boneless chicken
    breasts or thighs, about
    175 g each**

**125 ml chicken stock, hot**

**salt and freshly ground
    black pepper**

**Per serving**
kcal 332, protein 50 g, fat 11 g
(of which saturated fat 3 g),
carbohydrate 8 g (of which
sugars 2 g), fibre 1.5 g,
sodium 0.3 g

**1** Preheat the oven to 180°C (gas 4). Heat 1 tbsp of the oil in a large, deep frying pan, add the mushrooms and spring onions and sauté over a medium heat for 5 minutes until the mushrooms are tender. Stir in the spinach and cook, stirring, for 2 minutes, until wilted.

**2** Transfer the vegetables to a large bowl, using a draining spoon to drain off excess moisture from the spinach. Set the pan on one side. Add the breadcrumbs, Parmesan and salt and pepper to season, and toss together.

**3** Pound the chicken flat and thin between two sheets of cling film. Spread 2 heaped tbsp of the spinach filling onto each piece of chicken, to about 1 cm from the edges. Then, starting at one of the narrower ends, roll up and secure the roulades with cocktail sticks or string.

**4** Drain the vegetable cooking juices from the frying pan, then add the remaining 1 tbsp of oil and set the pan over a high heat. Add the roulades, seam-side down, and cook for 6 minutes or until browned all over. (Placing the roulades seam-side down first seals them closed.)

**5** Place the roulades in a shallow ovenproof dish and pour over the hot stock. Cover and bake for 15–18 minutes or until the chicken is cooked through.

**6** To serve, remove the cocktail sticks or string from the roulades and cut the chicken diagonally into 1 cm slices. Serve hot, drizzled with the cooking juices.

**COOK SMART**
• Portobello mushrooms are full grown chestnut mushrooms and are wonderfully flavoursome. Alternatively, use four chestnut mushrooms or large, white flats.

177

# chicken roulades with spinach and mushrooms

# jamaican jerked chicken salad

JERK SEASONING IS A SIMPLE WAY TO ENLIVEN GRILLED CHICKEN AND TRANSFORMS THIS SALAD INTO A SPICY, REFRESHING TASTE SENSATION. ENJOY IT WHILE THE CHICKEN IS STILL WARM.

££

**Serves 4**
Preparation  20 minutes
Cooking  about 15 minutes

4 spring onions, thinly sliced
3 garlic cloves, crushed
1 tsp dried thyme
1 tsp freshly ground black pepper
¾ tsp ground allspice
¾ tsp salt
4 tbsp red wine vinegar
2 tbsp Dijon mustard
2 tsp dark muscovado sugar
4 chicken breast fillets, about 150 g each
1 tbsp vegetable oil
220 g can pineapple chunks in juice, drained
4 kiwi fruit, peeled and cut into wedges
1 large red pepper, seeded and cut into thin strips
250 g mooli radish, peeled and sliced (optional)

**Per serving**
kcal 284, protein 38 g, fat 5.5 g (of which saturated fat 1 g), carbohydrate 21.5 g (of which sugars 21 g), fibre 2 g, sodium 0.7 g

**1** In a large bowl, stir together half the spring onions, the garlic, thyme, black pepper, allspice, and ½ tsp of salt. Stir in 2 tbsp of the vinegar, 1 tbsp of the mustard and the brown sugar and mix well. Add the chicken, rubbing the mixture into the chicken. Cover and set aside.

**2** In a separate bowl, whisk together the remaining 2 tbsp vinegar, 1 tbsp mustard, ¼ tsp salt and the oil. Add the remaining spring onions, the pineapple, kiwi fruit, pepper and radish, if using. Toss to combine.

**3** Preheat a medium grill. Grill the chicken, 5 cm from the heat, for 5–7 minutes on each side or until cooked through.

**4** When cool enough to handle, slice the chicken on the diagonal. Add the warm chicken to the salad and serve immediately.

## COOK SMART
• If you can't get mooli radish (it looks like a thin, smooth, white parsnip), use sliced red globe radishes for a crisp texture. Alternatively, look out for jicama (yam bean). This root vegetable from Central America looks like a turnip. It has a crisp, juicy texture and is good raw, peeled and sliced into salads.

**£ £**

**Serves 4**
Preparation 10 minutes
Cooking 15–20 minutes

**2 tsp olive oil**

**4 chicken breast fillets,
about 150 g each**

**2 oranges**

**2 shallots, finely chopped**

**1 tbsp lemon juice**

**1 tbsp tangy orange
marmalade**

**1 tsp chopped fresh
rosemary or ½ tsp
dried**

**1 tsp cornflour**

**salt and freshly ground
black pepper**

**sprigs of fresh rosemary
to garnish**

**Per serving**
kcal 223, protein 36 g,
fat 4 g (of which saturated
fat 1 g), carbohydrate 10 g
(of which sugars 9 g),

# pan-fried chicken with orange and rosemary sauce

**1** Heat the oil in a large frying pan over a medium heat. Add the chicken and cook gently for 5–6 minutes on each side or until golden brown and cooked through. Transfer the chicken to a plate and cover with foil to keep warm.

**2** Grate the zest from one of the oranges and squeeze the juice from both (there should be 1½ tsp zest and 150 ml juice). Add the shallots to the pan and cook, stirring, for 3 minutes until light golden. Stir in the orange juice and zest, lemon juice, marmalade and rosemary. Season with salt and pepper and bring to the boil.

**3** Mix the cornflour with 1 tbsp cold water to make a smooth paste. Add to the sauce and simmer for 1 minute, stirring, until slightly thickened.

**4** Slice the chicken on the diagonal and serve with the sauce spooned over the top. Garnish with sprigs of fresh rosemary.

**COOK SMART**
• To complete the meal, serve with rice char-grilled peppers and red onions.

**TANGY ORANGE AND FRAGRANT ROSEMARY GIVE THIS SIMPLE DISH A SOPHISTICATED EDGE.**

# chicken with creamy onion sauce

💷💷

**Serves 4**
Preparation 15 minutes,
  plus 1–2 hours
  marinating
Cooking 25 minutes

**4 chicken breast fillets,
  halved lengthways**

**½ tsp ground cumin**

**juice of 1 lemon**

**35 g packet onion sauce
  mix**

**1 tbsp vegetable oil**

**15 g butter**

**200 ml single cream**

**salt and freshly ground
  black pepper**

### COOK SMART
• For an extra flavour, some chopped fresh tarragon would be good added to this sauce.

• For a home-made onion sauce, see page 32. Make up a 300 ml quantity to use here.

**Per serving**
kcal 258, protein 20 g, fat 17 g (of which saturated fat 9 g), carbohydrate 7 g (of which sugars 2 g), fibre 0 g, sodium 0.3 g

1 Season the chicken breasts on both sides and sprinkle lightly with cumin. Place the chicken in a shallow bowl and pour over the lemon juice. Cover and leave to marinate in the fridge for 1–2 hours.

2 Make up the sauce mix with 300 ml boiling water, or according to the packet instructions, and set aside.

3 Heat the oil and butter in a frying pan. Pat dry the chicken breasts and reserve the marinade. Cook the chicken breasts over a medium heat for 5 minutes until golden brown, then reduce the heat and cook gently for a further 5 minutes on each side.

4 Remove the chicken from the pan, place on a heated serving dish and cover to keep warm.

5 Pour the reserved marinade into the frying pan and cook over a medium heat for 1–2 minutes until reduced slightly. Add the onion sauce to the pan, bring to the boil, then reduce the heat and stir in the cream. Simmer the sauce for 2–3 minutes until thickened, then spoon over the chicken breasts.

181

USING A SAUCE MIX TAKES ALL THE EFFORT OUT OF THIS LUSCIOUS DISH. SERVE WITH MASHED POTATOES AND GREEN VEGETABLES FOR A REAL FEAST.

**Serves 4**

Preparation 15 minutes,
 plus 2–3 hours
 marinating
Cooking 50 minutes

**200g natural low-fat
 yoghurt**

**3 tbsp lemon juice**

**2 tbsp mild curry paste**

**2 tsp chopped fresh thyme
 or ½ tsp dried**

**8 chicken thighs**

**30g butter**

**1 large red pepper,
 deseeded and diced**

**salt and freshly ground
 black pepper**

**sprigs of fresh thyme
 to garnish**

---

**COOK SMART**

• To accompany this dish, place four courgettes, cut in half lengthways, in an ovenproof dish. Baste with olive oil and sprinkle with fresh thyme. Bake for 25 minutes at 200°C (gas 6), then sprinkle with a little lemon juice and spread lightly with garlic purée. Serve with savoury rice.

**Per serving**

kcal 270, protein 39g, fat 10g (of which saturated fat 4.5g), carbohydrate 7g (of which sugars 6g), fibre 0.5g, sodium 0.3g

---

**1** Mix together the yoghurt, lemon juice, curry paste and thyme, then season with salt and pepper.

**2** Put the chicken pieces in a shallow ovenproof dish, cover with the yoghurt mixture and turn the chicken several times to make sure it is evenly coated. Leave to marinate in the fridge for 2–3 hours.

**3** Preheat the oven to 200°C (gas 6). Put a knob of butter on each chicken piece. Surround with the chopped pepper, then put in the oven and cook for 50 minutes or until cooked through, basting a couple of times. Serve immediately, garnished with sprigs of fresh thyme.

# spicy lemon chicken with peppers

**TAKING TIME TO MARINATE THE CHICKEN BEFORE COOKING ENSURES THAT IT WILL BE TENDER, JUICY AND MELTINGLY SUCCULENT.**

# caribbean chicken

££

**Serves 4**

Preparation  20 minutes
Cooking  1½ hours

**1 chicken, about 1.5 kg
(without giblets)**

**2 tbsp olive oil**

**225 ml chicken or
vegetable stock**

**250 g long-grain rice**

**227 g can pineapple pieces
in juice**

**1 star anise (optional)**

**3 firm bananas**

**15 g butter**

**3 tbsp single cream**

**salt and cayenne pepper**

**AN UNUSUAL TWIST ON
CLASSIC ROAST CHICKEN,
THIS RECIPE MAKES THE
MOST OF THE FLAVOUR OF
THE FRESH FRUITS.**

### COOK SMART

- For an extra special flavour, flambé the bananas with 2 tbsp dark rum.

- To test the chicken is cooked, pierce between the chicken breast and thigh with a knife – the juices should run clear.

**Per serving**
kcal 690, protein 64 g,
fat 15 g (of which saturated
fat 5 g), carbohydrate 74 g
(of which sugars 23 g),
fibre 1 g, sodium 0.2 g

1 Preheat the oven to 190°C (gas 5). Place the chicken on a rack, brush with 1 tbsp of the oil and season with salt and cayenne pepper. Roast for 1½ hours (or allow 20 minutes per 450 g plus 20 minutes, if your bird is bigger or smaller).

2 Tilt the cooked chicken over the roasting rack, to allow the juices to run from inside the bird into the tin. Remove the chicken and cover with foil to keep it warm. Allow to rest for 15–20 minutes before carving. Meanwhile, skim off the fat in the roasting tin, add the stock and place over a high heat on the hob. Bring to the boil, scraping the bottom of the pan with a spatula all the while, and boil for several seconds until reduced slightly. Set aside.

3 Meanwhile, cook the rice. Put the rice in a saucepan and cover with 600 ml boiling water. Drain the pineapple, put aside 2 tbsp of the juice, then pour the rest into the pan with the rice. Add a pinch of salt and the star anise, if using. Bring back to the boil, then reduce the heat and cover. Simmer for 12–15 minutes until all the water has been absorbed and the rice is just tender. (Add a little more boiling water if needed before the rice is cooked.) Drain, if necessary, cover and keep warm.

4 Carve the chicken, cover and keep warm. Cut the bananas in half widthways, peel and then cut in half lengthways. Heat the remaining oil in a frying pan, add the butter and sauté the bananas for a few minutes until golden. Remove from the pan using a draining spoon and keep warm. Add the pineapple to the pan, heat gently for 1 minute, then remove and keep warm.

5 Pour the reduced chicken roasting juices and the reserved 2 tbsp pineapple juice into the frying pan and bring to the boil. Reduce the heat, stir in the cream and season to taste. Pour into a jug or sauceboat.

6 To serve, arrange the chicken on top of the rice with the bananas and pineapple and serve the sauce on the side, to pour over.

# stir-fried chicken and broccoli with coconut milk

£ £

**Serves 4**
Preparation  25 minutes
Cooking  about 10 minutes

**Per serving**
kcal 343, protein 30 g,
fat 21 g (of which saturated
fat 12 g), carbohydrate 10 g
(of which sugars 8 g),
fibre 3.5 g, sodium 0.4 g

---

**COOK SMART**
• Thai curry paste is pretty
fiery, so use it sparingly. If
you do not have any paste,
use ¼ tsp crushed dried
chillies instead.
• Serve with boiled rice or
Chinese noodles.

---

1 lime

125 ml canned coconut
milk

1 tbsp soy sauce

15 g fresh root ginger,
peeled and finely
chopped

1 tbsp light muscovado
sugar

1 tsp cornflour

½ tsp Thai green curry
paste (optional)

2½ tbsp vegetable oil

1 onion, halved and sliced

6 garlic cloves, crushed

375 g broccoli, cut into
small florets and stems
thinly sliced

250 g button mushrooms,
halved

375 g skinless, boneless
chicken breasts or
thighs, cut into
thin strips

4 tbsp shredded fresh basil

**RICH WITH THE EXOTIC FLAVOURS OF
THAI CUISINE, THIS SPICY STIR-FRY
IS GOOD AT ANY TIME.**

**1** Grate the zest of the lime and squeeze 1 tbsp of
the juice into a small bowl. Add the coconut milk,
soy sauce, ginger, sugar, cornflour, and curry
paste, if using. Set aside.

**2** Heat 1½ tbsp of the oil in a wok or large frying pan
over a high heat. Add the onion and garlic and
stir-fry for 2 minutes until slightly softened. Add
the broccoli and mushrooms and stir-fry for a
further 2 minutes. Transfer to a bowl.

**3** Add the remaining 1 tbsp of the oil to the pan.
Add the chicken and stir-fry for 2 minutes until
light golden. Add the coconut milk mixture and
the vegetables and stir-fry for 1 minute to thicken.
Cover and simmer for 2 minutes or until the chicken
is cooked through and the vegetables are just tender.
Scatter with the basil and serve at once.

---

# devilled chicken drumsticks

**Serves 4 (makes 8)**
Preparation  15 minutes,
plus 1 hour or overnight
marinating
Cooking  30 minutes

**Per serving**
kcal 270, protein 37 g,
fat 2 g (of which saturated
fat 0.5 g), carbohydrate 25 g
(of which sugars 25 g),
fibre 0 g, sodium 1 g

---

**COOK SMART**
• Try turkey drumsticks
(a 700 g drumstick will
serve 2–3 people). Marinate
as above, then bake at
190°C (gas 5) for 1¼ hours,
covering with foil for the first
40 minutes.

---

8 large chicken drumsticks

1 garlic clove, crushed

1 fresh green chilli, seeded
and finely chopped or
½ tsp chilli powder

¼ tsp ground ginger

3 tbsp runny honey

3 tbsp dark muscovado
sugar

4 tbsp tomato ketchup

2 tbsp dry sherry or
1 tbsp sherry or
white wine vinegar

2 tbsp soy sauce

1 tbsp Dijon mustard

salt and freshly ground
black pepper

**1** Remove the skin from the drumsticks, if preferred.
Cut two or three slashes in the flesh of each drumstick
with a sharp knife, then place them in a large bowl.

**2** Mix together all the remaining ingredients in a small
bowl or jug. Pour this sauce over the drumsticks and
turn them with your hands to coat evenly and inside
the slashes. Cover and marinate in the fridge for at
least 1 hour, or overnight if more convenient.

**3** Preheat the oven to 200°C (gas 6). Place the
drumsticks in a lightly oiled roasting tin, preferably
non-stick, and cover the chicken loosely with foil.
Bake for 15 minutes.

**4** Remove the foil and baste the chicken with the
juices. Return to the oven uncovered for a further
15 minutes or until sizzling and cooked right through
(the juices should run clear when the flesh is pierced
with a skewer). Serve hot, or cool and keep chilled
until ready to pack up cold for a picnic or lunchbox.

**CHICKEN LEGS ARE GREAT
VALUE FOR MONEY, AND THEY ARE
DELICIOUS MARINATED IN A SWEET
AND SPICY SAUCE, THEN BAKED
UNTIL TENDER AND JUICY.**

# chicken with fresh tomato and garlic sauce

**Serves 4**
Preparation 15 minutes
Cooking 30 minutes

1 tbsp olive oil

8 chicken thighs, skinned

2 tbsp wine vinegar (red or white)

300 g ripe tomatoes, roughly chopped

100 ml chicken stock

3 sprigs of fresh thyme

4 large garlic cloves, crushed

½ tsp paprika or cayenne pepper

2 pinches of sugar

pinch of salt

sprigs of fresh thyme to garnish (optional)

**Per serving**
kcal 211, protein 37 g, fat 5 g
(of which saturated fat 1 g),
carbohydrate 3 g (of which
sugars 3 g), fibre 0.5 g,
sodium 0.1 g

**1** Heat the oil in a deep frying pan and fry the chicken for 5 minutes, over a medium heat, until golden brown all over. Remove the chicken to a plate.

**2** Pour the vinegar into the pan and cook until reduced by half, scraping the bottom of the pan all the while with a wooden spatula. Add the tomatoes, stock, thyme, garlic, paprika or cayenne and sugar. Bring to the boil, then reduce the heat and return the chicken to the pan. Cover and cook gently for 30 minutes until the chicken is tender.

**3** Remove the chicken and arrange on a heated serving dish and keep warm. Discard the thyme from the sauce. Tip the sauce into a blender or processor and whizz until smooth. Pass the sauce through a sieve if you prefer a smoother texture. Season to taste, then pour over the chicken. Garnish, if liked, with sprigs of fresh thyme.

**COOK SMART**
• Fresh basil would also be good in this sauce, in place of the thyme.

• Keep tomatoes on a sunny windowsill – chilling them in the fridge dulls their flavour.

• Serve with pasta, tossed with olive oil and black pepper or Champion Hash Browns (see page 281).

MAKE THIS DISH IN HIGH SUMMER WHEN TOMATOES ARE AT THEIR BEST: PLUMP, JUICY AND INTENSELY FLAVOURED.

186

# spicy chicken casserole with apricots

1 tbsp vegetable oil

4 chicken breast fillets, about 150 g each

1 small onion, thinly sliced

3 garlic cloves, crushed

1 tbsp curry powder or paste

400 g can chopped tomatoes

30 g ready-to-eat dried apricots, thinly sliced

2 tsp chopped fresh thyme or ½ tsp dried

salt and freshly ground black pepper

To garnish
2 tbsp toasted flaked almonds

sprigs of fresh thyme (optional)

£ £

**Serves 4**
Preparation 10–15 minutes
Cooking 20 minutes

**Per serving**
kcal 275, protein 39 g, fat 10 g (of which saturated fat 1 g), carbohydrate 8.5 g (of which sugars 7 g), fibre 2 g, sodium 0.2 g

1 Heat the oil in large flameproof casserole over a medium heat. Add the chicken and sauté for about 3 minutes on each side until golden brown. Transfer the chicken to a plate, using tongs or a draining spoon.

2 Add the onion and garlic to the casserole and cook for 4–5 minutes until the onion is tender.

3 Stir in the curry powder or paste and cook for 1 minute. Add the tomatoes, apricots, thyme and salt and pepper to season, and bring to the boil.

4 Return the chicken (and any accumulated juices) to the casserole. Reduce the heat to a simmer, cover and cook for 20 minutes or until the chicken is cooked through.

5 Serve sprinkled with toasted, flaked almonds and garnish with fresh thyme, if liked.

**DRIED FRUIT MAKES A WONDERFUL ADDITION TO SPICY CASSEROLES, AND IT IS A GREAT WAY TO BOOST YOUR INTAKE OF FRUIT.**

## COOK SMART

• To prepare ahead, make up to the end of step 4. Cool and chill, then reheat at 170°C (gas 3) for 30–40 minutes until thoroughly heated through.

• Fresh thyme is an easy herb to grow in the garden, or in a pot on a sunny windowsill. It is good with fish and chicken dishes, and for pasta sauces.

• Serve on a bed of nutty brown or fragrant white basmati rice.

# chicken hash with potatoes and peppers

£

**4 servings**
Preparation 25 minutes
Cooking 25 minutes

500 g small new potatoes, scrubbed
2 tbsp vegetable oil
1 onion, chopped
1 green pepper, seeded and chopped
1 red pepper, seeded and chopped
150 g cooked chicken, diced
1 fat garlic clove, crushed
1 tsp paprika
½ tsp dried thyme
salt and freshly ground black pepper

**To serve**
few shakes of Tabasco or sweet
   chilli sauce

**Per serving**
kcal 240, protein 14 g, fat 9 g (of which
saturated fat 2 g), carbohydrate 27 g (of
which sugars 8 g), fibre 2.5 g, sodium 0.05 g

**1** Cook the potatoes in their skins in a pan of lightly salted boiling water for 20–25 minutes until tender. Drain, allow to cool, then cut into small cubes.

**2** Heat the oil in a large frying pan over a medium heat. Add the onion and sauté for 4 minutes or until lightly softened. Add the peppers and cook gently for a further 4–5 minutes.

**3** Stir in the potatoes, cook for 5 minutes until beginning to brown, then add the chicken and garlic. Sprinkle with paprika, thyme, salt and pepper.

**4** Press the hash into an even layer over the bottom of the pan, using a spatula or the back of a wooden spoon to squash it down. Cook, without stirring, for 5 minutes, until the bottom is nicely browned and crispy.

**5** Break up the mixture, then leave to cook again for a further 5 minutes until a crust forms on the bottom. Spoon on to plates and serve sprinkled with Tabasco or sweet chilli sauce, if liked.

## COOK SMART
• You need to use a waxy variety of potato with a firm flesh, such as Pink Fir Apple, Estima or Charlotte, which will hold their shape while cooking. Peel off the skins, after boiling, if preferred. Roast beef hash is also delicious, made as above with potatoes, but include some cooked greens, such as broccoli, rather than peppers.

• Serve with wedges of crisp dessert apples.

LEFTOVER CHICKEN FROM A ROAST IS PERFECT FOR THIS CRISPY GOLDEN HASH. IT'S EASY TO MAKE AND IDEAL FOR A ONE-POT SUPPER.

# easy chicken curry

**£**

**Serves 6**
Preparation 20 minutes
Cooking 45 minutes

1 chicken, about 1.5 kg, jointed
    into 6 pieces
2 tbsp vegetable oil
2 large onions, finely chopped
3 garlic cloves, finely chopped
2 tbsp curry powder or paste
500 ml chicken stock
1 tbsp tomato purée
½ tsp sugar
2 tbsp Greek-style yoghurt
salt and freshly ground
    black pepper
chopped fresh coriander to
    garnish

**1** Remove the skin from the chicken joints, if preferred, and season them with salt and pepper.

**2** Heat the oil in a deep frying pan or flameproof casserole. Add the chicken and brown it on all sides for 6–8 minutes over a medium heat. Remove and set aside on a plate.

**3** Cook the onions in the pan for 5 minutes until golden brown, stirring regularly. Add the garlic and curry powder or paste and cook, stirring, for 1 minute.

**4** Add the stock, tomato purée, sugar and seasoning. Mix well and add the chicken. Bring to the boil, then reduce the heat, cover and simmer for 45 minutes or until tender, turning the chicken pieces halfway through cooking.

**5** Remove the chicken to a serving dish using a draining spoon. Heat the sauce over a high heat for 2–3 minutes until reduced and thickened. Take the pan off the heat and stir in the yoghurt. Check seasoning, then pour the sauce over the chicken. Scatter over the chopped coriander.

**USING A GOOD-QUALITY CURRY POWDER OR PASTE TAKES ALL THE WORK OUT OF MAKING THIS FABULOUS DISH. FOR THE BEST FLAVOUR, MAKE IT A DAY AHEAD AND REHEAT.**

190

**COOK SMART**

• Add a finely diced eating apple and a handful of raisins to the curry 15 minutes before the end of cooking. You can substitute cream for the yoghurt.

• For a coconut flavour, use a 400 ml can of coconut milk and just 100 ml stock.

• Serve with boiled rice or warm naan bread. Make a banana raita accompaniment, with sliced bananas tossed in Greek-style yoghurt.

**Per serving**
kcal 270, protein 44 g,
fat 8 g (of which saturated
fat 1.5 g), carbohydrate 5 g
(of which sugars 4 g),
fibre 0.5 g, sodium 0.2 g

**COOK SMART**

• This dish also works well with fish. Use chunky fillets of white fish and gently simmer in fish stock for 20–30 minutes.

• Use the leftover egg whites to make a sweet soufflé omelette. Whisk until the whites form soft peaks, then fold in one to two whole eggs and ½ tbsp caster sugar. Cook in a non-stick frying pan, then spread the omelette with warmed jam and fold in half.

# gardener's chicken

FOR WINTER COMFORT, SERVE THIS CREAMY CHICKEN AND VEGETABLE CASSEROLE WITH MASHED POTATOES OR POLENTA AND SEASONAL GREENS.

££

**Serves 6**
Preparation 40 minutes
Cooking about 1 hour

**Per serving**
kcal 450, protein 66g, fat 16.5g (of which saturated fat 6g), carbohydrate 10.5g (of which sugars 9g), fibre 5g, sodium 0.2g

2 tbsp vegetable oil

1 oven-ready chicken, around 1.8kg, jointed into 6 pieces

25g butter

400g carrots, peeled and cut into chunky batons

1kg leeks, white ends sliced and green ends shredded

25g fresh flat-leaf parsley

600ml chicken stock

2 egg yolks

2 tbsp crème fraîche

salt and freshly ground black pepper

1 Heat the oil in a large flameproof casserole or deep frying pan. Add the chicken and brown it on all sides for 8–10 minutes, over a medium heat. Remove and set aside. Melt the butter in the casserole or pan. Add the carrots and the whites of the leeks. Stir well, cover and cook gently for 10 minutes, over a low heat. Season with salt and pepper.

2 Place the chicken pieces on top of the vegetables. Scatter over about two thirds of the parsley sprigs and the shredded leek-greens. Pour over stock to cover, bring to the boil, then reduce the heat, cover and simmer for 1 hour or until the chicken is tender.

3 Discard the parsley. Lift out the vegetables and chicken using a draining spoon and put on a serving dish.

4 Boil the stock left in the pan over a high heat for 5 minutes until reduced by a third. Reduce the heat.

5 Mix the egg yolks with the crème fraîche. Gradually blend this mixture into the reduced stock and simmer gently, stirring for 2 minutes, until thickened. Do not let the sauce boil. Roughly chop the remaining parsley. Pour the sauce over the chicken and sprinkle with the parsley.

ADDING CHICKPEAS, DRIED FRUIT AND WARMING SPICES TO MEAT OR POULTRY STEWS IS TYPICAL OF MOROCCAN COOKING. SERVE WITH COUSCOUS OR FLATBREAD FOR A WHOLESOME MEAL.

# moroccan braised chicken

**Serves 4**

Preparation 15 minutes
Cooking 15–20 minutes

**50 g dried apricots**
**1 tbsp olive oil**
**4 chicken breast fillets**
**1 large onion, finely chopped**
**6 garlic cloves, crushed**
**2 celery sticks, thinly sliced**
**400 g can chickpeas, drained and rinsed**
**400 g can chopped tomatoes**
**2 tsp grated lemon zest**
**2 tbsp lemon juice**
**1½ tsp ground coriander**
**freshly ground black pepper**
**2 tbsp chopped fresh coriander**

**Per serving**
kcal 300, protein 40 g, fat 7 g (of which
saturated fat 1 g), carbohydrate 22 g (of
which sugars 9 g), fibre 5 g, sodium 0.3 g

**1** Put the apricots in a small bowl and pour over
250 ml boiling water. Leave to stand for 10 minutes,
then strain, reserving the soaking liquid, and chop
the apricots.

**2** Meanwhile, heat the oil in a large, deep frying pan
or flame-proof casserole over a medium heat. Add
the chicken and cook gently for 3 minutes until
golden brown all over. Transfer the chicken to a plate.

**3** Add the onion and garlic to the frying pan and cook,
stirring frequently, for 7 minutes or until the onion
is tender. Add the celery and cook for 3 minutes.

**4** Stir in the apricots, the reserved liquid, the
chickpeas, the tomatoes with their juice, the
lemon zest and juice, ground coriander and pepper
to season.

**5** Bring to the boil and return the chicken to the pan.
Reduce the heat to a simmer, cover and cook for
15–20 minutes or until the chicken is cooked
through. Taste to check the seasoning, then stir
in the chopped coriander just before serving.

**COOK SMART**

• This recipe could also be made with cubed lean lamb
but would need to cook for about 1 hour. Serve with flat
bread, rice or couscous and a vegetable dish such as
Carrots with Cumin (see page 258).

# baked barbecued chicken with vegetable fried rice

££

**Serves 4**
Preparation 15 minutes,
 plus at least 3 hours
 or overnight marinating
Cooking 30–35 minutes

**8 chicken thighs, about
 1 kg in total, skinned**

**Barbecue marinade**
**4 tbsp soy sauce**
**1 tbsp tomato purée**
**1 tbsp runny honey**
**1 tbsp Worcestershire
 sauce**
**2 tsp mustard powder**
**1 garlic clove, crushed**

**Vegetable rice**
**250 g long-grain rice**
**2 tbsp vegetable oil**
**1 red onion, halved and
 thinly sliced**
**1 garlic clove, crushed**
**75 g button mushrooms,
 quartered**
**50 g mange-tout, sliced
 lengthways**
**2 tbsp chopped fresh
 mixed herbs (such as
 parsley, oregano and
 thyme)**
**25 g butter**
**2 tbsp flaked almonds,
 toasted**
**salt and freshly ground
 black pepper**

**Per serving**
kcal 590, protein 45 g,
fat 20 g (of which saturated
fat 5.5 g), carbohydrate 62 g
(of which sugars 7 g),
fibre 1.5 g, sodium 1.3 g

**A TANGY BARBECUE
MARINADE TRANSFORMS
THESE SIMPLE BAKED
CHICKEN THIGHS INTO
A SPECIAL MEAL.**

**1** Arrange the chicken thighs in a shallow non-metallic dish. Mix together the marinade ingredients, add salt and pepper to season and pour over the thighs, ensuring they are well coated. Cover and leave in a cool place for at least 3 hours, or overnight in the fridge.

**2** Preheat the oven to 200°C (gas 6). Transfer the chicken to a roasting tin (preferably non-stick) and spoon over any remaining marinade. Put into the hot oven and bake for 30–35 minutes, basting from time to time, until the thighs are well browned and most of the marinade has evaporated, leaving a sticky glaze on the chicken.

**3** Meanwhile, cook the rice in a large pan of lightly salted boiling water for 12–15 minutes until just tender. Drain, rinse with cold water and drain again.

**4** When the chicken has cooked for 25 minutes, heat the oil in a wok or large frying pan. Add the onion and cook gently for 2–3 minutes, then add the garlic and mushrooms and cook for a further 2–3 minutes until the vegetables are just soft.

**5** Add the mange-tout and cook for a further minute, then stir in the rice. Reheat thoroughly, tossing all the time. Mix in the herbs, butter and almonds, and check the seasoning. Cover to keep warm.

**6** Test that the chicken is cooked – the juices should run clear when the thickest part of the meat is pierced with a skewer or a sharp knife. Pile the chicken on top of the rice and serve hot.

**COOK SMART**
• To accompany, roast two courgettes and two red peppers, cut into chunky pieces in a little oil in the oven.

# midsummer chicken

£ £

**Serves 4**
Preparation  20 minutes
Cooking  45 minutes

**4 chicken portions (such
as large thighs or
drumsticks)**

**1 tbsp vegetable oil**

**2 rindless, smoked bacon
rashers, chopped into
strips**

**2 large onions, thinly
sliced**

**2 red peppers, seeded and
diced**

**2 courgettes, diced**

**4 firm tomatoes, diced**

**4 garlic cloves, crushed**

**2 sprigs of fresh thyme or
½ tsp dried**

**pinch of cayenne pepper**

**pinch of salt**

**sprigs of fresh thyme to
garnish (optional)**

**Per serving**
kcal 300, protein 47 g,
fat 6 g (of which saturated
fat 1 g), carbohydrate 15 g
(of which sugars 13 g),
fibre 3.5 g, sodium 0.3 g

---

**COOK SMART**

• An easy way to skin
chicken portions is to
hold the chicken in one
hand, then tug the skin off
with the other hand, using
a piece of kitchen paper to
get a good grip.

• Some hot garlic bread
would make a delicious
accompaniment.

---

**1** Remove the skin from the chicken, if preferred. Heat
the oil in a large frying pan or flame-proof casserole
and brown the chicken and bacon over a medium
heat. Remove with a draining spoon and set aside.

**2** Add the onions to the pan and cook for 5 minutes
until softened. Add the peppers, courgettes,
tomatoes, garlic, thyme and cayenne pepper.
Cook gently for 5 minutes. Season with a little salt.

**3** Return the chicken and bacon to the pan. Cover
and cook gently for 45 minutes or until the chicken
is tender. Turn the chicken halfway through
the cooking.

**4** Serve each chicken portion on a bed of the
vegetables, with some of the vegetables spooned
on top. Remove the cooked thyme and garnish, if
liked, with extra fresh thyme.

**BRAISED CHICKEN
PIECES ON A BED
OF SUMMER
VEGETABLES
MAKE A PRETTY
DISH THAT IS
SIMPLY BURSTING
WITH FLAVOUR.**

POULTRY & GAME

# roast chicken with herb stuffing

WHEN IT COMES TO A SUNDAY LUNCH OR SPECIAL DINNER, YOU CAN'T BEAT ROAST CHICKEN. THIS VERSION, WITH ITS FRAGRANT FRESH HERB STUFFING, IS SIMPLY THE BEST.

## COOK SMART

• If you have the giblets, use them to make a flavoursome stock. Put them in a small pan and cover with water. Add some chopped onion, celery, a few fresh herbs and some seasoning, then bring to the boil. Reduce heat, cover and simmer gently for 30 minutes, then strain before using.

196

**Per serving**
kcal 443, protein 64g,
fat 11g (of which saturated fat 3.5g), carbohydrate 18g (of which sugars 1.5g), fibre 1g, sodium 0.3g

£ £

**Serves 6**
Preparation 30 minutes
Cooking 2 hours

1 large, free-range chicken, about 2kg (giblets removed)
1 lemon, cut into quarters

**Stuffing**
25g butter
2 tbsp olive oil
1 onion, finely chopped
2 celery sticks, finely chopped
100g fresh white breadcrumbs
2 tbsp chopped fresh herbs (such as thyme, sage, parsley or tarragon) or 2 tsp dried mixed herbs
1 egg, beaten
salt and freshly ground black pepper

**Gravy**
2 tbsp plain flour
300ml giblet stock (or vegetable cooking water)
150ml dry white wine or apple juice

**To garnish**
sprigs of fresh herbs
1 lemon, cut into wedges

1 Preheat the oven to 220°C (gas 7). To make the stuffing, gently heat the butter and 1 tbsp of the oil in a large frying pan over a medium heat and cook the onion and celery for 10 minutes until soft. Remove from the heat and tip into a bowl. Stir in the breadcrumbs, herbs, egg and seasoning, and mix well to bind the mixture together.

2 Loosely stuff the neck end of the chicken with half the stuffing, pushing it well up inside to make a neat shape. Fold the flap of skin underneath and secure with a small skewer or cocktail stick. Put the lemon quarters in the cavity of the bird and tie the legs together with kitchen string. Put the remaining stuffing in a small, lightly buttered dish and cook for the last 30 minutes of the cooking time.

3 Place the chicken, breast-side down, on a rack in a roasting tin. Pour about 250ml water under the rack. (This creates steam and helps to keep the bird moist. It will also collect the juices that drip down during cooking and can be used for making the gravy.) Roast for 30 minutes.

4 Remove the tin from the oven and carefully turn the chicken over so it is now breast-side up. Rub the remaining olive oil over the breast and season. Reduce the oven temperature to 150°C (gas 2). Roast the chicken for a further 1½ hours, basting every 20 minutes with the juices in the tin until it is cooked through. (To test, insert a skewer into the thickest part of the thigh — the juices should run clear.)

5 Tip the bird up slightly so any lemony juices inside the cavity run into the tin. Remove chicken, cover with foil and allow to stand for 10–15 minutes before carving.

6 Meanwhile, make the gravy. Blend the flour with a little water in a jug to make a paste. Gradually stir in the roasting juices, then pour into a saucepan. Add the stock and wine or apple juice, bring to the boil, stirring until smooth and thickened. Season to taste, then pour into a gravy jug. Place the chicken on a large plate and garnish with fresh herb sprigs and lemon wedges.

# onion roasted turkey drumsticks

£

**Serves 4**
Preparation 10 minutes,
    plus 2–3 hours marinating
Cooking 1½ hours

**2 turkey drumsticks**

**grated zest and juice of
    1 lemon**

**1 tbsp olive oil**

**2 tbsp mild curry powder**

**1 onion, finely chopped**

**1 tbsp vegetable oil**

**25 g butter**

**125 ml chicken stock**

**3 tbsp crème fraîche**

**salt and freshly ground
    black pepper**

**To garnish**
**1 lemon, cut into thin wedges**

**sprigs of fresh parsley**

---

### COOK SMART

• Instead of large turkey drumsticks, use four large or eight regular-sized chicken drumsticks. Cook for about 40 minutes, or according to the instructions on the pack.

• Serve with fluffy basmati rice – you could toss the cooked rice with the grated zest of one lemon and 2 tbsp chopped fresh parsley.

---

**Per serving**
kcal 350, protein 37 g,
fat 20 g (of which saturated
fat 8.5 g), carbohydrate 4 g
(of which sugars 1 g),
fibre 2 g, sodium 0.3 g

---

**1** Score several slits on each of the turkey drumsticks, using a sharp knife. Mix together the lemon zest, olive oil and curry powder, and rub it all over the turkey, working it well into the cuts. Season with salt and pepper and place in a shallow dish. Pour over 2 tbsp of the lemon juice, cover and leave in the fridge to marinate for 2–3 hours.

**2** Preheat the oven to 190°C (gas 5). Toss the onions with the vegetable oil, then spread them over the base of an ovenproof dish. Place the turkey on top.

**3** Roast for 30 minutes, then turn the turkey, spread with the butter and roast for a further 30 minutes. Turn the turkey drumsticks over again and baste with some of the cooking juices. Cook for a further 30 minutes or until the turkey is cooked through.

**4** Place the turkey on a heated serving dish. Pour the remainder of the lemon juice into the cooking dish and scrape up the onions with a wooden spatula. Pour into a small pan, add the stock, heat gently, then stir in the crème fraîche and warm through.

**5** Pour the sauce over the turkey and garnish with lemon slices and parsley. Grind some pepper coarsely over the top.

TURKEY DRUMSTICKS MAKE AN ECONOMICAL MEAL. HERE THEY ARE MARINATED WITH A SPICY BASTE, THEN ROASTED AND SERVED WITH A CREAMY ONION AND LEMON SAUCE.

# chicken and mushroom pie

A GOOD PIE IS PERFECT COMFORT FOOD, AND THIS ONE IS NO EXCEPTION. FOR A HEALTHY BALANCE, SERVE WITH PLENTY OF SEASONAL GREENS.

**Serves 4**
Preparation 40 minutes
Cooking 25–30 minutes

**25 g butter**
**225 g button mushrooms, halved**
**250 g mascarpone or full-fat cream cheese**
**150 ml semi-skimmed milk**
**½ tsp English mustard**
**500 g cooked chicken, cut into bite-sized pieces**
**3 tbsp snipped fresh chives**
**300 g ready-made puff pastry**
**salt and freshly ground black pepper**

**Per serving**
kcal 880, protein 39 g, fat 67 g (of which saturated
fat 34 g), carbohydrate 29 g (of which sugars 3 g),
fibre 0.5 g, sodium 0.6 g

**1** Preheat the oven to 200°C (gas 6) and place a baking sheet inside
to heat. Melt the butter in a large frying pan and gently cook the
mushrooms for 4–5 minutes until tender.

**2** Beat the mascarpone or cream cheese in a bowl until softened.
Reserve 2 tbsp of the milk, then mix the rest into the cheese
with the mustard to make a thick sauce. Add the chicken, chives
and the mushrooms with their juices to the cheese mixture. Season
to taste, then spoon the mixture into a 1 litre pie dish. Place a pie
funnel or an upturned ovenproof china eggcup, if you have one, in
the middle of the filling to support the pastry lid.

**3** Roll out the pastry on a lightly floured surface so that it is about
5 cm larger all round than the pie dish. Cut off a 3 cm strip around
the edge, then press this strip on to the rim of the pie dish. Lightly
brush with water, then lift the pastry lid on top, pressing the edges
together to seal.

**4** Trim the excess pastry, pinch to seal, then 'flake' the edges (see
below). Re-roll the pastry trimmings and cut out leaves to decorate
and stick them onto the pastry lid with a little of the reserved milk.
Glaze all over with the remaining milk and cut two slits in the top to
allow steam to escape.

**5** Place the pie on the hot baking sheet and bake for 25–30 minutes
or until the pastry is nicely puffed and golden brown. Leave to stand
for 5 minutes before serving, sprinkled with pepper.

**COOK SMART**
• For a chicken and leek pie, leave out the mushrooms and cook two sliced
leeks in the butter until soft.

• For cooked chicken, a hot roasted chicken from the supermarket is likely to
be cheaper, and more convenient, than buying chicken portions.

• To 'flake' the edges, hold a sharp knife horizontally to the side of the pastry
edge and make shallow cuts all the way round.

THIS HEARTY FRENCH, COUNTRY-STYLE CASSEROLE IS REDOLENT WITH THE FLAVOURS OF RED WINE, ORANGE ZEST AND AROMATIC THYME.

# chicken in red wine

£ £

**Serves 4**
Preparation 20 minutes
Cooking 1 hour

1 tbsp olive oil

15 g butter

1 oven-ready chicken, about 1.35 kg

2 small onions, sliced

2 carrots, peeled and diced

300 ml chicken stock

125 ml full-bodied red wine

2 sprigs of fresh thyme

grated zest of 1 small orange

¼ tsp ground nutmeg

2 tbsp crème fraîche

salt and freshly ground black pepper

sprigs of fresh thyme to garnish (optional)

### COOK SMART

• Ask your butcher for the chicken giblets. Add them to the casserole with the chicken – the flavour will enrich the sauce. Remove them at the end of step 3.

• If preferred you could use four chicken portions.

• Buy shallots when you see them and use whole in place of sliced onions.

**Per serving**
kcal 430, protein 61 g,
fat 14 g (of which saturated
fat 7 g), carbohydrate 8.5 g
(of which sugars 7 g),
fibre 2 g, sodium 0.2 g

**1** Heat the oil and butter in a large flameproof casserole over a medium heat. Add the chicken and brown it all over for 5 minutes, then remove to a plate.

**2** Put aside a few small onion rings for garnish, then add the rest of the onions and carrots to the casserole and cook gently for 5 minutes until lightly coloured.

**3** Pour over the stock and the wine. Add the thyme, orange zest, nutmeg and salt and pepper to season. Bring to the boil, then reduce the heat and put the chicken back in. Cover and simmer gently for 1 hour or until cooked through, basting the bird with the cooking juices from time to time.

**4** Lift out the chicken and carve into serving pieces. Cover and keep warm.

**5** Remove the cooked thyme from the casserole. Stir the crème fraîche into the cooking juices and allow to simmer gently, uncovered, for several minutes to thicken slightly. Put the chicken back on top and serve from the casserole or arrange on a serving dish. Garnish with fresh thyme and the reserved onion rings. Serve with lots of crusty French bread and a big green salad.

# sweet and sour turkey meatballs

£ £

**Serves 4**
Preparation 40 minutes
Cooking 15 minutes

**Meatballs**
450 g minced turkey
75 g fresh white
    breadcrumbs
1 egg, lightly beaten
¼ tsp ground ginger
¼ tsp ground cumin
salt and freshly ground
    black pepper
2 tbsp plain flour for
    dusting
sunflower oil for frying

**Fruit sauce**
75 g dried cranberries
430 g can pineapple pieces
    in natural juice
2 tbsp caster sugar
1½ tsp cornflour
3 tbsp cranberry sauce
    or jelly

**Per serving**
kcal 472, protein 28 g,
fat 13 g (of which saturated
fat 2.5 g), carbohydrate 64 g
(of which sugars 42 g),
fibre 1.5 g, sodium 0.3 g

1 Put the minced turkey in a bowl with the breadcrumbs, egg, ginger and cumin. Season with salt and pepper, then combine the ingredients with your hands until thoroughly mixed. Now lightly flour your hands and shape the mixture into sixteen small walnut-sized balls. Place these on a plate and chill until ready to cook.

2 For the sauce, put the dried cranberries in a small saucepan. Drain the pineapple, and add all but 1 tbsp of the juice to the pan. Stir in the sugar and heat gently, stirring occasionally, until the sugar has dissolved. Meanwhile, chop the pineapple into small pieces.

3 Blend the cornflour with the reserved pineapple juice and add to the saucepan, stirring all the time until the sauce clears and thickens. Add the chopped pineapple and cranberry sauce or jelly and warm through, stirring. Turn off the heat.

4 Heat a little oil in a large frying pan and gently fry the meatballs, in batches, until they are golden brown all over. Drain on kitchen paper. Wipe the pan clean, then return all the meatballs. Pour over the sauce, cover and simmer gently for 15 minutes or until cooked through. Serve hot with rice or spaghetti.

**COOK SMART**
• To make your own mince, use fresh turkey meat from either the breast or leg. Mince in a food processor or mincing machine or ask the butcher to do it for you. Use within two days. Minced chicken or pork makes a good alternative.

THE TANGY FRUIT FLAVOURS OF TROPICAL PINEAPPLE AND TART CRANBERRIES ARE THE PERFECT PARTNERS FOR THESE LIGHTLY SPICED MEATBALLS.

A PASTA BAKE IS THE PERFECT ONE-POT DISH FOR AN INFORMAL PARTY. THIS ONE IS HEALTHY, HEARTY AND UTTERLY DELICIOUS.

# turkey and vegetable pasta bake

**£**

**Serves 6**
Preparation 25 minutes
Cooking 25–30 minutes

**250 g penne**

**1 tbsp olive oil**

**1 large onion, chopped**

**375 g minced turkey**

**2 x 400 g cans chopped tomatoes with herbs**

**300 g frozen, sliced green beans, thawed**

**300 g frozen broccoli florets, thawed and chopped**

**150 ml soured cream**

**50 g Parmesan, freshly grated**

**salt and freshly ground black pepper**

**Per serving**
kcal 372, protein 29 g,
fat 11 g (of which saturated
fat 5.5 g), carbohydrate 41 g
(of which sugars 9 g), fibre 5 g,
sodium 0.2 g

**1** Cook the pasta in a large pan of lightly salted boiling water for 10–12 minutes, or according to the packet instructions, until al dente. Drain and transfer to a large bowl. Preheat the oven to 180°C (gas 4).

**2** Meanwhile, heat the oil in a large deep pan over a medium heat, add the onion and cook for 5 minutes or until softened. Add the turkey to the pan and cook for 4–5 minutes until lightly browned. Stir in the tomatoes with their juice and cook for 5 minutes or until the liquid has reduced by half.

**3** Stir the tomato mixture into the pasta and season with salt and pepper.

**4** Add the beans, broccoli and soured cream to the pasta mixture and stir everything together well.

**5** Spread the mixture in a large, deep baking dish, measuring about 33 x 23 cm. Sprinkle the Parmesan over the top.

**6** Bake for 25–30 minutes until golden and slightly crispy on top. Serve hot.

---

**COOK SMART**

• Canned tomatoes flavoured with herbs are a useful convenience product. However, if using regular canned chopped tomatoes, add ½ tsp dried thyme or mixed herbs to the mixture in step 2.

• For a vegetarian variation, use Quorn mince and replace the Parmesan with an alternative cheese.

• Serve with a mixed-leaf salad tossed with a fruity vinaigrette dressing.

# sausage and coleslaw pitta pockets

**Serves 4**
Preparation 15 minutes
Cooking 15 minutes

2 tsp soy sauce

2 tsp tomato ketchup

1 tsp Dijon mustard

1 tsp light muscovado
    sugar

450 g (8 thick) turkey
    sausages

4 large pitta breads

**Fruity coleslaw**
25 g sultanas

1 tbsp lemon juice

300 g firm white cabbage

1 eating apple

2 carrots, peeled and
    coarsely grated

3 tbsp mayonnaise

3 tbsp Greek-style yoghurt

salt and freshly ground
    black pepper

**204**

## COOK SMART

• Take care when grilling
the pitta breads. They
should be warm and
steaming, but don't brown
them or they will be
difficult to split open.

• Leftover coleslaw,
covered in the fridge, will
keep for 2–3 days. Use it
to fill out sandwiches for
packed lunches.

• This recipe suggests
turkey sausages but
you could use any good
plump ones.

**Per serving**
kcal 611, protein 45 g,
fat 20 g (of which saturated
fat 4.5 g), carbohydrate 69 g
(of which sugars 19 g),
fibre 6 g, sodium 0.9 g

1 Mix together the soy sauce, ketchup, mustard and
sugar in a small bowl and lightly brush over the
sausages. Set aside while making the coleslaw.

2 Put the sultanas in a large bowl and sprinkle with
1 tsp of the lemon juice. Remove any discoloured
leaves and core the cabbage, then shred as finely
as possible. Quarter, core and dice the apple, then
toss immediately with the remaining lemon juice.
Add to the bowl with the cabbage and carrots.

3 Mix together the mayonnaise and yoghurt, season
to taste, then stir into the coleslaw, using a large
spoon to combine thoroughly.

4 Put the sausages on a foil-lined grill pan and place
under a preheated moderate grill. Cook for about
15 minutes, turning frequently until browned all
over and cooked through. Remove the sausages
and thickly slice.

5 Grill the pitta breads for 1–2 minutes on each side
(or pop them in the toaster or microwave) to warm.
Cut them in half lengthways and spoon some
coleslaw into each. Pack in the sausage slices and
some more coleslaw and serve straight away, while
the pittas and sausages are still warm. Serve any
remaining coleslaw alongside.

PLUMP SAUSAGES BRUSHED WITH A STICKY GLAZE AND
SLICED MAKE A QUICK AND EASY FILLING FOR WARM
PITTA BREAD WITH FRUITY COLESLAW.

# turkey and leek frittata

**THIS FRITTATA IS A GREAT WAY TO USE UP LEFTOVER TURKEY AND PASTA, BUT IF YOU HAVE SOME LEFTOVER CHICKEN OR HAM, USE THAT INSTEAD.**

£ £

**Serves 6**
Preparation  15 minutes
Cooking  10 minutes

**3 tbsp olive oil**

**1 red pepper, seeded and diced**

**2 leeks, trimmed and finely sliced**

**25 g stoned black olives, halved (optional)**

**250 g cooked turkey, diced**

**100 g cooked pasta shapes (such as fusilli or macaroni)**

**6 eggs, beaten**

**3 tbsp chopped fresh parsley**

**75 g Gruyère or mature Cheddar, thinly sliced**

**salt and freshly ground black pepper**

**Per serving**
kcal 300, protein 24.5 g, fat 20 g (of which saturated fat 6 g), carbohydrate 5.5 g (of which sugars 2 g), fibre 1.5 g, sodium 0.3 g

**1** Heat the oil in a large, deep frying pan, about 25 cm in diameter, with a flameproof handle. Add the red pepper and leeks and fry gently for 10 minutes until softened. Toss in the olives, if using, the turkey and the cooked pasta, ensuring all the ingredients are well mixed.

**2** Beat the eggs with the chopped parsley and season well. Pour into the hot pan and swirl around to allow the eggs to settle evenly. Cook over a moderate heat for 4–5 minutes or until nearly set. Meanwhile, preheat a moderate grill.

**3** Arrange the cheese over the top of the frittata. Place under the grill for 5 minutes or until the cheese melts and bubbles.

**4** Slide the tortilla onto a hot plate and serve, cut into wedges. It can be eaten warm or cold.

**COOK SMART**

• If you don't have any leftover cooked pasta, use 50 g (dry weight) pasta and cook it first in a large pan of lightly salted boiling water, for 10–12 minutes, or according to the packet instructions, until al dente. Drain thoroughly.

SWEET, TENDER RABBIT MEAT IS PERFECT IN CASSEROLES, AND MAKES A GREAT ALTERNATIVE TO THE USUAL CHICKEN.

# creamy rabbit casserole

£ £

**Serves 4**
Preparation 30 minutes
Cooking 1¼ –1½ hours

4 rabbit joints, about 750 g in total
3 tbsp plain flour
2 tbsp vegetable oil
15 g butter
1 small onion, halved and sliced
2 large leeks, trimmed and
    diagonally sliced
1 garlic clove, crushed
200 ml dry cider
200 ml vegetable or chicken stock
3 tbsp wholegrain mustard
4 carrots, peeled and cut into
    chunky batons
½ head celeriac, peeled and cut
    into chunks
1 bay leaf
sprig of fresh thyme (optional)
4 tbsp crème fraîche
salt and freshly ground black pepper
chopped fresh parsley to garnish

**Per serving**
kcal 480, protein 43 g, fat 25 g (of which
saturated fat 10 g), carbohydrate 16 g (of
which sugars 6 g), fibre 4 g, sodium 0.3 g

**1** Preheat the oven to 170°C (gas 3). Season 2 tbsp of the flour with salt and pepper, then toss the rabbit joints in the flour to coat lightly, shaking off any excess.

**2** Heat the oil and butter in a large flameproof casserole over a high heat and brown the rabbit joints on all sides. Remove with a draining spoon and set aside.

**3** Reduce the heat to low, then add the onion and leeks to the casserole. Gently cook for 5 minutes, stirring frequently until beginning to soften. Add the garlic, then sprinkle over the remaining 1 tbsp of flour. Cook for a further minute, stirring all the time.

**4** Gradually stir in the cider, followed by the stock and mustard. Return the rabbit to the casserole with the carrots, celeriac, bay leaf and thyme, if using. Slowly bring to the boil. Cover the casserole and cook in the oven for 1¼–1½ hours or until the rabbit is very tender and the vegetables are cooked. Remove the bay leaf and thyme.

**5** Transfer the rabbit and vegetables to a heated serving dish to keep warm. Stir the crème fraîche into the cooking juices in the casserole and heat through on the hob. Taste and adjust the seasoning. Pour the sauce over the rabbit and vegetables and sprinkle with chopped parsley before serving.

## COOK SMART
• Choose a dry or medium fruity cider; most supermarkets sell it in small cans and bottles. Dry white wine makes a good alternative if you have some to hand.

• Chicken leg joints may be used instead of rabbit for this dish and three chopped celery sticks as an alternative to celeriac.

• Cook some extra vegetables in the oven at the same time as the casserole; braised finely shredded red or green cabbage flavoured with crushed juniper berries would be a good accompaniment.

# hunter's rabbit

£ £

**Serves 6**
Preparation  20 minutes
Cooking  50 minutes

2 tbsp olive oil

1 rabbit, about 1–1.3 kg,
  cut into 6 pieces

3 rindless smoked bacon
  rashers, chopped

200 g shallots, peeled

1 tbsp plain flour

300 ml dry white wine

100 ml vegetable or
  chicken stock

2 carrots, peeled and
  sliced

1 bouquet garni

300 g chestnut
  mushrooms, quartered

salt and freshly ground
  black pepper

---

**COOK SMART**

• Many large supermarkets stock rabbit, as do some butchers and game suppliers. If preferred off the bone, use 500 g boneless rabbit cut into large chunks.

• This casserole is delicious served with small fried potatoes and apple sauce (see page 34).

• First soak shallots in boiling water for 10 minutes so they are easier to peel.

---

**Per serving**
kcal 350, protein 42 g,
fat 12 g (of which saturated
fat 4 g), carbohydrate 10 g
(of which sugars 5 g),
fibre 2 g, sodium 0.4 g

---

**1** Heat the oil in a large flameproof casserole, add the rabbit pieces and the bacon and cook gently over a medium heat for 4–5 minutes or until browned. Remove from the pan and set aside.

**2** Add the shallots to the casserole dish and cook gently for a few minutes, then sprinkle over the flour and blend in. Pour in the wine, scraping up any crispy bits on the bottom of the casserole, using a spatula, then stir in the stock. Return the rabbit and bacon to the casserole.

**3** Add the carrots, bouquet garni and salt and pepper to season, then cover and cook gently for 30 minutes.

**4** Add the mushrooms, cover and cook for a further 20 minutes or until the rabbit is tender. Remove the bouquet garni before serving and taste to check the seasoning.

**COOKING RABBIT IN WHITE WINE WITH EARTHY CHESTNUT MUSHROOMS AND FRAGRANT HERBS GIVES IT A REAL TASTE OF THE FOREST.**

# citrus
# duck
# stir-fry

£ £ £

**Serves 4**

Preparation  30 minutes, plus at least
  20 minutes marinating
Cooking  7 minutes

**2 boneless duck breasts, skinned and
  cut into strips**

**¼ tsp Chinese five-spice powder**

**1 tbsp soy sauce**

**2 tsp toasted sesame oil**

**100 ml orange juice**

**2 oranges**

**1 tbsp caster sugar**

**1 tbsp red wine vinegar**

**1 tsp cornflour**

**1½ tbsp vegetable oil**

**4 spring onions, trimmed and diagonally
  sliced**

**125 g mange-tout, cut in half lengthways**

**200 g bean sprouts**

**Per serving**

kcal 260, protein 23 g, fat 12 g (of which
saturated fat 2 g), carbohydrate 18 g (of
which sugars 16 g), fibre 3 g, sodium 0.4 g

---

**COOK SMART**

• Five spice powder is a mixture of ground
star anise, Sichuan peppercorns, fennel,
cloves and cinnamon. It lends an exotic
fragrance to marinades. You'll find it in the
spice section at supermarkets as well as
Chinese grocers.

• Serve with rice noodles. Some prawn
crackers would would also be a fun
accompaniment for this dish.

• Use chopsticks, rather than cutlery, to
eat with.

---

208

---

1 Place the duck strips in a shallow dish. Mix together
the Chinese five-spice powder, soy sauce, sesame
oil and 2 tbsp of the orange juice. Pour over the
duck, stir to coat, then leave to marinate while
preparing the rest of the dish. (If time allows,
marinate the duck in the fridge for 2–3 hours. Let
it stand at room temperature for about 30 minutes
before starting to cook.)

2 Meanwhile, thinly pare the zest from half of one of
the oranges, then cut into fine strips. Add the strips
to a pan of cold water, bring to the boil, then drain
and set aside. Cut away all the peel and white pith
from the oranges using a sharp knife, then cut the
flesh into segments.

3 Heat the sugar and vinegar in a small saucepan until
the sugar has dissolved. Blend the cornflour with
1 tbsp of orange juice, then pour the remaining
orange juice into the saucepan. Bring to the boil,
then add the cornflour mixture, stirring all the time
until the sauce has thickened and cleared. Add
the strips of orange zest and turn off the heat.

4 Remove the duck from the marinade with a draining
spoon. Heat a wok or large frying pan, add 1 tbsp
of the oil, then, when hot, add the duck and stir-fry
for 2–3 minutes until tender. Remove and set aside.

5 Add the remaining oil to the wok, add the spring
onions and mange-tout and stir-fry for 1 minute.
Add the bean sprouts and stir-fry for a further
2 minutes or until cooked, but still crisp.

6 Return the duck to the pan with the orange
segments, sauce and any remaining marinade.
Bring to the boil and let it bubble for about
30 seconds or until everything is hot. Serve
straight away.

DISTINCTIVE, GAMEY-TASTING
DUCK BREASTS GO BEAUTIFULLY
WITH THE SWEET, JUICY APRICOTS.

# duck
# with apricots

£ £ £

**Serves 4**
Preparation  10 minutes
Cooking  50 minutes

**4 duck legs**
**1 tsp salt**
**1¼ tsp Chinese five-spice powder**
**411 g can apricot halves in juice, drained**
**1 tbsp caster sugar**
**2 tsp flour**
**100 ml chicken stock**
**1 tbsp white wine vinegar**
**2 tsp runny honey**
**piece of stem ginger in syrup, drained
    and sliced into thin sticks**

**Per serving**
kcal 250, protein 28 g, fat 10 g (of which
saturated fat 2 g), carbohydrate 12 g (of
which sugars 10 g), fibre 0.5 g, sodium 0.6 g

**1** Preheat the oven to 200°C (gas 6). Place the duck legs on a rack in a roasting tin, prick the skin all over with a fork, then sprinkle with salt and 1 tsp of the five-spice powder to help to crisp and flavour the skin.

**2** Roast for 50 minutes until crispy and cooked through. Spread the apricots in a shallow ovenproof dish (reserving the juice), sprinkle with the sugar and bake in the oven for the last 15 minutes of the duck cooking time until lightly caramelised.

**3** Remove the duck to a warmed serving plate and pour off all but 1 tbsp of fat from the tin and place on the hob. Stir in the flour and cook, stirring, until well browned. Add the stock, vinegar and reserved apricot juice and cook, stirring, until thickened. Stir in the honey, ginger and ¼ tsp of five-spice powder.

**4** Serve the duck with the hot apricots and spoon over the fruity sauce.

**COOK SMART**
• For a fruity variation, replace the apricots with canned peaches, plums or pineapple.
• This would be good served with basmati and wild rice and mange-tout.

£ £ £

**Serves 4**
Preparation 30 minutes
Cooking 50 minutes

**1 plump oven-ready pheasant, about
        600–800 g**
**2 smoked, streaky bacon rashers**
**1 tbsp vegetable oil**
**150 ml soured cream**

**Stuffing**
**15 g butter**
**2 shallots, finely chopped**
**2 dried figs, finely chopped**
**150 g sausage meat**
**salt and freshly ground black pepper**

**Per serving**
kcal 500, protein 39 g, fat 28 g (of
which saturated fat 15 g), carbohydrate
10 g (of which sugars 6 g), fibre 1 g,
sodium 0.6 g

---

**COOK SMART**
• Choose a plump hen pheasant for
preference; although smaller than a
cock pheasant, the meat will be more
succulent and tender.

• Creamy mashed potatoes and broccoli
would make a lovely vegetable
accompaniment.

• In season, you could also serve this
pheasant dish with fresh figs, trimmed
at the tip and baked in the oven at
200°C (gas 6) for 15 minutes.

---

**STUFFING A SMALL PHEASANT
WITH A ROBUST SAUSAGE-MEAT
MIXTURE HELPS TO MAKE IT GO
THAT LITTLE BIT FURTHER.**

# stuffed pheasant

1 Preheat the oven to 200°C (gas 6). Melt the butter
in a saucepan over a low heat, add the shallots and
cook very gently for 3 minutes. Add the figs, cook for
a further 2 minutes, then tip out into a bowl and mix
with the sausage meat. Season lightly.

2 Rub the pheasant all over with salt and pepper,
inside and out, then stuff the neck end with the
sausage meat mixture. Secure the flap of skin with
a small skewer or cocktail stick and fold the wing
tips underneath.

3 Tie the legs together with kitchen string. Lay the
bacon over the breast to cover it and also tie in
place with string.

4 Heat the oil in a large flameproof casserole that will
hold the bird comfortably. Turn the bird in the hot oil
for 3–4 minutes to sear it all over. Add 3 tbsp water,
then cover and bake in the oven for 40 minutes.

5 Remove the bacon and put the pheasant back in
the oven, uncovered for 10 minutes, to brown.

6 Remove the pheasant from the casserole, untie
the string and put the bird on a warmed plate.
Add the soured cream to the cooking juices and
stir on the hob to reduce slightly. Season to taste.

7 To serve, take out the stuffing and cut into slices,
then cut the pheasant into four portions and arrange
on plates with a piece of bacon on each. Drizzle
over the sauce.

# m

**tempting,
hearty meals
for every
occasion**

# eat

Clever cooking means that you can enjoy rich, meaty meals without breaking the budget. Make the most of cheaper cuts of meat in fabulous stews, casseroles, pies and bakes, or make prime cuts such as lean beef steak go further by slicing thinly and stir-frying with plenty of vegetables and noodles. Minced meat is great value and can be enjoyed in many guises, while a dish such as Toad-in-the-hole made with plump pork sausages baked in a batter pudding is always a firm favourite, and so economical.

# corned beef hash

**£**

**Serves 4**
Preparation  10 minutes
Cooking  25 minutes

**2 tbsp vegetable oil**
**25 g butter**
**1 onion, finely chopped**
**1 red or green pepper, seeded and diced**
**450 g firm boiled potatoes, diced**
**340 g can corned beef, roughly chopped**
**200 g can sweetcorn, drained**
**2 tbsp mango or fruity chutney**
**dash of Tabasco sauce**
**freshly ground black pepper**

**To serve**
**extra mango or fruity chutney**

**Per serving**
kcal 450, protein 26 g, fat 21 g (of which
saturated fat 9 g), carbohydrate 42 g (of
which sugars 13 g), fibre 3 g, sodium 1 g

**214**

1 Heat the oil and butter in a large frying pan,
preferably non-stick, until the butter has melted.
Add the onion and cook for 10 minutes until soft
and translucent and just starting to colour. Add the
diced pepper and cook for a further 2 minutes.

2 Stir in the diced potato, then scatter over the
corned beef and sweetcorn. Press down lightly
and fry, without stirring, over a medium heat for
3–4 minutes or until a golden brown crust has
formed on the underside.

3 Meanwhile, chop any large pieces of fruit in the
chutney and mix with the Tabasco sauce and black
pepper in a small bowl. Break up the hash in the
pan, add the chutney mixture, then press it down
again and continue frying for 3–4 minutes until
nicely browned and crusty.

4 Repeat once more, breaking it up, then pressing
it down and frying again.

5 Cut the hash into quarters and serve on warmed
plates with a little extra chutney.

---

**COOK SMART**
- Any cooked potatoes can be used in this
dish – boiled, baked or roast.
- Make a corned beef and egg hash by
adding eggs in step 4. Make four wells in
the hash and carefully crack an egg into
each. Cover the pan and cook gently for
4–5 minutes or until the eggs are lightly set.
- Some grilled tomatoes make a good
accompaniment.

££

**Serves 4**
Preparation 10–15 minutes
Cooking 20 minutes

**500g lean minced beef**

**1 large onion, finely chopped**

**1 large green or red pepper, seeded
and finely chopped**

**2 large garlic cloves, crushed**

**400g can chopped tomatoes**

**150ml beef stock**

**400g can red kidney beans, drained
and rinsed**

**½ tsp chilli powder, or to taste**

**½ tsp ground cumin**

**¼ tsp cinnamon**

**50g mature Cheddar, grated**

**salt and freshly ground black pepper**

**To serve (optional)**
**4 tbsp soured cream**

**1 small avocado, stoned and diced**

**2 tbsp chopped fresh coriander**

**4 soft flour tortillas, warmed**

**Per serving**
kcal 415, protein 41g, fat 18g (of which
saturated fat 8g), carbohydrate 23g (of
which sugars 10g), fibre 7g, sodium 0.6g

**1** Brown the minced beef in a large frying pan, for 4–5 minutes over a medium heat, without adding any fat.

**2** Add the onion, pepper and garlic and cook for a further 5 minutes until the onion is softened. Stir in the tomatoes with their juice, the stock, beans and spices. Bring to the boil, then reduce the heat and simmer for 20 minutes. Season to taste.

**3** Preheat a moderate grill. Divide the chilli among individual heatproof bowls or spoon into one casserole dish. Sprinkle the cheese in a mound in the centre, then grill for about 1 minute until the cheese begins to melt. (Alternatively, ladle the hot chilli into individual bowls and serve immediately, sprinkled with cheese.)

**4** If liked, serve topped with soured cream, diced avocado and chopped coriander with warmed tortillas on the side.

**COOK SMART**

• For a vegetarian version, omit the beef and use two 400g cans of red kidney beans and vegetable stock.

• Chilli is a useful dish so why not make up double quantity and put some in the freezer. It can be served in warmed tortillas, taco shells or pitta bread, piled on jacket potatoes or simply with rice.

# chilli pots with cheese

MAKING THIS CHILLI IN INDIVIDUAL DISHES TOPPED WITH MELTING CHEESE TURNS A SIMPLE SUPPER INTO A REAL TREAT. SERVE WITH A CRISP GREEN SALAD.

A POPULAR FAMILY FAVOURITE, BAKED WITH A TOMATO SAUCE FILLING.

# american meat loaf

£

**Serves 8**
Preparation 25 minutes,
  plus 10 minutes standing
  before serving
Cooking 1¼ hours

**1 tbsp vegetable oil**

**2 large onions, chopped**

**2 large celery sticks,
  chopped**

**1 large green pepper, seeded
  and chopped**

**3 garlic cloves, crushed**

**1 kg lean minced beef**

**75 g fresh breadcrumbs
  (white or wholemeal)**

**1 egg, lightly beaten**

**227 g can chopped tomatoes**

**4 tbsp tomato ketchup**

**salt and freshly ground
  black pepper**

## COOK SMART

• Breadcrumbs are often added to minced meat dishes, not only as a 'stretcher', but also as a 'lightener'. So never waste the ends of loaves, instead turn them into breadcrumbs and keep in the freezer, handy for when you need them.

• Serve with pasta and a green vegetable or a selection of side salads.

**Per serving**
kcal 310, protein 30 g,
fat 15 g (of which saturated
fat 6 g), carbohydrate 15 g
(of which sugars 6.5 g),
fibre 1 g, sodium 0.3 g

**1** Preheat the oven to 180°C (gas 4). Heat the oil in a large, deep frying pan, add the onions, celery, green pepper and garlic and cook gently for 5 minutes over a medium heat until soft. Transfer the vegetables to a large bowl.

**2** Add the beef, breadcrumbs and egg to the vegetables, season with salt and pepper and knead the mixture with your hands.

**3** Combine the tomatoes with their juice and the ketchup in a small bowl. Add half to the meat loaf mixture and mix again.

**4** Transfer the mixture to a lightly greased baking dish or roasting tin and shape to make a loaf, measuring about 25 x 18 cm, mounding it slightly in the centre. Make a lengthways groove down the centre with the side of your hand and pour the remaining tomato mixture into the groove.

**5** Bake for 1¼ hours or until cooked through to the centre. (If you have a meat thermometer, it should read 71°C when the loaf is cooked.) Allow to stand for 10 minutes before slicing, using a sharp knife.

# blue-cheese stuffed burgers

£

**Serves 4**
Preparation  10 minutes
Cooking  10–12 minutes

**375 g lean minced beef**
**90 g porridge oats**
**2 tbsp tomato ketchup**
**2 tsp Dijon mustard**
**¼ tsp freshly ground
   black pepper**
**30 g blue cheese, crumbled**

**To serve**
**4 soft rolls, split and
   toasted**
**4 crisp lettuce leaves**
**1 large firm tomato, sliced**
**1 small red onion, thinly
   sliced**

**TANGY, MELTING
BLUE CHEESE GIVES
THESE BURGERS A
SURPRISE CENTRE
– A REAL TREAT FOR
A MIDWEEK MEAL.**

**Per serving**
kcal 427, protein 30 g,
fat 15 g (of which saturated
fat 6 g), carbohydrate 46 g
(of which sugars 6 g),
fibre 3 g, sodium 0.6 g

**1** Preheat a moderate grill. Mix together the minced beef, oats, ketchup, mustard and pepper in a large bowl until well blended. Divide into eight equal pieces and flatten into thin patties.

**2** Place a quarter of the crumbled cheese in the centre of each of four patties. Top with the remaining patties and press the edges together to seal completely.

**3** Place on the grill rack and grill for 5–6 minutes on each side until nicely browned and cooked through.

**4** Serve the burgers hot in lightly toasted rolls, filled with lettuce, sliced tomato and onion.

### COOK SMART

• Stilton or Roquefort are good blue cheese choices. Alternatively use Gruyère or mature Cheddar.

• Top with sliced gherkins, if liked, and serve with extra salad and home-made oven chips. Cut peeled or scrubbed potatoes into thick wedges, then toss in vegetable oil, to coat them lightly. Sprinkle with seasoning and dried herbs, if liked. Bake for 45 minutes in a hot oven, preheated to 220°C (gas 7).

**MEAT**

SLOPPY JOES ARE AN ALL-AMERICAN FAVOURITE THAT WILL BE A HIT WITH THE WHOLE FAMILY. THEY ARE MESSY TO EAT BUT TASTE DELICIOUS.

# sloppy joes

**£ £**

**Serves 4**
Preparation  10 minutes
Cooking  25–30 minutes

**450 g lean minced beef**
**1 onion, finely chopped**
**1 celery stick, finely chopped**
**1 green pepper, seeded and finely chopped**
**400 g can chopped tomatoes**
**1 tbsp chilli sauce, or to taste**
**2 tsp Worcestershire sauce**
**2 tsp cider vinegar**
**freshly ground black pepper**

**To serve**
**1 large carrot, peeled and cut into thin matchsticks**
**¼ small head white cabbage, finely shredded**
**2 tbsp olive oil**
**1 tbsp cider vinegar**
**4 buns, split and toasted**

**Per serving**
kcal 430, protein 32 g, fat 18 g (of which saturated fat 6 g), carbohydrate 37 g (of which sugars 13 g), fibre 4 g, sodium 0.5 g

**1** Brown the mince in a large non-stick frying pan over a medium heat for 4–5 minutes, without adding any fat. Break up the meat with a wooden spatula and when it is no longer pink, add the onion, celery, and green pepper. Cook for a further 5 minutes until the vegetables are softened.

**2** Add the tomatoes with their juice, chilli sauce to taste, Worcestershire sauce, vinegar and black pepper. Cook for 15–20 minutes, stirring often, until the flavours are blended.

**3** Mix together the carrot and cabbage, sprinkle with the oil and vinegar and toss together.

**4** Put the bottoms of the toasted buns onto the serving plates and spoon the sloppy meat mixture on top. Top with a heap of the coleslaw and cover with the tops of the buns. Serve immediately.

## COOK SMART

• You could also include some chopped chestnut or button mushrooms in the mixture. Add about 200 g at the end of step 1.

• A little vinegar in the meat mixture perks up the flavour, but be careful not to add too much.

# chinese crispy beef stir-fry

**Serves 2**
Preparation 20 minutes
Cooking 6 minutes

**200 g lean beef steak**

**2 tsp cornflour**

**1 tsp Chinese five-spice powder**

**1 carrot, peeled**

**1 small leek, trimmed**

**6 spring onions, diagonally sliced**

**½ red pepper, seeded and cut into strips**

**100 g rice noodles**

**2 tbsp soy sauce**

**2 tbsp dry sherry or rice wine**

**2 tbsp vegetable oil**

**1 large garlic clove, finely chopped**

**2 cm piece fresh root ginger, peeled and finely chopped**

**1 fresh red chilli, seeded and finely chopped**

**To serve**
**soy sauce to sprinkle**

**Per serving**
kcal 511, protein 26 g,
fat 18 g (of which saturated
fat 4.5 g), carbohydrate 57 g
(of which sugars 11 g),
fibre 3 g, sodium 1.1 g

**COOK SMART**
• For a stir-fry, it is
important to have all the
ingredients ready prepared
before you start cooking.
It then takes just minutes
to toss everything together
over a high heat.

• Prime beef steak is
relatively expensive but you
only use a small quantity in
this stir-fry. Rib-eye steak
is terrific value compared
to fillet and even rump.

1 Cut the meat, across the grain, into 5 cm wide pieces, and then cut each piece into wafer-thin strips. Place in a small bowl with the cornflour and five-spice powder. Mix together well to coat the meat.

2 Cut the carrot and leek into 5 cm lengths, then cut each piece into fine matchsticks. Put all the prepared vegetables together in a bowl.

3 Soak the noodles in a bowl of lightly salted, boiling water for 3 minutes. Drain and refresh in cold water, then drain again. Combine the soy sauce, sherry and 2 tbsp water in a small jug or bowl.

4 Place a wok or a large frying pan over a high heat. When hot, add 1 tbsp of the oil, then when it is just smoking, toss in the meat and stir-fry for 2–3 minutes until cooked through. Remove with a draining spoon. Add the remaining oil with the garlic, ginger and chilli. Stir-fry for 30 seconds, then add the vegetables and toss these around for another 30 seconds.

5 Stir in the soy sauce mixture and as soon as the liquid is bubbling, mix in the drained noodles and finally the meat. Serve immediately, with extra soy sauce to sprinkle.

**MAKE THE MOST OF PRIME LEAN BEEF STEAK BY STIR-FRYING IT WITH HEALTHY VEGETABLES, WHOLESOME NOODLES AND AROMATIC ASIAN-STYLE FLAVOURINGS.**

# traditional cornish pasties

A HEARTY MEAL-IN-ONE, MAKE THESE
SATISFYING PASTIES FOR A PICNIC OR
PACKED LUNCH, OR ENJOY WITH SALAD.

💷💷

**Makes 8**
Preparation 30 minutes, plus 20 minutes
    resting (for the pastry)
Cooking 1–1¼ hours

**Shortcrust pastry**
**450 g plain white flour**
**250 g chilled butter, diced (or half butter
    and half white vegetable fat)**

**Filling**
**350 g lean chuck (casserole) steak,
    finely diced**
**1 small onion, finely chopped**
**1 potato, about 175 g, peeled and
    finely diced**
**175 g butternut squash or swede,
    peeled and finely diced**
**2 tbsp beef or vegetable stock**
**3 tbsp chopped fresh parsley**
**salt and freshly ground black pepper**
**beaten egg or milk, to glaze**

**Per serving**
kcal 515, protein 17 g, fat 29 g (of which
saturated fat 17 g), carbohydrate 50 g
(of which sugars 3 g), fibre 2 g, sodium 0.2 g

1 Sift the flour and a pinch of salt together into
a mixing bowl. Rub in the fat until the mixture
resembles fine breadcrumbs. Sprinkle 6 tbsp
chilled water evenly over the surface, then mix with
a round-bladed knife or fork. Add a little more water
if the mixture is too dry. Gather the dough together,
then lightly knead on a floured surface for a few
seconds until smooth. Wrap and chill in the fridge
for 20 minutes.

2 Meanwhile, make the filling. Put the steak, onion,
potato, squash or swede, stock and parsley in a
bowl. Season generously with salt and pepper and
mix well. Preheat the oven to 200°C (gas 6).

3 Divide the pastry into eight pieces, then roll out each
piece on a lightly floured surface to a 20 cm round.
Spoon an equal amount of the filling onto
the centre of each pastry round.

4 Brush the pastry edges with beaten egg or milk,
then bring together at the top. Press the edges
firmly together to seal, then crimp the edges or
pattern them with a fork.

5 Place the pasties on lightly greased or non-stick
baking trays and brush with beaten egg or milk.
Make a small hole in each to allow some of the
steam to escape. Bake for 15 minutes, then reduce
the oven temperature to 160°C (gas 3) and cook
for a further 45 minutes–1 hour or until the pastry
is nicely golden and the filling is cooked. (Test by
piercing in several places with a fine skewer – it
should go through with little resistance.) Serve hot,
warm or cold.

**COOK SMART**
• If time is short, use two 375 g packets of ready-made
shortcrust pastry.
• Add extra flavour by blending ½ tsp English mustard with
the stock. You could also make up the vegetable content
with some diced carrot or turnip.
• Pasties will freeze well for up to 2 months.

# beef stew with rosemary dumplings

SHIN OF BEEF AND SKIRT ARE WELL-PRICED, HAVE A GREAT FLAVOUR AND ARE IDEAL FOR USING IN SLOW-COOKED STEWS WITH FLAVOURSOME ROOT VEGETABLES.

££

**Serves 4**
Preparation  30 minutes
Cooking  2 hours 20 minutes

500 g lean stewing beef (such as shin or skirt), cubed
2 tbsp plain flour
3 tbsp vegetable oil
2 bay leaves
1 onion, chopped
1 garlic clove, crushed
750 g mixed root vegetables (such as carrots, parsnips, celeriac, swede or turnips), peeled and cut into chunks
2 celery sticks, sliced
750 ml beef stock
2 tbsp tomato purée
1 tbsp red wine vinegar
2 tbsp redcurrant jelly
½ tsp dried mixed herbs
salt and freshly ground black pepper

Rosemary dumplings
175 g self-raising flour
pinch of English mustard powder (optional)
75 g shredded suet
2 tsp finely chopped fresh rosemary or 1 tsp dried

**Per serving**
kcal 734, protein 51 g, fat 34 g (of which saturated fat 13 g), carbohydrate 62 g (of which sugars 20 g), fibre 7 g, sodium 0.4 g

1 Preheat the oven to 150°C (gas 2). Toss the cubes of beef in the flour, seasoned with a little salt and pepper. Heat 2 tbsp of the oil in a large heavy-based frying pan and brown the meat in batches over a high heat, turning frequently. Transfer to a large flameproof casserole, using a draining spoon. Place the bay leaves on top of the meat.

2 Add the remaining 1 tbsp of oil to the frying pan and gently cook the onion for 10 minutes until soft and translucent. Add the garlic, root vegetables and celery and cook for a further 2–3 minutes or until just starting to colour. Add to the casserole.

3 De-glaze the pan by pouring in a little of the stock. Bring to the boil, scraping up any crusty bits from the bottom of the pan, then stir in the tomato purée, vinegar, redcurrant jelly and herbs. When blended, pour over the vegetables, then add the remaining stock.

4 Bring the casserole to the boil, then cover tightly and cook in the oven for 2 hours or until the beef and vegetables are tender. Turn up the oven temperature to 160°C (gas 3).

5 To make the dumplings, sift the flour with the mustard, if using, and a pinch of salt into a mixing bowl. Stir in the suet and rosemary, then add about 100 ml cold water to make a soft, but not sticky dough. Divide into twelve equal pieces and lightly roll into balls with floured hands.

6 Remove the casserole from the oven after 2 hours and arrange the dumplings on top. (It is important that the liquid is hot and bubbling when the dumplings are added, to ensure that they rise well.) Cover again and cook in the oven for about 20 minutes or until the dumplings are well risen, light and fluffy. Serve straight away on warmed plates.

## COOK SMART
• Some red wine, stout or pale ale can be used to replace part of the stock.

• Redcurrant jelly adds a subtle taste and shine to the sauce, but is not essential. You can use ½ tsp sugar instead.

• The stew is suitable for freezing without the dumplings. Use within 3 months. Thaw in the fridge, then reheat gently.

COMFORT FOOD AT ITS BEST – THIS RICHLY FLAVOURED ITALIAN-STYLE BEEF IS PERFECT FOR A FAMILY MEAL OR RELAXED ENTERTAINING.

# italian braised beef with mushrooms

£ £

**Serves 6**
Preparation 20 minutes, plus 10 minutes standing before serving
Cooking 1½ hours

**15 g dried porcini mushrooms**

**1 tbsp olive oil**

**800 g lean, rolled beef brisket**

**3 carrots, peeled and cut into matchsticks**

**2 celery sticks, cut into matchsticks**

**227 g can chopped tomatoes**

**250 ml red wine or beef stock**

**2 tbsp tomato purée**

**4 garlic cloves, sliced**

**1 tbsp dark muscovado sugar**

**½ tsp dried oregano**

**salt and freshly ground black pepper**

## COOK SMART

• Brisket is an economical joint that becomes tender and succulent with long, slow cooking. Topside could also be used.

• For convenience, this dish can be made ahead. Put the sliced meat into the sauce with the vegetables, allow to cool, then keep in the fridge. Reheat at 130°C (gas ½) for 45 minutes–1 hour until it is thoroughly heated through.

**Per serving**
kcal 274, protein 29 g, fat 10 g (of which saturated fat 4 g), carbohydrate 10 g (of which sugars 8 g), fibre 1.5 g, sodium 0.1 g

**1** Preheat the oven to 180°C (gas 4). Soak the mushrooms in 250 ml boiling water in a small bowl for 20 minutes, until softened. Drain, reserve the liquid and coarsely chop the mushrooms.

**2** Meanwhile, heat the oil in a large flameproof casserole over a medium heat, add the beef and brown it all over. Add the carrots and celery to the casserole.

**3** Combine the mushrooms and their soaking liquid, the tomatoes with their juice, the wine or stock, tomato purée, garlic, sugar and oregano in a jug, then pour into the casserole. Season with salt and pepper, then bring to the boil over a medium heat.

**4** Cover the casserole and put it in the oven to bake for 1½ hours or until the meat is tender.

**5** Allow to rest for 10 minutes, then lift out the meat and carve into slices. Serve with the vegetables and sauce.

**A TENDER, JUICY POT-ROAST MAKES A LUXURIOUS MEAL AT A FRACTION OF THE PRICE OF A PRIME ROASTING CUT.**

# pot roast beef with braised vegetables

£ £ £

**Serves 8**
Preparation  30 minutes
Cooking  2 hours

**2 rindless smoked bacon rashers**

**1 tbsp vegetable oil**

**1.5 kg boned, rolled and tied beef topside or thick flank**

**8 large carrots, peeled and thickly sliced**

**2 onions, coarsely chopped**

**4 garlic cloves, crushed**

**2 x 400 g cans chopped tomatoes**

**250 ml red wine**

**250 ml beef stock**

**1 kg small new potatoes, scrubbed and halved**

**2 tsp cornflour**

**15 g fresh basil, chopped**

**salt and freshly ground black pepper**

**Per serving**
kcal 430, protein 51 g, fat 8 g (of which saturated fat 3 g), carbohydrate 34 g (of which sugars 13 g), fibre 4.5 g, sodium 0.4 g

**1** Preheat the oven to 160°C (gas 3). Cook the bacon in a large flame-proof casserole over a medium heat for 5 minutes or until crisp. Remove the bacon, drain on kitchen paper, then cut into pieces.

**2** Add the oil to the bacon fat left in the casserole, heat, then add the beef, turning it until browned all over. Transfer to a plate.

**3** Add the carrots, onions, and garlic to the casserole and cook in the meat drippings for about 8 minutes until lightly browned.

**4** Stir in the tomatoes, then return the meat to the casserole and pour in the wine and stock. Season with salt and pepper, bring to the boil, then reduce the heat. Cover with foil and then to create a tight seal with the lid. Transfer to the oven and cook for 1 hour, turning the meat once.

**5** Remove the casserole from the oven and add the potatoes and half the basil. Top up the liquid level if necessary with a little more stock. Return to the oven and cook for a further hour or until the beef and vegetables are tender. Put the bacon in the oven on a heatproof plate for 5 minutes to warm through.

**6** Slice the beef, arrange on a serving platter with the vegetables and keep warm. Put the casserole on the hob on a medium heat. Blend the cornflour with 2 tbsp cold water, then stir into the liquid and bring to the boil. Stir for 1 minute or until thickened. Ladle over the beef and vegetables and sprinkle over the bacon and remaining basil.

A REFRESHING YOGHURT DIP MAKES A PERFECT PARTNER FOR THESE CHUNKY, WARMLY SPICED MEATBALLS MADE FROM MINCED LAMB.

£ £

**Serves 4**
Preparation  30 minutes
Cooking  15 minutes

**500g lean minced lamb**
**1 onion, finely chopped**
**1 egg**
**¼ tsp ground cumin**
**¼ tsp ground cinnamon**
**2 tbsp olive oil**

**Cucumber yoghurt**
**150g Greek-style yoghurt**
**½ cucumber, coarsely grated**
**1 garlic clove, crushed**
**salt and freshly ground black pepper**

**Per serving**
kcal 365, protein 28g,
fat 27g (of which saturated
fat 11g), carbohydrate 3.5g
(of which sugars 3g),
fibre 0.5g, sodium 0.1g

# spiced lamb kofta

**1** Soak eight wooden skewers in cold water for 30 minutes. Alternatively, use metal skewers. Mix together the lamb, onion, egg, cumin and cinnamon in a bowl. Add salt and pepper, then quickly bind the mixture together in a food processor or by kneading with your hands.

**2** Divide the mixture into sixteen equal portions. Thread two meatballs on to each of the skewers, leaving a space of about 2cm between them. Lightly brush with half the oil. Preheat a medium grill.

**3** Blend the yoghurt with the remaining oil, then stir in the cucumber, garlic and salt and pepper to season. Mix well and chill until ready to serve.

**4** Put the kebabs on the grill rack and grill, about 12cm from the heat, for about 15 minutes, turning regularly, until golden brown and cooked through. Serve hot with the cucumber yoghurt.

**COOK SMART**
• If you are unable to buy ready-minced lamb, most butchers will mince meat for you. Shoulder of lamb or neck fillet make smart choices for flavour and price.

• Serve with savoury rice and grilled tomatoes, or pop the kebabs into split warm pitta bread, with shredded red cabbage and carrot. Drizzle with yoghurt.

**Serves 4**
Preparation 45 minutes
Cooking 15–20 minutes

**4 large courgettes, about 230 g each**
**150 g long-grain rice**
**2 firm tomatoes, seeded and chopped**
**1 egg, lightly beaten**
**2 tbsp chopped fresh mint (optional)**
**375 g lean minced lamb**
**1 onion, chopped**
**2 garlic cloves, crushed**
**250 g passata or a lightly diluted tomato sauce**
**1 tsp chopped fresh rosemary or ½ tsp dried**
**4 tbsp freshly grated Parmesan**
**salt and freshly ground black pepper**

**Per serving**
kcal 420, protein 28 g, fat 17 g (of which saturated fat 7 g), carbohydrate 42 g (of which sugars 9 g), fibre 3.5 g, sodium 0.1 g

**1** Preheat the oven to 190°C (gas 5). Cut each courgette in half lengthways and scoop out the pulpy centre with a teaspoon, leaving an outside shell, 1 cm thick. Reserve the pulp, and chop lightly.

**2** Place the courgettes in a shallow baking dish or roasting tin, cover with foil and bake for 20 minutes or until tender – they should pierce easily with a fork.

**3** Meanwhile, cook the rice in a pan of lightly salted boiling water for 12–15 minutes until just tender. Drain, allow to stand for 5 minutes, then add the chopped plum tomatoes, egg, mint, if using, and pepper to season. Set aside.

**4** Fry the lamb over a medium heat for 5 minutes or until browned. Add the onion and garlic, cook for a further 5 minutes until the onion has softened. Stir in the passata, reserved courgette pulp and rosemary. Bring to the boil, then reduce the heat and simmer gently for 10–15 minutes. Stir in the rice mixture and mix together.

**5** Spoon the stuffing mixture into the courgette 'boats' and sprinkle with Parmesan. Bake for 15–20 minutes until golden and crispy on top. Serve immediately.

**COOK SMART**
● You could use this filling to stuff other scooped-out vegetables such as aubergines, peppers or large beef tomatoes.

# baked stuffed courgettes

**COURGETTE 'BOATS' FILLED WITH A HEARTY RICE AND MINCED LAMB STUFFING MAKE A SATISFYING YET HEALTHY MEAL.**

# tex-mex shepherd's pie

**SPICY LAMB CHILLI WITH BEANS MAKES A GREAT BASE FOR THIS WARMING VERSION OF SHEPHERD'S PIE. THE CRISP, GARLICKY POTATO CRUST TOPS IT OFF FABULOUSLY.**

£ £

**Serves 4**
Preparation  30 minutes
Cooking  15 minutes

2 tsp olive oil

4 spring onions, thinly sliced

6 garlic cloves, crushed

1 large green pepper, seeded and chopped

300 g lean minced lamb

1 tsp chilli powder

1½ tsp ground coriander

1½ tsp ground cumin

400 g can chopped tomatoes

100 ml lamb or beef stock, hot

400 g can red kidney beans, drained and rinsed

750 g floury potatoes, peeled and sliced

3 tbsp chopped fresh coriander

salt

**Per serving**
kcal 415, protein 27 g, fat 13 g (of which saturated fat 5 g), carbohydrate 51 g (of which sugars 9 g), fibre 8 g, sodium 0.4 g

**1** Preheat the oven to 220°C (gas 7). Heat the oil in a large frying pan over a low heat. Add the spring onions and half the garlic and cook for 2 minutes, stirring frequently. Add the chopped pepper, increase the heat to medium and cook for 5 minutes, stirring until the pepper is just tender.

**2** Stir in the lamb, chilli powder, ground coriander and cumin and cook for 2–3 minutes, stirring occasionally to break up the meat, until it is no longer pink. Stir in the tomatoes with their juice, the stock and the kidney beans and bring to the boil. Reduce heat to a simmer, cover and cook for 15 minutes until the mixture is thick.

**3** Meanwhile, cook the potatoes with the remaining garlic in a pan of lightly salted boiling water for 10 minutes or until tender.

**4** Drain the potatoes, reserving 50 ml of the cooking liquid. Return the potatoes and garlic to the pan with this liquid and crush them using a potato masher or a large fork. Stir in the chopped coriander.

**5** Spoon the lamb mixture into a deep pie dish, about 1.5 litre capacity. Spoon the crushed potatoes over the top. Bake for 15 minutes until golden. Serve hot.

## COOK SMART

• This dish can be made ahead, then simply baked for the final 15 minutes, or until heated through, before serving.

• You can use lean minced beef and alternative canned beans if preferred.

# greek lamb and aubergine bake

💷💷

**Serves 6**
Preparation 40 minutes
Cooking 20–25 minutes

**400 g lean minced lamb**

**1 onion, finely chopped**

**3 garlic cloves, crushed**

**1 aubergine, cut into 1 cm chunks**

**200 ml lamb or vegetable stock**

**2 x 400 g cans chopped tomatoes**

**15 g fresh mint, chopped**

**15 g fresh dill, chopped (optional)**

**300 g spaghetti, broken into short lengths**

**300 g natural low-fat yoghurt**

**1 large egg**

**salt and freshly ground black pepper**

**Per serving**
kcal 360, protein 24 g,
fat 12 g (of which saturated
fat 5 g), carbohydrate 42 g
(of which sugars 6 g),
fibre 3 g, sodium 0.1 g

**1** Brown the lamb in a large frying pan over a medium heat. Add the onion and garlic, and cook for 5 minutes, stirring frequently, until the onion is soft. Then add the aubergine and stock and cook, stirring frequently, for 5 minutes, until the aubergine is tender.

**2** Stir in the tomatoes, half the mint and dill, if using. Season with salt and pepper and bring to the boil. Reduce to a simmer, cover and cook for 20 minutes or until the lamb is tender. Preheat the oven to 180°C (gas 4).

**3** Meanwhile, cook the spaghetti in a large pan of lightly salted boiling water for 10–12 minutes, or according to the packet instructions, until al dente. Drain. Beat together the yoghurt and egg in a small bowl.

**4** Stir the drained pasta into the lamb mixture, then spoon into a large baking dish, measuring about 28 x 18 cm. Spoon the yoghurt mixture over the top and bake for a further 20–25 minutes until piping hot. Sprinkle with the remaining mint and dill just before serving.

---

**COOK SMART**

• In Greece, this dish is made with orzo, a small tear-shaped pasta. Use in place of the broken spaghetti, if you have a packet, or you could use long-grain rice.

• Serve with a salad of lightly cooked green beans tossed with thinly sliced red onions.

228

THIS DISH IS TYPICAL OF GREEK CUISINE
– SIMPLE BUT WONDERFULLY FLAVOURED.
THE INGREDIENTS ARE SIMILAR TO MOUSSAKA
BUT WITH SOME PASTA INCLUDED.

COOKED GENTLY WITH RICE, VEGETABLES, DRIED FRUITS AND WARMING SPICES, THIS HEARTY CASSEROLE IS AN EXCELLENT WAY TO SERVE JUICY MIDDLE NECK OF LAMB.

£££

**Serves 4**
Preparation 25 minutes
Cooking 1 hour–1 hour 20 minutes

230

**1 tbsp vegetable oil**
**800 g middle neck of lamb, cut into pieces**
**2 onions, sliced**
**300 g carrots, peeled and cut into batons**
**2 tbsp wine vinegar**
**700 ml lamb or chicken stock, hot**
**½ tsp turmeric**
**½ tsp ground cumin**
**3 sprigs of fresh thyme**
**2 bay leaves**
**200 g long-grain rice**
**150 g dried apricots, halved**
**50 g sultanas**
**salt and freshly ground black pepper**

**Per serving**
kcal 800, protein 60 g, fat 31 g (of which saturated fat 12 g), carbohydrate 76 g (of which sugars 31 g), fibre 5 g, sodium 0.3 g

**COOK SMART**
• If you prefer lamb off the bone, use 450 g neck fillet and cut it into thick slices. Chump chops or leg steaks could also be used but the neck is more economical.

• Add a little ground paprika if you enjoy a spicy flavour.

**1** Heat the oil in a large flameproof casserole, add the meat and quickly brown on both sides, in two batches. Drain and remove to a plate. Add the onions and carrots to the casserole, cook for 5 minutes, then add the vinegar and cook over a high heat for 2 minutes, scraping up any meaty bits.

**2** Pour in the hot stock, add the turmeric, cumin, thyme, bay leaves and salt and pepper to season and bring to the boil. Reduce the heat, return the meat to the casserole, cover and simmer for 1 hour. (If more convenient, the casserole can be left to cook in the oven at 180°C/gas 4 for 1¼ hours.)

**3** Add the rice, apricots and sultanas to the casserole and cook for a further 20 minutes, stirring after 10 minutes, until the rice and meat are both tender. (The stock will be absorbed.) Remove the bay leaves and thyme, check for seasoning and serve hot.

**fruity one-pot lamb**

£££

**Serves 4**
Preparation  25 minutes
Cooking  1 hour

2 tsp olive oil

250 g lean boneless lamb,
    cut into cubes

2 tsp ground coriander

1 tsp ground ginger

2 tsp ground cumin

330 ml vegetable juice

100 ml vegetable stock

1 tbsp tomato purée

1 butternut squash,
    peeled, seeded and
    cut into cubes

3 courgettes, halved
    lengthways and thickly
    sliced

185 g couscous

salt and freshly ground
    black pepper

## COOK SMART

• Offer harissa (the traditional North African hot sauce), on the side. Some warm Arabic flat bread and a leafy green salad would make good accompaniments.

• Vegetable juice, in a can, is made from a blend of vegetable juices (principally tomato) with seasonings. Alternatively, use tomato or carrot juice.

**Per serving**
kcal 330, protein 19 g,
fat 9.5 g (of which saturated
fat 3.5 g), carbohydrate 45 g
(of which sugars 14 g),
fibre 3.5 g, sodium 0.1 g

**1** Heat the oil in a large saucepan or flameproof casserole. Add the lamb and cook over a medium heat for 5 minutes until the lamb is richly browned. Sprinkle over the spices and cook for a further minute, stirring constantly.

**2** Stir in the vegetable juice, stock and tomato purée and bring to the boil. Reduce the heat to a simmer, cover and cook for 30 minutes.

**3** Stir in the butternut squash and cook for 5 minutes, then add the courgettes. Cover and cook gently for a further 25 minutes or until the lamb and vegetables are tender.

**4** About 15 minutes before the lamb is ready, prepare the couscous. Cook following the packet instructions, then fluff up the grains with a fork.

**5** Divide the couscous among serving bowls and spoon the lamb stew over the top. Serve immediately.

# spiced lamb
# with couscous

**TREAT FAMILY AND FRIENDS TO SOMETHING A LITTLE MORE EXOTIC WITH THIS NORTH AFRICAN DISH OF LAMB AND VEGETABLES SERVED WITH FLUFFY COUSCOUS.**

# keema curry

**(£)**

**Serves 4**
Preparation  20 minutes
Cooking  55 minutes

**Per serving**
kcal 390, protein 35g,
fat 23g (of which saturated
fat 8.5g), carbohydrate 11g
(of which sugars 5g),
fibre 3.5g, sodium 0.2g

**COOK SMART**
• This dish is equally good
made with pork, beef,
turkey or Quorn mince.
• Frozen mixed vegetables
would make an alternative
to peas.

450g lean minced lamb
1 tbsp vegetable oil
1 large onion, finely
  chopped
2 garlic cloves, finely
  chopped
2.5cm piece fresh root
  ginger, peeled and
  grated
1 fresh green chilli, seeded
  and finely chopped
2 tbsp curry paste
2 tbsp tomato purée
350ml lamb or vegetable
  stock
225g frozen peas, thawed
1 tbsp lemon juice
3 tbsp roughly chopped
  fresh coriander
salt and freshly ground
  black pepper

1 Brown the minced lamb in a large non-stick frying
pan, without adding any oil. Fry over a medium
heat for 5–6 minutes until well-browned, stirring
frequently to break up larger pieces. Remove from
the pan using a draining spoon and set aside.

2 Heat the oil in the pan, then, when hot, add the
onion and cook for 10 minutes, stirring occasionally,
until soft and translucent. Add the garlic, ginger,
chilli and curry paste and cook for 2 more minutes,
stirring all the time. Return the meat to the pan,
add the tomato purée and stir until well mixed.

3 Pour in the stock, stir again, then reduce the heat,
cover and simmer gently for 45 minutes. Remove
the lid and cook for a further 10 minutes or until
the meat is very tender and the sauce is thick.

4 Add the peas and lemon juice and simmer for
3 minutes. Stir in 2 tbsp of the coriander and
season to taste with salt and pepper. Serve hot
with the remaining coriander scattered over the top.

MINCED MEAT IS EXCELLENT VALUE, VERY
VERSATILE AND UNIVERSALLY POPULAR.
IT IS USED HERE IN A QUICK INDIAN-STYLE
CURRY. SERVE WITH WARM NAAN OR
CHAPATTIS AND THICK, CREAMY YOGHURT.

# picadillo with rice

SPICY MEXICAN
GROUND PORK
COOKED WITH JUICY
RAISINS AND SPIKED
WITH HOT JALAPEÑO
PEPPERS MAKES A
MOUTH-WATERING
MAIN MEAL.

**(£)**

**Serves 4**
Preparation  15 minutes
Cooking  15–20 minutes

**Per serving**
kcal 536, protein 28g,
fat 17g (of which
saturated fat 5g),
carbohydrate 72g
(of which sugars 23g),
fibre 2g, sodium 0.3g

1 tbsp vegetable oil

1 large onion, finely
chopped

3 garlic cloves, crushed

450g lean minced pork

500ml passata

100g raisins

30g stoned green olives,
coarsely chopped

25g pickled jalapeño
peppers, finely chopped

1 tsp dried oregano

225g long-grain rice

salt and freshly ground
black pepper

**1** Heat the oil in a large frying pan over a medium
heat. Add the onion and garlic and cook for
5 minutes, stirring frequently, until the onion is soft.

**2** Add the pork and stir for 3 minutes until no longer
pink. Then add the passata, raisins, olives, jalapeño,
and oregano. Season with salt and pepper, bring
to the boil, then reduce the heat and simmer for
15–20 minutes, stirring frequently, until the pork
is cooked through.

**3** Meanwhile, cook the rice in a pan of lightly salted
boiling water for 12–15 minutes, or according to
the packet instructions, until just tender.

**4** Drain the rice and serve the minced meat mixture
over the top. Serve with a rocket salad.

## COOK SMART

• This also makes an
excellent filling for tacos or
soft flour tortillas. Chopped
fresh green chillies could
be used instead of the
jalapeño peppers. You
could also add some
toasted, flaked almonds.

• Passata is sieved
tomato pulp. It is readily
available in jars or cartons
from supermarkets.
Alternatively, use a tomato
pasta sauce diluted with a
little hot water or canned
tomatoes in rich juice.

SIZZLING STIR-FRIED STRIPS OF PORK AND MIXED PEPPERS, WRAPPED UP IN TORTILLAS WITH A ZINGY SALSA AND SOURED CREAM, MAKE A FUN, SERVE-YOURSELF DISH THAT THE WHOLE FAMILY WILL ENJOY.

# spicy pork fajitas

💷💷

**Serves 4**
Preparation 30 minutes
Cooking 8–9 minutes

**350 g pork fillet**

**Marinade**
**finely grated zest and
    juice of 1 lime**
**1 tsp caster sugar**
**1 tsp dried oregano**
**½ tsp ground cinnamon**
**¼ tsp cayenne pepper**

**Stir-fry**
**1 tbsp vegetable oil**
**1 onion, thinly sliced**
**1 red pepper, seeded and
    cut into strips**
**1 yellow pepper, seeded
    and cut into strips**

**Tomato salsa**
**4 ripe tomatoes, skinned,
    seeded and chopped**
**1 small red onion, finely
    chopped**
**¼ cucumber, diced**
**1½ tbsp olive oil**
**2 tsp lime juice**
**2 tbsp chopped fresh
    coriander**
**salt and freshly ground
    black pepper**

**To serve**
**8 soft flour tortillas**
**150 ml soured cream**
**paprika for sprinkling
    (optional)**

**Per serving**
kcal 618, protein 31 g,
fat 19 g (of which saturated
fat 7 g), carbohydrate 85 g
(of which sugars 14 g),
fibre 5.5 g, sodium 0.4 g

**1** Trim all visible fat from the pork fillet. Cut the pork widthways into slices, about 5 cm thick, then cut each slice into thin strips. Put the lime juice and zest in a shallow dish with the sugar, oregano, cinnamon and cayenne pepper. Add the pork strips and toss to coat, then leave to marinate while you prepare the rest of the ingredients.

**2** Now prepare the salsa. Combine the tomatoes, onion and cucumber in a bowl. Whisk together the olive oil and lime juice with a little salt and pepper in a bowl, drizzle over the salsa, add the chopped coriander and mix well. Cover and set aside.

**3** Heat the vegetable oil in a frying pan or wok until very hot. Add the marinated pork and stir-fry for 1 minute, then add the sliced onions and stir-fry for a further 3 minutes. Turn down the heat a little, then add the peppers and cook for a further 3–4 minutes until the pork is cooked through and the vegetables are tender.

**4** Meanwhile, gently warm the tortillas in a microwave for 1 minute or following packet instructions. (Alternatively, they can be warmed in a stack, wrapped in foil, in a preheated oven for 10 minutes.)

**5** Spoon the pork and pepper mixture into a warmed serving bowl and take it to the table with the tortillas, salsa and soured cream for diners to assemble themselves. Spread a little salsa over each tortilla, then pile on some of the pork and pepper mixture. Add a spoonful of soured cream, sprinkle with a little paprika if liked, then fold over or roll up and pick up to eat. Be sure to provide a stack of paper napkins.

**MEAT**

**235**

---

**COOK SMART**
• Use three skinless, chicken breasts instead of pork, if preferred.

• A mixed bean salsa could be served instead. Toss a drained and rinsed 400 g can of mixed beans (such as pinto and red kidney beans) with a finely chopped, fresh red or green chilli pepper and some vinaigrette dressing.

# sticky baked pork spare ribs

**Serves 4**
Preparation  10 minutes
Cooking  1 hour

**3 tbsp soy sauce**

**2 tbsp tomato ketchup**

**2 tbsp runny honey**

**2 garlic cloves, crushed**

**1 tsp paprika**

**grated zest of 1 lemon**

**1 kg pork spare ribs, each cut
    into 2 or 3 pieces**

**Per serving**
kcal 527, protein 47 g, fat 33 g
(of which saturated fat 13 g),
carbohydrate 10 g (of which
sugars 10 g), fibre 0 g,
sodium 1.2 g

## COOK SMART

• Use a blended honey, which
is cheaper than a delicately
flavoured, single flower variety.
Also, its strong flavour will
stand up to the heat better.

• Alternatively cook the pork
by simmering in a large pan of
water for 1 hour with 1 chopped
onion, 1 chopped carrot, a
bouquet garni and a pinch of
salt. Drain, then tip into a grill
pan and brush with a mixture
of 2 tbsp each of honey,
wholegrain mustard and soy
sauce. Finish under a medium
grill for about 5 minutes on each
side until glazed and sticky.

1 Preheat the oven to 200°C (gas 6). Put
the soy sauce, ketchup, honey, garlic,
paprika and lemon zest in a small pan.
Bring to the boil gently, then reduce the
heat and simmer for 2 minutes. Remove
the pan from the heat.

2 Place the pork in a lightly oiled roasting
tin, in a single layer, and brush with the
warm sauce.

3 Cook for 15 minutes, then lower the
temperature to 160°C (gas 3) and
cook for a further 45 minutes, turning
halfway through the cooking and basting
regularly with the sauce in the tin. Add
several spoonfuls of water to the tin
to prevent the juices sticking and
burning. When cooked, the ribs should
be golden and sticky on the outside.
Serve immediately with jacket potatoes
and seasonal salad.

RIBS IN A PIQUANT, STICKY SAUCE ARE BEST
EATEN WITH FINGERS. ENJOY THEM FOR AN
AL FRESCO MEAL, EITHER IN THE SUMMER
OR AT A WINTER BONFIRE PARTY.

PORK IS A LEAN MEAT THAT OFFERS GOOD VALUE FOR MONEY. SPARE-RIB STEAKS ARE PARTICULARLY WELL-PRICED, OR YOU COULD USE LOIN STEAKS.

# pork steaks with honey and mustard sauce

**££**

**Serves 4**
Preparation 10 minutes,
    plus 2 hours marinating
Cooking 15 minutes

4 lean pork steaks,
    trimmed of fat
1 tbsp runny honey
2 tbsp soy sauce
3 tbsp lemon juice
¼ tsp ground cinnamon
pinch of ground nutmeg
1 tbsp vegetable oil
1 tbsp grainy mustard
salt and freshly ground
    black pepper

**To serve**
baby spinach leaves, raw
    or lightly cooked

## COOK SMART

• To cook the spinach, lightly blanch it in a steamer over boiling water, for 30 seconds until just wilted.

• You could also serve this dish with some rice tossed with sautéed mushrooms for a change.

**Per serving**
kcal 270, protein 39g,
fat 10g (of which saturated
fat 3g), carbohydrate 4.5g
(of which sugars 4g),
fibre 0.5g, sodium 0.8g

1 Make regular nicks around the trimmed fat edge of the steaks using a sharp knife. This will ensure they stay flat while cooking.

2 Blend together the honey, soy sauce, lemon juice, cinnamon and nutmeg in a shallow dish. Lay the pork steaks in this mixture, turning them and basting well with a spoon. Cover with cling film and leave to marinate in the fridge for 2 hours.

3 Heat the oil in a large heavy-based frying pan. Drain the pork steaks, reserving the marinade, and fry over a gentle heat, for 6–7 minutes on each side, depending on their thickness.

4 Remove the meat from the pan and place on a warmed plate. Pour off the excess fat from the pan. Pour the reserved marinade into the pan, reduce it slightly over a high heat, then stir in the mustard and blend well. Season to taste, then pour over the pork and serve immediately, with baby spinach.

# toad-in-the-hole

£ £

**Serves 4**

Preparation  15 minutes
Cooking  30–35 minutes

**1 tbsp vegetable oil**

**8 thick pork sausages,
about 450 g**

**125 g plain flour**

**2 eggs, lightly beaten**

**300 ml semi-skimmed milk**

**2 tbsp chopped fresh
parsley**

**Onion gravy**

**2 tbsp vegetable oil**

**1 onion, thinly sliced**

**1 tbsp plain flour**

**600 ml beef stock**

**2 tsp Worcestershire
sauce**

**1 tsp made mustard**

**salt and freshly ground
black pepper**

**Per serving**

kcal 715, protein 27 g,
fat 54 g (of which saturated
fat 17 g), carbohydrate 45 g
(of which sugars 8 g),
fibre 2 g, sodium 1.2 g

---

**COOK SMART**

• Vegetarian sausages
can be used but they do
not need a pre-cook. Put
them in the hot oil just
before pouring over
the batter.

• If more convenient, mix
the batter ahead of time,
then keep in the fridge until
ready to start cooking.

---

**POPULAR WITH CHILDREN AND ADULTS ALIKE, THIS
TRADITIONAL BATTER PUDDING IS AN EXCELLENT WAY
OF TURNING A FEW SAUSAGES INTO A HEARTY MEAL.
SERVE WITH ONION GRAVY AND SEASONAL GREENS.**

**1** Pour the oil into a small roasting tin, measuring
about 30 x 25 cm, and put in the oven at 220°C
(gas 7). Heat for 5 minutes, then add the sausages
and cook for 10 minutes, turning occasionally, until
they are lightly browned and the fat is very hot. If a
lot of fat has come out of the sausages, carefully tip
some away, leaving about 1 tbsp in the tin.

**2** Meanwhile, sift the flour and a pinch of salt into
a mixing bowl. Make a well in the middle and add
the eggs with about half of the milk. Whisk the eggs
and milk together, gradually incorporating the flour
to make a smooth, thick batter. Whisk in the
remaining milk, then stir in half the parsley and
season with pepper.

**3** Pour the batter into the roasting tin around the
sausages. Immediately reduce the oven temperature
to 200°C (gas 6) and cook for 30–35 minutes, or
until the batter is well-risen and golden brown.

**4** While the pudding is cooking, make the onion gravy.
Heat the oil in a pan and fry the onion for 5 minutes.
Stir in the flour and cook for 1 minute. Gradually
add the stock, then the Worcestershire sauce
and mustard, stirring continuously until thickened.
Simmer gently on a low heat until the pudding
is ready.

**5** Serve the pudding straight from the oven with the
remaining parsley scattered over the top and with
lashings of onion gravy.

£ £

**Serves 4**
Preparation 40 minutes,
    plus overnight soaking
Cooking 1 hour (for
    the beans), plus
    40–45 minutes

- **225 g dried haricot beans, soaked in cold water overnight**
- **2 bay leaves**
- **a few parsley stalks**
- **a small sprig each of fresh thyme and rosemary (optional)**
- **2 onions**
- **2 whole cloves**
- **150 g thick-cut streaky bacon, diced**
- **400 g coarse-textured sausages**
- **1 leek, thickly sliced**
- **1 garlic clove, crushed**
- **2 carrots, peeled and thickly sliced**
- **400 g can chopped tomatoes**
- **½ tsp ground paprika**
- **salt and freshly ground black pepper**

**Garlic & herb crust**
- **75 g fresh white breadcrumbs**
- **2 tbsp chopped fresh parsley**
- **1 garlic clove, finely chopped**
- **15 g butter, diced**

**Per serving**
kcal 711, protein 32 g,
fat 37 g (of which saturated
fat 14 g), carbohydrate 66 g
(of which sugars 14 g),
fibre 13 g, sodium 1.5 g

**240**

# country cassoulet

**1** Drain and thoroughly rinse the beans, then put into a large saucepan with the bay leaves and parsley stalks. If using, tie the thyme and rosemary in a small bundle for easy removal, and add to the pan. Pour in 1 litre cold water and bring to the boil. Boil rapidly, uncovered, for 10 minutes. Skim off any scum that has risen to the surface.

**2** Skin one of the onions and stud with cloves. Add to the beans, cover and simmer gently for 50 minutes or until the beans are almost tender. Drain, reserving the stock, but discarding the herbs and onion.

**3** Meanwhile, gently fry the bacon in a large, flameproof casserole for 5 minutes or until the fat starts to run. Remove with a draining spoon and set aside, then add the sausages to the casserole. Turn up the heat to moderate and cook for 10 minutes, turning frequently, until lightly browned all over. Remove from the casserole and set aside.

**4** Drain all but 1 tbsp of fat from the casserole or add 1 tbsp oil if necessary. Finely chop the remaining onion and gently cook for 7–8 minutes until soft and translucent. Add the leek and garlic and cook for a further 2 minutes. Thickly slice the sausages and return to the casserole with the bacon. Add the carrots, canned tomatoes with their juice, paprika, haricot beans and 400 ml of the reserved stock. Season with salt and pepper.

**5** Preheat the oven to 160°C (gas 3). Bring the cassoulet to the boil, cover and simmer gently for 10 minutes. Meanwhile, mix together the breadcrumbs, parsley and garlic. Sprinkle over the cassoulet and dot with the butter. Cook uncovered in the oven for 45–50 minutes or until the vegetables are tender and the crust is nicely browned and crisp.

**INSPIRED BY THE CLASSIC FRENCH DISH, THIS VERSION IS LIGHTER AND LESS EXTRAVAGANT. IT COMBINES CHUNKY SAUSAGES, BACON AND BEANS WITH THE TRADITIONAL GARLIC AND HERB CRUST.**

**COOK SMART**
- If you're pushed for time, use two 300 g cans of haricot beans, drained and rinsed, and omit steps 1 and 2. Add pork or chicken stock in step 4, making up the quantity with 150 ml dry white wine, if liked.

# sausage hotpot with lentils

SAUSAGES HAVE SEEN A REVIVAL AND ARE BECOMING SOMETHING OF A GOURMET CHOICE. ENJOY THEM BRAISED WITH ONIONS, SWEET PEPPERS AND LENTILS.

£ £

**Serves 4**
Preparation  25 minutes
Cooking  15–20 minutes

1 tsp vegetable oil

8 good-quality sausages, about 450 g in total

2 red onions, sliced

2 red peppers, seeded and thickly sliced

300 ml beef or vegetable stock

420 g can green lentils, drained and rinsed

½ tsp dried mixed herbs

salt and freshly ground black pepper

## COOK SMART

• This dish would be equally good with a can of beans, such as flageolet or haricot, in place of the lentils. Use whatever you have in the cupboard.

• Serve this hotpot with fluffy mashed potatoes or creamy polenta (see page 115) and seasonal greens.

**Per serving**
kcal 500, protein 25 g, fat 30 g (of which saturated fat 12 g), carbohydrate 35 g (of which sugars 10 g), fibre 5 g, sodium 0.9 g

1 Heat the oil in a large frying pan, add the sausages and cook over a moderate heat for 5–6 minutes, turning frequently until lightly browned all over. Remove from the pan with a draining spoon and transfer to a flameproof casserole.

2 Add the onions to the frying pan and cook, stirring frequently, for about 10 minutes until soft and translucent. Add the peppers and cook for a further 2 minutes. Transfer both to the casserole.

3 Pour the stock over the sausages and vegetables, then add the lentils, dried herbs, salt and pepper. Bring to the boil, then reduce the heat. Cover with a lid and simmer gently for 15–20 minutes until the sausages are thoroughly cooked and the vegetables are tender.

242

# cheesy potato and ham gratin

£ £

**Serves 4**
Preparation  20 minutes
Cooking  1 hour

1 kg potatoes, peeled and thinly sliced

200 g lean cooked ham, shredded

100 g mature Cheddar, grated

2 tsp chopped fresh rosemary or thyme or 1 tsp dried

450 ml chicken or vegetable stock, hot

15 g butter

freshly ground black pepper

**Per serving**
kcal 430, protein 31 g, fat 15 g (of which saturated fat 9 g), carbohydrate 44 g (of which sugars 2 g), fibre 3 g, sodium 0.9 g

1 Preheat the oven to 200°C (gas 6). Arrange a layer of the potatoes in a greased, deep ovenproof dish. Scatter over some of the ham, cheese and herbs and season with pepper. Continue the layers until you have used up all the ingredients, finishing with a layer of potatoes.

2 Pour over the hot stock and dot with a little butter. Bake for 1 hour or until the potatoes are tender and the topping is crisp and golden. Serve hot, straight from the dish.

## COOK SMART

• If using new potatoes, they do not need peeling – simply scrub, then slice.

• This recipe is also good for using up leftover Christmas turkey and Stilton: use them to replace the ham and Cheddar.

• If made ahead, cover while cooking to prevent the gratin drying out. Reheat uncovered at 200°C (gas 6) for 20–30 minutes until heated through and golden brown.

A SIMPLE, COMFORTING DISH THAT IS GREAT FOR A COLD EVENING OR WEEKEND MEAL. IT IS PARTICULARLY GOOD FOR USING UP THOSE ODD BITS OF CHEESE AND HAM THAT YOU MAY HAVE IN THE FRIDGE.

# ham with madeira

£ £ £

**Serves 4**

Preparation  15 minutes, plus overnight
    soaking if necessary
Cooking  1¼ hours

**1 lightly cured gammon hock, about 1 kg**

**1 onion**

**2 cloves**

**green part of 2 leeks, roughly chopped**

**1 carrot, peeled and roughly chopped**

**3 sprigs of fresh parsley**

**1 bay leaf**

**2 tbsp wine vinegar**

**a few peppercorns**

**Madeira sauce**
**1 tbsp cornflour**

**3 tbsp Madeira (or medium-dry sherry)**

**3 tbsp whipping cream**

**1 tbsp Dijon mustard**

**1 tbsp chopped fresh tarragon**

**fresh tarragon to garnish (optional)**

**Per serving**
kcal 443, protein 45 g, fat 24 g (of which
saturated fat 9 g), carbohydrate 9 g (of
which sugars 5 g), fibre 2 g, sodium 2.2 g

---

### COOK SMART

• Leave the ham in the cooking water until
you're ready to carve, as this will keep it
moist and tender.

• Serve with baked jacket potatoes and a
dish of green vegetables, such as peas
and broccoli.

• Make a soup with the leftover cooking
liquid. If there is any ham left over, dice into
small pieces and add to the soup with some
canned haricot beans and frozen mixed
vegetables. Cook gently for 5–10 minutes.

---

**A SMALL GAMMON JOINT PROVIDES EXCELLENT VALUE,
AND TEAMED WITH THIS RICH, CREAMY MADEIRA AND
FRESH TARRAGON SAUCE IT MAKES AN EXTRA SPECIAL
MEAL – THE IDEAL ALTERNATIVE TO A ROAST.**

1 Soak the gammon overnight in cold water, if
necessary, to remove excess salt. (Check the
instructions on the packaging or ask the butcher
if soaking is required.)

2 Drain, throw away the water and put the meat in
a large saucepan and cover with fresh cold water.
Stud the peeled onion with the cloves and put in
the pan with the leeks, carrot, parsley, bay leaf,
vinegar and peppercorns. Bring to the boil slowly,
then reduce the heat and simmer gently for about
1¼ hours, depending on the size of the ham. (Allow
roughly 20 minutes per 450 g, plus 20 minutes.)

3 When the meat is tender, strain 400 ml of the
cooking juices and reserve. Carve the ham into
thick slices and arrange on a warm serving dish.

4 Pour the strained juices into a small pan and reduce
by half over a high heat. Blend the cornflour with the
Madeira, stir into the reduced juices and cook for
2 minutes, stirring, until thickened. Add the cream,
mustard and tarragon and heat through.

5 Coat the meat with a little of the sauce and
serve the rest in a sauceboat. Garnish, if liked,
with tarragon.

GAMMON, SLOW-COOKED WITH HARICOT BEANS, AND SERVED WITH CRUSTY BREAD AND GREENS, MAKES A LOVELY WEEKEND LUNCH.

# gammon pot roast with beans

££

**Serves 6**

Preparation  15 minutes, plus overnight soaking
   if necessary
Cooking  1 hour (for the beans), plus 2 hours

**225g dried haricot beans, soaked in cold water overnight**
**750g gammon joint, soaked overnight if necessary**
**1 sprig of fresh rosemary**
**1 carrot, peeled and finely chopped**
**2 garlic cloves, chopped**
**2 celery sticks, chopped**
**125g chestnut mushrooms, chopped (optional)**
**400g can chopped tomatoes**
**1½ tsp tomato purée**
**1½ tsp Dijon mustard**
**1 tbsp dark muscovado sugar**
**freshly ground black pepper**

**Per serving**
kcal 315, protein 31g, fat 10g (of which saturated
fat 3g), carbohydrate 25g (of which sugars 14g),
fibre 7g, sodium 1.2g

**1** Drain the soaked beans and put them in a large
saucepan. Pour over enough cold water to cover
them. Bring to the boil, without covering the pan
and boil for 10 minutes. Drain and return the beans
to the pan.

**2** Cover the beans with fresh water, add the rosemary,
bring to the boil, then reduce heat, cover and cook
gently for 50 minutes or until the beans are tender.
Preheat the oven to 160°C (gas 3).

**3** Drain the beans and tip into a large casserole.
Stir in the vegetables and the flavourings. (Because
of the salt in the gammon you do not need to add
extra salt.) Nestle the gammon joint, rind and fat
side up, in the beans. Cover the casserole with a
tight-fitting lid and cook in the oven for 1½ hours.

**4** Remove the lid and braise for a further 30 minutes
until the gammon is tender. Lift out the gammon
and carve into slices, then serve with the beans.

## COOK SMART

• When you buy the gammon, ask whether soaking is
required; most gammon is mildly cured, which means
soaking is not necessary.

• If you do not have time to soak dried beans, use two 300g
cans of haricot beans, drained and rinsed, and omit steps
1 and 2.

# liver with raisins

£

**Serves 4**
Preparation and cooking
15 minutes

450 g pig's liver, trimmed
2 tbsp plain flour
2 tbsp tomato purée
2 garlic cloves, crushed
1 bay leaf
200 ml beef or vegetable
     stock
2 tbsp raisins
1 tbsp vegetable oil
3 tbsp wine vinegar
salt and freshly ground
     black pepper

**COOK SMART**
• For a milder flavour, first soak the liver in milk for 30 minutes, then drain.
• Liver is very perishable so should be bought on the day of cooking and kept in the fridge until ready to cook.
• Serve with rice tossed with grilled pieces of smoked bacon and red pepper.

**Per serving**
kcal 270, protein 29 g,
fat 7 g (of which saturated
fat 3 g), carbohydrate 14 g
(of which sugars 6 g),
fibre 0.5 g, sodium 0.1 g

246

1 Rinse the liver, then pat dry with kitchen paper. If it is not already sliced, cut into thin slices. Now cut the liver into strips and toss in the flour, seasoned with salt and pepper. Put the liver in a dry sieve and shake briefly to remove excess flour. Set aside.

2 Put the tomato purée in a small saucepan with the garlic, bay leaf and stock. Simmer very gently for 5 minutes. Add the raisins to the sauce and leave simmering over a low heat.

3 Meanwhile, heat the oil in a frying pan and cook the liver gently for 3–4 minutes over a fairly high heat. Take care not to overcook it. Pour in the vinegar and scrape up any meaty bits with a wooden spatula.

4 Pour the sauce over the liver, stir and serve immediately.

**THIS RICHLY-FLAVOURED PAN-FRIED DISH IS A GREAT WAY OF PREPARING PIG'S LIVER. LAMB'S LIVER CAN BE COOKED IN THE SAME WAY.**

# liver and onions

£ £

**Serves 4**
Preparation and cooking
35 minutes

**Per serving**
kcal 360, protein 32 g,
fat 22 g (of which saturated
fat 8 g), carbohydrate 10 g
(of which sugars 5 g),
fibre 1 g, sodium 0.5 g

450 g lamb's liver, trimmed
2 tbsp plain flour
1 tbsp vegetable oil
25 g butter
4 rindless smoked streaky
     bacon rashers, chopped
2 onions, thinly sliced
227 g can chopped tomatoes
175 ml beef or vegetable stock
2 tbsp Worcestershire sauce
1 tbsp tomato purée
¼ tsp dried mixed herbs
salt and freshly ground
     black pepper

To serve
4 tbsp soured cream
2 tbsp chopped fresh parsley

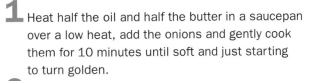

**MELTINGLY TENDER LIVER COOKED WITH ONIONS, BACON AND TOMATOES MAKES A QUICK AND EASY ECONOMICAL MEAL.**

**1** Heat half the oil and half the butter in a saucepan over a low heat, add the onions and gently cook them for 10 minutes until soft and just starting to turn golden.

**2** Meanwhile, rinse the liver, then pat dry with kitchen paper. If it is not already sliced, cut into thin slices. Toss each piece in the flour, seasoned with salt and pepper.

**3** Add the tomatoes with their juice, the stock, Worcestershire sauce, tomato purée and herbs to the onions and bring to the boil. Reduce the heat, cover and leave to cook on a gentle simmer, stirring occasionally.

**4** Meanwhile, heat the remaining oil and butter in a large frying pan over a moderate heat until sizzling. Add the liver and bacon and fry for 3–4 minutes on each side until the liver is just cooked and the bacon is lightly browned and crispy. Do not cook for too long or the liver will become tough.

**5** Remove the liver and bacon from the pan using a draining spoon and put onto warm serving plates, with the bacon scattered over the top of the liver. Spoon the onion and tomato sauce on the side, then top each serving with soured cream and sprinkle with parsley. Serve immediately.

### COOK SMART

• For lamb's liver with mushrooms, leave out the bacon and use one sliced onion with 100g halved button mushrooms, sautéed for just 5 minutes.

• Serve with pasta ribbons or creamed potatoes and seasonal greens.

# pan-fried lamb's kidneys

£

**Serves 4**
Preparation and cooking
15 minutes

**6 lamb's kidneys**
**15 g unsalted butter**
**1 tbsp wine vinegar**
**1 tbsp Dijon mustard**
**100 ml single cream**
**2 tsp chopped fresh tarragon**
**salt and freshly ground black pepper**
**fresh tarragon to garnish (optional)**

**Per serving**
kcal 150, protein 14 g, fat 10 g (of which saturated fat 6 g), carbohydrate 1 g (of which sugars 1 g), fibre 0 g, sodium 0.3 g

1 Remove the transparent membrane covering the kidneys. Cut them in half crossways and remove the core in the middle.

2 Melt the butter in a non-stick pan. Put the kidneys in the pan, cut side down. Cook on a fairly high heat for 2 minutes, then turn and cook for a further 2 minutes, pressing them flat with a spatula as they cook. Take care not to overcook the kidneys or they will be dry and rubbery. Remove kidneys to a plate.

3 Pour the vinegar into the pan and scrape up any meaty bits using the spatula. Cook on a high heat until most of the vinegar has evaporated. Add the mustard and cream and bring almost to boiling point, stirring all the time. Stir in the tarragon and season to taste with salt and pepper.

4 Return the kidneys to the pan, reheat for a few seconds, then serve immediately. Garnish with extra tarragon, if liked.

**COOK SMART**
• Alternatively, cook only four kidneys and add a grilled chipolata sausage per person.

---

£

**Serves 4**
Preparation  10 minutes
Cooking  6–8 minutes

**40 g butter, softened**
**1 tbsp chopped fresh parsley**
**1 garlic clove, crushed**
**450 g lamb's liver, trimmed and sliced**
**8 rindless smoked back bacon rashers**
**4 firm tomatoes**
**1 tbsp vegetable oil**
**freshly ground black pepper**
**sprigs of flat-leaf parsley to garnish**

**Per serving**
kcal 324, protein 28 g, fat 22 g (of which saturated fat 9 g), carbohydrate 3 g (of which sugars 3 g), fibre 1 g, sodium 0.5 g

# liver and bacon kebabs

1 First soak eight wooden skewers in cold water for 30 minutes. Alternatively, use metal skewers. Put the butter in a bowl, add the parsley and garlic and blend together using a fork. Chill in the fridge.

2 Cut the liver into 3 cm square pieces and cut the bacon into 3 cm strips. Cut the tomatoes into halves, then cut each half into three to give six wedges from each tomato. Scoop out the seeds.

3 Preheat a moderate grill. Arrange alternate pieces of bacon, liver and tomato (three wedges per skewer) on the skewers. Brush lightly with oil and season with pepper.

4 Lay the kebabs on the grill pan and cook for 6–8 minutes until the liver is just tender, giving them a quarter-turn every few minutes.

5 Put the kebabs on warm serving plates, top with knobs of the herb and garlic butter and serve hot garnished with parsley.

**COOKSMART**
• This recipe would also work well with small squares of steak or lean lamb.
• Serve with soft polenta and spinach.

LIVER AND BACON ARE A CLASSIC COMBINATION, BUT HERE THEY ARE SERVED IN A LIGHT, MODERN WAY – GREAT FOR A QUICK SUPPER.

# veget

**making the
most of
abundant
seasonal
ingredients**

# ables

From crisp lettuces and leafy greens to juicy tomatoes, sweet root vegetables and tender shoots, glorious seasonal vegetables are a must for anyone making the most of their budget. Incredibly versatile, utterly delicious and great value in season, you can make a fabulous variety of dishes using both fresh and frozen vegetables. Refreshing salads, creamy gratins, crisp stir-fries, golden pancakes and fritters, spicy curries, luscious soufflés, frittatas and quiches: the possibilities are endless.

# red, white and green bean salad

MAKE THIS GLORIOUS SALAD WHEN GREEN BEANS ARE IN SEASON. IT IS LIGHT, FRESH AND UTTERLY IRRESISTIBLE.

£ £

**Serves 4 as a side dish** V
Preparation 25 minutes

50 ml red grape or apple juice
3 tbsp tomato ketchup
2 tbsp red wine vinegar
1 tbsp Dijon mustard
2 tsp olive oil
¾ tsp ground ginger
¾ tsp salt
1 red onion, halved and thinly sliced
350 g green beans, cut into short lengths
400 g can red kidney beans, drained and rinsed
300 g can cannellini beans, drained and rinsed

**Per serving**
kcal 206, protein 12.5 g, fat 3 g (of which saturated fat 0.6 g), carbohydrate 34 g (of which sugars 13.5 g), fibre 11.5 g, sodium 1.2 g

1 Whisk together the grape juice, ketchup, vinegar, mustard, oil, ginger and salt in a large bowl. Add the onion, stirring to coat in the dressing. Set aside.

2 Cook the green beans in boiling water for 4 minutes or until just tender. Drain and refresh in a sieve under cold running water, to cool quickly and retain their bright green colour. Add to the bowl with the onions and toss to combine.

3 Gently fold in the red and white canned beans and stir everything together. Serve at room temperature or chilled.

## COOK SMART

• Serve as an accompaniment to cold cuts, or for an easy meal with some tasty cheese and rustic bread.

• This would also be good for a large supper or buffet party, or packed up to take on a picnic. For a heartier meal, add strips of cold roast chicken or beef.

• Use frozen green beans when fresh are not in season. Cook following pack instructions, then refresh in cold water.

# pumpkin ratatouille

SERVE AS A SIDE DISH, OR USE AS A FILLING FOR JACKET POTATOES OR A SIMPLE OMELETTE.

£ £

**Serves 4 as a side dish** V
Preparation 15 minutes
Cooking 30 minutes

**Per serving**
kcal 90, protein 3 g, fat 3.5 g (of which saturated fat 1 g), carbohydrate 11 g (of which sugars 10 g), fibre 3.5 g, sodium 0.01 g

1 tbsp olive oil
1 onion, chopped
1 green pepper, seeded and diced
500 g pumpkin, peeled, seeded and diced
1 courgette, diced
4 tomatoes, diced
2 garlic cloves, crushed
¼ tsp paprika
1 tsp fresh rosemary or thyme or ¼ tsp dried
salt and freshly ground black pepper
sprigs of fresh rosemary or thyme to garnish

1 Heat the oil in a large-lidded frying pan or saucepan. Cook the onion for 5 minutes or until light golden, then add the green pepper, pumpkin, courgette, tomatoes and garlic.

2 Sprinkle with the paprika, herbs and salt and pepper to season, then cover the pan and cook gently for 30 minutes, stirring occasionally, until all the vegetables are tender. Serve hot, garnished with fresh herb sprigs.

## COOK SMART

• For added protein, add a handful of roughly chopped cashew nuts plus some raisins at the end of cooking.

• Butternut squash could replace the pumpkin.

# warm spinach, mushroom and turkey salad

THIS WARM SALAD, WITH THE PERFECT BALANCE OF VEGETABLES, PROTEIN AND CARBOHYDRATE, MAKES A GREAT LIGHT LUNCH OR SUPPER. SERVE WITH PITTA BREAD.

**Serves 4 as a light meal**
Preparation 20–25 minutes

1 tbsp vegetable oil

4 smoked turkey or bacon rashers, cut crossways into narrow strips

225 g baby spinach leaves

1 yellow pepper, seeded and cut into small squares

1 small red onion, halved and thinly sliced

350 g button mushrooms, thinly sliced

2 x 300 g cans haricot or cannellini beans, drained and rinsed

125 ml vegetable or tomato juice

2 tbsp red wine vinegar

1 tbsp Dijon mustard

salt and freshly ground black pepper

### COOK SMART
• Loose, medium-sized button mushrooms are ideal for this salad. They needn't be the very small ones in supermarket packs, which tend to be more expensive. Check out local farm shops for buying mushrooms in bulk at bargain prices.

**Per serving**
kcal 235, protein 15 g, fat 9 g (of which saturated fat 2 g), carbohydrate 25 g (of which sugars 9 g), fibre 9 g, sodium 1 g

1 Heat the oil in a large frying pan over a medium heat. Add the turkey and cook for 5 minutes or until crisp. Lift out with a draining spoon onto kitchen paper.

2 Combine the spinach, pepper and red onion in a serving bowl and scatter over the turkey pieces.

3 Add the mushrooms to the pan and cook for 3–4 minutes until lightly coloured. Add the beans and stir-fry with the mushrooms to heat through.

4 Whisk together the vegetable or tomato juice, vinegar and mustard with salt and pepper to season. Pour over the bean and mushroom mixture and bring to the boil.

5 Immediately tip the hot vegetable mixture over the salad in the bowl and toss to combine. Serve at once with sesame pitta bread.

### COOK SMART
• You can buy sesame pitta bread or, to make your own, brush plain pitta with a little oil, sprinkle with sesame seeds and warm under the grill until lightly toasted.

# squash with honey and raisins

**Serves 6 as a side dish** Ⓥ

Preparation 10 minutes
Cooking 25–30 minutes

1 butternut squash, peeled, seeded
  and cubed

2 onions, chopped

2 garlic cloves, crushed

100 ml vegetable stock, hot

2 tsp *ras-el-hanout* spice mixture

50 g raisins

2 tsp honey

salt and freshly ground black pepper

a few fresh chives to garnish (optional)

**Per serving**

kcal 110, protein 4 g, fat 0.5 g
(of which saturated fat 0.1 g),
carbohydrate 24 g (of which sugars
16 g), fibre 3 g, sodium 0.01 g

**1** Put the squash, onions and garlic in a saucepan, pour over the stock, then cover and cook gently for 15 minutes.

**2** Sprinkle the vegetables with the *ras-el-hanout* spice mixture and add the raisins and honey. Season with salt and pepper, stir well, then cover and cook gently for a further 10–15 minutes until the squash is tender and the stock has evaporated. Serve hot, garnished with chives, if liked.

## COOK SMART

• *Ras-el-Hanout* is a Moroccan blend of aromatic spices including allspice, aniseed, cardamom, cloves, cumin, ginger, nutmeg and orris root – many of which are said to have aphrodisiac properties. You'll find it in the herbs and spices section in larger supermarkets.

• When ready to serve, add a little butter and perhaps a few whole almonds.

• This would be good served with grilled lamb chops, chicken or sausages.

BUTTERNUT SQUASH IS A REAL WINTER TREAT. MELTINGLY SWEET AND MOREISH, IT IS SO GOOD COOKED WITH WARMING MOROCCAN FLAVOURS.

# steamed sesame spinach

£

**Serves 4 as a side dish** Ⓥ
Preparation 10 minutes
Cooking 3–5 minutes

**450 g spinach, thick stems
removed**

**pinch of dried crushed
chillies**

**2 tsp toasted sesame oil**

**½ tsp salt**

**1 tsp lemon juice**

**1 tbsp sesame seeds,
toasted**

**Per serving**
kcal 65, protein 14 g,
fat 5 g (of which saturated
fat 0.5 g), carbohydrate 2 g
(of which sugars 1.5 g),
fibre 2.5 g, sodium 0.4 g

**1** Put the spinach in a medium saucepan with just the water clinging to the leaves after washing. Add the crushed chillies and cook for 3–5 minutes until just wilted. Drain thoroughly and transfer to a serving bowl.

**2** Sprinkle the spinach with the sesame oil, salt and lemon juice and toss to mix. Sprinkle with toasted sesame seeds, then serve at once.

**COOK SMART**
• This recipe would also work well for broccoli. Cut the spears into florets and slice the stems. Either cook in a little water or steam the broccoli with the chilli flakes for 3–4 minutes or until just tender. Complete as above.

• Dried crushed chillies are not the same as chilli powder and are readily available in jars.

• This would make a lovely dish to serve as part of a Chinese meal

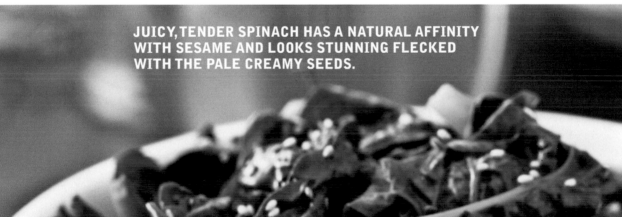

JUICY, TENDER SPINACH HAS A NATURAL AFFINITY WITH SESAME AND LOOKS STUNNING FLECKED WITH THE PALE CREAMY SEEDS.

AROMATIC SPICES, GARLIC AND FRESH PARSLEY
TRANSFORM CARROTS INTO A FABULOUS SIDE DISH.

## COOK SMART

• If possible, use flat-leaf parsley, which has a better flavour than curly parsley, and add a few chopped walnuts. Chopped fresh mint would also marry well with the carrots.

• For an extra spicy flavour, you could also sprinkle the cooked carrots with some cumin seeds, toasted in a dry frying pan for 1–2 minutes.

• Serve as a side dish with a spicy main course, such as Moroccan Braised Chicken (page 193).

# carrots with cumin

£

**Serves 4 as a side dish**  Ⓥ
Preparation  10 minutes
Cooking  20–25 minutes

**4 garlic cloves, crushed**

**½ tsp ground cumin**

**pinch of paprika**

**2 tbsp olive oil**

**750 g carrots, peeled and sliced diagonally**

**pinch of salt**

**1 tbsp chopped fresh parsley**

**sprig of flat-leaf parsley to garnish (optional)**

**Per serving**
kcal 115, protein 1 g, fat 6 g
(of which saturated fat 1 g),
carbohydrate 15 g (of which sugars
14 g), fibre 4.5 g, sodium 0.04 g

**1** Put the garlic, cumin, paprika, oil and 3 tbsp water in a saucepan, stir together and boil for 1 minute.

**2** Add the carrots to the pan, pour over 300 ml boiling water and add a pinch of salt. Cover and cook on a low heat for 20–25 minutes or until all the liquid has evaporated and the carrots are tender. If any liquid remains, uncover the saucepan to let it cook off.

**3** Tip the carrots into a serving dish and scatter over the chopped parsley. Garnish with a sprig of parsley, if liked.

# carrots with chestnuts

💷

**Serves 4 as side dish** Ⅴ
Preparation 30 minutes
Cooking 30 minutes

**300 g fresh chestnuts**
**2 tbsp vegetable oil**
**3 carrots, peeled and sliced**
**3–4 sprigs of fresh thyme**
**½ tsp fennel seeds**
**salt and freshly ground black pepper**

**COOK SMART**
- For a storecupboard variation on this dish, use a vacuum-pack or can of cooked and peeled chestnuts and omit steps 1 and 2.
- This would make a super accompaniment to roast chicken or turkey.

**Per serving**
kcal 200, protein 2 g,
fat 8 g (of which saturated
fat 1 g), carbohydrate 33.5 g
(of which sugars 11 g),
fibre 5 g, sodium 0.02 g

**FRESH CHESTNUTS ARE ONLY IN SEASON FOR A SHORT TIME, SO MAKE THE MOST OF THEM DURING THE WINTER MONTHS.**

1 Score all around each chestnut with the point of a knife. Bring a saucepan of water to the boil, add 1 tbsp of the oil and the chestnuts and boil for 10 minutes. (The oil helps to loosen the skins so they will be easier to peel.)

2 Remove the pan from the heat and lift out just a few chestnuts at a time with a draining spoon. Remove the outer shell and inner brown skin – they peel much more easily when piping hot, but you will need to wear rubber gloves for this operation.

3 Heat the remaining oil in a large frying pan, add the chestnuts and carrots and cook, stirring, for 5 minutes or until the chestnuts are golden brown.

4 Sprinkle with 100 ml water and add two thyme sprigs and the fennel seeds. Cook gently for 30 minutes, uncovered, shaking the pan occasionally. Add more water if needed, then drain if necessary when the vegetables are cooked. Season with salt and pepper.

5 Remove the cooked thyme and garnish with fresh sprigs to serve.

# balsamic baked tomatoes with parmesan crumbs

SOMETIMES ALL YOU NEED IS A FEW FINE INGREDIENTS TO PRODUCE A FABULOUS DISH. HERE, THE SIMPLE COMBINATION OF TOMATOES, BREADCRUMBS AND PARMESAN PRODUCE A DISH FIT FOR A KING.

**Serves 8 as a side dish**
Preparation 10 minutes
Cooking 25 minutes

4 large beef tomatoes, about
   250 g each
¼ tsp salt
50 g fresh wholemeal breadcrumbs
3 tbsp freshly grated Parmesan
1 tbsp olive oil
5 tbsp balsamic vinegar
2 tbsp light muscovado sugar

260

**Per serving**
kcal 90, protein 3 g, fat 3 g (of which
saturated fat 1 g), carbohydrate 12.5 g
(of which sugars 8 g), fibre 1 g,
sodium 0.1 g

**1** Preheat the oven to 200°C (gas 6). Cut the tomatoes in half horizontally, then place them, cut-side up, in an ovenproof baking dish large enough to hold them in a single layer. Sprinkle with salt.

**2** Combine the breadcrumbs, Parmesan and oil in a small bowl, then sprinkle evenly over the tomatoes.

**3** Bake for 25 minutes until the topping is golden and crispy and the tomatoes are cooked through.

**4** Meanwhile, combine the vinegar and brown sugar with 2 tbsp water in a small frying pan. Bring to the boil over a high heat and cook for 3 minutes until syrupy. Drizzle over the baked tomatoes and serve immediately.

### COOK SMART
• This versatile dish makes a lovely accompaniment to grilled meat or fish or could be served on a brunch table. As a starter or light meal, allow two tomato halves per person and garnish or serve with salad leaves.

• If preferred, use mature Cheddar in place of Parmesan.

# celeriac batons with tomato

**Serves 4 as a side dish** V

Preparation 15 minutes

Cooking 55 minutes

1 tbsp olive oil

2 onions, sliced

600 g tomatoes, skinned, seeded and chopped

2 garlic cloves, crushed

1 tbsp chopped fresh sage

½ tsp sugar

1 head celeriac, about 500 g

salt and freshly ground black pepper

sprig of fresh sage to garnish

**Per serving**

kcal 93, protein 3 g, fat 4 g (of which saturated fat 0.5 g), carbohydrate 12 g (of which sugars 10 g), fibre 6 g, sodium 0.1 g

**1** Heat the oil in a saucepan, add the onions and cook on a medium heat for 5 minutes. Add the tomatoes, garlic, sage and sugar, season with salt and pepper, then cover and cook gently for 30 minutes.

**2** Peel the celeriac, cut into slices, then cut these into thick 5 cm long matchsticks. Add to the tomato sauce with 4 tbsp water. Bring to the boil, cover and simmer gently for a further 20 minutes or until the celeriac is tender. Garnish with fresh sage.

## COOK SMART

• For a sweeter celeriac dish, cut the vegetable into sticks, then cook for 15 minutes in boiling, salted water. Drain, then cook gently in a pan with 30 g butter and 2 tbsp raisins for 5 minutes, stirring regularly.

CELERIAC HAS A SWEET, NUTTY FLAVOUR AND IS PARTICULARLY GOOD SERVED WITH PORK AND CHICKEN.

262

SWEET RED ONIONS BECOME WONDERFULLY TENDER
AND TAKE ON A GLORIOUS COLOUR WHEN COOKED WITH
BEETROOT – GREAT WITH PORK AND CHEESE DISHES.

# compote of red onions

£

**Serves 4 as a side dish** Ⅴ
Preparation  15 minutes
Cooking  35 minutes

**2 tbsp olive oil**

**500 g red onions, thinly
sliced**

**3 tbsp red wine (or sherry)
vinegar**

**1 tsp curry powder**

**1 tsp honey**

**2 sprigs of fresh thyme**

**pinch of salt**

**1 small cooked beetroot,
about 50 g (fresh or
vacuum packed)**

### COOK SMART
• To slice onions, cut the
peeled onions in half from
top to bottom, then remove
the hard base of the root.
Place cut side down on the
work surface and slice in
half-circles.

**Per serving**
kcal 110, protein 2 g,
fat 6 g (of which saturated
fat 1 g), carbohydrate 12 g
(of which sugars 9 g),
fibre 2 g, sodium 0.02 g

**1** Heat the oil in a large saucepan and cook
the onions for 8–10 minutes over a medium
heat, stirring, until they are golden.

**2** Pour the vinegar over the onions and scrape
the bottom of the pan with a wooden spatula.
Add the curry powder, honey, one sprig of thyme,
2 tbsp water and a pinch of salt. Cover and cook
gently for 20 minutes, stirring frequently.

**3** Peel and slice the beetroot, then finely chop it in
a food processor. Add to the onions and simmer
for 5 minutes. Remove the cooked thyme before
serving and garnish with a fresh sprig.

# roasted cauliflower with parmesan and almonds

£

**Serves 4 as a side dish**
Preparation 10 minutes
Cooking 25 minutes

**1 large cauliflower,
   cut into florets**
**100 g raisins**
**25 g dried breadcrumbs**
**2 tbsp freshly grated
   Parmesan**
**1 tbsp flaked almonds**
**1 tbsp olive oil**
**2 tbsp lemon juice**

### COOK SMART
• To make your own dried breadcrumbs, place slices of white or wholemeal bread on a baking tray and bake at 150°C (gas 2) until completely dried out but not browned. Let the toasts cool, then whizz them to fine crumbs in a food processor.

### Per serving
kcal 215, protein 9 g, fat 9 g (of which saturated fat 2 g), carbohydrate 26 g (of which sugars 21 g), fibre 3 g, sodium 0.2 g

1 Preheat the oven to 200°C (gas 6). Cook the cauliflower in a steamer, set over a pan of boiling water, for 5 minutes or until just tender.

2 Meanwhile, stir together the raisins, breadcrumbs, Parmesan, almonds and olive oil in a medium bowl.

3 Transfer the cauliflower to a lightly greased roasting tin. Sprinkle the breadcrumb mixture over the cauliflower, then roast for 20 minutes or until the crumbs are toasted.

4 Drizzle the lemon juice over the top and roast for a further 5 minutes. Serve hot or warm.

# cauliflower and spinach gratin

£

**Serves 6 as a side dish** Ⅴ
Preparation  35–40 minutes
Cooking  30 minutes (20 minutes
    for individual dishes)

**450 g frozen leaf spinach**
**600 g potatoes, peeled and quartered**
**1 cauliflower, cut into florets**
**pinch of ground nutmeg**
**60 ml semi-skimmed milk**
**25 g butter, softened**
**2 eggs**
**75 g mature Cheddar, grated**
**salt and freshly ground black pepper**
**sprigs of fresh parsley to garnish (optional)**

**Per serving**
kcal 240, protein 14 g, fat 11 g (of which
saturated fat 6 g), carbohydrate 21 g (of
which sugars 4 g), fibre 4 g, sodium 0.2 g

LAYERS OF CREAMY MASHED POTATO, TASTY
SPINACH AND CAULIFLOWER PURÉE, TOPPED
WITH MELTING CHEESE, MAKES A LUSCIOUS
SIDE DISH FOR A SPECIAL DINNER.

1  Preheat the oven to 200°C (gas 6). Put the frozen spinach in a saucepan, cover and cook over a low heat for 5 minutes or until thawed.

2  Meanwhile, put the potatoes in a pan of lightly salted water. Bring to the boil, then reduce the heat and cook for 15–20 minutes or until tender. Cook the cauliflower in a steamer, over the potatoes, for 10 minutes, or in a separate pan of boiling water.

3  Tip the spinach into a colander and press down with a vegetable masher to squeeze out excess liquid. Chop the spinach roughly and season with salt, pepper and nutmeg.

4  Drain and mash the potatoes with the milk and butter. Spread half the mashed potatoes in a 1 litre ovenproof baking dish (or six individual dishes). Layer the spinach on top of the potatoes.

5  Purée the cauliflower in a blender or food processor. Add the eggs and the remaining mashed potatoes and taste to check seasoning. Spread this mixture over the spinach layer.

6  Sprinkle the top with grated cheese, then put in the oven and bake for 30 minutes (20 minutes for individual dishes) or until golden. Serve hot, garnished with parsley, if liked.

## COOK SMART

• This could be served as a light lunch or supper dish for four.

• Floury varieties of potato, such as King Edward or Maris Piper, are best for mashing.

• If using fresh spinach, you will need 900 g. Remove stalks and coarse midribs, wash thoroughly, then put the wet leaves into a covered pan without adding any extra water and cook gently for 5 minutes.

# oriental stir-fried vegetables

£

**Serves 4 as a side dish**  Ⓥ
Preparation  10–15 minutes
Cooking  7 minutes

**2 tbsp soy sauce**
**2 tbsp dry sherry**
**1 tbsp runny honey**
**3 tbsp vegetable stock**
**3 tbsp vegetable oil**
**750 g mixed fresh vegetables, prepared and cut into similar-sized pieces**
**1 garlic clove, crushed**
**2.5 cm piece of fresh root ginger, peeled and grated**
**2 tsp toasted sesame oil**

266

**COOK SMART**
• For a main course, increase the protein content by stir-frying 100 g of nuts, such as unsalted cashews or peanuts, or 200 g cubed, smoked or marinated tofu in hot oil for a minute or two, before adding the vegetables.

• Serve with Chinese egg noodles or boiled rice.

**Per serving**
kcal 170, protein 7 g,
fat 11 g (of which saturated
fat 2 g), carbohydrate 9 g
(of which sugars 8 g),
fibre 3.5 g, sodium 0.6 g

**1** Put the soy sauce, sherry, honey and stock together in a jug and stir together. Set aside.

**2** Heat the vegetable oil in a wok or large deep frying pan. Add the tougher, slower-cooking vegetables (such as carrots, broccoli, celery, green beans and baby sweetcorn) and stir-fry over a high heat for 30 seconds. Add 1–2 tbsp of water, cover and cook over a high heat for 2 minutes.

**3** Next add the quicker-cooking vegetables (such as peppers, mange-tout, bean sprouts and spring onions) with the garlic and ginger and stir-fry for 1–2 minutes or until they are almost tender.

**4** Finally, stir in any delicate leafy vegetables (such as shredded greens or pak choi) and cook for just 1 more minute until all the vegetables are cooked but still retaining some bite and their bright colour.

**5** Pour in the soy sauce mixture, stir-fry for 1 minute, sprinkle with sesame oil then serve at once.

STIR-FRYING REALLY MAKES THE MOST OF VEGETABLES, RETAINING THE COLOUR, TASTE AND TEXTURE, WHATEVER YOUR SEASONAL CHOICE.

# spiced pan-fried vegetables

**COOK SMART**

• Other vegetables could be used, such as sliced leeks or small broccoli florets in place of the courgette, and petits pois instead of the beans.

• This dish makes a good accompaniment to serve with grilled chicken or fish, or could stand alone as a vegetarian meal for two served with rice, naan bread and yoghurt raita.

£

**Serves 4 as a side dish** Ⅴ
Preparation  15 minutes
Cooking  10–12 minutes

125 g fine green beans, cut in half
2 tbsp vegetable oil
2 shallots, finely chopped
2 garlic cloves, crushed
1 celery stick, chopped
2 carrots, peeled and cut into matchsticks
½ green pepper, seeded and thinly sliced
1 tsp curry powder
1 courgette, cut into matchsticks
2 tsp cornflour
150 ml vegetable stock
salt and freshly ground black pepper
sprig of fresh parsley or coriander to
    garnish (optional)

**Per serving**
kcal 125, protein 5 g, fat 7 g (of which
saturated fat 1 g), carbohydrate 11 g (of
which sugars 9 g), fibre 3.5 g, sodium 0.04 g

SERVE THIS LIGHTLY CURRIED SIDE DISH AS A STUNNING ACCOMPANIMENT TO EITHER PLAIN OR SPICY DISHES. IF THERE IS ANY LEFT OVER, SERVE IT AS A FILLING FOR A JACKET POTATO.

**1** Cook the green beans for 5 minutes, uncovered, in a pan of boiling water. Drain and refresh in a sieve under cold running water.

**2** Heat the oil in a large frying pan. Add the shallots, garlic, celery, carrots and pepper. Cook over a high heat for 3 minutes, mixing well.

**3** Sprinkle in the curry powder, cook for 1 minute, then add the beans and courgette.

**4** Blend the cornflour with a little cold water to make a paste, stir in the stock, then pour into the pan. Bring to the boil, then reduce the heat, cover and simmer for 5–8 minutes until the vegetables are tender and the sauce has thickened. Season to taste, then serve immediately, garnished with a sprig of parsley or coriander, if liked.

RED CABBAGE IS A PERFECT WINTER DISH. IT IS THE CLASSIC ACCOMPANIMENT TO ROAST PORK AND GAME DISHES AND ALSO GOES WELL WITH HAM AND SAUSAGES.

£

**Serves 6 as a side dish** V
Preparation 10 minutes
Cooking 30 minutes

1 tbsp vegetable oil

1 onion, thinly sliced

1 small head red cabbage, cored and coarsely shredded

120 ml red wine

¼ tsp ground allspice

2 tbsp red wine vinegar

1 tbsp light muscovado sugar

¼ tsp salt

15 g butter

**Per serving**
kcal 83, protein 1 g,
fat 4 g (of which saturated
fat 1 g), carbohydrate 7 g (of
which sugars 6 g), fibre 2 g,
sodium 0.1 g

**COOK SMART**
• You could also add
one peeled and chopped
apple to the pan. And if you
happen to have some fresh
cranberries, they could go
in too – 10 minutes before
the other vegetables
are cooked. For a twist,
replace the allspice with
one star anise.

# sweet and sour red cabbage

**1** Heat the oil in a large non stick saucepan over a medium heat. Add the onion and cook for 5 minutes until softened. Add the cabbage, red wine and allspice. Reduce heat, cover and cook gently for 20 minutes or until tender.

**2** Add the vinegar, sugar and salt and cook, uncovered, stirring occasionally, for 5 minutes or until almost all the liquid has evaporated. Stir in the butter and serve.

AUTUMN AND WINTER VEGETABLES ARE GREAT FOR ROASTING. BE
FLEXIBLE WITH THIS DISH AND VARY THE INGREDIENTS, DEPENDING
ON WHAT LOOKS APPEALING AND GOOD VALUE AT THE MARKET.

**Serves 4 as a side dish or
light meal** Ⓥ
Preparation 20–25 minutes
Cooking 40 minutes

**3 tbsp olive oil**

**6 garlic cloves, sliced**

**500g butternut squash, peeled
and cut into chunks**

**300g Brussels sprouts,
trimmed and halved**

**2 large, red dessert apples**

**25g sun-dried tomatoes,
drained, if in oil, and thinly
sliced**

**2 fresh rosemary sprigs or
1 tsp dried**

**pinch of salt**

**250g chestnut mushrooms,
halved**

**4 tbsp freshly grated Parmesan
or mature Cheddar
(optional)**

**Per serving**
kcal 280, protein 11g, fat 18g
(of which saturated fat 5g),
carbohydrate 20g (of which
sugars 14g), fibre 6g,
sodium 0.5g

# roasted harvest vegetables

1 Preheat the oven to 400°C (gas 6). Put the olive
oil and garlic in a large roasting tin and heat for
3 minutes in the oven.

2 Add the squash and Brussels sprouts. Cut the
apples into quarters, core, then thickly slice. Add to
the tin with the sun-dried tomatoes and rosemary.
Sprinkle with salt and toss to combine.

3 Place in the oven and roast for 20 minutes, turning
the vegetables after 10 minutes. Remove the
tin from the oven, add the mushrooms, toss with
the other vegetables, then roast for a further
15 minutes until everything is golden and tender.

4 Sprinkle over the cheese, if liked, and roast for
a further 5 minutes. Serve immediately.

---

**COOK SMART**
• You could make this dish with parsnips, carrots, swede
or turnip, peeled and cut into chunks, instead of the
squash, or throw in some small button onions – whatever
takes your fancy. For a special occasion, substitute thickly
sliced shiitake mushrooms in place of the chestnut variety.
• Fresh rosemary is an easy herb to grow and is a hardy
evergreen, so it can be used year round.

CREAMY GOAT'S CHEESE AND FRESH
SPINACH FORM A GLORIOUS PARTNERSHIP
IN THIS CROSS BETWEEN A THICK,
SPANISH-STYLE OMELETTE AND A PANCAKE.

# spinach and goat's cheese pancake wedges

£ £

**Serves 4 as a side dish** Ⅴ
Preparation 15 minutes
Cooking 13 minutes

500 g spinach, roughly
   chopped
1 tbsp chopped fresh
   parsley
¼ tsp ground nutmeg
pinch of sugar
pinch of salt
4 tbsp plain flour
125 g rindless, soft goat's
   cheese
2 eggs, lightly beaten
15 g butter

**COOK SMART**

• If you have a blini pan,
you can make four small
individual pancakes.

• These pancakes go well
as an accompaniment to
meat or fish. Alternatively
you could dry-fry some
sliced, spicy sausage and
serve it scattered over the
top of the pancakes.

**Per serving**
kcal 220, protein 13 g,
fat 12 g (of which saturated
fat 6 g), carbohydrate 14 g
(of which sugars 3 g),
fibre 3 g, sodium 0.4 g

1  Cook the spinach in a large saucepan using just
   the water clinging to the leaves after washing them.
   Cook for 3–4 minutes until just wilted, stirring from
   time to time. Drain off excess liquid.

2  Add the parsley, nutmeg, sugar and salt to the
   spinach, then stir in the flour.

3  Take the pan off the heat and beat in the goat's
   cheese, then the eggs.

4  Melt half the butter in a large non-stick frying pan and
   spread out the spinach mixture to a thickness of about
   1 cm. Cook for 5 minutes over a moderate heat, then
   for 3 minutes on a low heat until golden underneath.

5  Slip the pancake on to a plate and add the remaining
   butter to the pan. Turn the pancake over, then slide
   it back into the pan and cook for 5 minutes, over a
   moderate heat, on the other side. Cut into four
   wedges to serve.

# vegetable medley with bacon and kidney beans

£

**Serves 4 as a side dish**
Preparation 10 minutes
Cooking 25 minutes

2 rindless, smoked back bacon rashers
1 leek, trimmed and sliced
2 carrots, peeled and diced
½ small green cabbage, shredded
400 g can red kidney beans, drained
   and rinsed
2 tbsp snipped fresh chives or chopped
   fresh parsley
salt and freshly ground black pepper
fresh chives and sprigs of fresh parsley
   to garnish (optional)

**Per serving**
kcal 140, protein 9 g, fat 3 g (of which
saturated fat 1 g), carbohydrate 20 g (of
which sugars 9 g), fibre 7 g, sodium 0.5 g

1  Trim any fat from the bacon, then cut the lean
   rashers into dice. Put the bacon in a saucepan with
   the leek, carrots and cabbage. Pour over 4 tbsp
   water, season with salt and pepper, then cover
   and cook gently for 20 minutes.

2  When the vegetables are almost tender, add the
   kidney beans to the pan and heat through gently for
   5 minutes. Toss in the snipped chives or chopped
   parsley and garnish with chives or sprigs of parsley,
   if using.

**COOK SMART**
• For a variation, replace the cabbage with 400 g canned
tomatoes and a 200 g can of sweetcorn. Season with ½ tsp
each of ground cumin and coriander and a pinch of paprika.

• This dish would go well with a ham joint or pork spare ribs.

• For a vegetarian dish, omit the bacon and add 150 g button
mushrooms cooked gently in a knob of butter.

RED KIDNEY BEANS
AND SMOKED BACON
ADD A WONDERFUL
DEPTH OF FLAVOUR
AND EXTRA SUBSTANCE
TO THIS LOVELY DISH. IT
IS A GREAT CHOICE IN
WINTER AND AUTUMN.

THESE CRISP FRITTERS
MADE WITH SWEET AND JUICY
CORN KERNELS WILL MAKE
A POPULAR CASUAL DISH
SERVED WITH A COOLING
WATERCRESS DIP.

£

**Serves 4** Ⅴ
   **(makes about 12)**
Preparation  10 minutes
Cooking  15 minutes

**125 g plain flour**
**½ tsp baking powder**
**2 eggs, lightly beaten**
**150 ml semi-skimmed milk**
**400 g frozen sweetcorn,
   thawed and drained**
**1 fresh red chilli, seeded
   and finely chopped
   (optional)**
**salt and freshly ground
   black pepper**

**Watercress dip**
**85 g watercress, trimmed
   and chopped**
**juice of ½ lemon**
**200 g Greek-style yoghurt**

**COOK SMART**
• These fritters are also
good made with frozen
peas or frozen mixed
vegetables. If fresh corn
cobs are available, scrape
off the kernels and lightly
crush them, then add to
the batter. Or you can use
drained, canned sweetcorn.

• These fritters would also
be tasty served with
tomato salsa. Kids may
prefer ketchup.

**Per serving**
kcal 325, protein 15 g,
fat 11 g (of which saturated
fat 4 g), carbohydrate 44 g
(of which sugars 5 g),
fibre 2 g, sodium 0.2 g

1 Sift the flour, baking powder and a pinch of salt into
a bowl and make a well in the centre. Add the eggs
and milk and gradually beat in, using a balloon whisk
or a wooden spoon, drawing in the flour from the
sides to make a thick, smooth batter. Stir the
sweetcorn and chilli, if using, into the batter and
season with pepper. Put aside until ready to cook.

2 For the dip, stir the chopped watercress and lemon
juice into the yoghurt. Spoon into a serving bowl,
cover and keep chilled.

3 To cook the fritters, heat a greased griddle or large,
heavy-based frying pan. Drop large spoonfuls of the
batter onto the pan, making three or four fritters at
a time, and cook over a moderate heat for 2 minutes
until nicely browned and firm on the underside.

4 Using a palette knife or fish slice, turn the fritters
over and cook for a further 1–2 minutes or until
the flip-side is cooked. Remove and drain on kitchen
paper. Keep warm while cooking the rest of the
fritters in the same way, greasing the pan between
batches. Serve hot with the watercress dip.

# corn
# fritters with
# watercress
# dip

NOURISHING LENTILS ARE GREAT VALUE AND VERY GOOD FOR YOU. THE WARM SPICES AND RICH COCONUT MILK COMBINE TO CREATE AN INTOXICATINGLY FLAVOURED DISH.

# curried lentils

£

**Serves 6 as a light meal**
**(or 4 as a main course)**
Preparation  15 minutes
Cooking  30–40 minutes

**1 tbsp vegetable oil**

**15 g butter**

**1 onion, finely chopped**

**2 garlic cloves, crushed**

**1 red pepper, seeded and diced**

**1 tsp curry powder**

**200 g brown or green lentils**

**100 ml coconut milk**

**1 tbsp chopped fresh coriander (optional)**

**salt and freshly ground black pepper**

**Per serving (as a light meal)**
kcal 315, protein 14g, fat 16g (of which saturated fat 10g), carbohydrate 31g (of which sugars 5g), fibre 6g, sodium 0.05g

**1** Heat the oil in a deep frying pan, add the butter and cook the onion and garlic gently for 8–10 minutes until lightly golden. Add the pepper, sprinkle with the curry powder and mix well.

**2** Stir in the lentils and add 700 ml cold water. Bring to the boil, then reduce the heat, cover and cook gently for 20–30 minutes until the lentils are almost tender but not mushy, and the water has been absorbed.

**3** Stir in the coconut milk and simmer uncovered for a further 5–10 minutes. Season to taste and add chopped coriander, if liked. Serve hot.

**COOK SMART**

• Cooking times for lentils vary depending on the variety and their age. Red split lentils cook very quickly and can be easily puréed. Green and brown lentils take slightly longer and retain their shape well after cooking. Do not salt until the end of cooking as this will toughen the skins and prevent them from softening.

• Leftover canned coconut milk will keep in a tightly sealed container in the fridge and could be used for a Thai-style curry.

SERVE THIS TRADITIONAL AMERICAN DISH
WITH BARBECUED CHICKEN OR PORK OR AS A
MAIN COURSE WITH BREAD, RICE OR POTATOES.

£

**Serves 8 as a side dish
(or 4 as a main course)**
Preparation  1 hour, plus
    overnight soaking
Cooking  1 hour

**300 g dried haricot beans,
    soaked overnight**

**1 tbsp vegetable oil**

**2 smoked bacon rashers,
    cut in half crossways**

**1 large onion, chopped**

**4 tbsp tomato ketchup**

**4 tbsp black treacle**

**1 tbsp chilli sauce, or to
    taste**

**50 g light muscovado
    sugar**

**1 tsp wholegrain mustard**

**COOK SMART**
• Other dried beans could
be used, such as red
kidney or black-eyed.
Do not worry if the dried
weight doesn't look much
– they triple in volume
when cooked.
• For a quick version, use
three 300 g cans of haricot
beans and 100 ml stock.
Omit step 1.

**Per serving (as a side dish)**
kcal 193, protein 10 g,
fat 3 g (of which saturated
fat 0.5 g), carbohydrate 34 g
(of which sugars 16 g),
fibre 6.5 g, sodium 0.3 g

**1** Drain the soaked beans and rinse under cold
running water. Put them in a large saucepan, cover
with cold water and bring to the boil. Boil rapidly for
10 minutes, then reduce the heat and simmer for
50 minutes or until tender. Drain well, reserving
375 ml of the cooking liquid. Transfer the reserved
liquid and the beans to a large casserole dish.

**2** Preheat the oven to 150°C (gas 2). Heat the oil in
a frying pan over a medium heat. Add the bacon
and fry for 5 minutes or until crisp. Remove and
drain on kitchen paper, then cut up into small
pieces. Cook the onion in the bacon fat left in
the pan for 5 minutes or until soft. Add the bacon
and onion to the casserole.

**3** Combine the ketchup, treacle, chilli sauce, sugar
and mustard in a small bowl, then pour over the
casserole and stir to combine.

**4** Cover and bake for 1 hour, stirring once, until hot
and bubbling.

# boston baked beans

**THIS SIMPLE COMBINATION OF INGREDIENTS IS DELICIOUS SERVED AS A SIDE DISH OR AS A VEGETARIAN MAIN COURSE WITH BASMATI RICE OR WARM NAAN BREAD.**

£

**Serves 2 as a main course** V
**(or 4 as a side dish)**
Preparation 20 minutes
Cooking 20 minutes

1 small onion, cut into chunks
3 garlic cloves, peeled
5 cm piece fresh root ginger, peeled and sliced
1 tbsp vegetable oil
250 g chestnut mushrooms, halved
2 tsp curry powder (preferably Madras)
375 g small new potatoes, scrubbed and quartered
½ tsp salt
150 g frozen peas, thawed
125 g natural low-fat yoghurt

**Per serving (as a main course)**
kcal 325, protein 15 g, fat 9 g (of which saturated fat 1.5 g), carbohydrate 49 g (of which sugars 12 g), fibre 8 g, sodium 0.6 g

**1** Combine the onion, garlic, ginger and 3 tbsp water in a food processor or blender and process to make a purée.

**2** Heat the oil in a large frying pan over a medium heat. Add the onion purée and cook for 5 minutes or until the liquid has evaporated. Add the mushrooms to the pan and cook for 3 minutes, stirring frequently, until just tender.

**3** Stir in the curry powder. Add the potatoes and salt to the pan and stir so that the potatoes are well coated with the spice mixture. Add 250 ml water and bring to the boil. Reduce to a simmer, cover and cook for 15 minutes or until the potatoes are tender.

**4** Stir in the peas and cook for 2 minutes until heated through. Remove from the heat, stir in the yoghurt and serve immediately.

**COOK SMART**
• Chestnut mushrooms have a firm texture and hold their shape well when cooked. Fresh shiitake mushrooms would also be good for this curry, having a unique steak-like texture and subtle meaty flavour, but they do cost more. At the other end of the price range, check out cooking mushrooms at the supermarket for good value.

# potato curry with peas and mushrooms

# garlic and thyme potato gratin

**POTATOES ARE FILLING, COMFORTING, CHEAP AND VERSATILE. THIS LEAVE-TO-COOK DISH IS JUST AS GOOD FOR A MID-WEEK SUPPER AS FOR A DINNER PARTY.**

£

**Serves 4 as a side dish**  Ⓥ
Preparation  10 minutes
Cooking  45 minutes

**700 g potatoes, peeled and thinly sliced**

**3 garlic cloves, crushed**

**2 tsp chopped fresh thyme**

**100 ml vegetable stock**

**25 g butter**

**salt and freshly ground black pepper**

**sprigs of fresh thyme to garnish**

**Per serving**
kcal 190, protein 6 g, fat 6 g
(of which saturated fat 3 g),
carbohydrate 30 g (of which
sugars 1 g), fibre 2 g,
sodium 0.06 g

**1** Heat the oven to 200°C (gas 6). Mix the potatoes with the garlic and thyme, season with salt and pepper, then spread evenly in a 1 litre greased baking dish (or four individual ovenproof dishes).

**2** Pour over the stock and dot with knobs of butter. Put in the oven and bake for 45 minutes or until the potatoes are tender and golden on top. Serve hot, garnished with sprigs of fresh thyme.

**COOK SMART**

• The quickest way to slice potatoes thinly is using the slicing disc on a food processor, if you have one. Alternatively, use the smooth cross blade on a box grater.

• Charlotte or Pink Fir Apple are good potato varieties for this dish as they have firm flesh and hold their shape well when cooked.

• Serve with grilled meat, fish or a casserole.

# champion
# hash browns

£

**Serves 4 as a side dish**
Preparation  10 minutes,
    plus 10 minutes
    soaking
Cooking  25 minutes

**750g waxy potatoes, such
    as Estima, peeled**

**3 tbsp vegetable oil**

**3 rindless, smoked bacon
    rashers, chopped**

**1 onion, chopped**

**1 green pepper, seeded
    and chopped**

**¼ tsp paprika**

**salt and freshly ground
    black pepper**

CRISPY OUTSIDE AND TENDER
INSIDE, THESE GOLDEN BITES ARE
IRRESISTIBLE. ADDING BACON,
ONION AND GREEN PEPPER ADDS
A TWIST TO THE CLASSIC RECIPE.

## COOK SMART
• Soaking the potatoes
in iced water converts
some of the starch to
sugar, which helps the
spuds to brown faster and
absorb less fat. Squeezing
them dry ensures that they
fry properly and that you
achieve a crispy texture.

**Per serving**
kcal 280, protein 8g,
fat 12g (of which saturated
fat 2g), carbohydrate 36g
(of which sugars 5g),
fibre 3g, sodium 0.3g

**1** Coarsely grate the potatoes into a large bowl
of iced water. Leave to stand for 10 minutes.

**2** Meanwhile, heat 1 tbsp of the oil in a large frying
pan and fry the bacon over a medium heat for
5 minutes or until crisp. Remove with a draining
spoon and set aside.

**3** Add the onion and green pepper to the pan and cook
for 5 minutes or until soft. Remove from the pan and
set aside with the bacon.

**4** Drain the potatoes, squeezing out as much water
as possible, using your hands. Transfer to a clean
tea towel and pat dry. Combine the potatoes, bacon,
onion, green pepper and paprika in a large bowl and
season with salt and pepper.

**5** Add half the remaining oil to the pan and heat.
Spread the potato mixture evenly in the frying pan
and cook, without stirring, for 15 minutes or until
golden brown and crispy on the bottom.

**6** Place a large plate over the pan and invert. Heat
the remaining oil in the pan, slide the potatoes
back into the pan and cook for a further 10 minutes
until golden brown and crispy on the other side.
Serve hot, cut into wedges.

# pan haggerty

£

**Serves 4 as a side dish** V
**(or 2 as a main course)**
Preparation  15 minutes
Cooking  35–40 minutes

25 g butter

1 tbsp vegetable oil

100 g mature Cheddar, grated

450 g potatoes, peeled and
    thinly sliced

2 onions, thinly sliced

salt and freshly ground
    black pepper

**Per serving (as a side dish)**
kcal 280, protein 9 g, fat 15 g
(of which saturated fat 9 g),
carbohydrate 24 g (of which
sugars 3.5 g), fibre 2 g,
sodium 0.2 g

---

**COOK SMART**

• Use firm-fleshed potatoes
such as Desirée for this dish,
as they will keep their shape
during cooking.

• If liked, instead of the cheese
topping, scatter some chopped,
smoked streaky bacon or
lardons over the top and grill as
before until crispy and browned.

• For a really traditional flavour,
use beef dripping for frying.

---

1 Heat the butter and oil in a large heavy-based frying
pan (preferably non-stick) until melted. Remove the
pan from the heat and swirl the fat around the base
and slightly up the sides to coat evenly.

2 Set aside 25 g of the cheese. Layer up the potatoes,
onions and remaining cheese, starting and finishing
with a layer of potatoes and seasoning between
each with salt and pepper.

3 Put the pan over a low heat, cover and gently
cook for 30–35 minutes or until the potatoes and
onions are tender when pierced with the tip of a
sharp knife. Turn up the heat a little for the last
5–10 minutes to brown and crisp the bottom.

4 Uncover the pan and sprinkle the top with the
reserved cheese. Cook under a preheated,
moderate grill for 4–5 minutes or until the cheese
is browned and bubbling. (If your pan is not suitable
for placing under the grill, carefully turn the cake
over on to a plate, then slide it back into the pan,
greased with a little more butter. Sprinkle with
cheese and continue cooking for about 10 minutes
or until golden brown on the reverse side.) Cut into
wedges and serve hot.

THIS CLASSIC NORTHUMBERLAND
DISH OF LAYERED POTATO, ONIONS
AND CHEESE, SLOW-COOKED IN A
PAN UNTIL GOLDEN AND CRISPY,
WILL SATISFY EVEN THE
HEARTIEST OF APPETITES.

CRUMBLE TOPPINGS ARE NOT JUST GOOD WITH FRUIT. FOR A VEGETARIAN MAIN MEAL, TRY THIS TASTY CHEESE CRUMBLE, BAKED OVER VEGETABLES IN A RICH CREAM SAUCE .

# vegetable crumble

**Serves 4 as a main course**  V

Preparation  25 minutes

Cooking  30 minutes (20 minutes
   for individual dishes)

**400 g potatoes, peeled
   and diced**

**2 carrots, peeled and diced**

**200 g fine green beans, cut into
   short lengths**

**25 g cool butter, diced**

**100 g plain flour**

**100 g mature Cheddar, grated**

**2 garlic cloves, crushed**

**1 tbsp chopped fresh parsley**

**4 tbsp single cream**

**salt and freshly ground
   black pepper**

**Per serving**

kcal 412, protein 12 g, fat 22 g
(of which saturated fat 13.5 g),
carbohydrate 43 g (of which sugars 6 g),
fibre 4 g, sodium 0.2 g

**1** Preheat the oven to 200°C (gas 6). Cook the potatoes and carrots in a large saucepan of lightly salted, boiling water for 10 minutes.

**2** Add the beans to the pan and cook gently for a further 5 minutes. Rub the butter into the flour, either in a bowl using your fingertips or in a food processor. Stir the cheese into the crumb mixture.

**3** Drain the vegetables and toss them with the garlic, parsley and pepper to season. Tip into a large, greased baking dish or divide among four individual ovenproof dishes. Pour over the cream, then cover with the cheese crumble.

**4** Bake for 30 minutes (20 minutes for individual dishes) until golden and crispy. Serve immediately.

**COOK SMART**

• Use any fresh vegetables of your choice, such as chopped curly kale or cauliflower or broccoli florets, precooked in boiling water.

• The vegetable cooking liquid makes a delicious soup base; just add other vegetables and small pasta shapes.

# butternut and sweetcorn gratin

(£)

**Serves 4 as a side dish**
Preparation 15 minutes
Cooking 45 minutes

1 butternut squash, peeled, seeded
   and cubed

1 red onion, halved and thinly sliced

275 g frozen sweetcorn or 340 g canned
   sweetcorn, drained

1 tbsp olive oil

1 tbsp chopped fresh thyme or rosemary

4 tbsp freshly grated Parmesan or
   mature Cheddar

salt and freshly ground black pepper

**Per serving**
kcal 255, protein 11 g, fat 9 g (of which
saturated fat 3.5 g), carbohydrate 34 g (of
which sugars 14 g), fibre 5 g, sodium 0.2 g

**1** Preheat the oven to 200°C (gas 6). Combine the
squash, onion and sweetcorn in a large bowl, drizzle
over the oil, sprinkle with herbs and season with salt
and pepper. Toss together.

**2** Tip the vegetables into a baking dish or roasting tin,
measuring about 23 x 33 cm. Bake for 40 minutes
or until the squash is tender, stirring halfway through
the cooking time.

**3** Sprinkle over the cheese and bake for a further
5 minutes until golden. Serve immediately.

---

**COOK SMART**

• Bake the vegetables in an attractive oven-to-table baking
dish for simplicity of serving and to save on washing-up.

• For an unusual pasta dish, bake the vegetables as
above, then stir them into a bottled tomato sauce and
heat through. Toss with hot cooked pasta and sprinkle
with Parmesan.

• To serve as a vegetarian main course, accompany with
wholegrain bread, baked tomatoes and a green salad.

BUTTERNUT SQUASH HAS A SWEET, INTENSE FLAVOUR AND, WHEN ROASTED WITH BRIGHT YELLOW CORN KERNELS, MAKES A GLORIOUS VEGETABLE TREAT FOR AUTUMN AND WINTER. IT IS PARTICULARLY GOOD WITH ROAST CHICKEN.

# courgette soufflé

(£)

**Serves 4 as a main course**
Preparation 25 minutes
Cooking 40–45 minutes

**Per serving**
kcal 430, protein 16 g,
fat 34 g (of which saturated
fat 18 g), carbohydrate 16 g
(of which sugars 7 g),
fibre 1 g, sodium 0.3 g

**1 tbsp vegetable oil**

**2 courgettes, about 375 g
in total, coarsely grated**

**pinch of sugar**

**50 g butter**

**50 g plain flour**

**375 ml semi-skimmed milk**

**100 g soft cheese with
garlic and herbs**

**pinch of ground nutmeg**

**3 large eggs, separated**

**2 tbsp freshly grated
Parmesan or mature
Cheddar**

**salt and freshly ground
black pepper**

1 Heat the oil in a large frying pan. Add the courgettes and cook over a medium heat for 10 minutes, stirring frequently. Add the sugar and season with salt.

2 Put a baking sheet in the oven and preheat to 200°C (gas 6). Lightly grease a 1.5 litre soufflé dish with a small knob of the butter.

3 Melt the remaining butter in a saucepan over a low heat. Add the flour and cook for 30 seconds, stirring with a wooden spoon. Gradually pour in the milk and bring to the boil, stirring constantly, until thickened. Stir in the cheese until melted, then season with nutmeg, salt and pepper. Remove the pan from the heat and leave to cool.

4 Whisk the egg whites until stiff. Beat the egg yolks into the cooled sauce, then fold in the courgettes and egg whites. Pour the mixture into the buttered soufflé dish and sprinkle the cheese over the top.

5 Set the dish on the hot baking sheet and bake for 40–45 minutes or until risen and golden brown. Serve immediately.

# potato moussaka

(£)

**Serves 4 as a main course** Ⅴ
Preparation 30 minutes
Cooking 30 minutes

**1 kg potatoes, peeled and sliced into
5 mm rounds**

**3 tbsp vegetable oil**

**2 large onions, finely chopped**

**150 ml dry white wine or vegetable stock**

**700 g jar passata or sugocasa**

**1 tsp sugar**

**½ tsp ground nutmeg**

**2 tbsp chopped fresh parsley or 1 tbsp
chopped fresh rosemary**

**20 black olives, stoned and chopped**

**4 tbsp fresh breadcrumbs**

**salt and freshly ground black pepper**

**sprig of fresh parsley or rosemary to
garnish (optional)**

**Per serving**
kcal 280, protein 7 g, fat 7 g (of which saturated
fat 1 g), carbohydrate 45 g (of which sugars 9 g),
fibre 4 g, sodium 0.4 g

**1** Preheat the oven to 200°C (gas 6). Cook the potatoes in a large pan of lightly salted boiling water for 5 minutes or until just tender. Drain and set aside.

**2** Heat the oil in a deep frying pan and gently cook the onions for 5–10 minutes until light golden, stirring all the time.

**3** Add the wine or stock, passata or sugocasa, sugar, nutmeg and rosemary, if using, to the onions. Season lightly with salt and pepper, mix well, then cook gently, uncovered, for 15 minutes, stirring from time to time, until the sauce thickens. Stir in the parsley, if using, and taste to check the seasoning.

**THIS HEARTY ONE-POT DISH MAKES A SATISFYING VEGETARIAN SUPPER – PARTICULARLY GOOD WHEN IT IS COLD OUTSIDE AND YOU NEED A COMFORTING MEAL TO LIFT YOUR SPIRITS.**

**4** Make a layer with half the potatoes in a 2 litre baking dish (or four individual ovenproof dishes), cover with half the tomato and onion sauce, then scatter over most of the olives, reserving a few for garnishing. Repeat with a second layer of potatoes and tomato sauce.

**5** Sprinkle the breadcrumbs over the top, then bake for 30 minutes until golden and crispy. Serve hot, garnished with a sprig of fresh parsley or rosemary, if liked, and the reserved olives heaped in the centre.

**COOK SMART**

• Sugocasa is similar to tomato passata but is chunkier and more highly seasoned. Both are available from larger supermarkets – you can use either. Alternatively, use 2 x 400g cans of chopped tomatoes in rich juice.

THIS SAVOURY VERSION OF THE CLASSIC FRENCH BATTER PUDDING IS MADE WITH FROZEN VEGETABLES, WHICH ARE IDEAL WHEN YOU ARE IN A HURRY.

288

# vegetable clafoutis

ⓔ

**Serves 4 as a light meal** Ⓥ
Preparation  10 minutes
Cooking  35–40 minutes

**30 g butter**

**500 g frozen mixed vegetables, thawed and drained**

**4 tbsp plain flour**

**250 ml semi-skimmed milk**

**4 eggs**

**1 tbsp chopped fresh parsley**

**salt and freshly ground black pepper**

**sprigs of fresh parsley to garnish**

**Per serving**
kcal 267, protein 13g, fat 14g
(of which saturated fat 6g),
carbohydrate 23g (of which
sugars 9g), fibre 3g, sodium 0.2g

**1** Preheat the oven to 200°C (gas 6). Melt the butter in a large frying pan, add the vegetables and cook over a gentle heat for 2–3 minutes, stirring.

**2** Sift the flour into a bowl. In a jug, beat the milk with the eggs, then gradually whisk into the flour to make a smooth batter. Season with salt and pepper.

**3** Stir the parsley into the vegetables, then spread evenly in a 1.5 litre oven-to-table baking dish and smooth level with the back of a spoon. Pour the batter slowly over the vegetables.

**4** Bake for 35–40 minutes or until lightly set and golden. Serve hot from the baking dish, garnished with sprigs of fresh parsley.

## COOK SMART

• For individual clafoutis, bake in four 400 ml ovenproof dishes and cook for 20–25 minutes until set.

• This dish could also be made with leftover cooked vegetables, cut into dice. If you don't have quite enough, make up the quantity with drained, canned or thawed frozen peas, carrots or sweetcorn.

• Serve with a fresh tomato salad.

# baked cheesy-topped vegetables

CARROTS, BROCCOLI AND ONIONS, BAKED IN A CHEESY BÉCHAMEL SAUCE, ARE DELICIOUS SERVED AS A LIGHT VEGETARIAN SUPPER DISH, OR AS A SIDE DISH WITH MEAT OR FISH.

£

**Serves 4 as a light meal** ⓥ
**(or 6 as a side dish)**
Preparation  30 minutes
Cooking  20–25 minutes

**400 g carrots, peeled and sliced**

**2 onions, sliced**

**250 g broccoli, cut into small florets**

**25 g butter**

**1 tbsp plain flour**

**250 ml semi-skimmed milk**

**1 egg**

**few drops of Tabasco sauce**

**pinch of ground nutmeg**

**50 g mature Cheddar, grated**

**salt and freshly ground black pepper**

**fresh herbs to garnish (optional)**

**Per serving (as a light meal)**
kcal 235, protein 11.5 g, fat 13 g (of which saturated fat 7 g), carbohydrate 19 g (of which sugars 14 g), fibre 5 g, sodium 0.2 g

1. Preheat the oven to 200°C (gas 6). Cook the carrots and onions in a steamer, over a pan of boiling water, for 12 minutes. Add the broccoli florets and steam for a further 8 minutes.

2. Meanwhile, melt the butter in a small saucepan over a low heat. Add the flour and stir for 30 seconds. Gradually pour in the milk and bring to the boil, stirring constantly, until thickened.

3. Remove the pan from the heat and beat in the egg and half the cheese. Add a few drops of Tabasco and the nutmeg and season with salt and pepper.

4. Put the vegetables in a 1.5 litre ovenproof dish. Coat them with the béchamel sauce and sprinkle over the remaining cheese.

5. Bake for 20–25 minutes until bubbling and golden. Serve immediately, garnished with fresh herbs, if liked.

VEGETABLES

## COOK SMART
• For individual portions, bake in four 400 ml ovenproof dishes, at 200°C (gas 6), for 15–20 minutes, until golden.

• Gruyère has good melting properties and would make a delicious alternative cheese to Cheddar.

# baked stuffed marrow

MARROWS ARE WELL-PRICED WHEN IN SEASON.
THE JUICY FLESH CONTRASTS WELL WITH THE TASTY
STUFFING – PERFECT FOR A VEGETARIAN MAIN MEAL.

£

**Serves 4 as a light meal** Ⓥ
Preparation 30 minutes
Cooking 45 minutes

**1 short thick marrow,
    about 900 g**

**40 g butter**

**1 onion, chopped**

**2 celery sticks, chopped**

**1 garlic clove, crushed**

**2 x 400 g cans chopped
    tomatoes**

**3 tbsp shredded fresh basil**

**50 g fresh white
    breadcrumbs**

**25 g mature Cheddar,
    finely grated**

**salt and freshly ground
    black pepper**

**fresh basil to garnish
    (optional)**

**Per serving**
kcal 200, protein 6.5 g,
fat 11 g (of which saturated
fat 6.5 g), carbohydrate 20 g
(of which sugars 9 g),
fibre 2 g, sodium 0.3 g

**1** Preheat the oven to 190°C (gas 5). Cut the marrow into eight rings, each about 4 cm thick. Remove the peel, unless the marrow is very young and tender, and scoop out the seeds. Place the rings in a large, lightly greased ovenproof dish, arranging them in a single layer.

**2** Melt the butter in a large saucepan and cook the onion and celery for 5 minutes until softened. Add the garlic and cook for a futher minute. Stir in the chopped tomatoes with their juice and season with a little salt and pepper. Bring to the boil, then simmer uncovered for about 10 minutes or until the mixture is thick and pulpy. Stir in the shredded basil.

**3** Lightly season the marrow rings with salt and pepper before spooning the tomato mixture into the hollowed-out centres. Spread any leftover tomato mixture between the marrow rings. Tightly cover the dish with foil so that the marrow will cook in the steam, then bake for 30 minutes.

**4** Meanwhile, mix the breadcrumbs and cheese together. Remove the foil and sprinkle the crumb mixture over the tops of the marrow rings. Return to the oven and bake for a further 15 minutes or until the topping is golden and crisp and the marrow is tender and juicy. Serve hot, scattered with fresh basil leaves, if liked.

**COOK SMART**

• For ham and mushroom stuffed marrow rings, leave out the celery and cook 125 g chopped mushrooms with the onion. Add the garlic as above and 100 g chopped, lean ham. Add one can of chopped tomatoes and chopped fresh parsley instead of basil. A meat sauce would be good as a filling too (see Sloppy Joes, page 218).

• Use 1 tsp dried mixed herbs if unable to get fresh basil.

• Serve with wholegrain bread and a leafy salad.

# bubble and squeak

THIS SIMPLE DISH IS PERFECT FOR USING UP LEFTOVER COOKED POTATOES AND CABBAGE – OR EVEN BRUSSELS SPROUTS, KALE OR SPINACH. TOP WITH POACHED EGGS FOR A SCRUMPTIOUS LUNCH.

£

**Serves 4 as a light meal** V
Preparation  20 minutes
Cooking  15 minutes

**25 g butter**
**1 onion, finely chopped**
**450 g cold, cooked mashed potatoes**
**225 g cooked cabbage, roughly chopped**
**1 tbsp plain flour for dusting**
**1 tbsp oil for frying**
**1 tbsp vinegar**
**4 eggs**
**salt and freshly ground black pepper**

**Per serving**
kcal 300, protein 11 g, fat 20 g (of which saturated fat 9 g), carbohydrate 23 g (of which sugars 4 g), fibre 2.5 g, sodium 0.2 g

1 Melt the butter in a large, shallow, heavy-based frying pan (preferably non-stick). Add the onion and cook for 10 minutes, stirring frequently, until soft.

2 Tip the softened onion into a large bowl and add the potatoes and cabbage. Season generously with salt and pepper and mix together. With lightly floured hands, shape the mixture into four rough cakes, each about 2 cm thick.

3 Wipe the pan clean with kitchen paper, then add the oil and heat. Put the cakes into the pan and fry over a medium heat for about 15 minutes, turning once, until golden brown and crisp.

4 About 5 minutes before the end of cooking, prepare the poached eggs. Pour about 4 cm of boiling water into a large, wide frying pan. Add the vinegar and bring to the boil. Reduce the heat, so that the water bubbles gently. Crack an egg into a cup or small bowl, then gently tip it into the water. Repeat this with the remaining eggs.

5 Cook the eggs very gently for 1 minute, then gently spoon a little boiling water over the centre of each egg to cook the yolks. Poach for a further 2 minutes, then lift out the eggs with a draining spoon, allowing the water to drain.

6 Lay a poached egg on top of each bubble and squeak cake and break each yolk gently with the tip of a knife, so that it drizzles temptingly.

**COOK SMART**
• This dish is known as 'Colcannon' in Ireland, where it usually contains bacon. Chop four rashers of rindless back or streaky bacon and fry with the onions.

• You could be traditional and make one large cake. Serve cut into wedges with cold roast beef and lashings of gravy.

# vegetable quiche

A HOME-MADE QUICHE, MADE WITH CRISP SHORTCRUST PASTRY AND A TASTY FILLING, IS A SURE-FIRE WAY TO TEMPT APPETITES, WITHOUT BREAKING THE BANK.

£

**Serves 6** V
Preparation 30 minutes, plus 30 minutes chilling (for the pastry)
Cooking 30 minutes

**Shortcrust pastry**
150 g plain flour
75 g cool butter, diced

**Filling**
200 g carrots, peeled and diced
200 g broccoli, cut into small florets
3 eggs
300 ml semi-skimmed milk
3 tbsp grated Cheddar
salt and freshly ground black pepper
sprigs of fresh parsley to garnish (optional)

**Per serving**
kcal 300, protein 11 g, fat 17 g (of which saturated fat 10 g), carbohydrate 25 g (of which sugars 6 g), fibre 2 g, sodium 0.2 g

**COOK SMART**
• For individual quiches, use six 8 cm diameter, loose-based flan tins and bake for 20 minutes. Make as for the large quiche, but reduce quantities to 100 g broccoli, 2 eggs and 200 ml milk.

• Serve as a light meal with salad, plus new potatoes for a main course. Also good for a buffet table or to pack up for a picnic.

1 Make the pastry. Sift the flour and salt into a large mixing bowl, add the butter and rub into the flour, using your fingertips, until the mixture resembles breadcrumbs. Sprinkle with 2 tbsp of cold water and mix using a round-bladed knife. With your hands, gather together into a firm but pliable dough, handling as little as possible. (This can be done quickly in a food processor.) Wrap the pastry in greaseproof paper or cling film and chill for 20 minutes before rolling out.

2 Cook the carrots in a steamer for 10 minutes, over a pan of boiling water. Add the broccoli and steam for a further 5 minutes. The vegetables should be just tender and not soft.

3 Meanwhile, whisk together the eggs, milk and salt and pepper to season, in a jug. Stir in the cheese. Preheat the oven to 190°C (gas 5) and put a baking sheet in to heat.

4 Roll out the pastry thinly on a lightly floured surface and use to line a 24 cm diameter, loose-based, flan tin. Prick over the base with a fork, then chill in the fridge for 10 minutes. Spread the vegetables over the pastry, then pour over the cheesy egg custard.

5 Place the tin on the hot baking sheet and bake for 30 minutes or until the filling is lightly set and golden. Serve warm, garnished with sprigs of fresh parsley, if liked.

# hoppin' john
## with sweet
# peppers

£

**Serves 4 as a side dish
(or 2 as a main course)**
Preparation 20 minutes
Cooking 15 minutes

**1 tbsp vegetable oil**

**3 rindless smoked bacon
rashers, chopped**

**1 onion, finely chopped**

**2 mixed peppers (red, yellow,
green, or orange), seeded
and diced**

**2 garlic cloves, crushed**

**400 g can black-eyed beans,
drained and rinsed**

**75 g long-grain white rice**

**250 ml vegetable stock, hot**

**1½ tbsp red wine vinegar**

**2 tsp hot pepper sauce**

**salt and freshly ground
black pepper**

**Per serving (as a side dish)**
kcal 276, protein 16 g, fat 8 g
(of which saturated fat 2 g),
carbohydrate 36 g (of which
sugars 9 g), fibre 6 g,
sodium 0.6 g

**1** Heat the oil in a flameproof casserole or large saucepan over a medium heat. Add the bacon and cook for 5 minutes or until crisp.

**2** Add the onion and cook for 5 minutes, stirring frequently, until softened. Add the peppers and garlic, and cook for 4–5 minutes, stirring from time to time, until the peppers are just tender.

**3** Stir in the black-eyed beans and rice, then pour in the stock. Bring back to the boil and season with salt and pepper, then reduce the heat, cover and cook gently for 15 minutes or until the rice is tender.

**4** Sprinkle over the vinegar and hot pepper sauce and toss through.

**COOK SMART**

• Black-eyed beans are small and creamy-flavoured with a black scar where they have been joined to the pod. They are used a lot in American and African cooking and are an essential ingredient of this traditional dish. If dried beans are used, cook 125 g first before using in the recipe. Canned pinto beans could be used instead.

• This dish would be good served with sausages, burgers or grilled meats, plus a green salad tossed with vinaigrette dressing. Add orange segments to the salad for a fruity twist.

**THIS CLASSIC DISH FROM THE AMERICAN SOUTH HAS A BASE OF RICE AND BEANS, JAZZED UP WITH SMOKED BACON, SWEET PEPPERS AND HOT PEPPER SAUCE.**

# asparagus and potato frittata

USE NEW SEASON'S POTATOES AND ASPARAGUS TO MAKE THIS ITALIAN-STYLE OMELETTE AND SERVE IT FOR A LIGHT LUNCH OR SUPPER WITH SALAD.

£ £

**Serves 4 as a light meal**
Preparation and cooking
30–35 minutes

1 tbsp vegetable oil

250 g new potatoes, scrubbed and diced

450 g asparagus, cut into short lengths

6 large eggs, beaten

1 tbsp chopped fresh tarragon or ½ tsp dried

2 tbsp freshly grated Parmesan

salt and freshly ground black pepper

**Per serving**
kcal 261, protein 19 g, fat 15 g (of which saturated fat 5 g), carbohydrate 23 g (of which sugars 3 g), fibre 2 g, sodium 0.2 g

**COOK SMART**
• Be sure to use freshly grated Parmesan. It is quite expensive but you don't need to use a lot and the flavour is infinitely superior to ready-grated Parmesan in tubs.

• For a vegetarian frittata, use an alternative, strong-flavoured cheese.

1 Heat the oil in a large frying pan, over a medium heat. Add the potatoes and cook for 7–8 minutes, tossing occassionally.

2 Add the asparagus and 5 tbsp water, sprinkle with salt, cover and steam for 10–12 minutes or until the asparagus and potatoes are tender.

3 Meanwhile, in a large bowl, whisk together the eggs, tarragon and Parmesan with 1 tbsp of water and pepper to season.

4 Preheat the grill to moderate. Pour the egg mixture into the pan and swirl it around to cover the vegetables. Cook gently for 4–5 minutes or until the eggs are almost set, shaking the pan from time to time – there will still be some uncooked egg mixture on top.

5 Place the pan under the grill and cook the frittata for a further 2 minutes or until the top looks set. (If the pan doesn't have a flameproof handle, carefully upturn the fritatta onto a plate, then slide it back into the pan and put it back on the hob to cook the underside.)

6 Use a spatula to loosen the frittata from the pan and slide it onto a serving platter. Cut into wedges and serve hot or cold.

296

**COOK SMART**
• The roulade would be good served with a warm tomato sauce (see page 33).

• Use a serrated knife to slice the roulade, to prevent the filling from oozing out.

£

**Serves 4** V
Preparation 35 minutes
Cooking 15 minutes

200 g frozen chopped spinach, thawed

4 eggs, separated

pinch of grated nutmeg

25 g butter

225 g chestnut or button mushrooms, thinly sliced

2 tbsp plain flour

150 ml semi-skimmed milk

50 g mature Cheddar, finely grated

1 tsp wholegrain mustard

salt and freshly ground black pepper

**Per serving**
kcal 250, protein 15 g, fat 17 g (of which saturated fat 8 g), carbohydrate 9 g (of which sugars 3 g), fibre 2 g, sodium 0.3 g

# spinach and mushroom roulade

**1** Preheat the oven to 200°C (gas 6). Grease and line the base of a 33 x 23 cm Swiss roll tin with non-stick baking parchment. Put the spinach in a sieve and press with the back of a wooden spoon to remove as much liquid as possible, then put in a bowl. Add the egg yolks and nutmeg, season with salt and pepper and mix well together.

**2** Whisk the egg whites until stiff, then fold into the spinach mixture with a metal spoon. Spoon the mixture into the prepared tin and spread it out evenly. Bake in the oven for 15 minutes until firm to the touch.

**3** Meanwhile, melt the butter in a saucepan. Add the mushrooms and fry gently for 5 minutes until tender. Add the flour and cook over a low heat, stirring with a wooden spoon, for 1 minute.

**4** Remove the pan from the heat and gradually blend in the milk, stirring after each addition. Return to the heat and bring to the boil, stirring all the time, until the sauce thickens and is smooth. Remove from the heat and stir in the cheese, mustard and salt and pepper to taste.

**5** When the roulade is cooked, remove from the oven and quickly spread the mushroom sauce evenly over the surface. Roll up from one of the short ends by gently lifting the baking parchment. Serve hot, cut into slices.

**WHEN YOU NEED A CENTREPIECE FOR A SPECIAL VEGETARIAN MEAL, THIS STUNNING ROULADE WITH ITS CREAMY FILLING IS JUST THE THING.**

# cauliflower and lentil curry

(£)

**Serves 4 as a main course** Ⓥ
Preparation  10 minutes
Cooking  25 minutes

3 tbsp vegetable oil
1 onion, finely chopped
1 fat garlic clove, finely chopped
25 g fresh root ginger, grated
2 tsp ground coriander
2 tsp ground cumin
½ tsp ground turmeric
75 g red split lentils
150 ml vegetable stock, hot
1 cauliflower, cut into small florets
1 large carrot, peeled and diced
400 ml can coconut milk
75 g frozen green beans, thawed
3 tbsp chopped fresh coriander
1 tbsp lemon juice
salt and freshly ground
    black pepper
sprig of fresh coriander to garnish

**Per serving**
kcal 550, protein 15 g, fat 45 g
(of which saturated fat 31 g),
carbohydrate 22 g (of which
sugars 9 g), fibre 4 g, sodium 0.05 g

**1** Heat 2 tbsp of the oil in a large saucepan and gently cook the onion for 10 minutes, stirring frequently, until soft and translucent. Add the garlic, ginger, ground coriander, cumin and turmeric and cook for 2 minutes, stirring all the time.

**2** Stir in the lentils, then pour in the stock. Bring to the boil, then reduce the heat, cover and gently simmer for 10 minutes.

**3** Meanwhile, heat the remaining 1 tbsp oil in a frying pan and fry the cauliflower for 2–3 minutes until lightly browned. Add to the lentil mixture with the carrots and coconut milk.

**4** Bring the curry back to a gentle simmer and cook for a further 10 minutes or until the vegetables are tender. Stir in the beans and cook for 3–4 minutes.

**5** Stir in the chopped coriander and lemon juice, then season to taste with salt and pepper. Spoon onto a warmed serving dish and garnish with a sprig of fresh coriander.

## COOK SMART
• If canned coconut milk is unavailable, use 175 g chopped creamed coconut, which comes as a block, dissolved in 350 ml boiling water. Alternatively, you could use a carton of coconut cream and make up to 400 ml with stock or water.

A STAPLE DISH IN INDIAN CUISINE, THIS VEGETARIAN 'DHAL' WITH VEGETABLES IS ENRICHED WITH COCONUT MILK, GIVING IT AN EXOTIC, ENTICING FLAVOUR. SERVE WITH RICE, WARM NAAN OR CHAPPATIS.

# lentil stew with browned onions

£ £

**Serves 4 as a main course** Ⅴ
Preparation 10 minutes
Cooking 35 minutes

**2 tbsp vegetable oil**

**3 carrots, peeled, quartered lengthways, then thinly sliced crossways**

**8 garlic cloves, thinly sliced**

**75 g fresh shiitake mushrooms, sliced**

**125 g red split lentils**

**227 g can chopped tomatoes**

**600 ml vegetable stock**

**¾ tsp ground cumin**

**¾ tsp ground ginger**

**½ tsp dried sage**

**150 g frozen peas, thawed**

**1 large onion, halved and thinly sliced**

**2 tsp sugar**

**salt and freshly ground black pepper**

**Per serving**
kcal 310, protein 24 g,
fat 10 g (of which saturated
fat 2 g), carbohydrate 35 g
(of which sugars 13 g),
fibre 6 g, sodium 0.1 g

### COOK SMART
• For a more substantial dish, crumble some cheese over the top to serve. Goat's cheese, feta or grated Gruyère would all be suitable.

**1** Heat 1 tbsp of the oil in a large saucepan over a medium heat. Add the carrots and garlic and cook for 5 minutes or until softened.

**2** Stir in the mushrooms and lentils, then add the tomatoes with their juice, the stock, cumin, ginger and sage. Bring to the boil, then reduce the heat to a simmer, cover and cook for 35 minutes or until the lentils are tender. Add the peas and cook in the stew for the last 5 minutes of the cooking time.

**3** Meanwhile, heat the remaining oil in a large frying pan. Add the onion, sprinkle over the sugar and cook for 15–20 minutes over a medium heat, stirring frequently, until the onion is lightly browned.

**4** Season the stew to taste with salt and pepper, then serve hot with the onions heaped on top.

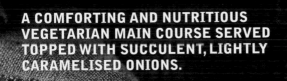

**A COMFORTING AND NUTRITIOUS VEGETARIAN MAIN COURSE SERVED TOPPED WITH SUCCULENT, LIGHTLY CARAMELISED ONIONS.**

# dess

**sweet,
luscious
and utterly
irresistible**

# erts

Whether it is a fresh and fruity finale or a rich, decadent dessert that you are looking for, cooking on a budget doesn't mean you need to miss out on delicious desserts. Take advantage of fresh seasonal fruits when they are in abundance and enjoy great-value fruity pies, tarts, puddings and gratins. Alternatively, use canned, frozen and dried fruits when fresh are out of season, or indulge in luxurious ingredients such as good quality cream and chocolate to make chocolate mousse or crème brûlée.

# fresh pineapple with strawberry sauce

💷💷

**Serves 4** Ⅴ
Preparation 30 minutes

1 small pineapple
250g strawberries
100g caster sugar
1 tbsp lemon juice
4 scoops vanilla ice-cream
pineapple leaves to
    decorate (optional)

**COOK SMART**
• For an extra special
flavour, steep the
pineapple slices in a little
Kirsch liqueur in step 1.
• A ripe pineapple should
smell sweet and tropical.

**Per serving**
kcal 300, protein 3g,
fat 9g (of which saturated
fat 5g), carbohydrate 56g
(of which sugars 52g),
fibre 2g, sodium 0.05g

**1** Remove the leafy top and base of the pineapple, using a large knife. Cut away the skin, collecting the juice into a bowl. Cut the pineapple widthways into six thick slices. Remove the fibrous core, then cut the slices in half and put in a shallow dish. Set aside in a cool place.

**2** Pureé the strawberries, with the reserved pineapple juice, in a blender or food processor. Then pass the strawberry purée through a sieve to remove the tiny pips, if preferred smooth.

**3** Put the sugar in a small pan with 2 tbsp of water and dissolve over a low heat. Bring to the boil, then stir occasionally until the caramel mixture turns a pale amber colour. Remove from the heat. Add the lemon juice and strawberry purée, taking care that the caramel does not splash. Stir until all the caramel is incorporated, then leave to cool.

**4** When ready to serve, arrange three half slices of pineapple on each plate and place a scoop of ice-cream on top. Pour over the strawberry sauce, decorate with pineapple leaves, if liked, and serve immediately.

**TRANSPORT YOURSELF TO A FAR-FLUNG TROPICAL BEACH WITH THIS REFRESHING FRUITY DESSERT.**

# normandy baked apples

£

**Serves 4**  V

Preparation  10 minutes
Cooking  30–40 minutes

**4 Bramley cooking apples**
**juice of ½ lemon**
**4 tsp honey**
**15 g butter, cut into four**
**pieces**
**100 ml medium-dry cider**

**Per serving**
kcal 120, protein 0.6 g,
fat 3 g (of which saturated
fat 2 g), carbohydrate 22 g
(of which sugars 22 g),
fibre 3 g, sodium 0.03 g

HOT AND FLUFFY
BAKED APPLES,
WITH A HONEYED
BUTTER CENTRE,
ARE A SENSATIONAL
NO-FUSS DESSERT.

**COOK SMART**
• If liked, you could serve
the apples on slices of
toasted brioche. You
will find brioche in the
bakery section of larger
supermarkets or in
continental grocers.

• For a spicy flavour,
sprinkle a pinch of ground
cinnamon into the apple
cavities and decorate with
pieces of cinnamon bark.

1 Preheat the oven to 180˚C (gas 4). Core and peel
the apples. Sit the apples in a lightly buttered,
shallow ovenproof dish and brush over the outsides
with the lemon juice to prevent them from browning.

2 Spoon the honey and the butter into the cavities
of the apples. Pour the cider into the dish.

3 Bake for 30–40 minutes or until the apples are
tender, basting them several times with the cider
while cooking.

4 Leave to rest for 5–10 minutes before serving,
with the buttery cider syrup spooned over to
moisten them.

# baked bananas

£

**Serves 4**  V

Preparation  10 minutes
Cooking  10–15 minutes

**1 large orange**
**4 firm bananas**
**1 tbsp dark rum or brandy**
**(optional)**
**2 tbsp light muscovado**
**sugar**
**25 g butter, cut into small**
**pieces**

**Per serving**
kcal 193, protein 1.5 g,
fat 5.5 g (of which saturated
fat 3.5 g), carbohydrate 34 g
(of which sugars 32 g),
fibre 2 g, sodium 0.04 g

1 Preheat the oven to 180°C (gas 4). Use a citrus
zester to take fine shreds of zest from half of
the orange, or thinly remove the zest with a
vegetable peeler and then cut it into fine shreds.
Cut the orange in half and squeeze the juice from
both halves.

2 Peel the bananas, slice them lengthways and lay
them in a shallow ovenproof dish. Pour over the
orange juice and rum or brandy, if using. Sprinkle
with the sugar and scatter over the butter and
orange zest.

3 Bake for 10–15 minutes until the bananas are
just lightly cooked and the sauce is syrupy.
Serve immediately.

**COOK SMART**
• These bananas are delicious served hot with vanilla
ice-cream.

• Slices of fresh pineapple are equally good cooked in
this way.

• For an exotic flavour, sprinkle with crushed seeds of
shelled cardamom pods.

BANANAS BAKED IN A BUTTERY ORANGE
SYRUP COULDN'T BE SIMPLER TO MAKE
AND THEY TASTE UTTERLY DIVINE. FOR AN
EXTRA TREAT, ADD A SPLASH OF LIQUEUR.

HOME-MADE ICES ARE RICH AND CREAMY, AND ALWAYS A LUSCIOUS TREAT. THIS ONE, SERVED WITH HOT APRICOTS, IS NO EXCEPTION.

# caramel ice-cream with apricots

£

**Serves 4** Ⓥ

Preparation 20 minutes, plus freezing (varies according to method used)

**Caramel ice-cream**
250 ml full-fat milk
3 egg yolks
150 g caster sugar
100 ml single cream

**To serve**
25 g unsalted butter
16 ready-to-eat dried apricots, halved
2 tbsp caster sugar
juice of ½ lemon

**Per serving**
kcal 380, protein 6 g, fat 16 g (of which saturated fat 9 g), carbohydrate 55 g (of which sugars 55 g), fibre 0.5 g, sodium 0.08 g

304

1 Heat the milk in a saucepan over a low heat until almost boiling, then remove from the heat, cover and set aside. Whisk the egg yolks with 50 g of the sugar in a large bowl until the mixture is pale and frothy.

2 In another saucepan, dissolve the remaining 100 g of sugar for the ice-cream with 4 tbsp of water over a low heat. Bring to the boil, then cook over a high heat for 2–3 minutes, stirring occasionally, until the syrup turns a deep golden caramel. Remove the pan from the heat and carefully stir in the cream.

3 Pour the caramel cream into the hot milk, then gradually whisk this mixture into the egg yolks. Return to the pan and cook gently, stirring constantly with a wooden spoon until the custard coats the spoon, taking care that the mixture does not boil.

4 Remove the pan from the heat and plunge the base into a bowl of cold water to cool quickly. Pour the mixture into a plastic container and place it in the freezer. Remove and whisk after 2 hours, refreeze, then repeat whisking a second time. Freeze again until completely frozen.

5 Just before serving, melt the butter in a frying pan. Add the apricots and sprinkle with the sugar. Heat gently for 5 minutes, turning halfway through, until the apricots are glazed with the buttery syrup. Pour over the lemon juice.

6 Scoop the ice-cream into serving dishes and spoon over some of the warm apricots and syrup.

**COOK SMART**

• If you have an ice-cream machine, pour the mixture into the machine in step 4, and churn according to the manufacturer's instructions until thick and slushy. Put into a plastic container and freeze for several hours until firm.

• To use up the egg whites, you could make meringues. Allow 50 g caster sugar to each egg white. Whisk the egg whites until stiff, add a little of the sugar, whisk, then continue adding sugar and whisking until two-thirds of the sugar has been used. Fold in the remainder. Spoon or pipe the meringue onto baking sheets lined with baking paper. Bake for 1 hour in a preheated oven at 140°C (gas 1).

# pears with chocolate sauce

1 Put the sugar in a large, deep saucepan with 1 litre of water and dissolve over a low heat, stirring.

2 Peel the pears and remove the cores by cutting in through the base using a paring knife. Leave the stalk attached to the fruit. Sprinkle lemon juice over the pears as soon as they are peeled, to prevent them from browning.

3 Split the vanilla pod in half, scrape out the pulp into the sugar syrup and add the pod. Bring the syrup to the boil and add the pears. Reduce heat and poach the pears gently for 15–20 minutes or until they are just tender. Leave to cool in the syrup.

4 Shortly before serving, put the cream in a heatproof bowl with the chocolate and liqueur, if using, and heat over a pan of simmering water, stirring from time to time, until the chocolate has melted. (Alternatively, heat gently in the microwave.)

5 Divide the hot sauce among serving bowls and sit a pear in each one. Serve immediately.

£

**Serves 4** V
Preparation  10 minutes
Cooking  15–20 minutes

**250 g caster sugar**
**4 dessert pears**
**juice of 1 lemon**
**1 vanilla pod**
**100 ml single cream**
**100 g plain chocolate, broken into pieces**
**2 tbsp Grand Marnier or brandy (optional)**

**Per serving**
kcal 500, protein 2.5 g, fat 12 g (of which saturated fat 7 g), carbohydrate 97 g (of which sugars 96 g), fibre 4 g, sodium 0.02 g

### COOK SMART
• Instead of the liqueur, you could add 2 tbsp fresh orange juice.

• If the pears don't sit upright, cut a small slice from across the base to steady them.

• Reserve the pear poaching syrup to use for a fruit salad.

PEARS AND CHOCOLATE ARE ONE OF THOSE CLASSIC, HEAVENLY COMBINATIONS. ENJOY THIS SEDUCTIVE DESSERT DURING THE AUTUMN, WHEN JUICY PEARS ARE ABUNDANT.

SUMMER FRUITS CLOAKED IN ZABAGLIONE AND GRILLED UNTIL GOLDEN MAKE AN IRRESISTIBLE DINNER PARTY DESSERT.

# summer fruit gratin

💷💷

**Serves 4** Ⅴ
Preparation and cooking
30–35 minutes

**3 ripe nectarines**

**4 ripe apricots**

**250g strawberries**

**1 tbsp lemon juice**

**4 egg yolks**

**50g caster sugar**

**4 tbsp dessert wine, Marsala or sweet sherry**

**100ml whipping cream**

**To decorate**

**4 whole strawberries**

**sprigs of fresh mint**

---

**COOK SMART**

• Sweet dessert wines are sold in half-size bottles. This wine can also be served chilled as an aperitif

• Make a batch of meringues to use up the leftover egg whites (see page 304), or make Floating Islands on Red Berry Coulis (see page 309) to serve another day.

---

**Per serving**
kcal 280, protein 5g,
fat 15g (of which saturated
fat 8g), carbohydrate 28g
(of which sugars 28g),
fibre 2g, sodium 0.02g

**1** Cut all the fruits into slices and drizzle with the lemon juice. Divide equally among four individual, heatproof gratin dishes.

**2** Put the egg yolks in a large heatproof bowl, add the sugar and whisk using an electric hand mixer until the mixture is pale and creamy.

**3** Place the bowl over a saucepan of simmering water and continue whisking until the mixture thickens, adding the wine or sherry a little at a time, followed by the cream. (It is important that the water in the pan does not boil; if it is too hot, the egg yolks will cook too quickly.)

**4** Preheat the grill to its hottest setting. Pour the thick, mousse-like mixture over the fruits and place the dishes under the grill. Leave to brown for a few minutes, then serve immediately, decorated with a whole strawberry and a sprig of mint on each dish.

# apple and blackberry pancakes

£
**Makes 6** Ⓥ
Preparation and cooking
40 minutes

**75 g plain flour, sifted**

**¼ tsp ground cinnamon**

**1 egg**

**200 ml semi-skimmed milk**

**1 large cooking apple, about 225 g**

**125 g blackberries**

**25 g caster sugar plus extra for dusting**

**15 g unsalted butter**

**To serve**
whipped cream, crème fraîche, Greek-style yoghurt or ice-cream

## COOK SMART
- Both the pancakes and the blackberry compote are suitable for freezing. Interleave the pancakes with greaseproof paper, then pack into a polythene bag.
- If you have a bottle of cider or apple juice, use 3 tbsp to cook the blackberries in place of the water.

**Per serving**
kcal 129, protein 4 g,
fat 4 g (of which saturated
fat 2 g), carbohydrate 20 g
(of which sugars 11 g),
fibre 1 g, sodium 0.04 g

1 Sift the flour and cinnamon into a bowl and make a well in the centre. Crack in the egg, working it into the flour together with the milk to form a smooth batter. Peel, core and grate the apple into the batter.

2 Heat the blackberries with 3 tbsp water in a small saucepan. Bring to a steady simmer, then sprinkle on the caster sugar and stir until dissolved. Continue to simmer for 2–3 minutes until the juices become syrupy and the blackberries have softened, but still hold their shape. Remove from the heat.

3 Melt the butter in an 18 cm non-stick frying pan, swirling it around to coat the base and sides. Pour off the excess and reserve. Drop 2 tbsp of batter into the pan, and shake the pan to ease the mixture over the base. Cook until crisp and nutty brown at the edges, then flip over with a spatula, and cook the other side until crispy. Keep warm.

4 Repeat with the rest of the batter to make six pancakes, greasing the pan with the reserved butter. Serve warm, sprinkled with a little caster sugar and topped with a spoonful of the blackberries and syrupy juices. Offer whipped cream, crème fraîche, Greek-style yoghurt or ice-cream as accompaniments.

307

YOU CAN TAKE ADVANTAGE OF NATURE'S HARVEST FOR THIS DESSERT, AND PICK THE BLACKBERRIES WHERE THEY GROW WILD IN HEDGEROWS.

THIS TROPICAL TWIST ON THE CLASSIC NURSERY
PUDDING IS GREAT FOR USING UP LEFTOVER
BREAD. TOPPED WITH STICKY MERINGUE, IT IS
SURE TO BECOME A FAMILY FAVOURITE.

£

**Serves 4** V
Preparation 15 minutes,
    plus 15 minutes standing
Cooking 40–50 minutes

**75g fresh white breadcrumbs**
**25g desiccated coconut**
**425ml semi-skimmed milk**
**25g butter**
**2 eggs, separated**
**75g caster sugar**
**2 tbsp raspberry jam**
**pinch of salt**

**Per serving**
kcal 380, protein 14g, fat 18g
(of which saturated fat 9g),
carbohydrate 45g (of which
sugars 31g), fibre 1g,
sodium 0.3g

1 Mix together the breadcrumbs and coconut in a large bowl. Warm the milk with the butter in a small pan or in the microwave until just simmering.

2 Whisk the egg yolks lightly in a bowl with 25g of the sugar, then pour in the hot milk, stirring continuously. Pour this warm custard mixture over the breadcrumb mixture and stir to combine.

3 Pour into a greased 1 litre ovenproof dish and leave to stand for 15 minutes so that the breadcrumbs can absorb some of the liquid. Preheat the oven to 180°C (gas 4).

4 Bake for 25–30 minutes or until lightly set, then remove from the oven. Just before the end of the cooking time, warm the jam, then carefully spread it over the pudding when set.

5 In a clean, grease-free bowl, whisk the egg whites with the salt until stiff but not dry, then whisk in half the remaining sugar. Fold in the last of the sugar, using a large metal spoon. Pile the meringue on top of the pudding to cover it completely and swirl it into peaks with a fork.

6 Bake for a further 15–20 minutes until golden. Serve immediately.

**COOK SMART**
• Traditionally, lemon zest is added to the custard mixture. Use the grated zest of one lemon in place of the coconut, or you could add 1 tsp pure vanilla extract.

• Any red fruit jam, such as plum, cherry or strawberry, will work well.

• To make individual puddings, bake them in large ramekin dishes, first for 20 minutes until set, then for 15 minutes with the meringue topping.

# coconut queen of puddings

FLUFFY POACHED
MERINGUES FLOATING
IN A GLORIOUS FRUIT
SAUCE IS THE IDEAL
CHOICE WHEN JUICY
SUMMER BERRIES ARE
IN SEASON.

💷💷

**Serves 6** Ⅴ
Preparation and cooking
30 minutes

**300 g strawberries**
**150 g raspberries**
**100 g caster sugar, plus**
    **1 tbsp**
**2 tbsp blackcurrant cordial**
**1 tbsp lemon juice**
**3 egg whites**
**pinch of salt**
**6 whole strawberries**
    **to decorate**

**Per serving**
kcal 107, protein 2g,
fat 0g (of which saturated
fat 0g), carbohydrate 26g
(of which sugars 26g),
fibre 1g, sodium 0.04g

---

**COOK SMART**
• Greater volume is
achieved from fresh eggs,
so check the 'best before'
date on the box.

• If you have a bottle of
cassis, use it to replace
the blackcurrant cordial.

• For more traditional
floating islands, serve
the meringues on a
vanilla Custard Sauce
(see page 34).

---

# floating
# islands on
# red berry coulis

**1** Put the strawberries and raspberries
in a blender or food processor and
whizz together to make a purée.
Pass the purée through a fine sieve
to remove the seeds.

**2** Place the 100g of caster sugar in a
small saucepan with 2 tbsp of water.
Dissolve over a low heat, then slowly
continue heating until it caramelises
and looks a rich golden colour.
Remove from the heat. Carefully add
the blackcurrant cordial, lemon juice
and fruit purée, stir until the caramel
is incorporated, then leave to cool.

**3** In a clean, grease-free bowl, whisk
the egg whites with the salt into stiff
peaks, using an electric hand mixer.
(The salt makes the whites easier to
whisk to firm peaks.) Sprinkle over
the remaining sugar and continue
whisking until the meringue is glossy.

**4** Two-thirds fill a deep frying pan with
water and heat to just below boiling
point. Using a tablespoon, float six
dollops of the meringue mixture on
to the simmering water. Cook gently
for 30 seconds, then turn them over
using a draining spoon and cook
for 30 seconds on the other side.
Remove them from the pan with
the draining spoon, place on a clean
cloth and leave to cool.

**5** When ready to serve, pour the fruit
sauce into individual serving dishes
and float a meringue on top of each.
Decorate each dessert with a whole
strawberry, sliced from the tip almost
to the stalk end and fanned out.

## COOK SMART

• For a more sophisticated flavour, sprinkle a few raisins steeped in dark rum in the bottom of the dishes. Or add 1 tbsp rum to the creamed coconut and melt it separately over a low heat, before blending it into the chocolate.

• Use a good quality plain chocolate with at least 70% cocoa solids.

• To melt chocolate in a microwave, break into squares, put into a bowl and microwave for 3–4 minutes on low power. Time will vary depending on the power of the microwave, so keep an eye on it as it melts.

# chocolate and coconut mousse

£

**Serves 4**  V

Preparation and cooking  15 minutes, plus 6 hours or overnight chilling

**75g plain chocolate, broken into pieces**
**40g creamed coconut, cut into pieces**
**75g icing sugar, sifted**
**3 eggs, separated**
**40g unsalted butter, cut into pieces**
**pinch of salt**
**grated creamed coconut to decorate**

**To serve**
**small dessert biscuits (optional)**

**Per serving**
kcal 380, protein 7g, fat 25g (of which saturated fat 15g), carbohydrate 32g (of which sugars 32g), fibre 0.5g, sodium 0.1g

**1** Put the chocolate in a heatproof bowl and place over a saucepan of simmering water to melt, stirring occasionally. (Alternatively, melt gently in the microwave.)

**2** When the chocolate has melted, add the creamed coconut and stir until blended. Gradually add the icing sugar and continue stirring, still above the saucepan of water, until the mixture is quite runny.

**3** Beat the egg yolks into the chocolate, then take the bowl off the heat. Add the butter gradually, then allow the mixture to cool.

**4** Add a pinch of salt to the egg whites and whisk until they stand in stiff peaks. Carefully fold into the chocolate mixture, then divide among four individual dishes and chill in the fridge for 6 hours or overnight until firm.

**5** Decorate each mousse with a little grated, creamed coconut sprinkled on top and serve, if liked, with small dessert biscuits.

**A RICH AND INDULGENT DESSERT THAT IS GUARANTEED TO DELIGHT CHOCAHOLICS.**

# chocolate caramel cream

**Serves 4** V

Preparation and cooking
30 minutes, plus at least
1 hour chilling

**125 g caster sugar**

**170 g can evaporated milk**

**200 g plain chocolate, broken
into pieces**

**3 eggs, separated**

**Per serving**
kcal 510, protein 12g, fat 23g
(of which saturated fat 12g),
carbohydrate 68g (of which sugars
68g), fibre 1g, sodium 0.1g

**1** Put the sugar into a large heavy-based saucepan with 3 tbsp of cold water. Heat gently, stirring occasionally, until the sugar dissolves, then simmer for 10–12 minutes until caramelised and a rich golden colour.

**2** Gradually and carefully (as the mixture will froth up), pour the evaporated milk into the pan on a low heat and stir until the caramel dissolves into the milk. (The caramel will harden when the cold evaporated milk is first poured in, but will then dissolve again on heating.) Remove pan from the heat to cool.

**3** Meanwhile, melt the chocolate in a bowl over a pan of very hot water or in the microwave for 1–2 minutes, stirring occasionally. Allow the melted chocolate to cool for 5 minutes, then beat in the egg yolks, one at a time, followed by the caramel mixture.

**4** Whisk the egg whites, not too stiffly, then gently fold them into the chocolate mixture. Divide among four individual glass dishes or little pots. Chill in the fridge for at least 1 hour or until ready to serve.

**PERFECT FOR A
DINNER PARTY,
THESE ELEGANT
DESSERTS CAN
BE MADE AHEAD.**

# citrus surprise pudding

£

**Serves 6** Ⅴ
Preparation 15 minutes
Cooking 35–40 minutes

**75 g butter, softened**
**175 g caster sugar**
**finely grated zest and juice of 2 lemons**
**finely grated zest and juice of 1 small orange**
**3 eggs, separated**
**75 g self-raising flour**
**450 ml semi-skimmed milk**
**2 tsp icing sugar, sifted**

**Per serving**
kcal 505, protein 11 g, fat 22 g
(of which saturated fat 12 g),
carbohydrate 59 g (of which
sugars 55 g), fibre 0.5 g,
sodium 0.3 g

THIS OLD-FASHIONED CLASSIC IS SURE TO DELIGHT. AS THE PUDDING COOKS, IT MAGICALLY SEPARATES INTO TWO LAYERS, WITH A SMOOTH SAUCE UNDERNEATH AND A LIGHT SPONGE ON TOP.

1 Preheat the oven to 190°C (gas 5). Lightly grease a 1.75 litre shallow ovenproof dish.

2 Beat the butter in a mixing bowl until creamy, then add the sugar and beat again until the mixture is light and fluffy. Beat in the lemon and orange zests, then the egg yolks, one at a time.

3 Sift the flour over the mixture and stir it in with the milk, lemon and orange juice. The mixture will be quite runny and have a slightly curdled appearance, but don't worry, it is meant to look like this.

4 Whisk the egg whites, using an electric hand mixer, until they hold stiff peaks, then gently fold into the citrus mixture, half at a time.

5 Pour into the prepared dish, then place in a roasting tin and pour in enough warm water to come just over halfway up the sides of the dish.

6 Bake for 35–40 minutes or until the top is lightly set and golden brown. Remove the dish from the roasting tin, dust with icing sugar and serve hot.

**COOK SMART**
• Make a chocolate and orange pudding by using light muscovado sugar instead of caster sugar, substituting 20 g sifted cocoa powder for the same amount of flour and using the grated zest and juice of three small oranges.

# orange mousse

£

**Serves 4** Ⓥ
Preparation and cooking  15 minutes,
    plus 30 minutes cooling
    and 1 hour chilling

**3 eggs, separated**
**125g caster sugar**
**1 tbsp cornflour**
**grated zest of 1 lime**
**250ml freshly-squeezed orange juice**
**1 tbsp Cointreau or Grand Marnier**
    **(optional)**
**pinch of salt**

**To decorate**
**fine strips of orange and lime zest**
**sprigs of fresh mint**

**Per serving**
kcal 240, protein 6g, fat 5g (of which
saturated fat 1g), carbohydrate 43g
(of which sugars 39g), fibre 0g,
sodium 0.07g

---

**COOK SMART**
• To cool the sauce quickly at the
end of step 3, plunge the base of the
saucepan into a bowl of cold water.

---

**MAKE THIS LIGHT AND FLUFFY MOUSSE WHEN
ORANGES ARE IN SEASON. A SPLASH OF FRUITY
LIQUEUR GIVES IT AN INDULGENT KICK.**

**1** Put the egg yolks in a bowl with 50g of the sugar and
whisk using an electric hand mixer until the mixture is
pale and creamy. Blend in the cornflour and lime zest.

**2** Gradually pour the orange juice into the egg yolk mixture
and mix well.

**3** Pour the mixture into a non-stick saucepan and cook
gently on a low heat, stirring constantly with a wooden
spoon, until the sauce begins to bubble and thicken.
Remove the pan from the heat and add the liqueur,
if using. Leave to cool for 30 minutes, stirring
occasionally to prevent a skin forming.

**4** Whisk the egg whites, with the pinch of salt, in a
clean, grease-free bowl to form soft peaks. Gradually
sprinkle in the remaining sugar and continue whisking
until the meringue is glossy.

**5** Fold the meringue mixture into the cooled orange sauce.
Divide among four dessert glasses and chill in the fridge
for at least 1 hour or until ready to serve.

**6** Decorate with strips of orange and lime zest, and fresh
mint sprigs.

MELT-IN-THE-MOUTH
ZABAGLIONE MAKES
A DIVINE BASE FOR
THIS DESSERT. THE
SWEET-SHARP TASTE
OF PERFECTLY RIPE
RASPBERRIES IS A
GREAT PARTNER.

# zabaglione fruit sundaes

**£ £**

**Serves 6**

Preparation and cooking
20 minutes, plus
2 hours chilling

**2 eggs, plus 1 egg yolk**

**50 g caster sugar**

**100 ml dessert wine,
Marsala or sweet
sherry**

**2 tsp powdered gelatine**

**100 ml whipping cream**

**150 g strawberries,
chopped**

**100 g raspberries**

**sprigs of fresh mint
to decorate**

**Per serving**

kcal 166, protein 5 g,
fat 10 g (of which saturated
fat 4 g), carbohydrate 12 g
(of which sugars 12 g),
fibre 0.7 g, sodium 0.04 g

**1** Break one whole egg into a large mixing bowl. Separate the remaining whole egg, pouring the egg white into another clean bowl and the yolk into the mixing bowl, together with the third egg yolk and the sugar. Whisk the egg yolk mixture until it is pale and frothy, using an electric hand mixer.

**2** Place the mixing bowl over a pan of simmering water and continue to whisk for about 10 minutes, adding the wine a little at a time, until the mixture has tripled in volume and is warm to the touch. Do not allow the water in the saucepan to boil while you are whisking. Remove the bowl from the heat.

**3** Sprinkle the gelatine into 3 tbsp hot (not boiling) water in a jug, stir briskly until thoroughly mixed. If it does not fully dissolve because the liquid has cooled, stand the jug in a pan of hot water and continue to stir until fully dissolved. Do not allow the gelatine mixture to boil.

**4** Pour the dissolved gelatine into the egg mixture and whisk in. Sit the bowl over a pan of cold water and continue whisking for a further 5 minutes until the zabaglione mixture is cold.

**5** Whip the cream until lightly thickened and doubled in volume, then fold into the egg mixture. Whisk the egg white into stiff peaks, then also fold into the mixture. Spoon into six dessert glasses and chill in the fridge for at least 2 hours.

**6** Just before serving, scatter the strawberries and raspberries evenly over the top of the desserts and decorate with sprigs of mint.

# honeycomb mould

£

**Serves 6**
Preparation 20 minutes,
    plus 30 minutes cooling
    and overnight setting

600 ml full-fat milk
**thinly pared zest of
    1 lemon**
**1 tbsp (1 sachet)
    powdered gelatine**
**2 eggs, separated**
**40g caster sugar**
**2 tbsp runny honey**

**Per serving**
kcal 140, protein 6g,
fat 6g (of which saturated
fat 3g), carbohydrate 15g
(of which sugars 15g),
fibre 0g, sodium 0.07g

316

---

### COOK SMART

• This jelly can be set in
a simple ring mould, but
looks stunning when made
in a more decorative one.
Serve with strawberries
and raspberries in the
summer months, hedgerow
blackberries in autumn
and orange segments
during winter.

• If using leaf gelatine, use
15g (about four sheets)
and follow the pack
instructions for preparation.

---

**1** Put aside 3 tbsp of the milk in a cup, then pour the rest into a saucepan and add the lemon zest. Heat the milk in the pan on a low heat until it is steaming hot, but not boiling. Remove from the heat, cover and leave to infuse for 10 minutes.

**2** Meanwhile, heat the 3 tbsp of milk in the microwave (or stand the cup in a pan of boiling water) until very hot but not boiling. Sprinkle over the gelatine and stir briskly until dissolved.

**3** Lightly whisk the egg yolks, sugar and honey together in a bowl until pale in colour. Remove the lemon zest from the milk and reheat the milk to boiling point. Slowly pour the milk into the egg yolk mixture, whisking all the time. Return the mixture to the pan and cook over a low heat, stirring continuously, until lightly thickened.

**4** Strain the hot custard through a sieve into a clean bowl and stir in the gelatine liquid. Allow the custard to cool for 30 minutes, stirring frequently to prevent a skin forming.

**5** Whisk the egg whites in a clean bowl until they stand in stiff peaks, then gently fold them into the custard. Pour the mixture into a wetted 1 litre mould. Chill in the fridge overnight until set.

**6** To turn out the honeycomb mould, quickly dip the mould, right up to the rim, in a bowl of hot water. Place a serving plate on top, then invert the mould and the plate together, giving the mould a sharp tap. Chill until ready to serve.

**MILK JELLIES FIRST BECAME POPULAR
IN VICTORIAN DAYS, ADORED FOR THEIR
DELICIOUS FLAVOUR AND LOW COST. THIS
LEMON AND HONEY VERSION TURNS OUT
WITH THE JELLIED LAYER ON TOP AND THE
LIGHT AND FLUFFY MOUSSE BELOW.**

RICH AND CREAMY CUSTARD WITH A CRISP, GOLDEN CARAMELISED TOPPING IS ALWAYS POPULAR, AND MAKES A DELIGHTFUL DISH FOR ENTERTAINING.

# spiced crème brûlée

£

**Serves 6**  V

Preparation  20 minutes, plus
    2 hours or overnight chilling
Cooking  about 1¼ hours

**250 ml full-fat milk**
**250 ml double cream**
**5 egg yolks**
**100 g caster sugar**
**½ tsp mixed spice**

**Caramel topping**
**12 tsp caster sugar**

**To serve**
**small dessert biscuits**

**Per serving**
kcal 390, protein 4.5 g, fat 28 g
(of which saturated fat 16 g),
carbohydrate 31 g (of which sugars
31 g), fibre 0 g, sodium 0.04 g

1 Preheat the oven to 110°C (gas ¼). Gently heat the milk and cream in a saucepan and bring to just below boiling point. Immediately remove the pan from the heat.

2 Place the egg yolks, sugar and mixed spice in a large mixing bowl. Whisk with an electric hand mixer until the mixture is pale and frothy.

3 Slowly add the hot creamy milk to the egg yolk mixture, stirring to mix. Strain the custard into a jug, through a sieve.

4 Pour the custard mixture into six 150 ml heatproof individual dishes or ramekins. Place on a baking sheet and bake for 1¼ hours or until just set.

5 Remove from the oven and leave to cool at room temperature, then place in the fridge for at least 2 hours or overnight, to chill thoroughly. (The desserts must be very cold when put under the grill in the next step to achieve the contrast between hot and cold, creamy and crunchy.)

6 A few minutes before serving, preheat the grill to high. Sprinkle 2 tsp of sugar evenly over the top of each dessert and place them under the grill for 30–40 seconds until the sugar caramelises. Cool slightly, then serve immediately with small dessert biscuits. (For crunchy tops, do not put the desserts back in the fridge, or the sugar will dissolve.)

**COOK SMART**
• Make the most of the low oven temperature to make meringues, using the leftover egg whites (see page 304).

# creamy citrus and vanilla rice pudding

**Serves 4** Ⓥ
Preparation 10 minutes,
   plus about 2 hours
   chilling
Cooking 50 minutes

1 litre semi-skimmed milk
strip of orange zest
strip of lime zest
1 vanilla pod, split
100 g pudding (short-grain)
   rice
4 tbsp caster sugar
2 egg yolks

**COOK SMART**
• For a dairy-free rice
pudding, simply substitute
a soya or rice alternative to
cow's milk. Both are readily
available from larger
supermarkets.

**Per serving**
kcal 300, protein 12g,
fat 8g (of which saturated
fat 4g), carbohydrate 49g
(of which sugars 27g),
fibre 0g, sodium 0.1g

1 Pour the milk into a large saucepan and add the orange and lime zests. Scrape the seeds from the vanilla pod into the milk, then add the pod too. Add the rice and bring to a simmer over a low heat, watching it carefully so that the milk doesn't boil over. Cover and simmer gently for 30 minutes, stirring occasionally.

2 Meanwhile, whisk together the sugar and egg yolks in a bowl.

3 Uncover the rice and cook, stirring frequently for a further 15 minutes or until the rice is very tender. Remove the citrus zests and the vanilla pod.

4 Whisk some of the hot rice mixture into the egg mixture to warm it, then whisk the egg mixture into the pan. Cook for 3–4 minutes, stirring constantly, or until the pudding is slightly thickened.

5 Transfer the pudding to a bowl and leave to cool, then cover and chill in the fridge until ready to serve. Alternatively, divide among individual dishes before chilling.

# spiced semolina with walnuts

**Serves 4** Ⓥ
Preparation 10 minutes
Cooking 15 minutes

50 g semolina
30 g caster sugar
600 ml semi-skimmed milk
15 g unsalted butter
grated zest of ½ lemon
½ tsp mixed spice

**To serve**
30 g walnut pieces,
   chopped
4 tsp maple syrup, golden
   syrup or runny honey

**COOK SMART**
• Other nuts could be
sprinkled on top,
depending on what you
have in the cupboard, such
as almonds (toasted) or
hazelnuts. You could also
stir 50 g raisins or sultanas
into the semolina, if liked.

**Per serving**
kcal 263, protein 8g,
fat 14g (of which saturated
fat 6g), carbohydrate 28g
(of which sugars 18g),
fibre 1g, sodium 0.1g

1 Put the semolina and sugar in a saucepan. Pour in the milk, add the butter, lemon zest and mixed spice, then bring to the boil on a medium heat, stirring occasionally.

2 Immediately reduce the heat and simmer the semolina gently for 15 minutes, stirring from time to time, until thickened.

3 Allow to cool slightly, then pour the semolina into four ramekins or individual serving dishes. Sprinkle the walnuts over the top and drizzle each dessert with 1 tsp of the syrup or honey. Serve warm.

SEMOLINA IS ONE OF THOSE UTTERLY MOREISH DESSERTS THAT IS NOT EATEN NEARLY ENOUGH. TRY THIS SPICY, NUTTY VERSION AND SEE HOW GOOD IT CAN BE.

£

**Serves 4** ☑

Preparation 20 minutes, plus
   30 minutes resting (for the pastry)
Cooking 30–35 minutes

**75 g cool butter, diced**

**150 g plain flour, sifted**

**25 g caster sugar**

**grated zest of 1 lemon**

**½ tsp ground cinnamon**

**pinch of ground cloves**

**1 egg yolk**

**250 g good quality red fruit jam (such as raspberry, strawberry or plum)**

**fresh raspberries to decorate (optional)**

**Per serving**

kcal 505, protein 5 g, fat 17 g
(of which saturated fat 10 g),
carbohydrate 88 g (of which sugars
59 g), fibre 1 g, sodium 0.1 g

**USING WARMLY SPICED, ZESTY PASTRY FOR THIS YUMMY TART TRANSFORMS AN OLD FAVOURITE INTO A MODERN TREAT.**

**1** First make the pastry. With your fingertips, rub the diced butter into the flour until the mixture resembles breadcrumbs. Stir in the sugar, lemon zest and spices. Make a well in the centre and stir in the egg yolk and 1–2 tbsp cold water, using a round-bladed knife to bind the mixture together. (This can be done in a food processor.) Lightly knead to form a firm dough, then wrap in cling film or greaseproof paper and leave to rest in the fridge for 20 minutes.

**2** Preheat the oven to 190°C (gas 5) and put a baking sheet in to heat. Roll out the pastry on a lightly floured surface to a thickness of 2 mm and use to line a loose-based 24 cm shallow tart tin. Prick the base all over with a fork and chill for a further 10 minutes. Cover the pastry with a circle of greaseproof paper and weigh down with dried or baking beans. Place the tin on the baking sheet and bake for 12–15 minutes until the pastry is set and pale golden.

**3** Remove the pastry case from the oven and remove the beans and greaseproof paper. Reduce the oven temperature to 180°C (gas 4). Spread the jam evenly over the pastry, then return to the oven and bake for a further 15–20 minutes.

**4** Leave to cool slightly to set before removing from the tin. Decorate, if liked, with a few fresh raspberries. Serve warm or cold.

**COOK SMART**

• To make individual jam tarts, use the pastry to line four 12 cm fluted tart tins. Bake blind for 10 minutes, then fill with jam and return to the oven for a further 10–15 minutes.

• This spiced pastry is also very good for making mince pies.

• If you have pastry trimmings left over, gather them together, re-roll, then cut into narrow strips and arrange over the jam to form a lattice pattern. Brush with a little milk and bake as in step 3.

# jam tart

# luscious lemon tart

£

**Serves 8** V
Preparation 30 minutes,
  plus 30 minutes resting
  (for the pastry)
Cooking 30 minutes

**Sweet shortcrust pastry**
**100 g cool butter, diced**
**175 g plain flour, sifted**
**2 tbsp caster sugar**
**pinch of salt**
**1 egg yolk**

**Lemon filling**
**2 unwaxed lemons, grated**
**zest and juice**
**115 g butter, melted**
**3 eggs**
**150 g caster sugar**
**25 g plain flour, sifted**
**10 g cornflour, sifted**

**To serve**
**crème fraîche**

**Per serving**
kcal 419, protein 0.6 g, fat 25 g
(of which saturated fat 15 g),
carbohydrate 44 g (of which
sugars 24 g), fibre 0.8 g,
sodium 0.2 g

**1** First make the pastry. With your fingertips, rub the diced butter into the flour until the mixture resembles breadcrumbs. Stir in the sugar and salt, then the egg yolk and 1 tbsp cold water, and mix to a firm dough. (This can be done in a food processor.) Wrap in cling film or greaseproof paper and leave to rest in the fridge for 20 minutes.

**2** Preheat the oven to 190°C (gas 5) and put a baking sheet in to heat. Roll out the pastry on a lightly floured surface to a thickness of 2 mm and use to line a loose-based 24 cm flan tin. Prick the base all over with a fork and chill for a further 10 minutes. Cover the pastry with a circle of greaseproof paper and weigh down with dried or baking beans. Place the tin on the baking sheet and bake for 12–15 minutes until the pastry is set and pale golden.

**3** Meanwhile, make the filling. Mix together the lemon zest and juice, melted butter, eggs, sugar, flour and cornflour in a large bowl and beat until smooth.

**4** Remove the beans and greaseproof paper from the pastry case and reduce the oven temperature to 180°C (gas 4). Pour in the lemon mixture and bake for 15 minutes or until the filling has set. Leave to cool for 10 minutes before removing from the tin. Serve warm or cold, cut in slices, with crème fraîche, if liked.

## COOK SMART
• Decorate the tart with caramelised lemon slices. Lay the slices on lightly oiled foil, sprinkle with icing sugar and pop under the grill.

• Make a meringue topping. Whisk 1 egg white (leftover from the pastry) until stiff and peaky, then fold in 50 g caster sugar. Gently spread this meringue over the cooked tart, sprinkle with icing sugar and bake gently at 150°C (gas 2) for 10–15 minutes until golden.

**NOTHING BEATS THIS RICH, TANGY TART FOR FLAVOUR. IT IS A POPULAR DESSERT IN RESTAURANTS, BUT YOU CAN MAKE IT YOURSELF FOR FAR LESS AT HOME.**

# rhubarb tart

£

**Serves 4** V

Preparation  30 minutes, plus
    30 minutes resting (for the pastry),
    plus 5 minutes cooling before
    serving
Cooking  35 minutes

**Shortcrust pastry**
**75 g cool butter, diced**
**150 g plain flour, sifted**
**pinch of salt**

**Filling**
**500 g rhubarb, chopped**
**5 tbsp caster sugar**
**pinch of ground cinnamon**
**1 egg yolk**
**2 tbsp crème fraîche or double cream**

**Per serving**
kcal 400, protein 6 g, fat 21 g (of which
saturated fat 13 g), carbohydrate 50 g
(of which sugars 21 g), fibre 3 g,
sodium 0.1 g

---

### COOK SMART
• You can make the pastry case a day
in advance, but do not fill and bake with
the rhubarb filling until shortly before
serving, or the pastry case will be soggy.

• Ceramic baking beans stop a pastry
case from rising, when baking 'blind'.
They conduct heat for even cooking and
will last for years. However, if you don't
have them, simply use dried beans, peas
or rice.

---

**EARLY RHUBARB MAKES THE PRETTIEST
PALE PINK FILLING FOR THIS TEMPTING
TART. IF USING MAINCROP RHUBARB, YOU
MAY NEED TO ADD A LITTLE MORE SUGAR.**

**1** First make the pastry. Rub the butter into the
flour and salt in a large mixing bowl with your
fingertips until the mixture resembles breadcrumbs.
Sprinkle over 2–3 tbsp of cold water, then using a
round-bladed knife, stir to bind the mixture together.
(This can be done in a food processor.) Knead lightly
to form a dough, then wrap the pastry in greaseproof
paper or cling film and leave to rest in the fridge for
20 minutes.

**2** Meanwhile, put the rhubarb in a saucepan with
3 tbsp of the sugar and cook gently for about
10 minutes, so that it is tender but still holding
its shape. Drain well, add the cinnamon and leave
to cool.

**3** Preheat the oven to 200°C (gas 6) and put a baking
sheet in to heat. Roll the pastry out on a lightly
floured surface and use to line a loose-based 24 cm
fluted tart tin. Prick the base all over with a fork and
chill for a further 10 minutes. Cover the pastry with
a circle of greaseproof paper and weigh down with
dried or baking beans. Place the tin on the baking
sheet and bake for 12–15 minutes until the pastry
is set and pale golden.

**4** Beat the egg yolk with the remaining sugar, then
beat in the crème fraîche or cream.

**5** Remove the beans and greaseproof paper from
the pastry case. Pour the crème fraîche mixture
into the pastry case, spreading it evenly, then
arrange the rhubarb on top.

**6** Return the tart to the oven and bake for a further
15 minutes. Allow to cool for 5 minutes, then
carefully remove the tart from the tin. Serve warm.

£

**Serves 4** V

Preparation 15 minutes,
plus 30 minutes resting
(for the pastry)
Cooking 40 minutes

**Shortcrust pastry**
**75 g cool butter, diced**
**150 g plain flour, sifted**
**pinch of salt**

**Filling**
**50 g unsalted butter**
**50 g caster sugar**
**2 egg yolks**
**25 g plain flour**
**50 g ground almonds**
**411 g can pear halves**
**in juice, drained**

**Per serving**
kcal 572, protein 9 g,
fat 36 g (of which saturated
fat 18 g), carbohydrate 57 g
(of which sugars 23 g),
fibre 4 g, sodium 0.2 g

A PÂTISSERIE-STYLE TART MADE WITH PEARS AND BAKED IN
AN ALMOND FRANGIPANE FILLING WON'T COST A FORTUNE AND
IS SURE TO IMPRESS.

# pear and almond tart

**1** First make the pastry. Rub the butter into the flour and salt in a large mixing bowl with your fingertips until the mixture resembles breadcrumbs. Sprinkle over 2–3 tbsp of cold water, then using a round-bladed knife, stir to bind the mixture together. (This can be done in a food processor.) Knead lightly to form a dough, then wrap the pastry in greaseproof paper or cling film and leave to rest in the fridge for 20 minutes.

**2** Preheat the oven to 200°C (gas 6) and put a baking sheet in to heat. Roll out the pastry on a lightly floured surface and use to line a 24 cm loose-based, fluted tart tin. Prick the base all over with a fork, then chill in the fridge for 10 minutes. Cover the pastry with a circle of greaseproof paper and weigh down with a layer of dried or baking beans. Place the tart case on the baking sheet and bake for 10 minutes. Remove from the oven, lift off the beans and paper, then return to the oven for a further 5 minutes.

**3** Meanwhile make the filling. Cream together the butter and sugar in a mixing bowl using a wooden spoon. Beat in the egg yolks, followed by the flour and ground almonds. Cut the pear halves into parallel slices, but do not separate, so as to keep the pear shape.

**4** Spread the almond mixture over the base of the tart. Using a spatula, place each pear half in the tart tin, without dislodging the slices, with the pointed ends towards the centre.

**5** Bake the tart for 25 minutes until golden and firm. Leave to cool slightly before removing from the tin. Cool completely on a wire rack before serving.

**COOK SMART**

• Before cooking, sprinkle the tart with a few crushed macaroons, mixed with 1 tbsp light muscovado sugar.

• To make individual tarts, use the pastry to line four 12 cm loose-based tartlet tins. Bake blind for 5 minutes, remove the beans and paper, then bake for a further 5 minutes. Fill with the almond mixture and place one sliced and fanned pear half in each tartlet. Bake for 20 minutes.

# kiwi slices

£ £

**Makes 4**
Preparation  20 minutes
Cooking  15–20 minutes

**300 g ready-made puff pastry**
**3 tbsp icing sugar, sifted**
**4 large firm kiwi fruit**
**300 ml whipping cream**
**½ tsp pure vanilla extract**

**To decorate**
**sifted icing sugar**
**sprigs of fresh mint**

**Per serving**
kcal 330, protein 4 g, fat 22 g
(of which saturated fat 12 g),
carbohydrate 31 g (of which
sugars 12.5 g), fibre 0.5 g,
sodium 0.2 g

324

1 Preheat the oven to 200°C (gas 6). Roll out the pastry very thinly, on a lightly floured surface, to a rectangle measuring 30 x 20 cm. Use a sharp knife to cut the pastry into twelve equal rectangles, each measuring 10 x 5 cm. Arrange on a lightly wetted baking sheet and place a wire rack on top, so they rise evenly during baking. Bake for 10 minutes until lightly puffed and golden.

2 Remove the wire rack, sprinkle the pastry with 1 tbsp of the icing sugar and continue to bake for a further 5–10 minutes until the sugar has caramelised. Lift off on to a wire rack and leave to cool.

3 Peel the kiwi fruit and cut widthways into even slices.

4 Whip the cream until it is thick and holding its shape. Fold in the remaining 2 tbsp icing sugar and the vanilla extract.

5 Just before serving, spoon or pipe half the whipped cream in a layer onto each of four pastry rectangles and cover with one third of the kiwi slices. Top each with another pastry rectangle, the remaining cream and more kiwi slices, to make a second layer. Place the last four pastry rectangles on top, finishing with remaining slices of kiwi fruit.

6 Dust with icing sugar, decorate with sprigs of mint, if liked, and serve immediately.

**COOK SMART**
• Use whole raspberries or sliced strawberries instead of the kiwi fruit, or even just a red fruit jam.

£

Serves 4  Ⓥ
Preparation  20 minutes
Cooking  12–15 minutes

**40 g caster sugar**

**1 tbsp lemon juice**

**3 nectarines, halved and stoned**

**4 slices ginger cake, about 130 g in total**

**2 tbsp light muscovado sugar**

**125g filo pastry**

**30 g unsalted butter, melted**

**sprigs of fresh mint to decorate (optional)**

**Per serving**
kcal 330, protein 4 g,
fat 12 g (of which saturated
fat 7 g), carbohydrate 54 g
(of which sugars 40 g),
fibre 2 g, sodium 0.2 g

## COOK SMART

• For a variation, make these parcels with poached plums or peaches and use 1 tbsp toasted flaked almonds in place of the cake crumbs.

• The nectarine cooking syrup will keep in a jar in the fridge for 1 week. Use to drizzle over a sponge cake or for a fruit salad.

• The weight of filo pastry varies depending on the thickness and size of the sheets. If it is very thin, make each parcel with three squares of filo.

# nectarine parcels

1 Put the caster sugar in a saucepan with 400 ml water and heat gently until the sugar has dissolved. Bring slowly to the boil, then add the lemon juice. Reduce the heat, place the nectarines in the syrup and poach for 5 minutes.

2 Preheat the oven to 180°C (gas 4). Toast the ginger cake under a moderate grill, then turn into crumbs using a food processor. Add the brown sugar to the crumbs.

3 Cut the filo pastry into eight squares, each measuring about 20 x 20 cm. Stack two squares of filo on top of each other, brushing lightly between the layers with a little of the melted butter and placing them so that the corners are offset, making a star shape. Repeat with the remaining filo squares. Sprinkle half the crumbs evenly over the centre of the four pastries.

4 Drain the nectarines and cut each nectarine half into four slices, giving twenty four slices in total. Arrange six slices in the centre of each pastry and sprinkle with the remaining crumbs.

5 Pull the edges of the filo pastry up to the centre to make little parcels and scrunch together to hold in shape. Brush with the remaining butter and place on a non-stick or lightly greased baking sheet.

6 Bake for 12–15 minutes until golden. Serve immediately, decorated, if liked, with sprigs of fresh mint.

**CRISP, GOLDEN FILO PARCELS FILLED WITH JUICY POACHED NECTARINES AND CAKE CRUMBS ARE A GREAT SUMMER DESSERT.**

# filo fruit baskets

**Serves 4** V

Preparation 30 minutes
Cooking 8–10 minutes

**350 ml full-fat milk**

**2 egg yolks**

**50g caster sugar, plus 1 tbsp**

**25 g plain flour, sifted**

**1 tbsp brandy (optional)**

**100 g redcurrants**

**4 firm kiwi fruit, peeled, sliced and quartered**

**125g filo pastry**

**25 g unsalted butter, melted**

**2 tbsp double cream (optional)**

**sprigs of fresh mint to decorate**

**Per serving**
kcal 359, protein 7 g,
fat 16 g (of which saturated
fat 9 g), carbohydrate 45 g
(of which sugars 34 g),
fibre 2 g, sodium 0.2 g

**1** Gently heat the milk in a saucepan until just coming to the boil. Meanwhile, whisk the egg yolks in a bowl with the 50 g of sugar until the mixture is pale and frothy. Fold in the flour, then pour in the boiling milk, whisking constantly. Pour the custard back into the saucepan and cook over a low heat until it returns to the boil, stirring constantly with a wooden spoon until thickened. Remove the pan from the heat, stir in the brandy, if using, and leave to cool.

**2** Put the redcurrants in a shallow dish and sprinkle with the remaining 1 tbsp of sugar.

**3** Preheat the oven to 180°C (gas 4). Cut the filo pastry into eight squares, each measuring about 20 x 20 cm. Stack two squares of filo on top of each other, brushing lightly between the layers with a little of the melted butter. Repeat with the other filo squares. Place the pastry in four lightly buttered, large ramekin dishes, each about 150 ml capacity.

**4** Place dishes on a baking sheet and bake for 8–10 minutes until golden. Carefully turn out the baskets and transfer them to serving plates.

**5** Just before serving, whip the cream, if using, until thick and beat into the custard. (The cream is not essential but gives the custard a silky smooth richness.) Fill the baskets with the custard cream and top with the redcurrants and kiwi fruit slices. Decorate with sprigs of fresh mint and serve immediately.

## COOK SMART

• Alternative fruits could be used such as mixed berries, or halved seedless grapes with clementine segments.

• For a pretty zigzag edging on the pastry, use crimping scissors to cut before baking.

• See note on filo pastry (page 325).

**FILO PASTRY BASKETS MAKE PRETTY CONTAINERS FOR A FILLING OF CRÈME PATISSIÈRE WITH FRESH SUMMER REDCURRANTS AND KIWI SLICES.**

# autumn crumble

£

**Serves 6** Ⅴ
Preparation 20 minutes
Cooking 50 minutes
(25–30 minutes for
individual dishes)

**2 cooking apples (such
as Bramleys), peeled,
cored and diced**

**2 ripe pears, peeled, cored
and diced**

**250 g plums, halved,
stoned and chopped**

**50 g light muscovado
sugar**

**1 tsp ground cinnamon**

**Crumble topping**
**85 g cool butter, diced**
**175 g plain flour**
**75 g demerara sugar**

**Per serving**
kcal 340, protein 3.5 g,
fat 12 g (of which saturated
fat 7 g), carbohydrate 58 g
(of which sugars 36 g),
fibre 3.5 g, sodium 0.09 g

**EVERYONE LOVES
A HOME-MADE
CRUMBLE – AND
THIS ONE, MADE WITH
JUICY SEASONAL
FRUIT AND A
CRUNCHY TOPPING,
IS JUST DELICIOUS.**

## COOK SMART

• This basic crumble
mixture can top any fruit
filling such as rhubarb with
strawberries, gooseberries,
or apples with blackberries.
Demerara sugar in the
crumble gives a lovely
crunchiness, otherwise
use light muscovado.
You could add 50 g flaked
almonds to the topping or
replace 50 g of the flour
with porridge oats.

• Serve with cream,
crème fraîche, custard,
vanilla ice-cream or
Greek yoghurt.

**1** Preheat the oven to 190°C (gas 5). Combine the
fruits in a 2 litre ovenproof dish. Sprinkle with the
light muscovado sugar and ½ tsp of the ground
cinnamon. Spoon over 3 tbsp of water, then level
the fruit. (For individual crumbles, divide the fruit
among six large ramekin dishes on a baking sheet.)

**2** Rub the butter into the flour using your fingertips
(or use a food processor) until the mixture is
crumbly. Stir in the demerara sugar and the
remaining cinnamon.

**3** Sprinkle the mixture evenly over the fruit – don't
press it down. Bake in the oven for 50 minutes until
the crumble is nice and golden and the fruit juices
have started to bubble up around the edges. (Bake
individual crumbles for 25–30 minutes.) Serve warm.

# apple and blackberry cobbler

£ £

**Serves 4**  V
Preparation  25 minutes
Cooking  30 minutes

**700 g cooking apples, peeled,
    cored and thinly sliced**

**25 g butter, melted**

**4 tbsp caster sugar**

**1 tbsp orange or apple juice**

**225 g blackberries**

**Cobbler topping**
**225 g self-raising flour**

**¼ tsp ground cinnamon**

**a pinch of salt**

**100 g cool butter, diced**

**50 g caster sugar**

**5 tbsp semi-skimmed milk**

**1 egg, lightly beaten**

**1 tbsp demerara sugar, for sprinkling**

**To serve**
**cream or custard**

**Per serving**
kcal 650, protein 9 g, fat 28 g (of which
saturated fat 17 g), carbohydrate 95 g (of
which sugars 53 g), fibre 6 g, sodium 0.1 g

328

1 Preheat the oven to 200°C (gas 6). Put the apple slices in a bowl and drizzle over the melted butter. Sprinkle with the sugar and fruit juice, then mix together to coat the slices.

2 Layer up the apple slices and blackberries in a well-buttered, deep ovenproof dish (about 1.5 litre capacity), starting and finishing with apple slices.

3 To make the cobbler topping, sift the flour, cinnamon and salt into a mixing bowl. Add the butter and rub in using your fingertips until the mixture resembles fine breadcrumbs. (This could be done using the pastry blade on a food processor.) Stir in the caster sugar.

4 Reserve 1 tbsp of the milk, then mix the rest with the egg and add to the dry ingredients. Stir together with a round-bladed knife or fork to make a soft dough. Lightly knead on a floured surface for a few seconds until smooth.

5 Roll out the dough to 1 cm thick and cut into about twelve 4 cm rounds. Arrange the scones, overlapping as necessary, on top of the fruit, brush with the reserved milk and sprinkle with demerara sugar. Bake in the oven for 10 minutes.

6 Reduce the oven temperature to 180°C (gas 4) and continue to bake for another 20 minutes or until the scones are cooked and golden brown and the fruit is tender. Serve hot or warm with thick cream or custard.

**COOK SMART**

• For a gooseberry cobbler, gently heat 700 g gooseberries, 100 g caster sugar, 1 tbsp apple juice or elderflower cordial and 15 g butter in a saucepan until the sugar and butter have melted. Turn up the heat a little, cover and cook for 1 more minute. Make the cobbler with ¼ tsp ground ginger instead of cinnamon.

• Other seasonal fruits would also be delicious, such as plums or pears.

# tarte tatin

**£**

Serves 4  [V]
Preparation  45 minutes,
    plus 20 minutes resting
    (for the pastry) and
    15 minutes cooling
    before serving
Cooking  25–30 minutes

**Pastry**
**75 g cool butter, diced**
**150 g plain flour, sifted**
**50 g caster sugar**
**1 egg yolk**

**Apple topping**
**800 g dessert apples**
    **(such as Cox's or**
    **Granny Smith)**
**juice of 1 lemon**
**75 g unsalted butter**
**150 g caster sugar**

**Per serving**
kcal 700, protein 5 g,
fat 33 g (of which saturated
fat 20 g), carbohydrate
104 g (of which sugars
76 g), fibre 5 g,
sodium 0.2 g

**1** Rub the butter into the flour in a large mixing bowl with your fingertips until it resembles breadcrumbs. Stir in the sugar, then make a well in the centre and stir in the egg yolk and 1–2 tbsp cold water, using a round-bladed knife to bind the mixture together. (This can be done in a food processor.) Lightly knead to form a firm dough, then wrap the pastry in greaseproof paper or cling film and leave to rest in the fridge for 20 minutes.

**2** Preheat the oven to 200°C (gas 6). Peel the apples and cut into quarters. Remove the core and pips, cut in half again, then toss well in the lemon juice.

**3** Melt the butter for the topping in a large frying pan, sprinkle over the sugar, then add the apples. Cook over a medium heat for 10–15 minutes, shaking the pan regularly, until the apples are just tender and the buttery syrup has caramelised.

**4** Tip the apples into a 22 cm shallow cake or flan tin, pressing them well down to fill the tin and with the rounded sides upper-most. (If your tin is loose-based, line it first with foil.) Leave to cool.

**5** Roll out the pastry on a lightly floured surface to a circle, 25 cm in diameter. Lay the pastry over the top of the apples, tucking the surplus pastry down the sides of the tin. Make three to four nicks in the pastry with a knife, to allow the steam to escape. Bake in the oven for 25–30 minutes until golden.

**6** Let the tart rest for 15 minutes before turning out, upside down onto a serving dish, so that the apples are on the top. Serve warm.

**COOK SMART**
• This upside-down tart can also be made with dessert pears.

• Make in a cast-iron or ovenproof frying pan, if you have one, using it to first cook the apples in step 3.

• To make individual tarts, divide the apples among six 12 cm tins. Cut out six pastry circles, each 14 cm in diameter, to cover over the tops. Bake for 15–20 minutes.

**HOME-GROWN APPLES ARE ONE OF THE GREAT PLEASURES OF AUTUMN. USE THEM TO MAKE THIS RICH UPSIDE-DOWN TART.**

# pineapple upside-down cake

**A FAVOURITE TREAT, THIS VERSION USES CRÈME FRAÎCHE RATHER THAN BUTTER.**

£

**Serves 4** V
Preparation 15 minutes,
  plus 5 minutes cooling
  before serving
Cooking 35–40 minutes

**2 tbsp light muscovado sugar**
**227g can (4 slices) pineapple in juice, drained**
**a few glacé cherries, halved**
**3 eggs**
**175g caster sugar**
**100ml crème fraîche**
**125g plain flour**
**1½ tsp baking powder**

**Per serving**
kcal 505, protein 9g, fat 15g
(of which saturated fat 8g),
carbohydrate 88g (of which
sugars 03g), fibre 1g,
sodium 0.3g

**1** Preheat the oven to 200°C (gas 6). Lightly grease a 20cm diameter, 4cm deep sponge tin and sprinkle with the brown sugar. Lay the pineapple slices flat over the base and fill any gaps with half cherries, with the cut side facing upwards.

**2** Beat together the eggs and sugar in a mixing bowl until light and fluffy, then beat in the crème fraîche. Sift the flour and baking powder over the mixture and fold in gently but thoroughly.

**3** Carefully pour the mixture into the tin, making sure not to dislodge the fruit. Bake for 35–40 minutes until well risen and golden brown and springy to the touch.

**4** Leave the cake to cool in the tin for 5 minutes before turning out, upside-down onto a serving plate, so that the pineapple is uppermost. Serve warm.

### COOK SMART
• For a variation, use well-drained halved canned pears instead of pineapple.

• You could also bake this cake in a 20cm diameter cake tin or a deep sandwich tin with the above dimensions. Ideally the tin should have a fixed base.

• To make individual sponges, put a ring of pineapple and a cherry in the bases of four greased 275ml mini pudding basins. Divide the sponge mixture among the basin, then bake for 25 minutes.

£

**Serves 4** Ⅴ

Preparation 15 minutes
Cooking 15 minutes

**425 g can pineapple pieces in juice**

**2 tbsp raisins**

**2 tbsp runny honey**

**3 tbsp Kirsch (or brandy or dark rum)**

**2 eggs, separated**

**4 tbsp caster sugar**

**1 tbsp cornflour**

**½ tsp pure vanilla extract**

**pinch of salt**

**COOK SMART**

• To make individual puddings, divide the mixture among four 200 ml, lightly buttered ramekin dishes. Place on a baking sheet and cook the fruit for 3–5 minutes, then cook with the soufflé topping for 10 minutes.

• If liked, flavour the pineapple with a piece of finely chopped stem ginger and add 1 tsp of the ginger syrup.

**Per serving**
kcal 512, protein 50 g, fat 19 g (of which saturated fat 11 g), carbohydrate 79 g (of which sugars 76 g), fibre 4 g, sodium 0.2 g

**1** Preheat the oven to 190°C (gas 5). Drain the pineapple, reserving the juice, and spread the fruit in the bottom of a lightly buttered 1 litre ovenproof dish. Sprinkle over the raisins.

**2** Blend the honey with 2 tbsp of the pineapple juice and 2 tbsp of the liqueur and pour over the fruit. Put the dish in the oven and cook for 5 minutes.

**3** Meanwhile, put the egg yolks in a bowl with 2 tbsp of the sugar and whisk, using an electric hand mixer, until the mixture becomes pale and foamy. Stir in the cornflour, the rest of the liqueur, 3 tbsp of pineapple juice and the vanilla. Set aside.

**4** Add a pinch of salt to the egg whites in a clean bowl and whisk into stiff peaks. Carefully fold the egg whites into the egg yolk mixture, then pour it all over the warm fruit, spreading it gently with a spatula. Sprinkle with the remaining sugar.

**5** Return the dish to the oven and cook for a further 10 minutes until golden brown and lightly risen. Serve immediately.

**A SPLASH OF KIRSCH AND A FLUFFY SOUFFLÉ TOPPING TRANSFORMS A HUMBLE CAN OF PINEAPPLE INTO AN IMPRESSIVE PUDDING.**

# pineapple pudding

THIS DESSERT IS
A FABULOUS WAY
TO USE UP STALE
OR BROKEN BISCUITS.
THEY MAKE THE
MOST DELICIOUS
TOPPING FOR TART,
TANGY RHUBARB.

**Serves 4**  Ⅴ
Preparation  10 minutes
Cooking  25–30 minutes

**675 g rhubarb, chopped**

**75 g caster sugar**

**grated zest and juice of
1 orange**

**200 g digestive biscuits**

**50 g hazelnuts, roughly
chopped**

**Per serving**
kcal 400, protein 6 g,
fat 18 g (of which saturated
fat 5 g), carbohydrate 56 g
(of which sugars 28 g),
fibre 4 g, sodium 0.3 g

# quick
# rhubarb biscuit
# crumble

**1** Preheat the oven to 190°C (gas 5). Toss the rhubarb
with the sugar, orange zest and juice in a bowl, then
divide among four shallow heatproof dishes.

**2** Place the biscuits in a plastic bag and crush with
a rolling pin. Combine with the nuts and sprinkle
evenly over the fruit.

**3** Bake for 25–30 minutes or until the fruit is tender.
Leave to cool for a few minutes before serving.

**COOK SMART**
• Variations are numerous.
Use other fruits, like sliced
apples or mixed berries,
different nuts, or alternative
biscuits like gingernuts.

• If the biscuits are soft,
crisp them up in a hot oven
for 5 minutes before turning
into crumbs.

HEARTY TRADITIONAL PUDS ARE BACK IN FASHION AND ARE IDEAL ON CHILLY DAYS. THIS STEAMED SPONGE DOTTED WITH CURRANTS AND SERVED WITH A WARM LEMONY SYRUP IS A REAL TREAT.

# spotted dick with lemon syrup

£

**Serves 6**
Preparation  20 minutes
Cooking  1¾ hours (if steamed),
       1 hour (if baked)

**Sponge pudding**
**175 g self-raising flour**
**pinch of ground cinnamon**
**pinch of salt**
**50 g caster sugar**
**75 g shredded suet or coarsely
    grated chilled butter**
**75 g currants**
**finely grated zest of
    ½ lemon**
**1 egg, lightly beaten**
**5 tbsp semi-skimmed milk**

**Lemon syrup**
**4 tbsp golden syrup**
**finely grated zest of
    ½ lemon**
**2 tbsp lemon juice**

**Per serving**
kcal 316, protein 5 g,
fat 13 g (of which saturated
fat 7 g), carbohydrate 49 g
(of which sugars 26 g), fibre 1 g,
sodium 0.2 g

---

**COOK SMART**

• If using grated butter, chill
it first in the freezer for about
20 minutes, then hold the end
in a piece of foil while grating,
to prevent it melting with the
warmth of your hand.

• To microwave, leave
uncovered and cook on full
power at 650 watts for about
5 minutes (depending on the
power of your microwave oven).
Leave to stand for 3–4 minutes
before turning out. To check if it
is cooked through, a cocktail
stick inserted in the middle
should come out clean.

---

1  Sift the flour, cinnamon and salt into a mixing bowl.
Stir in the sugar and the suet or butter, followed
by the currants and lemon zest. Make a well in
the middle, add the egg and the milk and mix to
a soft dropping consistency, adding a little more
milk if needed.

2  Line the base of a well-greased 1 litre pudding basin
with a circle of greaseproof paper, then spoon in the
mixture. Place a double thickness of greaseproof
paper, pleated in the centre, over the pudding, then
tie securely with string. (The pleat allows room for
the pudding to rise.)

3  Put the basin on a trivet or an upturned saucer in
a saucepan and pour in enough boiling water to
come halfway up the sides of the basin. Cover the
pan and steam for 1¾ hours, topping up with boiling
water as necessary. (Alternatively, the pudding can
be baked, uncovered at 180°C/gas 4 for 1 hour or
until well-risen. Cover with foil towards the end of
cooking if the pudding is browning too much.)

4  When the pudding is almost cooked, make the
lemon syrup. Put the golden syrup, lemon zest and
juice in a small saucepan and gently heat, stirring
occasionally until the mixture just begins to bubble.
Turn off the heat.

5  Remove the basin from the pan and ease round
the edge of the pudding with a round-bladed knife
to loosen it. Turn out onto a warmed plate, then
pour the hot lemon syrup over the top. Serve cut
into wedges.

# plum sponge pudding

£

**Serves 6** V
Preparation  10 minutes
Cooking  35–40 minutes

**570 g can red plums in syrup,
    drained, halved and stoned
    (about 250 g stoned fruit)**
**100 g butter, softened**
**75 g caster sugar**
**75 g self-raising flour, sifted**
**1 tsp baking powder, sifted
    with the flour**
**75 g ground almonds**
**2 eggs, beaten**
**1 tbsp semi-skimmed milk**
**2 tbsp demerara sugar**

**Per serving**
kcal 370, protein 7 g, fat 23 g
(of which saturated fat 10 g),
carbohydrate 35 g (of which
sugars 27 g), fibre 1 g,
sodium 0.3 g

> **COOK SMART**
> • Serve with the syrup from
> the plums, and with custard
> sauce (see page 34).

336

1  Preheat the oven to 190°C (gas 5). Put the plums
in a lightly greased 1.3 litre ovenproof dish, about
6 cm deep. Drizzle with 3 tbsp juice from the plums.

2  Put all the remaining ingredients, except the
demerara sugar, into a bowl and beat them well
together for about 2 minutes until thoroughly
blended.

3  Spoon the sponge mixture over the plums and
smooth the level with the back of the spoon.
Sprinkle over the demerara sugar.

4  Bake for 35–40 minutes, or until the sponge is
well-risen and golden brown and will spring back
when lightly pressed with your finger. Serve warm.

**THIS ALL-IN-ONE SPONGE
PUDDING MADE WITH CANNED
PLUMS MAKES A COMFORTING
STORECUPBOARD DESSERT FOR
A COLD, GLOOMY DAY.**

# sponge cake

£

**Cuts into 6 slices** V
Preparation  25 minutes
Cooking  30–35 minutes

**4 eggs**
**125 g caster sugar**
**125 g plain flour, sifted**
**50 g butter, melted**
**3–4 tbsp raspberry jam**

**To decorate**
**sifted icing sugar**
**6 fresh raspberries (optional)**

**Per serving**
kcal 300, protein 7 g, fat 12 g
(of which saturated fat 6 g),
carbohydrate 45 g (of which
sugars 29 g), fibre 0.5 g,
sodium 0.1 g

---

**COOK SMART**
• To make a chocolate sponge
cake, replace 1 tbsp of the flour
with the same quantity of cocoa
powder and sift in with the flour.

---

**1** Preheat the oven to 180°C (gas 4). Lightly
grease a deep, 23 cm sponge tin with a fixed
base and dust with a little flour.

**2** Break the eggs into a heatproof bowl
and add the sugar. Place the bowl over a
saucepan of simmering water (not boiling),
and whisk for about 15 minutes, using an
electric hand mixer, until the mixture is
thick and leaves a ribbon trail when the
beaters are lifted. Remove the bowl from
the heat and continue beating until the
mixture is cold.

**3** Sift the flour over the top of the mixture
(this is a second sifting), then very gently
pour the cooled, melted butter around
the edge of the mixture. Gently fold in the
butter and flour using a large metal spoon,
ensuring there are no pockets of flour left.

**4** Pour the mixture at once into the sponge
tin and quickly spread flat. Bake for
30–35 minutes until well risen and golden
brown, and springy to the touch when lightly
pressed with a finger. Cool for 2–3 minutes
in the tin, then turn out onto a wire rack
and leave to cool completely.

**5** When the sponge is cold, cut in half to
make two equal layers. Fill with jam and
dust the top of the sponge with icing sugar.
Decorate if liked with fresh raspberries.

**THIS CLASSIC SPONGE CAKE CONTAINS LESS
FAT THAN ORDINARY CAKES AND MAKES
A GREAT CHOICE FOR A WEEKEND TEA.**

IDEAL FOR USING UP SLIGHTLY STALE
BREAD, THIS HEARTY PUDDING INCLUDES
DRIED APRICOTS, ALTHOUGH YOU COULD
USE CURRANTS OR SULTANAS INSTEAD.

**£**

**Serves 6**  Ⓥ

Preparation  20 minutes,
    plus 30 minutes soaking
Cooking  40–50 minutes

**600 ml semi-skimmed milk**
**grated zest of 1 lemon**
**75 g butter, softened**
**6 thick slices white bread**
**100 g ready-to-eat, dried**
    **apricots, thinly sliced**
**3 eggs**
**50 g caster sugar**
**1 tbsp demerara sugar**
**1 tsp ground cinnamon**

**Per serving**
kcal 353, protein 11 g,
fat 16 g (of which saturated
fat 9 g), carbohydrate 43 g (of
which sugars 25 g), fibre 2 g,
sodium 0.4 g

**338**

---

**COOK SMART**
• If you have a jar of
mincemeat, spread a layer in
between the layers of buttered
bread in place of the apricots.

• This pudding can be served
with cream, but is better still
with vanilla ice-cream.

---

1 Heat the milk with the lemon zest to just below
boiling point. Remove pan from the heat and set
aside to infuse.

2 Meanwhile, butter the slices of bread and cut each
slice into quarters to make twenty four triangles
in total, leaving the crusts on. Arrange the bread in
layers, buttered side up, neatly overlapping in a well
greased, 1.5 litre rectangular, ovenproof dish,
scattering the apricots in between the layers.

3 Beat together the eggs, caster sugar and flavoured
milk. Pour the mixture over the bread and leave to
soak for 30 minutes. Gently push the bread down
into the custard so that each piece is soaked.

4 Preheat the oven to 180°C (gas 4). Mix together the
demerara sugar and cinnamon and dust over the top
of the pudding.

5 Bake for 40–50 minutes or until the custard is lightly
set and the top is golden brown and crusty. Leave
for 5 minutes before serving.

# apricot bread and butter pudding

£

Serves 6 Ⓥ

Preparation 20 minutes,
   plus at least 2 hours chilling

**200 g ricotta cheese or
   fromage frais (8% fat)**

**125 g caster sugar**

**½ tsp pure vanilla extract**

**few drops of pure almond
   extract**

**24 trifle sponge fingers
   (boudoir biscuits)**

**6 tbsp cherry jam**

**To decorate**

**1 tbsp cocoa powder, sifted**

**6 whole fresh cherries (optional)**

**sprigs of fresh mint (optional)**

**Per serving**

kcal 302, protein 8 g, fat 7.5 g
(of which saturated fat 3.5 g),
carbohydrate 55 g (of which
sugars 46 g), fibre 0.6 g,
sodium 0.1 g

**1** Beat the soft cheese with 75 g of the sugar and the vanilla extract.

**2** Gently heat 6 tbsp of water in a saucepan with the remaining sugar, stirring with a wooden spoon until the sugar has dissolved. Immediately remove the pan from the heat, add the almond extract then pour into a shallow dish and leave to cool.

**3** Line a rectangular loaf tin, measuring 20 x 10 cm and 7 cm deep, with cling film, leaving enough excess hanging over the sides so as to cover the dessert before chilling it.

**4** Briefly dip eight of the sponge fingers in the syrup. Arrange them, side by side, in the tin, sugar side down. (Dip the biscuits just enough to flavour them, but do not soak or they will break up.)

**5** Spread with half the cherry jam, then half the soft cheese mixture. Put another layer of eight syrup-dipped biscuits on top, the rest of the jam, then the remaining cheese mixture.

**6** Finish with the remaining biscuits, dipped in the syrup. Wrap the film over the top, put a rectangular piece of cardboard on top and lightly weigh it down. Chill in the fridge for at least 2 hours.

**7** When ready to serve, peel back the film and carefully turn the cake upside down onto a serving plate. Remove the film. Sprinkle with cocoa powder and decorate with fresh cherries and sprigs of mint, if liked. Serve cut into six slices.

**COOK SMART**

• For an adult flavour, replace the almond essence with 1 tbsp Kirsch.

# cherry
# sponge layer cake

# squidgy chocolate muffins

££

**Makes 8 muffins** V
Preparation 10 minutes
Cooking 8 minutes

**Per serving**
kcal 250, protein 5g,
fat 17g (of which saturated
fat 8g), carbohydrate 20g
(of which sugars 18g),
fibre 0.5g, sodium 0.09g

**125g plain chocolate
(with at least 70%
cocoa solids), broken
into pieces**
**75g butter, diced**
**3 eggs**
**60g icing sugar, sifted**
**2 tbsp ground almonds**
**1 tbsp plain flour, sifted**
**1 tbsp brandy (optional)**

**1** Preheat the oven to 250°C (gas 9). Line a muffin tray with eight paper muffin cases.

**2** Melt the chocolate in a heatproof bowl over a saucepan of simmering water (or melt gently in the microwave). Stir well, then remove the bowl from the heat and stir in the butter – it will melt in the warmth of the chocolate.

**3** Break the eggs into a separate clean bowl and whisk them for 3–4 minutes, using an electric hand mixer, until thick and foamy. Stir in the sifted sugar, ground almonds and flour. Now fold in the melted chocolate mixture and the brandy, if using.

**4** Divide the mixture among the paper muffin cases. Bake for 8 minutes or until well risen and firm to the touch.

**5** Lift the muffins out of the tray onto a wire rack and allow to cool. Serve warm.

**COOK SMART**
• For double chocolate muffins, push a square of dark chocolate into the centre of each muffin just before baking. You could also stir a handful of raisins into the mixture in step 3.

AN EXTRA-NAUGHTY VERSION OF CHOCOLATE MUFFINS WITH A SUBTLE TANG OF BRANDY – JUST RIGHT WHEN YOU NEED A TREAT.

YOU MIGHT NEED
TO MAKE A DOUBLE
BATCH OF THESE. THEY
ARE SO GOOD THAT
THEY WILL GO IN NO
TIME AT ALL.

# chocolate
## chip
# cookies

£ £

**Makes 18 cookies**  V
Preparation  15 minutes
Cooking  12–15 minutes

**100 g butter, softened**
**100 g caster sugar**
**1 egg, beaten**
**175 g plain flour**
**½ tsp baking powder**
**150 g plain chocolate, coarsely chopped**

**Per serving**
kcal 145, protein 2 g, fat 7 g (of which
saturated fat 4.5 g), carbohydrate 19 g
(of which sugars 11 g), fibre 0.5 g,
sodium 0.06 g

**1** Preheat the oven to 200°C (gas 6). Cream together
the butter and sugar in a mixing bowl, using an electric
hand mixer, until the mixture is light and fluffy. Gradually
beat in the egg, then sift in the flour and baking powder
and mix together.

**2** Stir the chopped chocolate into the mixture so that it
is evenly distributed.

**3** Using two teaspoons, place about eighteen dollops
of the mixture on to two lightly greased baking sheets,
leaving enough space between them for the cookies
to spread, without touching, while cooking. Smooth
down the top of each cookie with the back of a
teaspoon dipped in cold water.

**4** Bake for 12–15 minutes until they feel soft and springy.
Allow to cool on the baking sheets for 5 minutes, then
lift on to a wire rack to cool completely. They will keep
in an airtight container for up to 5 days.

**COOK SMART**

• For chocolate and nut cookies, replace half the chopped
chocolate with chopped walnuts, hazelnuts or pecan nuts.

• To save time, you can use 150 g milk or dark chocolate chips
rather than chopping a block of chocolate.

# index

342

344

# acknowledgments

*Amazing Meals for less than £2.50 a Person* Published in 2011 in the United Kingdom by Vivat Direct Limited (t/a Reader'sDigest), 157 Edgware Road, London W2 2HR

*Amazing Meals for less than £2.50 a Person* is owned and under licence from The Reader's Digest Association, Inc.

An adaptation of a hardback originally published by Sélection de Reader's Digest, France as *La Bonne Cuisine avec Trois Fois Rien*, using additional new material and recipes from *Cooking Smart for a Healthy Heart*, *Vegetables for Vitality* and *Fight Back with Food*, all published by The Reader's Digest Association, Inc.

We are committed both to the quality of our products and the service we provide to our customers. We value your comments so please feel free to contact us on **0871 351 1000** or via our web site at **www.readersdigest.co.uk**
If you have any comments or suggestions about the content of our books you can contact us at **gbeditorial@readersdigest.co.uk**

**Created by Amazon Publishing Limited**
7 Old Lodge Place, Twickenham TW1 1QR

| | |
|---|---|
| Editor | Maggie Pannell |
| Copy editors | Susannah Blake, Jill Steed |
| New recipes created especially for this UK edition | |
| | Catherine Atkinson, Maggie Pannell |
| Recipe Testers | Carol Tenant, Jayne Cross, Catherine Atkinson, Emma Patmore, Susanna Tee, Christine France |
| Adaptation of US recipes | Anna Brandenburger |
| Designers | Vivienne Brar, Colin Goody |
| Nutritionist | Fiona Hunter |
| Indexer | Hilary Bird |

**For Vivat Direct**

| | |
|---|---|
| Editorial Director | Julian Browne |
| Art Director | Anne-Marie Bulat |
| Managing Editor | Nina Hathway |
| Picture Resource Manager | Sarah Stewart-Richardson |
| Pre-press Technical Manager | Dean Russell |
| Production Controller | Jan Bucil |
| Product Production Manager | Claudette Bramble |

**Photography**
All images RD copyright © 2005

Abbreviations are used as follows; **t** top, **c** centre, **b** bottom, **l** left, **r** right.

For the following images, photography is by William Lingwood, food stylist Lucy McElvie, props stylist Luis Peral: 30 **cl**, **cr**, **bc**, 37 **l**, **c**, 39 **bl**, **bc**, 40 **bl**, **bc**, 41 **tl**, **tr**, 42 **bl**, 50-51 **l**, 64 **c**, 104–105 **r**, 108–109 **l**, 134 **bl**, 137 **tc**, 139 **c**, 143 **tr**, 149 **tc**, 150 **bc**, 152–153 **l**, 160 **c**, 162–163 **tr**, 169 **c**, 174–175 **tr**, 198–199 **l**, 209 **c**, 210 **tc**, 212 **bl**, 220 **c**, 234–235 **l**, 238 **c**, 240–241 **r**, 244–245 **l**, 246–247 **tr**, 249 **c**, 250 **bl**, 266–267 **r**, 274–275 **l**, 290 **c**, 296 **tc**, 302 **bc**, 320–321 **l**, 331 **c**, 334 **c**.

For the following images, photography is by Christian Adam, food stylist Catherine Nicolas: 22 **br**, 30 **tr**, **bl**, 37 **br**, 38 **tr**, **br**, 39 **tc**, **br**, 40 **br**, 44 **t**, 45 **b**, 46 **tl**, 47 **t**, 48 **t**, 49 **br**, 52 **tr**, 63 **tr**, 64 **c**, 65 **tr**, 66 **t**, 67 **br**, 68 **tr**, 69 **b**, 71 **tl**, 72 **tl**, 73 **t**, 76 **tl**, 77 **tr**, 78 **tl**, 79 **c**, 80 **c**, 82 **tl**, **br**, 83 **t**, 84 **bl**, 85 **tr**, 86 **tl**, 88 **tl**, 89 **b**, 92 **tl**, 94 **tr**, 95 **tr**, 96 **bl**, 97 **br**, 98 **tl**, 99 **tr**, 102 **t**, 103 **tr**, 106 **br**, 110 **t**, 115 **b**, 118 **tl**, 119 **c**, 129 **tl**, 122 **tl**, 123 **c**, 126 **br**, 127 **t**, 128 **tr**, 133 **b**, 141 **t**, 148 **tl**, 151 **tr**, 157 **bl**, 172 **t**, 173 **tr**, 181 **b**, 182 **b**, 183 **tl**, 190 **br**, 191 **tr**, 195 **br**, 197 **bl**, 200 **t**, 206 **tr**, 207 **b**, 225 **tr**, 230 **tr**, 237 **t**, 243 **tr**, 253 **tr**, 256 **bl**, 258 **tl**, 259 **b**, 262 **br**, 263 **t**, 265 **bl**, 268 **tl**, 273 **c**, 276 **tl**, 280 **tl**, 283 **tl**, 287 **t**, 288 **t**, 289 **br**, 293 **br**, 300 **bl**, 303 **tl**, 304 **bl**, 305 **tl**, 306 **t**, 309 **tr**, 310 **tr**, 311 **b**, 313 **tr**, 314 **c**, 317 **tr**, 319 **b**, 323 **b**, 324 **tr**, 325 **bl**, 326 **t**, 327 **br**, 329 **tr**, 332 **br**, 333 **tr**, 337 **tr**, 339 **b**, 340 **br**, 341 **tr**

Colour origination FMG
Printed and bound by Neographia, Slovakia

Concept code FR 1508/IC-15C
Book code 400-049 UP0000-4
ISBN 978 0 276 44008 3